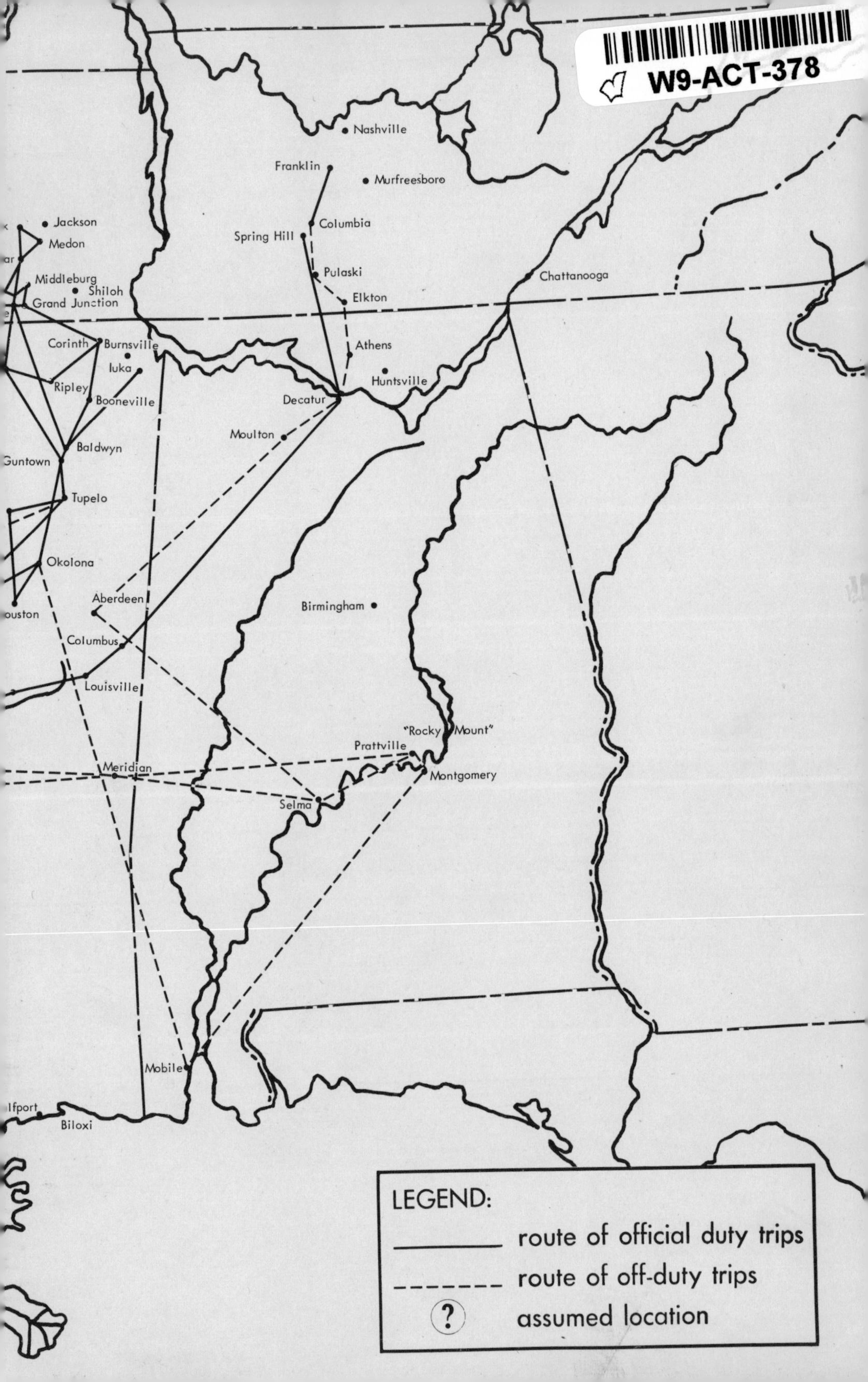
W9-ACT-378
Nashville
Franklin
Murfreesboro
Jackson
Medon
Columbia
Spring Hill
Pulaski
Middleburg
Shiloh
Grand Junction
Elkton
Chattanooga
Corinth
Burnsville
Iuka
Athens
Huntsville
Ripley
Booneville
Decatur
Moulton
Baldwyn
Guntown
Tupelo
Okolona
Aberdeen
Birmingham
Columbus
Louisville
"Rocky Mount"
Prattville
Meridian
Montgomery
Selma
Mobile
Biloxi
LEGEND:
route of official duty trips
route of off-duty trips
assumed location

THIS FIRST PRINTING

OF

"This Infernal War"

IS SIGNED

BY THE EDITORS

Bell W. Wiley

Lucy E. Fay

"This Infernal War"

The Confederate Letters of
SGT. EDWIN H. FAY

Sarah Shields Fay
(*about 1862*)

"This Infernal War"

The Confederate Letters of
SGT. EDWIN H. FAY

Edited by Bell Irvin Wiley
With the Assistance of Lucy E. Fay

AUSTIN · UNIVERSITY OF TEXAS PRESS

Library of Congress Catalog Card No. 58–12021

Published with the assistance of a grant
from the Ford Foundation
under its program for the support of publications
in the humanities and social sciences

Manufactured in the United States of America
by the Printing Division of the University of Texas

IN LOVING MEMORY OF

E. H. F. AND S. S. F.

Contents

Contents

"This Infernal War"

Introduction

THE CONFEDERATE LETTERS of Edwin H. Fay are remarkable documents, bearing little resemblance to the average run of missives that poured from Southern camps during the course of the Civil War. The spelling and grammar reveal a sound education. The handwriting is neat, almost to the point of daintiness, the lines straight and even, and the ink—only a few were written with pencil—uncommonly good for the C.S.A. The phraseology and style are superior; Latin and French are used in a manner which reflect mastery of those languages. Instead of following the usual pattern of beginning with "I take pen in hand to drop you a few lines" and ending with "your affectionate husband until death do us part," with a few stilted phrases about health, homesickness, and weather thrown in between, these letters are easy-flowing communications that have a character all their own. What other Rebel private would have begun a letter thus: "I commence now while the afflatus of letter writing is on me lest delay might prove dangerous"?

Some of the letters run to great length—one of them exceeding 4,000 words. Fay was a close and sensitive observer, and there was hardly a detail of soldier life that escaped his attention and comment. His letters tell much about food, clothing, diversions, equipment, morale, mail service, postal rates, substitutes, body servants, officers, marches, cavalry skirmishes, and the daily routine of camp. They also afford interesting insight into the conditions, activities, and attitudes of civilians. The correspondence derives special value from the fact that it deals with the western theaters of operations and a substantial portion of it with that least known segment of the Confederacy, the Trans-Mississippi country.

The letters owe their distinctiveness largely to the fact that they were written by an exceptional person. Among Johnny Rebs Edwin H. Fay was *sui generis.*

Fay, named for a great-uncle, Levi Hedge, who taught logic at Harvard, was born in Autauga County, Alabama, on March 17, 1832. His father, Edwin Fay, a native of Vermont, had migrated to Georgia shortly after graduating from Harvard in 1817.

In 1820 the elder Edwin Fay moved to Alabama and settled near Prattville, where he met and married Harriet White, a native of New York and a graduate of the Emma Willard School at Troy. In addition to running his farm, "Rocky Mount," he taught a school for boys and practiced law. He was said to be the first teacher and lawyer to settle in Autauga County. His versatility, apparently much talked of by his acquaintances, was the subject of a humorous, though somewhat erroneous, comment by Harriet Martineau in one of her books.[1] At the time of the Civil War his children numbered four: Edwin Hedge Fay, William Henry Fay, Sarah Fay (Mrs. Samuel) Stoddard, and Dunham Fay.

After a period of instruction by his father, Edwin Hedge Fay entered Harvard, from which he graduated in 1852. He taught school for a while in Alabama before returning to Harvard for an M.A. degree, which was conferred in 1855. He then moved to Minden, Louisiana, and became headmaster of a boys' school. On March 13, 1856, he married Sarah Elizabeth Shields, whose father, William Shields, manufactured cotton gins and corn mills in Minden.

Sarah Shields was a native of Lumpkin County, Georgia. While attending a female academy at Madison, Georgia, she studied logic from a book written by Levi Hedge. After she became Fay's wife she asked her husband if there was any connection between his middle name and the author of the book that she had used in school. When informed that the Hedge for whom her spouse was named was the author of her logic text, she teasingly remarked: "If I had known that I should not have married you."

[1] Harriet Martineau, *Society in America* (New York, 1837), I, 231. Miss Martineau, who saw Fay get out of his buggy to pick up a horseshoe as he was taking a basket of eggs to a friend in Montgomery, reported: "I saw this day, driving a wagon, a man who is a schoolmaster, lawyer, almanack-maker, speculator in old iron and dealer in eggs, in addition to a few other occupations. His must be a very active existence."

Fay became a partner in the business of his father-in-law, but operation of the school, which in 1862 had fifty pupils, continued to be his principal activity.

In the 1850's Minden's inhabitants numbered fewer than 1,000. But the village and the surrounding community, both of which appear to have shared fully the prosperity enjoyed by the South in the late antebellum period, supported two colleges for women as well as the male academy taught by Fay and an assistant, who also held an M.A. degree from Harvard.[2]

James A. L. Fremantle, the English army officer who traveled through the South in 1863, noted in his diary that Minden was a charming little town. He also commented on the beauty and productivity of the surrounding country.[3]

Life in this cultured and thriving community must have been pleasant for the young educator and his attractive wife. Their happiness was enhanced when a son, William Edwin, was born to them in 1857 and a daughter, Eleutheria, in 1859. Eleutheria died in 1860 but a second son, Thornwell, was born in March, 1861.

Despite his Northern antecedents and his Harvard education, Fay seems to have subscribed wholeheartedly to prevailing Southern views about slavery and state sovereignty. He owned a few Negroes, including Cynthia, a household slave, and Rich, who accompanied him in the Confederate Army as a body servant. Once he wrote of giving Rich "a good whipping" and on another occasion he reported that he had "tried to bump his [Rich's] brains out against a hogshead of sugar" for leaving camp to go "skylarking" after some colored women.[4] Fay became greatly annoyed with Cynthia because of her

[2] Edwin W. Fay, *History of Education in Louisiana* (U.S. Bureau of Education, Circular of Information No. 1, Washington, 1898), 159. One of the women's institutions was the Minden Female College. See D. W. Harris and B. M. Hulse, *History of Claiborne Parish, Louisiana* ... (New Orleans, 1886), 99–100.

[3] James A. L. Fremantle, *Three Months in the Southern States, April–June, 1863* (Mobile, 1864), 45.

[4] Fay's letters give more insight into the character and activity of an enlisted man's body servant than any other source known to the editor. Rich seems to have been a person of considerable individuality. A sidelight on his "skylarking" bent is afforded by the following comment of Harriet White Fay to her son, October 10, 1863: "I don't altogether like Rich's conduct since he has been

infertility. "Tell Cynthia if she does not have a *young one* . . . I intend to whip her almost to death," he wrote his wife on December 21, 1862. For fear that Sarah Fay might not take him seriously, he wrote again on January 24, 1863:

Tell Cynthia that if she does not begin to show some signs that way when I come home that I'll either whip her most to death or sell her to the meanest man I can find on Red River. Be sure you tell her so, for I am not going to be fooled with by her any longer. I bought her to breed and I know no good reason why she should not do it and she shall or I won't own her long.

A balder statement on the "breeding of slaves" probably could not be found in all the writings about the peculiar institution. And the fact that such a sentiment could be held by a cultured and religious person like Fay helps to point up the blinding hold that slavery had on the minds of men less than a century ago.

Louisiana's move to leave the Union after Lincoln's election was strongly supported by Fay, who became a candidate for a seat in the secession convention. But he did not join the hordes of his fellow citizens who rushed into the service on the fall of Fort Sumter. Not until the war was nearly a year old did he take up arms for the Southern cause. The fact that conscription was soon to be initiated may have contributed to his decision to enter the service. It turned out that Fay as a teacher of more than twenty pupils would have been exempted under a law passed two weeks after his enlistment, but this he could not foresee.

On April 4, 1862, Fay enlisted as a private in a cavalry company then in process of organization in his home community. This unit was commanded by Captain F. D. Wimberly and was known as the Minden Rangers. After the Rangers were mustered into Confederate service at Monroe, Louisiana, on April 6, they proceeded to Grand Junction, Tennessee, where they remained about three weeks "rotting in camp." The sojourn at Grand Junction led Fay to conclude that he

---

here. Aunt Flora provided him with a good bed but he saw fit to take a bed with Fanny most of the time & when I learned about it a week or two since, I spoke to him about it & he said that was nothing, he was in the habit of doing such things. I told him I should tell you & so I do." MS. in possession of Miss Lucy E. Fay, Chapel Hill, North Carolina.

knew "absolutely more about military matters than any man in the company" and made him "determined not to be a private throughout this war." Further experience was to strengthen these views.

Late in April the Rangers moved to the vicinity of Corinth, where on the first or second of May Fay had his baptism of fire in a skirmish featured by lively musketry and shelling. "I was as cool as a cucumber," he wrote afterward to his wife though "the boys say my face was spotted white and red."

During the next few weeks, as Halleck slowly invested Corinth and forced the Confederates under Beauregard back to Tupelo, the Minden Rangers, as a part of Van Dorn's division, devoted themselves to reconnoitering, scouting, picketing, and protecting the flanks and rear of the army. This duty was at times very strenuous. On two occasions during May and June, 1862, Fay wrote his wife that he had not been able to change his shirt for a fortnight. He rode thirty miles a day for three successive days. After an exhausting experience helping to pull wagons up hills and through mud holes, he reported that he was "soldier, negro, mule, all three." These hardships were the more onerous, because some of the soldiers played sick. Many others, including Fay, were genuinely ill during a part of this trying period.

These experiences were extremely disillusioning to Fay and his associates. On May 20, 1862, Fay wrote: "I think that the patriotism of our Co. at least is about consumed. If they were at home I don't know a man who would volunteer with his present knowledge, unless I did." Before the end of May, Captain Wimberly, who while recruiting his company at Minden had told his men that he would stay with them for twelve months or twelve years as needed, announced his intention of returning home under provisions of the conscript law which allowed release of men over thirty-five years of age.

On May 20 Fay indicated to his wife his own desire to get out of the service. He stated that he could probably obtain release as a teacher, but preferred hiring a substitute to take his place in the ranks. The thought of going home, once expressed, rapidly became more appealing, and in a short time ripened into a firm resolution. From mid-June, 1862, until his transfer to the engineers nearly two years later he was an unwilling member of the Confederate Army; and even after his transfer he manifested little enthusiasm for soldiering.

Once he made up his mind to get out of the army Fay concentrated his efforts on obtaining a substitute. To guard against "the flings and arrows of outraged women" at home he tried to obtain a statement from the school trustees requesting his return to the classroom. In this he was unsuccessful. Procurement of a substitute proved much more difficult than he anticipated, and before a replacement could be found the Confederate War Department adopted a rule that only those soldiers who were unfit for further service would be allowed to obtain proxies.

After his hopes of obtaining a substitute were blasted early in July, 1862, Fay redoubled his efforts to obtain discharge as a school teacher. In April, 1863, he petitioned Van Dorn to release him from service, but when the paper was forwarded to Bragg, the army commander disapproved it on the ground that the law exempting school teachers did not apply to those already in the army. Fay was infuriated by the rejection of his request, and he wrote a strong letter to his Congressman, John Perkins, protesting the injustice of holding in the service one who admittedly would be exempted if he was still a civilian. But the protest was of no avail.

While Fay was trying unsuccessfully to get a discharge he and his company were engaged in varied and far-ranging activities. In late May, 1862, as a part of a general reorganization resulting from the Confederacy's resort to conscription, the company held a new election of officers. Wimberly declined to stand for re-election and Junius Y. Webb was unanimously chosen captain in his stead. L. B. Watkins, Nathaniel M. Martin, and J. J. Carter were elected respectively first, second, and third lieutenant. Fay refused to be a candidate for office because acceptance of a commission would commit him to three years of service and he was still hoping to get a substitute and go home. In June, 1862, Captain Webb appointed him orderly sergeant, the highest noncommissioned position in the company. In the discharge of his duties, which included keeping the company records, Sergeant Fay was closely associated with the officers, often eating with them and sharing their bunks. On one occasion he wrote his wife that Captain Webb and he were "as intimate as two brothers." In the fall of 1863 two comrades who were jealous of Fay and desirous of improving their status, talked the Captain into ordering an election of noncommissioned officers. But Fay, who had been forewarned of the effort to displace him, was supported by the Captain and returned to his position.

Fay once wrote to his wife that Captain Webb could not get along without him, and he undoubtedly performed well the duties of his responsible position. His abilities were recognized by occasional detail to higher headquarters for performance of such duties as copying orders, serving as provost marshal in an army court, and supervising construction of a military road.

In February, 1863, Fay came very near to getting a commission. He was actually appointed quartermaster of his battalion, a position which called for a captain's rank. But illness prevented his immediate assumption of the duties; and by the time he recovered, the job had been given to someone else.

The Minden Rangers experienced several changes of assignment in the period following their reorganization under Captain Webb. In August, 1862, they and a mounted unit from Bossier, Louisiana, known as Fuller's (later Harrison's) Company, were combined with five companies of Forrest's old regiment to form a battalion. This battalion, commanded by Lieutenant Colonel Robert M. Balch, was a part of General Frank C. Armstrong's cavalry brigade, Dabney H. Maury's Division, Sterling Price's Corps (known also as the Army of the West). For a time in early October, 1862, Price's command was a part of General Earl Van Dorn's Army of West Tennessee. But when John C. Pemberton on October 12, 1862, took over command of the newly created Department of Mississippi and East Louisiana, Van Dorn became his subordinate in charge of the cavalry.

In mid-December, 1862, the Rangers were detached from their battalion to serve as an escort for Brigadier General Albert Rust, who temporarily was commanding John C. Breckinridge's Division with headquarters near Grenada. Two months later the company became the escort of Brigadier General George B. Cosby of Van Dorn's (later William H. Jackson's) Cavalry Division. The Rangers continued as Cosby's escort as long as Fay remained a member of the company.

These various assignments kept Fay and his associates on the move. In August and early September, 1862, the Rangers accompanied General Armstrong on a long raid through North Mississippi into

Tennessee, almost to Jackson. This expedition was featured by sharp skirmishes on August 30 and September 1 near Bolivar and Denmark, Tennessee. At Denmark, Fay's horse got away from him early in the fight when he dismounted to lower a fence. Later he reported to his wife: "We captured a Yankee drummer about ten years old, a beautiful little fellow, but I presume hardened in sin as all little boys are." The drummer was paroled along with the enlisted men captured on this raid.

On September 14, 1862, the Rangers and the other elements of Armstrong's Brigade marched with Price into Iuka, Mississippi, where they took over a vast amount of supplies abandoned by the Federals. Fay was impressed by the variety and abundance of the captured provisions. "The Yankees had everything," he wrote Sarah. "They have mixed vegetables pressed and hermetically sealed so you have only to put on water and break off a cake and throw in and you have excellent soup. Coffee, concentrated milk, and sugar in the same way, only put a small piece into a coffee pot with water and you have coffee ready for drinking."

The sojourn at Iuka was of short duration. On the afternoon of September 19 Rosecrans attacked Price's forces south of the town, and a desperate encounter ensued. Early the next morning Price, threatened by Rosecrans on the south and Ord of Grant's army on the west, withdrew to Baldwyn.

On October 3–4, 1862, Van Dorn, re-enforced by Price, made a bloody but unsuccessful attempt to recover Corinth from the Federals. Fay's company, assigned to help cover the left flank, were "not much exposed" during the battle, but during the withdrawal they had to fight hard to save Van Dorn's wagon train. Fay rejoiced that "we piled the ground with Moslem slain," but was strongly critical of the Confederate leaders for their mismanagement of the campaign.

Between October 26 and November 18 Fay was home on furlough. Shortly after he returned to duty at Tupelo his company moved to the vicinity of Holly Springs to help oppose Grant's drive toward Vicksburg. At Abbeville, just north of Oxford, the hard pressed Confederates burned much of their equipment and baggage to keep it from falling into Federal hands. Among items destroyed were the record books and muster rolls of the Minden Rangers, and some clothing and personal articles belonging to Fay. During the retrograde movement to Grenada, General Rust put Fay in charge of a pioneer detail of ten men to "corduroy" the road, so that wagon trains would not mire down. This assignment was executed so successfully, according to Fay, that Rust proposed to appoint him engineer, and General Lloyd Tilghman remarked that Fay ought to be a colonel instead of an orderly sergeant.

Escort duties with General Rust at Grenada prevented the Minden Rangers from participating in Van Dorn's spectacular raid on Grant's base at Holly Springs on December 20. The company remained at Grenada until late January 1863, when they were ordered to report to Van Dorn for service in Middle Tennessee. Enroute to the new assignment Fay became ill at Okolona, Mississippi, and remained there for several weeks. During his sickness and convalescence he spent much time with the E. C. Madry family, who were exceedingly hospitable. For diversion he attended meetings of the Masonic lodge, read Bulwer and the Bible, and wrote long letters to his wife.

In March 1863, Fay was detailed to accompany the wife of an officer from Okolona to Montgomery. This assignment enabled him to visit his parents at "Rocky Mount," as well as numerous other relatives and friends in the Prattville-Selma area. Early in April, 1863, he rejoined his company at Spring Hill, Tennessee. General Cosby required only light duty of his escort during the next few weeks, and Fay and his associates found life relatively pleasant in the beautiful country south of Nashville. A sensational incident of this period was the shooting of General Earl Van Dorn by Dr. George B. Peters of Spring Hill. In reporting the killing to his wife, Fay stated flatly that Van Dorn had been too intimate with the doctor's wife and added: "It may be a great gain to the Confederacy. I do not think it was a great loss."

On May 20 General Cosby and his command headed for Mississippi to assist in the defense of Vicksburg. Enroute Fay spent a night at Columbus, Mississippi, where he was the guest of his wife's uncle, ex-Governor James Whitfield. The Rangers reached Canton, Mississippi, on June 4 and the next morning were reviewed, along with other elements of Jackson's cavalry division, by General Joseph E. Johnston. They then settled down to dull routine, which Fay sought to relieve by chess played with a set of men which he and Captain Webb had carved from sassafras wood with their pocket knives. They could not afford cards, which because of scarcity and inflation at that time cost from five to ten dollars a pack. Fay, who was still smarting from the rejection of his petition for discharge, found camp life at Canton almost intolerable. "I am a bond slave worse than any negro," he wrote his wife on June 27; "in fact, I would deem myself fortunate to exchange with any slave I ever saw."

As the Federal stranglehold on Vicksburg tightened, Fay and his comrades received glowing reports of Confederate triumphs in other parts of the South. The skepticism with which these dispatches were received was indicated by Fay's comment to his wife: "I dislike to think Confed[erate] authorities would lie so wilfully. A cause must be desperate indeed that seeks alone to bolster itself by falsehood."

The fall of Vicksburg on July 4 was a stunning blow to most Confederates, and especially to families separated by the Mississippi River. The effect on Fay, who viewed with horror the prospect of being unable to communicate with his wife and children, is vividly revealed in the letters that he wrote in July and August, 1863. One result was to cause him for a time to despair of Southern independence. A second consequence was an increasing dissatisfaction with army life and an upsurge of his determination to go home, or at least to get assigned to the Trans-Mississippi Department. On July 23 he wrote his wife: "I have submitted to military despotism as long as I intend to and when I get ready am coming for good. I want to get into service on that side and if I do not the Confederacy may go to the devil as for me. I will not support a government when my rights depend on the caprice of first this general, then that." A few weeks later he asked his wife to go to see General E. Kirby Smith with a view of effecting his transfer. He added: "I am tired of Cosby's drunkenness and Jackson's slothfulness." On September 19 he complained: "This cavalry has done nothing for a year but hold reviews for generals and dress parades for a few lonesome and garish young ladies."

The loss of Vicksburg also tended to intensify Fay's hatred of the Yankees. In subsequent letters he referred to them as vandals, demons, and vile villains. On July 10, 1863, he wrote his wife: "I expect to murder every Yankee I ever meet when I can do so with impunity if I live a hundred years and peace is made in six months. Peace will never be made between me and any Yankee if I can kill him without too great risks. . . . There can be no fellowship between us forever." On several occasions after Vicksburg he indicated that in the event of Confederate defeat he would take his family abroad rather than live again in a country dominated by the despised Yankees.

During the six months following the fall of Vicksburg the Minden Rangers, still acting as escort for General Cosby, devoted most of their time to scouting, patrolling, and other routine cavalry activities. Late in December Fay went to "Rocky Mount" on furlough to visit his father, who was critically ill. Enroute he was joined at Meridian by his brother, William Henry, of the First Alabama Infantry Regiment. His other brother, Dunham, who since December, 1862, had been employed in a leather shop at Selma, also obtained leave; so the elder Fay had the three sons together at home for the first time in several years. The ailing father improved considerably during the period of the visit, and his sons were back at their posts of duty early in 1864.

In the meantime, Edwin H. Fay had intensified his efforts to obtain transfer to the Trans-Mississippi Department. On March 14, 1864, apparently at Kirby Smith's request, orders were issued by the Adjutant General's Office at Richmond transferring him in the grade of sergeant to the Engineer Bureau of Smith's command.

Fay had arrived home on furlough the first day of March, 1864, and he was still in Minden when report of his transfer reached him on March 25. The effect of the good news is indicated by his wife's entry in her diary on March 27: "My heart did not recover from the shock for a long time."[5]

The new assignment was to the Office of the Chief of the Topographical Bureau, District of West Louisiana and Arkansas. Fay's duties, which consisted mainly of reconnoitering and surveying military roads, drawing maps, and keeping records, took him to various places in the District, but he apparently spent most of his time in the vicinity of Camden and Princeton, Arkansas, and Shreveport, Louisiana. His colored aide, Rich, did not accompany him in the new position. The reason is suggested in a statement appearing in Fay's home

[5] This diary, a small manuscript volume covering the period November 18, 1862–April 29, 1864, is in possession of Miss Lucy E. Fay.

letter of May 22, 1864: "If he went to the Yankees I hope they have killed him ere this."

The engineer assignment gave to Fay much more freedom of movement than he had known as a cavalryman, and also made considerably better use of his exceptional talents. These circumstances, along with the fact of his being closer home and on the same side of the Mississippi as his family, made him a better-adjusted soldier than he had been before. His morale received a further boost late in 1864 when he was promoted to captain's rank and made assistant quartermaster, Officer of Tax-in-Kind, Fourth District, at Opelousas, Louisiana. This office supervised the collection of the tithe of agricultural produce required by the Confederate tax law of April 24, 1863. Fay's work consisted largely of compiling records and preparing reports. Except for a brief period at the beginning of each month his duties were light. During his spare time he wrote poetry, read, and visited in the homes of congenial acquaintances in Opelousas. On January 29, 1865, he wrote his wife that "Dr. George Hill . . . has taken a powerful liking to me because I can quote Horace and Homer."

As prices soared with the continuing depreciation of Confederate money, Fay found it increasingly difficult to live on a captain's salary of $140 a month. He was tempted to speculate in flour and other scarce commodities, but none of his plans for supplementing his army pay seems to have progressed beyond the point of hopeful contemplation.

If his wife had been able to join him, he could have obtained allowances that would have raised his monthly compensation to $450. But his efforts to establish a home in Opelousas were defeated by a combination of circumstances including difficulties of transportation and the precarious state of his wife's health following the birth of a son on January 1, 1865.

During the final months of the war Fay seemed to be strangely blind to the Confederacy's impending defeat. On February 5 he wrote his wife: "Tell your Father to buy you a negro girl *at any price* and I will pay him." And as late as mid-March he was still trying desperately to buy a slave. On May 5, 1865, even after receiving reports of Lee's surrender, he wrote: "I firmly believe that the

Confederacy will gain its independence." He was still making hopeful statements on May 13, though he admitted that "everybody but me is whipped."

On May 25, he wrote that quartermaster depots under his supervision had on hand 1,600 pounds of excellent sugar and 32 pounds of tobacco. "I have no orders from above," he added, "nevertheless, I shall start home just as soon as I dispose of this produce. . . . I will never accept a parole. I shall fight them to the last." This was his last Confederate letter. He probably went home soon afterwards and, once there, practical considerations doubtless caused him to abandon his previously stated intention of taking his family to South America. There is no indication that a prediction made on May 13, 1865—"My faith in God is bound to be destroyed if the South is at last subjugated"—ever materialized. This statement, like the vow to fight the Yankees to the last and then leave the country, was the impulsive outburst of a man confronted by inescapable doom.

Reunited with his family, Fay, like most of his fellow Southerners, settled down, accepted defeat, endured Reconstruction, and eventually became an American again.

The 115 letters here reproduced, with the exception of three or four that were lost in transit, are all that Fay wrote to his wife during his three-years of Confederate service. Frequency of writing varied considerably with circumstances. When the military situation was static and avenues of communications were open Fay wrote home once or twice a week. During periods of active campaigning the flow of correspondence sometimes slowed down to one or two communications a month. After the fall of Vicksburg frequency of writing was influenced to some extent by the schedules of official couriers to whom the carrying of mails was entrusted or the coming and going of furloughed soldiers, civilian visitors, and other informal agents of communication. The longest interval in Fay's correspondence was between January 9, 1864, and his arrival home on March 1. This hiatus was probably due in part to interruption of mail services and in part to the fact that Fay throughout this period was expecting the furlough that he finally obtained in late February.

The paper on which these letters were written is better than that used by most Johnny Rebs. Fay's position as orderly sergeant gave him exceptional opportunities for obtaining writing materials. His relatives from time to time sent stationery to him. Many of the envelopes that he used bore the imprint of the business in which he held a partnership: "William Shields & Co., Manufacturers of Cotton Gins & Corn Mills, Minden, La."

Despite the relative abundance of his writing materials, Fay deemed it advisable to economize. This he did by writing on both sides of the sheets, cross-writing, interlining, and writing in the margins. When forwarding to his wife letters received from his mother, he sometimes wrote a message of his own around the edges and between the lines.

Fay's army letters reveal much of the man. Like his wife, his mother, and other members of his family, he was deeply religious, though he sometimes fell short of the high standards that he set for himself. Soon after entering the army he wrote his wife: "To God I daily commit you and my children. . . . Don't let Will forget his father in his prayers, for I don't believe a bullet can go through a prayer." Three weeks later he wrote: "Remember me in your prayers. . . . I fear I am far from the right road and I fear will not find it."

He was thoroughly devoted to his family. He sometimes appears petty and unreasonable, however, in chiding his wife for not writing more frequently, making errors in spelling, and failing to keep him informed as to home activities, and other minor shortcomings. She had once been his pupil and he apparently had some difficulty forgetting the teacher-student relationship. But his criticisms derived in large measure from his idealization of the woman to whom his life was joined. As he once put it: "I would fain have her whom I hold dearest on earth come quite up to my ideal of perfection and she can do it too I feel sure."

His fault-finding was the obverse of a deep and abiding affection. This affection manifested itself in many tender passages. "Oh, darling, you don't know how much I love you," he wrote soon after leaving home. Six months later he stated: "My own darling, I wish I could bear things as well as you do, but I am not half so good as you are, nor do I think I ever can be. You are my own noble wife, and if I am spared to come home alive I know that I shall appreciate you more than ever."

Almost every letter contains a testimonial of Fay's devotion to his children. On May 14, 1862, he wrote: "It rejoices me to hear such good accounts of Will Ed and Thornwell. You know that my heart is wrapped up in them." A week later he enjoined: "Do not let them forget me. Show my picture to Thornwell and teach him to say Father." On July 3, 1862, he instructed his wife to "kiss the children 40 times for me and talk to them about their father."

The advice that he gave his wife from time to time about the rearing of the children throws interesting light on parent-child relationships of the period and the ideals and standards of an educated, middle-class, Southern father. During the infancy of his second son he wrote Sarah: "Our loving him . . . won't do any harm. . . . I do hope you are teaching him to mind. Be particular to make him stop fretting and crying when anything displeases him. . . . Don't let anyone talk baby-talk to him, teach him to speak plainly at once."

On April 13, 1862, he wrote concerning his first-born, then five years old: "Govern him strictly for the army shows up need of every man being governed while young." A month later he requested: "Teach Will to make letters on a slate preparatory to learning to write." On May 27, 1862, he advised: "Tell Will Ed he must be a good boy and mind his mother and not play on Sunday, say his prayers every night and not forget his father." Two weeks later he counseled: "Tell Will Ed that his 'Favy' [Father] wants him to say lessons and learn to read but my dear do not keep him so closely confined as to give him a distaste to his books. . . . Don't disgust him with his lessons but try and make him love his books for his father's sake and for yours. Tell him stories and interest him with them. I place my greatest hope in my children. . . . Teach him [Will Ed] the importance of system and regularity. These are lessons he should learn early and be taught to appreciate the value of them. You must govern him firmly and Thornwell too. Children should be taught to obey."

Be good, mind your parents, study your lessons, say your prayers —these admonitions of Edwin H. Fay for his sons are to be found in thousands of other letters written from both Southern and Northern camps during the Civil War. In them are manifested fundamental ideals of Nineteenth Century America.

The greatest blow suffered by Edwin H. Fay during the war, and indeed, one of the most overwhelming sorrows of his entire life, was the death in July, 1862, of his eldest child, Will Ed. When the report of the tragedy reached him at camp near Tupelo on August 5, he immediately wrote the bereaved mother: "Could not God have afflicted us in some other way . . . My heart is bursting. I almost fear I will go crazy—I don't see how I can stand it. It would not have been so hard to give him up if I could have been there and heard his last words and seen his last breath, held him in my arms . . . When our little daughter died I could become reconciled because I had seen her suffer so much but to lose my Will Ed whom I left in blooming health, my misery is greater than I can bear. . . . My heart is bursting, my brain is on fire." Similar expressions of grief appeared in many subsequent letters, and, while time brought some assuagement, the loss of this beloved son weighed heavily on Fay's mind throughout his Confederate service.

Stonewall Jackson was said to have turned down a subordinate's request to visit a dying spouse by vehemently asking the anxious officer if he was more devoted to his wife than to his country. If this question had been put to Fay, the answer would have been disappointing, for Fay did not measure up to Stonewall's high standard of patriotism. His love for the Confederacy was secondary to his devotion to his wife and children. On October 8, 1863, he wrote: "A man's family is dearer to him than anything in the world, at least mine is and 40 Confederates may go to the Devil if I am going to be kept away from all I hold dear the rest of my life."

Another characteristic repeatedly manifested by Fay in his letters is frankness. He shows no inclination to shy away from unpleasant topics or to gloss over the seamy side of army life. He is exceptionally candid in pointing up the evils that flourished in camp, the shortcomings of comrades, the harshness of discipline, and the incompetency of officers. He represents one associate from his home community as a drug addict, and reports that another shot his hand off to get out of the army. Of one doctor who obtained a discharge after a brief stint of service he wrote: "Between us he did no duty whatever;" and of another whom he charged with feigning disability in hopes of going home, he wrote: "I hope he will fail [though] he might as well be discharged for all the good he has ever done as he has never done any duty of any kind but eating."

Fay also gives occasional glimpses of the degeneration of civilian morality during the war. On April 20, 1863, he wrote from Spring Hill, Tennessee: "This is a most beautiful country but I am sorry I cannot say much for the morals of it from the way I hear the boys speaking of going out to see the women." On another occasion he informed his wife: "I have heard a report that makes me heartsick. A young lady who lives near Homer that I always thought was the pink of perfection has been delivered of a bastard and a *black one* at that. I shall call no names but her mother was your mother's friend. . . . It is said that another woman will have one before long. . . . Illegitimacy, I fear, will not be the least curse of this war." While on a visit to his parents' home in Alabama he reported encountering one of his childhood acquaintances, a woman of respectable background, *"drunk as a fool."*

Fay's most scathing comments were about the military. He loathed the regimentation and the discipline, and resented the privileged status accorded to rank. After a slight illness early in his service he wrote: "Anyone here may lie here and die for want of attention. I have never seen so selfish a place as a camp." He pronounced the army a "despotism" and the Confederacy a "tyranny." The system of passes he detested as a token of slavery. "It is a surprising thing to me," he wrote his wife in May, 1862, "that the Southern soldiers will fight with so much valor when they are so badly treated. No negro on Red River but has a happy time compared with that of a Confederate soldier."

Officers—high and low, in general and in particular—were frequently the object of Fay's vehement denunciation. After the Corinth fight of 1862 he wrote: "Our retreat was conducted with the greatest confusion and Van Dorn was drunk all the time and Villipique too and I expect Price too. . . . Such demoralization was never seen in an army before. I think the cause of the Confederacy is lost in the West. . . . We were led into a trap. I could see the want of Generalship but I could say nothing for I am not an *officer.*"

Late in 1862 Fay found himself under a different set of generals, but the change brought no softening of his attitude toward the high brass. On December 9 he wrote his wife: "By the By, I saw Pemberton, and he is the most insignificant 'puke' I ever saw. . . . His head cannot contain sense enough to command a Regt, much less a Corps." Concerning William H. Jackson, whom he thought to have been badly outgeneraled in a recent clash with the Federals, he added: "He runs first and his cavalry are well-drilled to follow their leader. He is not worth shucks. But he is a West Point graduate and therefore must be born to command." Fay's disesteem for Confederate leadership extended all the way to the commander-in-chief, of whom he wrote in this same letter: "I tell you Dearest, our Country is gone up unless God interposes by taking away Jeff Davis and lets some other than a West Pointer hold the reins of Govt." In July, 1863, he stated: "Jeff Davis thinks Richmond is heaven or nearly so while the loss of Vicksburg is incomparably greater than 40 such cities as Richmond."

Fay considered his generals, as a group, to be heartless, high-handed, and self-seeking. The one leader for whom he expressed great admiration was Albert Rust, to whom he was assigned as escort in December, 1862, and whom he immediately sized up as "a gentleman and a soldier and a humane man." After three months' service with Rust, Fay wrote: "I know but one [general] in the Confederacy that I would trust far and that is Gen'l Rust. He is one of my favorites. He would fight if he only drew a private's pay and he is a fighter, too." For Fay this was high praise indeed.

Peace, even though the circumstances by which it came seemed calamitous at the time, proved an inestimable blessing to Fay. The happiness that ensued from restoration to his family offset in large degree the misery of Reconstruction.

Early in the postwar period Fay moved from Louisiana to Mississippi, where he became principal of Fayette Academy. In 1872 he accepted the presidency of Silliman Female Collegiate Institute at Clinton, Louisiana. Seven years later he was elected State Superintendent of Public Education of Louisiana, a position which he held from 1880 to 1884. During his absence from Silliman, his wife was acting president of that institution.

Fay's education, experience, personality, and general ability made him exceptionally well qualified to direct the educational program of his adopted state. Despite limited funds, inadequate facilities, shortage of trained teachers, and many other difficulties encountered by educational leaders during the lean years following Reconstruction, Fay was able to carry forward the program of rehabilitation that had been initiated by his illustrious predecessor, R. M. Lusher. With the aid of the Peabody Fund he further developed teachers' institutes in towns and parishes. He advocated establishment of a teacher-training department in the Louisiana State University to supplement and strengthen the programs provided by the New Orleans and state normal schools. His exceptional interest in the schooling of women was evidenced by his declaration in 1881 that another great need for promoting progressive education was the establishment in Louisiana of "a second 'Vassar' or 'Wellesley' for the education of our daughters." "Thoroughly (not fashionably)," he continued, "educate the daughters of our State and you are sowing a good seed in a field that will return an abundant harvest. It will open new avenues of support to women. Better, far better, give the future mothers of Louisiana a good State College like Mt. Holyoke than to give them the ballot. Do this and your children will rise up and call you blessed."[6]

The problems that he encountered as state superintendent, the means by which he sought to meet them, and the educational philosophy which guided his course are vividly revealed in the annual reports that he prepared for the legislature. These reports give an impression of slow but steady progress during his incumbency; they also indicate that he laid a solid foundation for future building.

At the expiration of his term as state superintendent, the Fays retired to "Elfinwood," their family plantation in East Feliciana Parish. But love of teaching was too deeply rooted in both Edwin and Sarah to enable them to be content with their new way of life. In 1885 they

[6] Louisiana State Superintendent of Education, *Report for 1880–1881* (Baton Rouge, 1881), 1 ff.

established the Baton Rouge Seminary. They continued to operate this school for four years, when Fay's greatly impaired health forced them again to retire to "Elfinwood."

Edwin Fay died December 27, 1898, and Sarah Shields Fay January 19, 1919. The enormous good that they did for education in their day lived on after them in the enriched lives of the men and women whom they taught as well as those instructed by their children. One son, Edwin W. Fay, was Professor of Latin, at the University of Texas from 1899 until his death in 1920. A son-in-law, H. A. Morgan (husband of Sarah Elizabeth Fay) taught at Louisiana State University from 1889 to 1905 and then moved to the University of Tennessee, where he served successively as professor of zoology, dean of the School of Agriculture, and president. In 1933 he was appointed to the Tennessee Valley Authority, and in 1938 he became chairman of that organization. The youngest child, Lucy E. Fay, who is a member of Phi Beta Kappa and co-author of *Instruction in the Use of Books and Libraries,* had a distinguished career as university librarian and teacher of English and library science. At the time of her retirement in 1942, she was Associate Professor of Bibliography, School of Library Service, Columbia University. She now resides at Chapel Hill, North Carolina.

Two sons of Edwin and Sarah Fay attained eminence in the business world. Thornwell Fay, who died at Houston, Texas, March 31, 1932, rose from telegraph operator to the presidency of the Southern Pacific Railway. Charles Spencer Fay, who was born October 23, 1867, and who died May 30, 1946, at Lake Charles, Louisiana, served for eight years as Freight Traffic Manager of the Louisiana lines of the Southern Pacific. From 1929 until his retirement in 1934 he was vice president of the Southern Pacific.

In editing the letters I have tried to make only those changes that would facilitate reading without altering meaning. I have arranged the letters into chapters, paragraphed some of the longer passages, spelled out confusing abbreviations, and, where possible, supplied missing first names or initials. Information about relatives and other non-military persons mentioned in the letters is given in the list of Relatives and Acquaintances (p. 451). Most of the members of the

Minden Rangers, to many of whom Fay made frequent reference, are listed on the official Roster (pp. 453–459) and on the unofficial Supplementary Roster (pp. 460–461). Other persons are identified in footnotes when a useful purpose could be served and the necessary data could be found.

Fay's limited opportunities for obtaining accurate information caused him to make some errors of fact. I have cited in footnotes only those misstatements which seemed of sufficient importance to merit correction. I have not deemed it necessary to cite the inaccuracy of all the extravagant rumors that he passed on to his wife.

The unhappiness resulting from Fay's separation from his family and his inability to adjust himself to soldier life tended to warp his judgment and to make him hypercritical of people and events. It is assumed that the reader will make due allowance for this distortion, as well as for the very intimate character of some of the statements that Fay addressed to his wife. The uninhibited, personal manner in which this sensitive and articulate man records his experiences, reactions, and relationships in the crisis of war enhances the distinctiveness and importance of his letters and helps to justify their publication.

The principal sources used in the editing were the muster rolls of the Minden Rangers, obtained from the National Archives; *Records of Louisiana Confederate Soldiers and Louisiana Confederate Commands,* compiled by Andrew B. Booth; *List of Field Officers, Regiments and Battalions in the Confederate States Army, 1861–1865; Battles and Leaders of the Civil War,* edited by R. U. Johnson and C. C. Buel; *Confederate Military History,* edited by Clement A. Evans; *War of the Rebellion: Official Records of the Union and Confederate Armies;* Edwin Whitfield Fay's recollections of his father published in the July, 1916, issue of the *Texas Review* under the title "A Father of the Seventies"; a war-time diary of Sarah Shields Fay; and some manuscript letters written by her, Fay's mother, and his soldier brother, William Henry, all in the possession of Lucy E. Fay.

The originals of the Edwin H. Fay letters, too, are in the possession of Miss Lucy E. Fay. To her is due credit for recognizing the historical importance of these exceptional documents; performing the laborious and time-consuming task of transcribing them; and last but not least, making them available for publication without expurgation. I am also indebted to her for providing background information about her father and other members of the Fay family, and for furnishing pictures for illustration. Grateful acknowledgment is also given to James I. Robertson, student and colleague at Emory University, for valuable assistance in identifying persons, places, and incidents mentioned in the correspondence. Without the encouragement, advice, and assistance given by Frank Wardlaw and his able associates at the University of Texas Press this book could never have come into being.

BELL I. WILEY

1

"I Find Camp Life Pretty Hard"

Monroe, La. Apr. 6, 1862
Quartermasters Room

My Dear One:

We are in Monroe as you see and I have been busy writing almost all day. You have probably heard of my horse being foundered but he is getting better. Was appraised at $250 today. I find camp life pretty hard but am mustered into Confederate Service today and am obliged to go for 12 months. We go tomorrow at daybreak to Vicksburg and go up to Memphis on the "Alonzo Child." Will probably start up on Sunday. I don't know how I shall stand it. My throat is very sore and I believe I shall have bronchitis before long though I hope not. All the Company[1] are well my dear one and I wish I had time to write you a long letter, but I have not as fifteen or twenty men are talking around me at 12 o'clock at night. Oh my dear One I wish I could see you tonight—and dear Willy & Thornwell but God bless you for my heart is too full. I can say no more. Yours truly and lovingly.

Edwin H. Fay

Tell Lou I shall probably not go to Vicksburg at all as we camp on this side of the River.

[1] Muster rolls in the National Archives show that Fay's company, known variously as the Minden Rangers, Wimberly's Cavalry, Webb's Cavalry, and Company "A," Louisiana Cavalry Regiment, was enlisted at Monroe, Louisiana, on April 4, 1862. The formal mustering into Confederate service, which included reading the Articles of War and taking the Oath of Allegiance to the Confederate States of America, occurred on April 6.

Tuesday Night Mar [April] 8th
On board str Alonzo Child
35 miles below Memphis
9½ o'clock at night

My own One:

Well dear, you see by the extensive heading where we are or where at least I am, for I am egotistical enough to believe that where I am most concerns you. I wrote you a hasty scrawl in the Quartermaster's office in Monroe and will now take up my narrative from that point. Well, after leaving the office I went to a freight car where our saddles were packed and after scrambling over five or six sleeping men, I laid down with Julius Lancaster on his blankets and slept soundly till a storm rising brought J. Y. Webb[2] down to the car for shelter. After getting to sleep once more the next alarm was P. P. Bates coming running down to the car from camp saying the cars for Vicksburg had gone and Webb was left, the Capt.[3] having called for Webb to go in the 5 o'clock train, our horses and men not going till 8 A.M. in a special train. Webb started and here came Rich saying the Capt. wanted me to go with him. I hurried up and found that the cars had not gone and that the Capt. had detailed Loye Webb and myself to go with him to Vicksburg to make arrangements for the Company. We got off the train three miles from Vicksburg and walked 3 or 400 yards across a field to the Boat and had to go 5 miles to Vicksburg.

Got there and found our "Here's your Ham and your Lamb, your Jelly and your Jamb" man,[4] as Quartermaster so overrun with business that he could do nothing for us, so Webb and I trotted about all the Flat Boats but could find none. We then went up street and got on track of some and got it. I bought all Lou's music except Leesburg

[2] Junius Y. Webb, one of the original members of the Minden Rangers, and initially 1st sergeant, was elected captain of the company in May, 1862. He was still in command when Fay was transferred from the company in 1864. See D. W. Harris and B. M. Hulse, *History of Claiborne Parish,* 237.

[3] Capt. F. D. Wimberly, who commanded the company from its original enlistment in April, 1862, until its reorganization in May, 1862. Wimberly, whose wife was in poor health, returned to Minden in June, 1862, and apparently remained there for the duration of the war.

[4] A hotel keeper in Vicksburg who met trains and boats and called out this invitation to prospective guests, and who apparently became a quartermaster in the Confederate service.

March for $2.10 and mailed it, which I hope she has got before this. You remember De Soto City opposite Vicksburg, well it was five feet deep under water and from Vicksburg up here we have seen all the pictures of Harper's Weekly fully realized. Such destruction never was seen anywhere. People living in houses whose floors were 8 in. deep in water. Stock of all kinds moored in flat boats close to the doors. Such is the scene on both sides of the River as far up as this place. Napoleon and Helena, Ark. are both almost under water.

Well Mother, we had to take deck passage but Capt. Wimberly made an arrangement for us to go into the cabin and sleep on the floor on our blankets, eat at the table &c for $3.00 apiece, which we are doing. Some of the men like Rathbun & Hudson (drunkards) grumble a great deal but we found when we reached Vicksburg even that our fame had preceded us—that of being the most orderly well-behaved company that had ever passed through that place. We have been treated very well and I could relate many little incidents, if I could sit by your side, which would interest you very much, but I have neither time or space to write all I could.

You will doubtless ere this have heard of the great battle at Corinth and how badly the federals ran.[5] I had a copy of yesterday's Appeal[6] given me. We have driven them back and taken all of their Artillery. Sidney Johnson killed.[7] How great our losses are had not been ascertained. We did not get a chance in the fight but if we get there tomorrow night we can see some of the effects. I anticipate a hard time now, for if the Feds. are driven back we will have a great deal of scouting to do and in all weathers. It is raining again tonight and was last night and I am afraid we are going to have bad weather and a great deal of it. I wrote you my horse was foundered but was valued at $250. I think he has recovered and will be as good as ever. I was greatly troubled but called on Him who relieves all of our troubles and He heard me. We left Vicksburg on Saturday night and on Sun-

[5] The reference is obviously to the battle of Shiloh, April 6–7, 1862.

[6] The *Memphis Daily Appeal.*

[7] Albert Sidney Johnston, Commanding General of the Confederate forces in the West, was mortally wounded at Shiloh on the afternoon of April 6, 1862. Fay's erroneous statements about the outcome of the battle accord with Southern newspaper accounts which continued for several days after the Confederates yielded the field to the Federals to represent Shiloh as a great Southern victory.

day I got out my Bible to read and found your Note. I thank you for it my dear Sarah and will read it when I can but I find already that I shall have little time for reading anything.

We will go to Corinth and you must write me there, if not there it will be forwarded to us. I can write you all night but the light is dim and I shall have to be on guard at 5 o'clock in the morning and shall not have time to write much more. Doc B. G. Brantley has been sick with mumps but is getting better now. Lynn Boyd [Watkins] has had a slight attack but I believe is convalescent now. A. F. Minchew is complaining tonight and a man by the name of Dabney[8] also. We are as a general thing quite healthy. I have no cold but a terrible sore throat but I think I'll get better of it in a few days. I wish you could step into this cabin tonight and see the floor covered with soldiers from the forward to the ladies saloon. In every conceivable posture you will see the Minden Rangers. At one table Dr. Patillo[9] on one side, J. Y. Webb on the other and your own husband on a third side all writing their dear ones at home. [John C.] Loye and Jim Simmons at another table, I presume doing the same thing. Thus dear you see I have given you a slight Daguerreotype of our Company at present. But [P. P.] Bates has gone to sleep and the cabin is looking all over my paper so I must stop. This letter I don't wish read around for it is for you alone. At Helena, Ark. today I saw a little boy who reminded me of Thornwell and I assure you I could not refrain from tears. I wish you to be sure to hear Will Ed's lessons regularly and remember that your child's education is of more importance than any visiting or anything else. Try, too, and see if Thornwell can't be taught to talk and teach him too. Don't let Will Ed forget his prayers—to say them every night. Give my love to your Mother and Father and the children all. Tell Lou she can write to a soldier now as she has been

[8] Dabney is unidentified. When the Minden Rangers were reorganized in late May, 1862, several members were at home. This fact explains the omission of their names from the official roster. No complete roster for the early period is available.

[9] Dr. W. C. Patillo, of Minden, was 1st lieutenant of the Minden Rangers when the company was mustered into Confederate service. At the time of reorganization in May, 1862, he declined to stand for re-election and returned home with Captain Wimberly. See Harris and Hulse, *History of Claiborne Parish,* 236.

wanting to for a long time. Good Bye dearest. May God bless and keep you. Kiss our children. Yours always, Ed.

I cannot look for mistakes in this, so you see it is for your eyes alone, for the eye of love overlooks all faults. Goodbye. A kiss to you dearest.

Grand Junction, Tenn. 11 Apr. 1862

My dearest One:

I mailed a letter to you at Memphis, which I hope you have got before this time, and gave you a description of events up to that time, and as I am off guard now for four hours I will pick up the end of my yarn. We reached Memphis Wednesday about 11 A.M. and found there 4100 prisoners from Shiloh, the battlefield, Gen'l Prentiss[10] among them. He said they would have Memphis in 20 days, also said that the great fight at Corinth would decide the war. He is a great brag and a great fool withal. There are rumors that Buell was killed and that Magruder had whipped McClellan and killed him on the Peninsula. There are a thousand and one rumors here and I got more reliable information of the battle from Alex Goodwyn just from N.O. than any I could find in Memphis or here only 40 miles from the battleground. We took the cars at Memphis at 6 P.M. and reached Grd. Junction at 3 A.M. and here our engines were taken from us and we had to lie over all day yesterday with our horses on the cars with no chance to feed or drink. Last night after night we declared we would stand it no longer and took our horses off the cars, watered and fed. I tell you our horses do not look as fine as they did the day we left although we still get the credit of being the best mounted company in the Confederacy. All this does not amount to anything though for

[10] Brig. Gen. Benjamin M. Prentiss commanded the 6th Division of the Federal Army of the Tennessee at Shiloh. He and most of his command were captured on the afternoon of April 6, after gallantly executing a delaying action which helped save the day for Grant's hard pressed forces. See Robert U. Johnson and Clarence C. Buel, eds., *Battles and Leaders of the Civil War* (4 vols., New York, 1884–1887), I, 505–506. To be cited hereafter as *Battles and Leaders.*

a report has just come in that 10,000 fresh troops had reached Corinth and were on their own expenses, so "they say."

We will stay here and pitch our camp for a few days at least. How true it may be I cannot say, for I have learned since I left home, to believe nothing that I do not see with my eyes or hear &c. I mentioned Alex Goodwyn who was going with two female nurses and some physicians to attend the sick and wounded. He has at home a little girl 3 yrs old named Annie. Sends much love to you. I hope I shall see or hear from William Henry before many days. I shall write this other half sheet to him at Corinth as I have casually heard that the 1st Ala. was in the battle.

We hear that the 19th La. was engaged in the fight. Parson Winfrey B.[11] was wounded in the calf of the leg, glory enough to send him to the Legislature if he ever returns. M. Leverett the 3rd Lieut. was killed and two others whom we did not know, Beauregard is at Corinth in an entrenched camp trying to draw the enemy from his Gun Boats as they run so fast back that our boys can't catch them in a four mile race, but if he can get them—15 or 20—thinks he will get all. Our men are confident of victory but I am very sorry to find but very little attention is paid the wounded.

Our soldiers are not treated right. I think they pay more attention to Yankee prisoners than our own wounded. This is only a surmise of my own from what I have seen. My dear I could tell you of camp life and if I could give you a true picture you would be miserable so I'll only say that I think I can stand it as long as any in the Co. I did not set out to complain. I believe all the sick are convalescent. It has rained all night and the worst storm now you almost ever saw, as cold as Chloe to boot tho thanks to your consideration I do not suffer any.

If I write to William Henry I must say goodbye to you. You must take good care of Yourself as well as of our darlings. Don't let them forget their Father. I don't think I shall write again till I can give

[11] Probably Winfrey B. Scott, the "Parson Scott" referred to in Fay's letter of April 13, 1862. Scott, a member of the 19th Louisiana Infantry Regiment, was wounded at the battle of Shiloh and mortally wounded at New Hope Church in Georgia May 27, 1864. See Harris and Hulse, *History of Claiborne Parish,* 200–201, 205.

you something definite about our movements. You must write to Corinth. My sore throat is improving and I feel pretty well except loss of sleep. However after tonight at 10 o'clock I shall have no guard duty to do for three days. Remember me kindly to your Father and Mother, Lou and the rest. Take good care of yourself my dearest for I may come home again. To God I daily commit you and my children. Kiss them for their Father and an hundred kisses to you my love. Write me good long letters. Your affectionate husband, Ed. H. Fay.

Write me good long letters and write to Mother. Don't forget Will Ed's lessons.

Camp Wimberly near
Gd Junction Tenn Monday
Morn 7½ A.M. [April 13,1862]

My Own dear One:

I mailed a letter to you on Saturday but nothing was certain of our movements and consequently I write this morning as I have an opportunity of sending it direct to Monroe by "Bill Oliver" who came back from the battlefield yesterday where he was engaged the Sunday previous. He says he saw enough to satisfy him altho he was but an independent in Ruggles Brigade. Captured one Yankee prisoner and *knows* that he killed eight or ten. That's glory enough for him so he goes back home to carry back "Jasper" who is sick and I think he is sick too of battles. "Mais revenons à nous moutons."

After leaving off my letter last Saturday (I believe it was Friday) at night I was on watch from 8 to 10 and after getting off had just stretched my blankets preparing to lie down when the order came to get our horses on board cars for Corinth. So out we paddled in the rain and mud to a lot a ¼th of a mile and got our horses. I thought Rich would get my horse but after all got up Rich was nowhere to be found so I got my horse and had to hunt all over Gd. Junction for him. Gave a boy a quarter to find him but at last he was brought in—gone skylarking to see some women. I tried to bump his brains out against a hogshead of sugar and since then he has done pretty well. We got our horses on but did not get the cars off owing to some reason or other and at 11 A.M. Saturday the order came down from Corinth pressing our engines again. Capt. Wimberly then ordered our horses off again and detailed me to hunt a camping ground and a pleasant one I found just on the corporation line of this place—an excellent spring and branch for washing. We moved out and divided our tents and mine was the first of the snowy houses erected on the plain although I had never seen a tent pitched in my life. [P. P.] Bates [N. M.] Martin, [P. Y.] Morrow, [John] Lackey and myself occupy a little 7 by 9 tent and find it quite comfortable so far. At least I have had two very good nights sleep in it.

I presume you will have had a rumor of Lewis Peters shooting his hand off. From all the circumstances attending it I think and I may say it is a general impression that he did it on purpose to get to go back home. Most persons say he is not in his right mind but he stole a saddle on board the boat with all the shrewdness of an accomplished veteran. I like Peters as well as a great many of the company and don't say this with any malice towards him. 'Tis simple truth but must be kept in the family. No gossiping neighbors should know anything about my saying it. He goes home this morning with Mr. [A. B.] Oliver on a discharge from the Post Surgeon.

Yesterday was as beautiful a day as ever dawned on the earth and as I had lost a great deal of sleep I made it up before dinner and after I made Rich take my valise and went to the branch and took a good bath and got on clean clothes. It was refreshing I tell you, you don't know what a luxury to be clean once more. In the evening Capt. Wimberly drilled the company but I begged off and minded camp. Before the drill we attended the funeral of a soldier who died in an adjoining camp of Tennesseans. The band played the dead march in Saul and I thought it the most beautiful music I ever heard. A drunken or crazy man fired at us and we heard the ball whistle over our heads very distinctly. The music is not pleasant I assure you. Oliver advised the Capt. to remain here and report in person to Beauregard and last night we received orders from Corinth to remain here until further ordered so we consider ourselves a fixture here for the time being at any rate.

I have written to William Henry but have not heard from him yet tho I hope to get an answer this morning if he is not killed or wounded for the 1st Ala. covered themselves with glory under Gen. [Braxton] Bragg. I think camp life will agree with him. A telegraphic dispatch came yesterday that the Yankees admit a loss of 12,000 in the Battles of Sunday & Monday.[12] Our loss in dead is not over 1500 but in wounded heavy. The dead will finally amount to 2000. I have heard many descriptions of the Battle from participants and Oliver says that we took their batteries before we fired a gun—just charged their camp while they were getting their breakfasts and got their victuals, coats and other clothing. I bought me a large sized Colt's revolver for which I paid $45.00 as I was determined to be as well armed as any of the company and if I could buy another I would do it to carry in my holsters. Money is nothing where my safety is concerned.

This is the rainiest country I ever saw, yesterday being the only pleasant day we have had. Today it looks cloudy but I hope it will not rain for I want Rich to do some washing. He had just passed the door of my tent where I am writing on my valise on my knee, sitting as cross legged as any Turk, and wants to know if I want anything washed. Camp life is dirty enough I assure you but I have set out with a determination to keep clean and I intend to persevere. Our Mess is no. 2 and I am the head of it, my business is to draw provisions from the Commissary who for the time being is Jim Simmons. This last page is peculiarly an Ollapod.[13] Joe Hamilton has thrown away the mouth piece of his Horn so as not to have to blow. He tries to take the command out of Capt. Wimberly's hands on all occasions and has the happiest faculty of making himself hated of any one I ever saw. I'd hate to go into battle if I was in his place for he will certainly be between two fires. I am sorry for him for he don't intend to do wrong but he is twice as big a fool as Peters.

Now my dearest I am most through my sheet. You know how I love you and I believe it increases more and more every day. What would I not give to see you and our own dear children or even get a letter from you this morning. You must direct your next letter to Grd. Junction for I don't know how long we may stay here but long

[12] The reference is to Shiloh.

[13] In George Colman's *Poor Gentlemen* Dr. Ollapod was an erratic apothecary and wit. But the word used by Fay is probably an abbreviation of *olla podrida,* a stew of meat and vegetables—hence a conglomeration.

enough I hope to get a letter from you. Parson [Winfrey B.] Scott passed through here yesterday morning en route for home, wounded in the fleshy part of his thigh. Glory enough for him. I did not see him. Mother I expect I repeat a great many things in my letters but they are not for publication so no import. Give a great deal of attention to Will Ed's studies and remember to govern him strictly, for the army shows the need of every man's being governed while young. Try and teach Thornwell to walk and in fact devote most of your time to your children for my sake. Don't let Will forget his father in his prayers, for I don't believe a bullet can go through a prayer and it is a much better shield than the steel armor with which Oliver says many Yankees were clad for he saw their coats of mail. Keep Willy in the house on Sundays and read to him and tell him stories. Teach him to reverence the Sabbath. Now my dear one I must say Good Bye. I have written you a long letter. I don't know that I shall have time to write as often in future but shall write when I can. Give much love to your Mother and Father from me. A kiss to Willy and Thornwell from their Father and your husband. Ed. H. Fay

In Camp, near Grand Junction
Monday 1 P.M. April 21st, 1862

My own dear One:

Again I seat myself in my tent to write you but have little new or interesting to tell you for we are experiencing that bane of a soldier's life, inactivity or in other words "rotting in camp." I thought when I volunteered in a Cavalry Co. that I should at least escape that disagreeability but find that the "Minden Rangers" are bound to carry out their already established character of moving slowly. We are here and here we are bound to stay till Capt. Wimberly gets tired. I find my dear, (this is for no other eyes than your own) that I (egotistical isn't it?) know actually more about military matters than any man in the company. Don't breathe this to anybody for I am far from saying it to any but you.

Pardon this interlude but I am spoiling for a fight, something I have dreaded heretofore, yes, actually dreaded, but now I am anxious for. I must tell you that in all human probability the Yankee villains have got Wm. Henry a prisoner in their pest holes of dungeons. He was basely surrendered at Island No. 10 by a fool Gen'l who for some reason or other assumed command a few days before the surrender.[14] All the 1st Ala. Regt. were given up except 180 who are said to have escaped. Capt. Whitfield's Co. were among those given up so William Henry is in all probability in the power of the Yankees. This my dear has changed my whole feelings about going into battle and I am anxious now to get me a big Yankee to swap for him. Nothing less than a Col. will suit me for I think any member of the "Fay" family is worth a dozen Yankee Cols. I did think never to take a prisoner but now I want a hostage or more for my brother. You beg me, my dear Wife, not to expose myself, but I have always believed the most daring came off with fewest wounds. It's not exposing myself unnecessarily and I may feel differently on the eve of battle but I am now determined to accomplish something should an opportunity ever offer. I am determined not to be a private throughout this war and I will have no office dependent on elections for I confess the principle though originally right is now entirely too democratic for me. Of late years office is not the reward for merit but a Sychophancy and my spirit as you know abhors that as "Nature does a vacuum."

You would have been uneasy enough had you been in camp for the last 48 hours. It has done nothing but rain and our camping ground is almost overshoe deep in mud and the coldest driving wind I ever felt at this season. It reminded me of the icy winds of Lake Erie while at Hudson, Ohio. Friday night I was on guard but had on India rubber cloak and kept dry. Saturday it rained all day so we had no supper or dinner and yesterday it held up long enough for me to take a wagon to an old gin house and get out the floor to put a floor in our tent. Sunday though it was I went and believe I have preserved my health by it for the rain was in our tent and last

[14] The Confederate leader who surrendered Island No. 10 in the Mississippi River, near New Madrid, Missouri, April 7, 1862, was Brig. Gen. W. W. Mackall, but he had been in command only a week and could do little to prevent capture of the place. The person most responsible was Brig. Gen. John P. McCown, whom Mackall had succeeded on March 31, 1862. See Stanley F. Horn, *The Army of Tennessee* (Indianapolis, 1941), 144–145.

night we had things dry. This morning it has rained off and on and now is sleeting as hard as you ever saw it and we were driven from our dinners by a storm of sleet. It is as cold as you would wish to see too, but inside a tent, wrapped up in blankets I defy the weather as long as my tent stands. I am looking every minute for it to blow down but still I intend to write on till it does fall for I have a chance to send this letter by Mr. Vickers who will return from Corinth on his way back to Minden tomorrow or next day and I have a kind of belief that letters go faster by private conveyance than by Cousin Sallie's Mail Boys.

I haven't told you yet my dearest how delighted I was on Saturday when lying down in a tent Rich told me there was a letter for me. I wanted to break his head for not bringing it and sent him to the Capt's tent for it. I knew it was from you long before I saw it. The tent was full but it was raining and so I was obliged to read it there and I must confess that only the presence of so many kept back my tears and did not quite do it at that for I was asked several times what was the matter. I told them that the smoke had made my eyes sore and they would run water. True enough. Indeed I was glad to hear that you were all well but I am troubled about "Will Ed." You cannot be too careful of his health. I trust him entirely to you and you know how my soul is wrapped up in him. Am glad *Forms*[15] has more teeth and hope he will walk soon. Poor fellow he wont know me should I live to come home for in three years he will be a good big boy if he lives.

I suppose you know we are all in for 3 years under this late conscription act. I think the act tyrannical but am satisfied that it is the speediest way to put an end to the war. It will get a good many who are hurrying back and will at any rate stop young speculators under 35. I fear it will not reach John D. Watkins but hope it may, for it will kill him. The very thought of a battle will be his death. So Ardis has got an office at last and Dr. Harper too.[16] Well some folk are born

[15] Pet name for Thornwell Fay.

[16] Ardis may be C. H. Ardis, who in January, 1865, was a colonel in charge of the Clothing Bureau for Louisiana. *War of the Rebellion: Official Records of the Union and Confederate Armies* (128 vols., Washington, 1880–1901), XLVIII, pt. 1, 1313. This source will be cited hereafter as *O.R.*, and unless otherwise indicated, all references will be to series 1. Dr. Harper may be

lucky for Joe Hamilton's old horse that Joe Bangs sold him was valued at $250.[17] The conscript act makes it necessary to hold an election of Officers in 40 days and the aforesaid Joe's Commission will do him very little good I opine for he will never get another office, I think, though there is no telling, the "Luck of a lousy calf" and he is emphatically one.

I wish now I had brought my watch for I need it to prevent these Corporals & Sergeants keeping me on guard too long. If you can send it to me by Martin Rawls take off the chain but send the key. I wish I had a good silver double cased watch in its place for all camp watches should be double cased. If you could buy me a good one cheap I'll give you mine, and send it by Rawls instead of my gold one. It should not cost over $50 and if some fellow is going off it might be got cheaper. I used to laugh at careful mothers sending eggs, butter, etc. to their sons in the army but such presents now I can appreciate could they be carried. I am hungry at meal times but must say I have not had anything fit for a negro to eat since I came to camp. Rich cant cook a bit and is more bother than he is worth. I wish I had brought Henry. Tho Rich does do tolerably well considering after all. You know he is careless and inattentive. Last night he went to sleep over the fire and dropped his hat in and burned it up, so he is hatless. Send him Jim's old hat in the closet at home, by Rawls. I expect I shall have to buy him one before that time though. The Govt. has furnished us with no wagons yet and if we have to move will have to throw away our baggage I am afraid for our Tents and Govt. property will have to go and our Wagons cant haul all. If it was not for this I would write for more things but I will wait and see.

Our officers have tents with flies and are large enough to accommodate ten or fifteen men while ours have no flies and are so small that

---

Francis A. Harper, lieutenant and captain, Company I, 1st Louisiana Cavalry Regiment. See Andrew B. Booth, compiler, *Records of Louisiana Confederate Soldiers and Louisiana Confederate Commands* (3 vols. in 4 parts, New Orleans, 1920), III, pt. 1, 194. This source will be cited hereafter as Booth, *La. Confed. Soldiers.*

[17] This reference may be to Joseph B. Hamilton, who later became a lieutenant in Company E, 13th Battalion, Louisiana Partisan Rangers. See Booth, *La. Confed. Soldiers,* III, pt. 1, 167.

hardly four men can occupy them conveniently and our saddles then have to be out of doors. There is too much difference made between officers and privates in the army as regards conveniences. We have tried to buy a fly or officers tent but cant be bought anywhere. Nat Martin is writing home for his hunting tent and you must tell Martin Rawls to bring it by all means and we will make a fly out of it. Tell Mr. Shields[18] to send us a lot of good rope for tie ropes for our horses, the size of bed cords. He will know what kind. Jack has broken my halter all to pieces. If that trifling Homer would take my leather and make me another and not charge three prices for it I would like it.

The weather is so disagreeable that eleven are on the sick list but I think it is mostly to get rid of duty this weather. Giles Monzingo is worst off at present. [A. B.?] Oliver [Butler?] has been pretty bad but is better. Bowel complaint is the principal disease. As for myself I am ready and willing to eat my allowance if it was only clean, an improbability in camp. The Va. boys bragged of nice biscuit &c. I don't believe a word of it. There are none here.

As regards your not getting a line in Lou's Music. I had it sealed up at the very time I bought it by the dealer himself and consequently could not get you in a line. I hardly had time in Vicksburg to get the music everything was in such a hurry and confusion. Am sorry you were disappointed. Am glad Will Ed is getting along so well with his lessons. Do not neglect him. Get him a slate and pencil. Mr. Webb says tell him that he left *positive orders* for his old negro to bring him a lamb the very first time he came from the plantation. You must be sure to get it for him and then Will will have a little lamb. Mrs. Webb knows about it. You must call on her. You must tell me how long my letters are coming.

The next day after writing you I went to La Grange, Tenn. 2½ miles from here. Learned that Dr. Waddel preached there.[19] He is president of the Synodical College there. It is a beautiful place. The

[18] William Shields, Fay's father-in-law.

[19] John N. Waddel, prominent Presbyterian educator and minister, helped found the University of Mississippi, taught ancient languages there from 1848 to 1857, and was chancellor of that institution from 1865 to 1874. From 1860 until 1862 he was president of the Synodical College at LaGrange, Tennessee. After the Federals occupied the town in 1862, he fled to the Confederate

college buildings are at present used as a hospital. There is a fine Female College there too. I calculated yesterday to go down and hear the Dr. preach but it rained so I could not. Will next Sunday if it is good weather and I am here. Fuller's Co. got here Saturday. Their tents have gone on to Corinth but they will stay here and send for them. What we will do I know not. Capt. Wimberly wants to form a Regiment of Cavalry here. I had rather do some fighting. I believe I wrote you that I had bought a Navy repeater for $45. I go out and kill rabbits with it almost as well as if I had a rifle. It carries the same ball. I don't think the Confederacy treats her troops right. She feeds us three days out of four on pickled Beef that even our negroes will not eat. Nasty stinking blue stuff a dog will hardly smell it. We have saved our meat from home along so that we have not suffered yet.

The report has just come to camp that our Cavalry had retaken Nashville and 5000 prisoners stacked their arms saying they would not fight for Lincoln any more. They will also bag the 10,000 Feds who are at Huntsville. There is great trouble of some kind in the Yankee army and Mr. Webb coming in from Grenada this morning says it was reported there that the Yankees had made proposition for peace on the basis that eight states should go out and the border states take a vote of their own people on the subject. There are so many rumors one hardly knows what to believe. Anything to close the war but a sacrifice of our honor or claims. I want them to pay our War debt too. I will write a little more between the lines on this page.

I am sorry that our trees blowed down but am glad it was no worse. I want you to have the little wagon fixed up for Thornwell, be sure to have it done no matter what it costs, have him a pretty painted body put on. You can get it done at Chaffe's. Springs might be easily put to it. See what you can have it done for and let me know. I wrote Mother a long letter before I heard William Henry was taken prisoner and asked where he was. I learned he was at Corinth then at Ft. Pillow, then on Island no. 10. Poor Boy. If I was in his place I should be able to get along better for I know the ways of the world better than he and the Yankees need some body who would talk to them.

---

lines and later became Chief of Chaplains in Joseph E. Johnston's Army of Tennessee.

Perhaps it is for the best as all things turn out for the best in the hands of our Dear Redeemer.

Well Mother dear, I must stop for I want to write Spencer this evening and my eyes are now sore from this smoke. Take good care of our children. Govern them with strictness and care and let nothing influence you that you do not your whole duty towards them. You know my wishes and my fears for my children therefore guard them as you love me. Keep Will Ed in the house on Sunday and read to him. You cannot employ your time more profitably than by instructing him. Teach Thornwell his prayers as soon as he can talk and teach him to read as early as possible. Should I never return you know all my wishes and I shall depend on your fulfilling them. Oh my Darling Wife I must say goodbye. Love to all the children and to your Father & Mother. Write to me often at Grand Junction till further orders. Yours and yours only, Ed. H. Fay

Tuesday Morn. Please send me two *heavy* plates that wont break. I cant endure tin ones.

In Camp Grand Junction
Friday April 25, 1862

My own dearest:

Rain Rain Rain and the coldest meanest muddiest rain! the day a fit emblem of the events which it has just ushered in. Last night at Roll Call we were ordered to be prepared at 5½ A.M., as on dress parade to attend the execution of a deserter from Col. Hannon's Regt.[20] stationed here. I hoped for a headache or to be sick in some way for I did not desire to witness the execution. Suffice it to say he was either the most hardened wretch I ever saw or an insane person. He marched on to the ground laughing and dreaded death no more than I do wetting nor as much for you know I am opposed to water for the outer man but for the inner am a strong advocate. He fell without a groan or a struggle. Poor fellow! and this is the beginning of war for 3 yrs. for

[20] Lt. Col. Moses W. Hannon at this time commanded the 1st Alabama Cavalry Regiment; he later commanded the 53rd Alabama Partisan Rangers.

me. My home will be doubly dear to me should I ever see it again which I think extremely doubtful.

We received orders last night to report without delay at Headquarters near Tuscumbia. The enemy hold it. We go in the morning and this I should not have written you but I know others will so you had better hear it from me. We'll probably join Jack Morgan's Regt.[21] Col. Sandidge[22] came from Corinth yesterday morning and described an interview he had had with Gen'l Beauregard who said he was going to send all the Cavalry to retake Huntsville, Ala. So you see that in all probability my first fighting will be in defense of my *native* state. Also that we must be attached to some Regt. and Col. Sandidge preferred Jack Morgan's. Scott's La. Regt.[23] Cavalry have nearly all died and their horses have been starved to death. The Phillips Rangers from Washita have been dismounted and there has been a rumor that we were to be too and turned into infantry. Sandidge drew from Gen'l Beauregard that we should retain our horses. Quite a favor in a *despotism,* for such is an army. Capt. Wimberly sat on the Court Martial that tried the deserter. There was no help for him for he had deserted three times and drawn three bounties of 50 each for re-enlistment in different Co's.

I have nothing to tell you of news for it is scarce. I have eaten nothing hardly lately until yesterday I went to La Grange and at the Tavern I got a good dinner. We have nothing but dry beef and it rotten, only 5 lbs. of Bacon for ten men for six days, just enough to cook once—the rest, beef that dogs wouldn't eat. Imagine horrors of

[21] Col. John Hunt Morgan's 2nd Kentucky Cavalry Regiment was at this time stationed at Corinth, Mississippi.

[22] Probably Col. John M. Sandidge, who is mentioned in *O.R.,* XXIV, pt. 2, 484, as a volunteer aide serving on the staff of Gen. Daniel Ruggles in North Mississippi, June, 1863. Sandidge served as a colonel in the Mexican War, was a member of the Louisiana legislature 1846–1855, and served in the United States House of Representatives during the 34th and 35th Congresses (March 4, 1855–March 3, 1859). *The Biographical Directory of the American Congress, 1774–1949* (Washington, 1950), 1776, states that he served throughout the Civil War as a colonel of the Bossier Cavalry. But his name does not appear on the *List of Field Officers, Regiments, and Battalions in the Confederate States Army, 1861–1865* (n.d., n.p.) or in Booth, *La. Confed. Soldiers.* His Civil War service may have been of a voluntary, unofficial character and the title of colonel may have been a carry-over from the Mexican War.

[23] The 1st Louisiana Cavalry Regiment, commanded by Col. John S. Scott.

horrors and you can't come up to camp life. I make no complaint openly for it does no good. We can't buy anything about here—musty bacon 30 cents per lb. and hard to find at that. I shan't starve, though you can imagine my breakfast when I tell you it consisted of 2 spoonsful of Rice and a little molasses. I shall soon be the "little dandy school teacher" again if I keep falling off. I can stand it as long as anyone I think in the Co. and I intend to do it too. I don't wish you to read my letters or show them to any one as you love me. Burn them for I can't write for other eyes than your own. To you, my dear, you know I always speak without reserve. I want you to tell me if you read or send my letters to be read to any one. I want Minden impressions of the camp life of the Minden Rangers to be derived from other pens than mine and then you will have an advantage over the rest in knowing the truth or falsity of such impressions. Learn the lesson I am now trying to learn, viz., to see, hear and find out all I can but contribute nothing to the general stock of information. I intend henceforth to let only "the sacred few" I call friends know what I do think or feel.

You do not know how disappointed I was at not getting a letter from you yesterday. Capt. Wimberly got one dated the 19th and there were one or two others came to camp in answer to letters written from this place but I have got none save the first. Don't let the like occur again. If any one in camp gets letters let that one be me. Shall I be disappointed this morning or not is the question I am as yet unable to answer. Webb has gone to the Post Office and I am anxiously awaiting his return. Heaven grant my letter may come. I'll write on though I have nothing more to say.

Van Dorn and Price have been up to Fort Pillow but I learned that their forces passed up Corinth yesterday. Another battle will occur there in all probability and we shall be beyond, but Beauregard and Bragg have disciplined the army again and will whip them certainly. These rains may put it off for several weeks but it must come or the Yankees are done. Money will give out and they complain that owing to increased expense of transportation in our country their expenses are $5,000,000 per day. Washington letter writers already hoot at the idea of ever paying the principal and doubt the interest being paid. Something will put an end to the war before long I hope for I acknowledge I am satisfied with what I have seen, but if the weather would stay good and we had "good to eat" I could even discover pleasure in camp life. Rich is sick this morning, had a chill and complains of his head and back. I have asked Dr. Patillo to fix some medicine for him which he has promised to do. 'Tis as cold as Chloe this morning, my breath steams up just as if there were white frost. I hope warm weather will come after a while—

11½ A.M. I quit writing a while ago and went out in hopes of getting a letter but Webb came and only brought one for Browder Oliver. What is the reason you don't like me as well as David Caufield's wife. He got a letter of the 19th and also of the 21st since I got mine whose latest date was the 14th. If we get off tomorrow I don't expect to hear from you in 6 or 8 weeks because no letter was written me on the 21st. But I'll not complain for it does no good. What would I not give to see you and my children this stormy morning. This blowy raining weather increases. What will poor us do for the life of me I can't conceive. I have said so much in previous letters about the children that I can say nothing more in this but that you must not forget what I have previously written. Do dear Mother take care of Will for I don't think him a hardy child. Thornwell's constitution is stronger. I dreamed of you last night, a painful pleasure, even in a pleasant dream. I hope *your health* continues *good*. Does it? Write me all about it when you can. Your letters I shall destroy soon after getting them so that should I fall no villainous Yankee shall ever behold your fair hand or gloat in ridicule over the expression of your love so dear to me. Tomorrow I burn the one already received. I am glad you wrote me about our dogs. I don't often think of them since there are objects so much dearer where they are. Well now Mother I must close for I am cold, almost frozen writing on my valise in my lap in my tent enduring what I have never endured before. I shall endeavor to write you as soon as I find where our Headquarters are to be, in the mean time write to this place and they will be forwarded to us I hope. Tell Lou she must write and be sure there is a letter sent every week at any rate. I shall write when I can. Give much love to your Parents, Brother & Sisters for me. May God bless and protect you and our children is my prayer. *Yours* Ed.

I may put in a few words in pencil in the morning if I get a letter.

Sat. Morn. This letter must go to the office before I can hear so don't know whether I shall get your Letter or not. Rich is still sick but I hope he will get better. The rain is over and the sun shining brightly. Start tomorrow for Tuscumbia. God Bless you.

Camp 6½ oclock P.M.
Sat Eve Feby [April] 26 1862

My own dear wife:

I have a chance to send a word by Mr. John L. Vickers although I mailed a letter to you this morning. I hope you will get it for in it I wrote you particulars of our intended march overland to the vicinity of Tuscumbia, Ala. where there are 8000 Federals and we will go on to Huntsville. Gen'l Beauregard has ordered all his Cavalry on and we are to join some Regiment up there—probably Jack Morgan's or Wirt Adams'.[24] We leave at daylight tomorrow morning. Rich has been quite sick but I think is getting better. We have to send our baggage by Rail to "Iuka" and I fear we will never see it again. I have wrapped up my two shirts (blue ones), a pair of pants, 3 prs. socks in my leggings and am to carry them on my horse. My blankets and oil cloth I shall wrap around them. We drew these little valises to put behind our saddles and they will not hold but a pair of my pants and a pair of socks. I have strapped it to my valise and sent it in the cars.

Send me if you can a yard of oil cloth. My buggy boot would be the very thing, if you would cut it out. Send me by Rawls a strong bottle of strong pepper sauce or some good catchup. John Lackey has done very well until he went to the Hospital and he got laudanum and I think he is most dead although he came back to camp this morning. I had hoped we were to make a man of him. I might write a week but it is so dark I can't see so must close. Take good care of our little ones. Write me at Gd. Junction till further notice. Give much love to all for me. Excuse this dearest for I mailed four full pages to you this morning. Yours most affectionately Ed. H. Fay.

Kiss our children for me.

[24] Col. Wirt Adams commanded a regiment of Mississippi cavalry in the Army of Tennessee.

2

"Just As Cool As a Cucumber"

Corinth, Miss. May 5, 1862

My own dearest:

More than one month has elapsed since I imprinted the farewell kiss upon your lips and this 5th of the month finds me alive and well at Corinth and you need not be surprised that I tell you and that, too, a participant in one battle in behalf of southern Independence. Yes the roar of musketry and the booming of cannon are sounds now well known to my ear. I do not wish to give you an exaggerated account and so will simply make a plain statement of facts and you may judge of their significance.

I last wrote you a hastily penned note by Mr. John Vickers of Bienville, on the eve of leaving Grand Junction for, as we supposed, Tuscumbia. After three days hard travelling we reached this place, a distance of only 40 miles. We had to dismount and with ropes pull the wagons up every hill and through every mud hole and some time they were so bad that we had to take out the mules and hitch in the men to get out. That day, the last, I waded in mud knee deep trying to get the wagons through. I was soldier, negro, mule, all three. Wednesday we rested in Corinth and Thursday morn drew 40 mules from the Quartermaster's department and struck tents, sent them to the railroad for Tuscumbia. Were just getting on our horses when a dispatch came that the train which had gone out had found the enemy about 6 miles and had turned back. Our baggage we had sent from G'd Junction was gone forward and may be for all I know in the hands of the enemy, so I am short of clothing having sent most of it to relieve my horse from the weight. We were then ordered to report to Gen'l [John S.] Marmaduke on the Farmington road 5 miles from here near the advanced outposts of the enemy. We got out after dark and 12 men were detailed to go on picket duty.

The lot fell on Jonah, of course, and we marched over a branch, hitched our horses all saddled and marched on foot across a creek obstructed in every possible manner by fallen timber, burned bridges, torn up crossways to the other side. Dr. Patillo was our officer and the Lieut. of 8th Ark. then on duty took Nat Martin and myself and put us on the very advance. We had not reached our post before snap went a cap at us. I kneeled determined if he fired to try and kill him by his own fire, but the Lieut. said it was his own picket, who was a cowardly fool, which was at once proved by his rushing back on his next man who fired in reality at him the Ball whistling over our heads through the leaves. We remained almost without breathing for 6 hours constantly on the alert, but not a stick cracked during the time although I found next day we were in 250 yards of a Yankee picket, saw the place where he lay concealed. Also saw a horse that our men killed the eve before. The next day the Col. of the brigade advanced me some 400 yards farther, further, too, than he was willing to go himself though an aid of Gen'l [William J.] Hardee went with me and looked at the horse which had been killed. Col. Sandidge went through the enemy's pickets somehow or other and went a mile to within sight of their Cavalry camp. He was accompanied by Lieut. Smith of his Co. When he came back he removed the Picket who was stationed in my place 300 yds. further back, saying he was liable to be cut off by the enemy's Cavalry.

That evening we returned across the creek, got our horses, went back to our bivouac in an old orchard, slept soundly expecting to be aroused every moment by the firing of our pickets but were not until the next day. The Col. said we might kill some hogs, for the enemy would get them if we didn't. About 12 M. we had killed 6 hogs and were skinning them when our pickets commenced firing rapidly and falling back. I left my pig half skinned and rushed to saddle my horse. We were formed in line of battle and soon received orders to gallop across to another road about 2 miles and try and prevent the enemy from turning our left flank. This we did in haste and found they had got above us already. Capt. Wimberly dispatched a courier "McArthur" (who joined us at Monroe) to Gen'l Marmaduke to announce the discovery. This man we have not seen since or heard of and the probability is that in his haste he galloped right into the jaws of the enemy as he had already occupied the spot where we had left Gen'l Marmaduke an hour before. The Artillery say they saw a courier shot from his horse. We came back and scouted through the woods and to prevent the advance of the Yankee pickets and finally fell in line of battle in an old field.

By this time the enemy much to my surprise had crossed their Artillery over what I deemed an impassable swamp and planted their battery in about 400 yds. of us. Our Infantry ambushed in the woods fired a sharp volley on them and according to Gen'l Beauregard's orders fell back. The Artillery opened on the woods and such a roar I never heard in my life before. You have heard and read descriptions of the whizzing of Parrot Shells but words cannot describe them. The Minnie balls came like the single buzz of a bumble bee, and you would have been amused to see Capt. Wimberly dodge when one passed near his head. He was in advance of us and we were protected partially by being in a hollow. Our artillery soon opened on our right and I tell you the roar of the duel was terrific. Our Guns less in number were heavier than those of the Yankees and were better handled for I heard the explosion of one of our shells in their battery and such a shriek as rent the air from the Yankees you never heard. Our Artillery filed back after firing some fifty or sixty shots and the infantry, too, and then we saw a Yankee picket on a fence, within range of my rifle at home, wave his hand and the battery turned loose on us a few shells, but they passed harmlessly over our heads we being at this time in a hollow. When the Infantry had fallen back some ¼ of a mile Capt. Wimberly ordered us to the woods and we filed through into an old field 200 yds. in rear of our previous position and formed again. Capt. Wimberly remained up at the woods and a federal officer rode up in fifty yards of him. Capt. Wimberly looked calmly at him and never once thought of his pistols, till the Federal spying him, dashed off. Capt. Wimberly is I think a brave cool man but far too forgetful. He kept us in range of that battery 5 minutes too long, tho I admire the spirit he showed on the occasion. He is a brave man sure: too daring sometimes.

We then fell back again and had not left our position 4 minutes when on rising another hill about 5 or 600 yds. there was the enemy's line of battle, 6 regiments strong drawn up on the very ground we had occupied but 4 minutes before. We formed again though the infantry were double quicking behind us and our Artillery rattling off down the road. The order for us to retreat soon came and determining to have a good look at the Yankees I rode to the top of the hill to see them. Then bidding them good evening I retired. That night we were kept out scouting, the enemy having followed us within 3 miles of Corinth, and all day yesterday, when it commenced raining and late we came back to camp, tired, wet, worn out and glad to get back safe. Fuller's Co.[1] protected the right flank and one time were in some danger. (I will write between the lines on the first page.) They had one man thrown from his horse who lay in a brier patch and the enemy came all around it and camped in 60 yds. of it. He came off this morning having secreted his Gun and accoutrements and passing off as a citizen—George Hearn—your father knows him. A Yankee asked him for fire to light his pipe, he having crawled up to an old house to secrete himself.

Now dearest, I have given you a succinct account of the whole affair. I was not alarmed in the least till we commenced our headlong gallop reconnoitering. Then I feared we might rush on the enemy before we knew it. During the cannonading I felt just as cool as a cucumber and my only fear was that we should stay till the enemy moved his battery to the top of the hill. I did not like to retreat under fire but would have been willing to charge the battery for it would have been the safest of the two plans. The boys say my face was spotted white and red but I know how I felt and to you I would express it, tho I have no doubt they were right but I had company in it. All the men acted bravely I think. So much for the battle. The plan of Beauregard is to draw the enemy on to Corinth and I think he will succeed. They are within 3 ms. We had only 3 small Regts. 3 pieces of Artillery and our 2 companies of Cavalry. The enemy had 6 Regts. of Infantry and how much Artillery I don't know—6 pieces at least. I saw no Cavalry. They will record it as a great victory in the N.Y. Herald I've no doubt.

[1] Capt. E. W. Fuller commanded the St. Martin's Rangers. At this time Fuller's and Wimberly's companies were in the same squadron.

Now dear Mother do you know that I have had but one letter from you since I left home. Others have had 3 or 4 from their wives. What does it mean my dearest? I cannot tell you half of what I want to say. Rich is quite sick with flux. I never saw him look half as bad in my life. I hope he wont die for I assure you I don't know what I should do without him. 'Tis hard enough I assure you to get along with him. You have never read or heard of half of the hardships of camp life. We have a good deal of duty to do for some will play off on the plea of sickness and that throws it harder on those who are not sick. I cannot do it tho there are many who can. I detest the spirit and it is not those altogether who you would suppose who do it but those who you would think would do their whole duty.

The Conscript Law will let off those who are over 35 yrs. and all are coming home I expect. P. P. Bates is I think tho I don't know when. I am in such utter confusion I can't write what I want. I believe I have told you all about my probably losing my clothing in the car in my valise. One of my overshirts, one Marseilles, and 3 prs. of socks. My needles and thread &C. My Bible I have with me tho I assure you I have but little time to read it. I have not changed my clothing in two weeks but intend this evening to try and put on some clean ones if I can find a place to wash in. The water around here is only the sweepings of 10,000 camps distilled and would sicken a carrion crow. I drink as little as possible. Oh dirt, dirt I have eaten more than my bushel already and if I ever get back I assure you that I must have things clean in future as an atonement. You must write here your next letter for I think the probabilities are that we shall remain here till after the great battle which may not come off in a week owing to the heavy rains yesterday and last night. Write me often my dearest. Take good care of our darlings for my sake, remember what I have told you about them. They must be governed. Write often dearest. Tell me all matters of little moment and as much "school girl sentimentality" as you call it, as you please. Remember me in your prayers my own one. I fear I am far from the right road and I fear I will not find it. Kiss our dear ones for their Father. Remember me to all my friends. Love to your parents, sisters & brother. I wish I could see you and kiss you. Your affectionate husband. Ed. H. F.

Wednesday 14 May 1862
In Bivouac Van Dorns Hd Qrtrs
2½ miles from Corinth
Near the Enemy

My own dearest Wife:

I wrote you a week ago a long letter which I sent by Mr. W. P. Mabry as also my picture but when I came back from advanced picket I found that Mabry had not got his papers fixed up right and had not gone. He will make one more trial today and I shall send this by him to town and if he does not get off I'll have it put in the Office though I presume that letters will be stopped from leaving here as a battle *is said* to be imminent though I cannot discover that it is any nearer than it was 10 days ago. I presume you have seen in the papers an account of the battle on Friday the 10 inst.[2] and know much more about it than I do although we were drawn up in battle line all day but got no hand in the fight. It is reported that 800 Yankees were taken prisoners and a Capt. Kitchen of Missouri Cavalry told me that he witnessed a charge of a Regt. of Yankee Cavalry on four pieces of the Washington Artillery and out of 800 troopers only 40 or 50 regained their saddles, the rest being killed or wounded. He saw this with his own eyes being a support of the Battery.

We have been out on Pickett for 6 days no sleep or rest and are entirely worn out and still the order comes to prepare 3 days rations for it again after a rest of one night only, though I got sick and came in to camp the day before the rest, so I have had 2 nights rest. Only 25 or 30 men report fit for duty and the consequence is that we who do go have it all to do. Capt. Wimberly can stand and suffer his men to stand anything rather than protest against the unjust exactions of higher officers. He is not afraid of the enemy but is "mighty afraid" of a rebuke from higher Officers. He has not enough confidence in himself from the fact that he does not sufficiently understand Military Law. However you will see him and Dr. [W. C.] Patillo both at home before very long *I think*. The Conscript Law releases both and I think both intend to go. Bert Harper will hire "Cahill" as a substitute and

[2] The engagement to which Fay refers was that at Farmington, Mississippi; it occurred on May 9, 1862 (which was Friday), instead of May 10, as Fay states. See *O.R.*, X, pt. 1, 807 ff.

I don't know what we shall do. This is not to go out in the family at least to the children for it may prove unfounded. It would not surprise me if our company disbanded entirely.

If I can get a transfer I shall go to Spencer and join his Artillery Co.[3] in case my above predictions prove true. I wish I could be released I should go as Independent henceforth sure. This living on nothing and not being allowed to go buy for yourself I cant stand. You would have been amused to have seen me living on picket on one biscuit a day and a little piece of *raw* bacon, you would have thought "how are the mighty fallen." I have been right sick for a day or two but feel a great deal better today so I am going out again. Capt Wimberly does not want any body to come back even if they are sick and we had some words the other morning about my coming back to camp. He *insinuated that I did not feel very badly* and I have never before failed to perform any duty since I left home. I told him in plain terms what I thought of it. That I should never ask him to go back if I was not really sick. It is a surprising thing to me that the Southern soldiers will fight with so much valor when they are so badly treated. No negro on Red River but has a happy time compared with that of a Confederate soldier. Yet strange to say I am getting more and more used to it, and in fact have got so I like to sleep in the open air. If I come home I think I shall bivouac for the future in your flower yard. News item!!! One of Fuller's men yesterday killed while on picket a Yankee, so he says. I would not be surprised though if he was not a Confederate Scout. Fuller's Co. have not established an excellent reputation and I don't know but the same blame attaches to us as we are in the same squadron. Don't mention this as I want nothing to come from me. Don't let my letters be read out any way.

And now about writing letters. Mail them to me just as often as you can. I shall get them scattering enough anyhow. Don't worry or feel bad if you don't hear from me every week as facilities for mailing letters are not good and sometimes I may be gone on picket 8 or 10 days at a time. If anything happens you will hear from me. I have

[3] Letters of Harriet White Fay to her son Edwin, Dec. 3, 1862, and Aug. 11, 1863, show that Spencer, whose family was then residing in the Prattville area, served in Capt. John C. Semple's Battery, Army of Tennessee.

got all your letters except the one sent by Dr. Harper but when the mail comes and I don't get a letter I feel right bad. Yesterday letters came from Minden as late as May 7 to Webb and David Caufield but none for poor me although I got one from Mother and Spencer but that was not from you by any means. I'll send them by Mabry to you. I burned all your letters before going on picket though I answered all your questions in that letter I believe. I wish you would neglect no opportunity of writing or sending such little things as I have mentioned in my letters. When is Martin Rawls coming. What has become of Johnson? You must write me all the news transpiring in and about Minden.

My Daguerreotype I send you is not like me for I have fallen off a great deal and then my whiskers cover my face, but it is the best I could do. It cost only $8.00 and I think you will burn it when you see it, at least you ought to. You had better get your Father to make a deed to you or me of that 20 acres of land on which our house stands not forgetting to include the strip in front to the branch. This had better be fixed at once as my life as well as your father's is uncertain. I would send you some of the money I have if I had a good opportunity as I have no use for it in camps. If I should get severely wounded I may go to Ala. though I shall send for you at once if I do. I feel in better spirits about a battle and feel as if I should live to see you again, and as Virgil says: "Et forsitan haec meminisse juvabit." I wish I knew something to tell you but I assure you if you get the Whig you know more about matters and things than I do.

When you answer my letters read them over and answer my questions, at least make me some reply. It rejoices me to hear such good accounts of Will Ed. and Thornwell. You know that my heart is wrapped up in them. My bible you put up is too large. I cant carry it in my pocket. Send me a small pocket testament. My bible I have to leave in my pack of clothes. Take care of Will Ed. and Thornwell. Teach Will to make letters on a slate preparatory to learning to write. Does Thorn try to talk any? Write me every day a little. You can very easily send two sheets of that thin paper and don't neglect to send a letter once a week anyhow. Tell your Father to write to me too, and Lou. I don't care how many letters I get but do how many I write for facilities are limited I assure you.

I am sitting on my blankets leaning against a tree writing on my knee I believe I told you the Prattville Dragoons were here but I have not been able to see them yet. Don't know when I will. I must close this as they are starting to the Office. You know that you have my whole heart dearest. Keep well and don't expose yourself my dear for it would hurt me greatly to hear you were sick. Take good care of the children. God bless you my own dear wife. Kiss all the children for me. Much love to your father & mother. Don't forget to pray for me. Your affectionate Husband. Ed. H. Fay.

Rich has got well again. The Yankees will be badly whipped if they attack us here. They are entrenching 10 miles from here. We wont attack them there. The Tenn. River is going down rapidly. Some things will have to be done soon. Good Bye. Ed

Camp Churchill Clark
Van Dorn's Hd.Qrtrs. May 20, 1862

My own dear One:

I have a few minutes to spare this morning dearest and although I can get no letters from you yet I will write. Why is it dearest that others in camp have dates from Minden as late as the 7th of May and mine is the 29th of April. This makes me feel badly, I assure you. I try to make excuses for you but I find it hard to satisfy myself with myself. I do not doubt your affections yet 21 days without any letters and not the fault of the mails for dates of the 7th have come through in 7 days at that. But I'll no more of complaints but try and write you some thing of interest.

I sent you a scrap of a note tucked around my Picture which I hope you have received ere this reaches you. I also enclosed two letters in an Envelope and the day before I mailed one to you so you see I have been faithful in writing to you and I intend to be when I can but you must not expect as much from me in Camps as I from you where all conveniences are. I see several of the boys lying flat on their stomachs writing to their wives, they having no other place. When I last wrote you we were just starting out on picket duty, a great deal of which our Co. have to do, in fact the squadron of our two companies have to do the duty of a whole regiment and we can not find out of both companies over 75 men fit for duty. In fact there is reported 38 sick out of our company this morning and Fuller's is in like proportion. I am happy to say I don't think any of ours are dangerous but some are quite sick. I have been commanded not to report names of sick in my letters and will only say that two of *whom I think most* have camp fever and yesterday I was alarmed about them but I find them better this morning.[4] So much for sick report.

Do you wish a running description of our picketing. Supposing you do, here goes. On Sat. morning we started out thinking to go to the same place as before but were ordered out on the Farmington Road again, where we were in or rather in the rear of the battle last Friday a week ago. I went on Post at 5 P.M. and had not been there over half an hour when looking out into an old field I saw 10 Yankee Cavalry advancing as skirmishers, this I reported to the Col. Comdg. and he came with his glass and said he thought they were after a drove of hogs which we saw in the field. I told him I thought it was a cautious advance with a view to occupying the old field and planting a battery on the brow of the Hill and subsequent events proved I was right for the next day we saw their earthworks. I watched till after dark but they still remained. I could distinctly hear the orders they gave and heard a scout tie his horse and advance to reconnoitre and tried to shoot him but could not find him. I could also hear the challenge of their pickets so you see we were in proximity to them.

The next morning their sharp shooters opened on our men when our sharp shooters came up with their Belgian guns and there was a continuous fusilade all day at from 6 to 900 yards. Our reserve was stationed in the woods some 2 or 300 yds behind our sharp shooters and the Yankee balls would fly over our heads and bury themselves

[4] This is the first instance noted by the editor of the censoring during the Civil War of soldier comments about health. A heavy incidence of sickness during the first few weeks in camp was common among both Johnny Rebs and Billy Yanks. Units most seriously affected were those made up of rural men, many of whom had not previously been exposed to epidemic diseases. Officers came to regard "putting their commands through the measles" as a normal phase of adjustment to army life. See Bell Irvin Wiley, *The Life of Johnny Reb* (Indianapolis, 1943), 244–262, and *The Life of Billy Yank* (Indianapolis, 1952), 124–140.

in oaks above and under our horses. While on post in the morning three balls were fired at me but a kind Father in Heaven shielded me and the balls whistled harmlessly by tho I confess in closer proximity to my head than was altogether agreeable. I could see the villains across an old field some 8 or 900 yds. and I would step out in plain sight and draw their fire and then get behind a tree before their balls came and I then proved Philosophy at fault, for sound travels faster than a bullet at 600 yds. distance. I could see the flash, hear the report and the bullet would not come along till after a second or more. One of Capt. Fuller's horses was shot through the thigh at least 400 yds. behind our sharp shooters and full ¾ of a mile, and a Tennessee trooper had his horse killed outright fully 400 yds. farther, nearly a mile distant. They use Sharps and Colts rifles but our Belgian Guns do equally as well as all long ranges depend upon elevation and my Rifle at home would shoot as far as any with raised sights.[5] There is no accuracy in it, but one of our men downed a Yankee for there came two and carried him off the field.

Sunday Night the moon rose at 12 M. and just as soon as the disk arose above the horizon the Yankees commenced firing, our horses kept stamping and snorting and a volley of at least 50 guns was fired into the woods where we were on post. The Balls came almost as fast as the hail that night you remember at home when the stones were so large, but again we were all mercifully preserved. Not even horses receiving a scratch. I found out one thing on that trip and that is that I am not more and not as much afraid of Balls as some of the high officers. Col's, Maj's, Aides, etc. for I saw them tried. Picketing is dangerous work but there is something exciting in it. I had rather do it than go into a regular engagement.

Now about the Conscript Law and the effect it will have on our company. All who are over age will go home. Capt Wimberly and Dr. Patillo if he can get off which I think he can, and Harper will try and hire a substitute so we will have no officers. We will have an election if it is not kept off too long. I think Webb will be Capt. I

[5] Fay's estimate of the Belgian rifle was much more favorable than that of most Civil War soldiers. Billy Yanks contemptuously referred to the Belgian guns as "pumpkin slingers." See Fred A. Shannon, *Organization and Administration of the Union Army* (2 vols., Cleveland, Ohio, 1928), I, 125.

shall run for 1st Lieut, but I think the election will be kept off by Gen'l Beall[6] and if so the President will appoint whomsoever Capt. Wimberly recommends. I don't think he will recommend me to any office altho he treats me much better for a few days past. I don't think he ought to leave us for he promised in Minden to go 12 mos. or 12 yrs. if necessary and all present remember it. I am exempt from the Conscript act for all teachers of schools of 20 scholars are exempt and if they all claim their exemption I ought to do it too. What think you, my dear? I shall in a great measure be governed by you. I am willing to serve 12 mos. but to be pressed in for 3 yrs. seems a long time especially having such hard times.

The boys who have been to Virginia now in our Co. say they in 6 mos. did not suffer the hardship and privation they do here in 6 days. Money does no one any good for you cannot buy anything and they serve out to us rations of stinking pork and beef that I saw an entire barrel looked over yesterday for one streak a single spot of fat and in vain. The Confederacy ought not to thrive unless they would treat soldiers better. I think too the patriotism of our Co. at least is about consumed. If they were at home I don't know a man who would volunteer with his present knowledge, unless I did. My health keeps good and I can get along, for I come home every night in my dreams.

You need not be surprised if you hear of the evacuation of this place for in my judgment we are no nearer a battle than we were 3 weeks ago. An aid to Gen'l Hardee, an acquaintance of Carter's told us the Yanks were bringing heavy Guns, building plank roads & were going to shell Corinth from 4 mis. distance and our plan was to attack them just as soon as they commence to mount those guns. Troops have been ordered to send all their baggage to the depot save what they could carry on their backs, and cook 5 days provisions. This was done 3 days ago and yesterday when we came in we found masked batteries planted and everything in readiness as if the enemy were following us close behind, and we knew they had no notion of attacking us for we had been watching them 2 days and nights. I confess my

[6] Brig. Gen. W. N. R. Beall was at this time in command of the Confederate cavalry forces about Corinth. He later commanded an Arkansas brigade at Port Hudson; he was captured when Port Hudson surrendered on July 9, 1863.

military prescience is at fault. I don't think we have a Gen'l who is worth a baubee. No not one. This is my opinion of the war. I believe I will except Price.

Apropos of Price I have an anecdote. After his arrival here Gen'l Beauregard invited him to ride round and look at the breastworks. Beauregard, his Aids, Price and his rode round all day and scrutinized everything carefully, came back late in the evening and drew up in front of Beauregard's quarters when Gen'l Beauregard said: "Gen'l you have seen my works! What think you of them?" Gen'l Price with great sang-froid replied: "Gen'l I never saw but *two breastworks* before at Lexington and Springfield, Mo. and I took them." this conversation is said to have actually transpired. I do not vouch for it, though it is characteristic of the man.

Well, dear, I have filled out my sheet and not a word have I said about the children. As I said before I come home every night in my dreams and Will Ed sleeps on my arm and Thornwell wakes me up every morning. Bless my dear children. I do love them devotedly. If I could hire a substitute I would gladly do it and come home. I will give my horse, bridle and saddle and $400 per year as long as the war lasts to any healthy man to take my place. If your Father can find such a man send him on to me by all means. Tho I really believe this war cannot last 12 mos. longer. If it does, I cannot, I know. Now my dearest do write to me often and write long letters.

It has been very dry and dusty for two weeks. Last night we had a pleasant rain and I think we will have more this evening. I will not seal this letter till tomorrow for I do hope to hear from you today. If I do not I shall *"cry."* You know I can't bear disappointment well. I am glad Will Ed gets along so well. Does he mind well, is he obstinate or bad. Let me know everything. Also when you write look over my last letter and answer questions for I sometimes ask them and would be glad to get a reply. Give my love to all. Kiss the children for me and do not let them forget me. Show my picture to Thornwell and teach him to say Father. I will commend you to the keeping of our Heavenly Father and will say Good Bye for the present. Your loving Husband, Ed. H. Fay.

Vicksburg is taken. I know not how this will reach you but I will send it with a prayer that it may reach you in safety. Dr. Patillo and

J. Y. Webb go down to Webb's brother's at Scooba on the Mobile and Ohio Railroad for 15 days. I think they are both a great deal better. Oh my dear the horror of being sick in camp and the horror of being cut off in communication with those we love. Oh our country to what have you come. Can we not drive back the invader. Is God against us? Have you seen the proclamation of Picayune Butler relative to the ladies of New Orleans.[7] But my heart sickens and yearns for you my dear. It seems to me that I must come to you. I am homesick for the first time this morning. Oh, darling. Good Bye. Yours only E——

Near Van Dorn's HdQrtrs. May 25, 1862

My own dear Wife:

I have just finished a letter to Mother this beautiful Sabbath morning and I now turn to you as the only being to whom it is more pleasant to write than to my own Mother, but dear, what good does it do to write you for I hear from Minden as late as the 11th of May that you have heard nothing from us since we left Gd. Junction. What can it mean? for I have written you faithfully every four or five days but my dear I have not heard from you since the 29th of April. David Caufield has got dates as late as the 7th and 11th, but not I. You asked in one of your letters how often you should write and I told you every week, but I find now that if at that rate I don't get letters in 21 days, you must mail me at least two letters every week.

Under the Confederate Law as a teacher of a school of over 20 scholars I am exempt from the Conscript Law and I shall claim my exemption for I know well that if I attempt to go through with what I have already gone through, for 3 years, that you are a widow and my children orphans. I know I cannot stand it. In my last I wrote you something about a substitute. In case you do not get that letter I will say it again. I will give any sound man over 35 years of age my

[7] This was the notorious "General Order No. 28" issued by Gen. Benjamin F. Butler at New Orleans on May 15, 1862. It directed "that hereafter, when any female shall by word, gesture or movement, insult or show contempt for any officer or soldier of the United States, she shall be regarded and held liable to be treated as a woman of the town plying her avocation."

horse, saddle and bridle and 400 a year for 3 yrs. if the war lasts so long, to take my place. I am willing and anxious to stay the 12 mos. but so many are going home that they have got me in the notion. I don't want to be bound on this side the River for three years, for I believe there will be need of soldiers about Minden before 3 years.

I have just been out and heard some thirty letters called but none for me. Oh this heart sickness! Can I stand it much longer? Why can I not hear from home. It has entirely discomposed me. I don't know that I can finish this letter. A good many of those letters were from Bossier and must have passed through Minden. But none for me. Have you forgotten me so soon? But I'll cease to murmur.

The last letter was sent you by Mr. Mabry and since then we have again been on picket for 3 days and under fire of the Yankee sharp shooters. I saw plenty of them but as I did not have a long range gun I did not fire. We were ordered out the other eve, 21st together with Van Dorn's and Price's army and after standing picket most of the night we were ordered forward in the morning at daylight and 20 were detailed as skirmishers to go forward and find the enemy. I of course happened among the 20 and we rode through the thick woods about 20 paces apart for nearly two miles. I saw a Yankee but he was too far. By and by we jumped four or five and several of us got shots. About 2 P.M. we came to a pond where they watered their horses and watered ours and stopped to rest. The Yankees endeavored to slip up on us but we were too fast for them and commenced firing on them. I was asleep at the root of a tree when the firing commenced but in less time than it takes me to write it, I was on Jack, and spying a Yankee across the pond loading his gun I pulled down on him with a load of buckshot. I cannot say whether I hit him or not but he rubbed his thigh as if I had sprinkled him. We would have charged them but were ordered not to do it. Forrest's Cavalry by another road went into their rifle pits but found them deserted by all but an Illinois Parson, who was riding a very fine horse.[8] They took the clerical

[8] In a letter to D. C. Trader May 23, 1862, Forrest reported this skirmish thus: " I had a small brush with the Enamy on yesterday I Suceded in gaining thir rear. . . . they wair not looking for me I taken them by suprise they run like Suns of Biches I captured the Rev Dr Warin from Ilanois and one fin Sorel Stud." R. S. Henry, *As They Saw Forrest* (Jackson, Tennessee, 1956), 287–288.

gentleman prisoner and brought him in. His name was Dr. Warren. I saw him and he said Lincoln was the best man in the world.

I see by the papers that Dr. Palmer preaches in Corinth four times a week but I am so far out that I cannot hear him.[9] In fact a man has to go to three or four different officials to get permission to go into Corinth and consequently I never attempt to go. But to finish the story of the battle.

About 15 or 20,000 men, 50 pieces of artillery and 3 or 4000 cavalry went out and slept on their arms, hunted the Yanks till 3 P.M. and marched back into their camps again, not having been able to find them on our right wing. The boys in camp said they had heard heavy cannonading on the left, but we knew nothing about it, nor have I heard anything of it. There is more or less skirmishing every day and a son of Mr. Vickers on the Lake, by whom I sent one letter to you from Gd. Junction was killed one day last week. I see also by Mobile papers that Thos. J. Ormsby of Prattville was killed in the Thursday skirmish I wrote you about. When will this horrid war cease? No one who has not been in a large camp has any idea or can conceive of the horrors and suffering of war. Why does God scourge this people? Now if ever England and France should intervene and I do hope from the signs of the times they will do it. Or do they rejoice at our distress and think that when we are worn out with the struggle they will come in and take both combatants. Every Christian should pray earnestly to the Almighty Disposer of events to put an end to this unholy war.

I could write you a great deal better if I had a letter of yours to answer, but as I have not I must try and fill out this sheet anyhow. I suppose of course you hear of the situation of Vicksburg. I presume ere this the gunboats are bombarding it as they have utterly refused to deliver it up. I wish I was on the other side of the Miss. River or you were on this side of it. If you were only at my Father's now and I got sick I could go there. If I get very sick I have written Father to

[9] Benjamin Morgan Palmer, minister of the First Presbyterian Church at New Orleans for many years and one of the leading proponents of slavery and secession, served for a time after Federal occupation of New Orleans as Presbyterian Commissioner to the Army of Tennessee. See T. C. Johnson, *Life and Letters of Benjamin Morgan Palmer* (Richmond, 1906), 171–296.

come after me. I am not exactly sick but have been unable for duty for the last two or three days tho we have had no duty to do. I shall lie up till I feel better at any rate. Any one may lie here and die for want of attention. I have never seen so selfish a place as a camp. No one seems to care much for any one else. Capt. Wimberly will come home I presume before long and I expect Webb will be Captain. To-day is our last day of grace for an Election and then we will probably have officers appointed over us but I presume they will be appointed from the company. I would not be a Captain for a thousand dollars and I don't intend to take any part in it for if I do I waive my right of exemption for three years. I could get a Lieutenancy but I don't know that I want even that if I have to waive my exemption for it and only a chance at it anyhow. I am not well and so shall not take part in the election. Besides Officers have to undergo an examination before a Military Board and John Maples was elected Capt. but could not undergo the examination and was rejected so I was told. This would hurt me more than being a private. You must not let this get out from me, however.

Now dear Mother, I want you to write me long, long letters and tell me all the news about crops, mill, hogs, etc. and also about Johnson and family. Everything of the kind interests me you know. You must tell me a great deal about the children for you know my heart is bound up in them. Don't let them forget their father but talk to them often of me. How does the school get on? Does Mr. Jones please the people? Paper is only worth $1.25 a quire and I cannot afford to throw this sheet away especially as I have written almost four pages. When is Martin coming? We are anxiously looking for him to see what news he will bring. If I do not hear from you before long I shall be for coming home to see what is the matter with you all. Tell your father to write me and Lou too. I would ask your Mother but I know she doesn't often write anyone. I would give every dollar I possess in the world if this war would end. I could come home in peace. Oh, my children, how I do want to see them. When I think of it I feel almost as if I should have to come home anyhow. But I have seen one deserter shot so I don't think I'll desert.

Don't think dearest I am complaining for I don't mean to do it and I don't want to distress you, for I would shield you from every pang. In my fevered sleep last night I was with you again and I thought all war was over and I was at home, but waking moments prove the falsity of dreams and I was lying cold on the ground wrapped in my shawl and a soldier still. I'll write more this evening. I'm exhausted now. I have just learned that I can send this by Lt. Humble of the Culwell Guards who goes direct to Monroe, La. this evening or tomorrow morning and I accordingly will send it by earliest opportunity. As I want you to hear from me whenever it is possible. Oh Mother how I wish it was me who was going to Monroe, La. and how soon I would be with you again.

Out of our whole company only 20 were at roll call this morning. I don't know any dangerously sick. Bill Smith has got the Measles good so I am told. I have not seen him but I believe most of the company have had them so I don't fear they will spread. Rich has been very well lately for two weeks—but is still the careless inattentive negro of old. He sends love to Mary and says "How'dy" to all the other negroes. Now darling I hope you will get this by next Sunday at any rate and don't let it be 26 days again before I hear from you. How is the wheat crop, it would have been good here but we have cut it up for our horses. Corn is scarce and fodder we haven't seen for 3 weeks. Our horses are fast starving to death and I presume we shall be dismounted if we have to stay here long. I have no idea of a general engagement here. I don't think Halleck or Beauregard either are willing to make the attack. Both are equally well fortified and yet the Battle may be over long before this reaches you. No one can tell anything about it. A newspaper correspondent says any one to hear Dr. Palmer will feel assured of the success of the Confederacy—I would like to hear him and have my faith re-established.

But this must be sealed and sent. Good Bye my dearest and best of Wives. Kiss our darlings many times for me. Write me often. Remember me to everyone. Mr. Wimberly and Dr. Patillo both wish to be remembered to you all. Mr. Bates is well, tell his wife. I can't name the sick ones. Dr. Patillo and J. Y. Webb are getting convalescent again. Nat Martin is writing to his wife. John Lackey is getting along finely as he can't get any opium. Good Bye. Pray for me my dear, for I hope I am getting to be a better man.

Your Edwin.

3

"Generals Override All Law"

Tuesday Morn. May 27, 1862

My Own Dear One:

After sending your letter on Sunday by Lieut. Humble, I find that this morning I have an opportunity of sending by Mr. Henry who is discharged and as I am willing to omit no opportunity of writing you I write again. About 15 minutes after sending off your last I received yours of the 4th inst. mailed in Monroe the 15th. I can't imagine why Mr. Ardis did not mail it at once. I have heard but very seldom from you of late and my dear I cannot imagine why I can't hear as often as anyone. David Caufield gets two or 3 letters every week from his wife but she don't say anything about you ever. I wish I could hear oftener from you than anyone else could from their wives. But I will not complain. I got your dear letter and that is enough.

I wrote you all the news in my Sunday letter so now I will devote this to answering your letter. You must not write me about green peas and onions &ç, for if you do, I'll be sure to desert for we have nothing at all to eat. I have not seen any meat for 3 days and then for 3 days before we had lived on hogs that the negroes had killed in the woods. I've got so I don't complain about biscuits now for we don't have any grease or even tallow to make them up with. We have nothing, but can buy soda at $1.00 per lb. but soda without grease or even buttermilk won't make biscuits. If we had anything to eat at all I would not complain. We cannot draw bacon or pickled pork but could draw pickled beef such as it was but we had rather do without, at least I had, for although the story about the mule leg was all 'gammon' yet there is not one streak of fat in any of the beef we draw and most is spoiled at that, so you see that writing about your good things is only an aggravation to us. Officers are allowed to purchase bacon and pork for themselves but not for privates, and you may indeed say that there is too great a distinction made between them. Yet such are the usages of war and I can't say from what I have seen that I envy the officers for they have some cares too.

Capt. Wimberly is heartily sick of his bargain but I can't say when he will come home for they have allowed us to have no election and the 40 days are out and I contend now that at the end of 12 mos. we are released by virtue of our enlistment.[1] Should anything turn up however that Exempts come home (for Generals override all law) I shall endeavor to come too and fight in La. if anywhere, for I believe there will be need of an army there. This army is falling back from Corinth, we sent off our baggage and part of the tents yesterday for what I don't know unless it was to fall back. They were sent to Okolona, Miss. on the Mobile & Ohio R.R. I believe. I think the movement is to flank the Yankees on the right and left and get into their entrenchments behind, which are said to be very formidable.

You ask me about my clothing and tell me to take care of my heavy jeans pants. I have worn them all the time and I find them very comfortable tho I suffer some from cold when on picket even then. As regards wearing my woolen shirts, I have only one and it is torn clear across the back having commenced under the arms. The gores were not large enough. I am afraid to sew it up for it will tear again. I have worn it every day since leaving Vicksburg. I hope I may get my valise again and get the other one. If I have to stay this winter you can make me some shirts out of such plain cloth as my brown pants are made of. Several have them. But I hope for the best and hope I may see you ere that time comes. My socks hold out very well as I do not walk about very much. My boots and shoes do very well. I wish I had not brought my cap for I don't use it and it is in my way. Our horses have fallen off greatly you would hardly recognize them. They

[1] The Confederate draft law of April 16, 1862, which extended the service of twelve-months units to three years, gave to those units the privilege of reorganizing under officers of their own choice, provided the new elections were held within forty days after the law was approved. Thus, the elections should have taken place on or before May 26. See J. M. Matthews, ed., *Statutes at Large of the Confederate States of America* (Richmond, 1862–1864), 30.

are getting more corn now, but no fodder and they suffer for roughness.

If you have not already sent my watch do not send it as I have no pockets to carry it in and it is in my way. I don't need it at all and it will be a useless bother. If you have sent it I shall send it back if Capt. Wimberly goes home. I do not want more than 3/4 yd. of oil cloth and there should be strings or straps or buttons and strings sewed on it so as to fasten the ends together when I roll my clothes in it. I shall have a pair of pants, 3 shirts, 2 drawers, 4 prs. socks to roll in it and that is all. I was going to send back 50 dollars of my money but yesterday I bought a Double Barrell Gun from Mr. Henry who carries this, paid 30 dollars, so shall not send any till we draw I don't know when. While on the subject of money tell Mary that Rich has sent home 2 1/2 by Capt. Wimberly $2 another time and 4 1/4 by Linn Watkins in a letter to her so he says.[2] I told him he was a fool. Why did he not bring it to me and let me send it off for him. I will make him do it in future so she will be sure to get it.

You wrote me a little news in your last but did not tell me anything about our garden or what our orchard was doing nor your raspberries. I want that corn and fodder taken care of that I left at the Ratliffe house for it is going to be a large item if this war continues. I want you to have everything you need and Thorny's wagon must be fixed anyhow for I know he will enjoy it so much. You don't write me enough about the children. I hope ere this that the Miss. River is down so that the cars will resume their trips across the swamp. We have not had any late papers in camp for several days so I don't know the state of affairs at Vicksburg. Letters have come from Comi Bluff as late as the 17th and of course they crossed at Vicksburg. The gunboats were 7 miles below the city on the 21st inst. You ask if Jim

[2] Mary, Rich's "wife" (slave marriages were not recognized by law) was a domestic servant in the home of Fay or his father-in-law in Minden. Like most body servants who accompanied their masters to camp, Rich had opportunity to make money by performing small services for officers and soldiers other than his owner. Fay seems to have allowed Rich to send these earnings to Mary. But when Rich was regularly hired out for a period of services at brigade headquarters at $1 a day, his wages were paid to Fay, in accordance with established practices governing the hire of Negro bondsmen. See Bell Irvin Wiley, *Southern Negroes, 1861–1865,* 2nd ed., (New York, 1953), 134–135.

Blackmon's son came? I think he did. We have a Jeff Blackmon [Blackman?] in our Co. I am sorry your father did not buy more molasses for I fear it will be very high. We get molasses, usually enough and sometimes rice, but living on dry provisions has laid me up. I am not very sick as you may know by my writing but I have not stirred round much for 2 or 3 days nor have I eaten as much in 10 days as I eat at one hearty meal at home.

If there was to be a fight *certain* today I should go out to it. They are skirmishing every day and taking and losing prisoners on both sides. We caught two yesterday morning and they say our man we lost, [A. M.] McArthur,[3] was captured and not killed we are glad to hear that. I hope ere this, my dearest, you have got my picture but I fear you wont be pleased with it as it don't look much as I did when I left home. I don't think I weigh over 175 lbs. now for I am sure I have lost 30 lbs., but so much the better on my horse for the other day I was on him for 30 hours almost every minute of the time. Of course you have learned ere this that your Yorktown battle was all a *canard*. We heard similar reports here. You need not believe anything for I believe our people are almost as much given to lying as the Yankees. This is beginning to make me doubt our success. Our pickets are in speaking distance of each other and yesterday the following took place: "How do you like sassafras tea as you were out of coffee?" "Oh, we have had coffee a plenty since we took your camps at Shiloh!" "Can send you some if you are tired of sassafras"—

I want you to buy a good gold pen and mail letters at least twice a week. Persons are passing through Minden to Fuller's Co. frequently and if your letters were always ready you could find frequent chances of sending but don't let this interfere with your mail letters. They do come through the mails sometimes. I wrote you faithfully every 3 or 4 days and if you don't hear from me it is the fault of the mail not mine, but you have not the same excuse, for letters do come from Minden much later than yours. You don't know how much I love you my dear nor can you imagine how much good your letters do me.

Do you ever hear from Nat Martin's wife. If you do be sure to

[3] Muster rolls of the Minden Rangers show that McArthur was captured at Farmington, Mississippi, May 3, 1862, and that he was later exchanged and returned to duty.

mention it. I hope you keep my buggy over at the Carriage House. I want you to use it all you see fit but if it is left at your father's the cows will eat up the harness and you will have another to buy. Ask your father to mend the bow of the top that is broken. He can screw a piece of steel on both sides. You had better have our house painted if you can for the paint is wasting. About Thorny's wagon: see what Chaffe will do it nicely for. I think five dollars would put a nice body on it and perhaps a top. See yourself anyhow for I want you to become a *business woman.* You must answer all my questions. Read over my letters before writing and answer. You find this a very disconnected thing but it may be more interesting for it, as the novelists think, when they are constantly breaking off their stories.

Rich keeps pretty well now tho he had a desperate time after coming to Corinth. I thought he would die. Flux. P. P. Bates has gone with our Tents, baggage and says he will write today but I don't think he will. He is well. The sickest man and the only dangerous one is Ben Fuller, tho he is said to be better this morning. Several have got measles. Bill Smith roaming round caught it and Oliver Butler has it too, and I don't know but more for I have not been out for 3 days. Don't be alarmed about me for you know I am a good hand to complain if anything much is the matter with me. If I do not come home it will be a bullet of the enemy that gets me I think.

Tell your father to save every pound of meat that he can this winter for it will all bear a very high price. Raise all the hogs he possibly can. Do try and get the mites off our chickens if possible and raise everything you can. There is no chance to make any money so you must raise everything you can and sell it. I fear there will be a great scarcity of provisions and I fear the army will be disbanded on account of famine. I think you need have no fears of putting Will Ed in 2d Reader. I thought Alice had got a long way ahead of him going to Bally's. How is it? Tell Will Ed. he must be a good boy and mind his Mother and not play on Sunday, say his prayers every night and not forget his Father. Does anyone see my letters? Yours are far too precious for any one's eyes but mine to look on. Tell your father to write to me about crops, his in particular. What is Wade Barrington doing? Did Mr. Shea take those hogs? If not, do sell them or have them got up. I dislike to lose them.

You do not write your letters as full as I do mine and yet I know you have a great deal more to write. You don't have time enough I fear but too much work to do. Remember letters are to be attended to before work. Work can be put off.

You ask about cottonade pants? If we don't have a great deal hotter weather than we have had my heavy jeans pants will last me this campaign but if you have a good opportunity you may send me a pair tho blue is a bad color unless it is very light blue. I shoot at blue clothes myself.

I have had my attention called off and I don't know how I can finish this page now unless I turn to sentimentality of which I feel a great deal just now. Our lives channels have flowed on very smoothly since they have commingled and I cannot see now why the vast island of this war should have arisen to separate two streams which had indeed mingled into one, but such has been the case and God only knows if they will ever reunite again in this world or if they are divided clear on down to the great gulf of Eternity not again to commingle except around the throne of our heavenly Father. Oh if I had no children the thought would not be so harrowing but I trust that God in his good Providence will order all for the best.

Mother dearest I could write you till tomorrow night but letters like everything else must come to an end. Tell Lou that she may consider all my letters as written to her for I think she is quite considerate since her return from Columbia and will do to be trusted, consequently she must write to me for all the time I have I must write to you. She may claim all the letters if she will write me some. Tell Bud to write too for it will improve him and he can tell me about the school. Have you got the slate and pencil for Will Ed. I want him to learn to write and he will make letters quicker on a slate. Well Mother Good Bye has got to come. Give my love to your father & Mother, Ella & Alice. The 20 kisses mentioned in your last I imagined but could not receive. Your letters should be more frequent and longer and they will give your loving husband that much more pleasure. God bless my wife and children and protect them too. Ed.

The election has come off and [J. Y.] Webb was unanimously elected Captain and Lynn Boyd Watkins 1st Lieut., [Nathaniel M.]

Martin 2d [Lieut.] and [John J.] Carter 3rd [Lieut.] The other officers are appointed. I took no part in the election for I expect I shall come home in 90 days anyhow though it is not certain for the Captain who held the election said to me that the will of the Commander was superior to all Laws of Congress. If so, I am coming home. All these elected officers have to pass an Examination and I do hope Lynn Boyd may fail tho it will keep Dr. Patillo. I did not dream of his election nor did any one else. Only 39 votes were polled and he got only 22.

Houston Chickasaw Co. Miss.
June 5, 1862

My dearest Wife:

Well dearest I do hope you have rec'd the letter I sent by Mr. Henry for I told you in that that I *believed* the Army would fall back from Corinth. You have doubtless heard of it through the papers ere this. The Retreat was conducted in good order tho Yankees pressed pretty strongly on our rear. We fell back some 35 miles to Baldwin a small town on the M.&O. R.R. I was detached as a guard to the waggons and thought that as I was sick this was one time when I would get out of an engagement. But when we got to Booneville 25 miles south of Corinth the 2d Iowa Cavalry 800 strong led by a spy dashed in about daybreak and burned a train of ammunition, the depot & stores. One Co. of cavalry came by our Camp and the Col. ordered every man capable of sitting on his horse to mount and fall in. We dashed into town ¼ of a mile and raised a yell and found the Yankees had made a breastwork of our 4000 sick men to keep us from charging them. The sick opened and we passed through and drew up in battle line facing them 100 yds., but did not fire, ordered the sick to scamper to the woods and hide, which they did. The Yankees dismounted one Co. to turn our flank and they advanced to 150 yds. and we faced them when they fired on us, wounding Nat Martin in the cheek, slightly cutting his ear, breaking the arm of one of Fuller's men, Morris, and wounding the calf of the leg of Clark, another. Owing to the preserving care of our Heavenly Father I was graciously shielded from harm and received no scratch though a ball grazed my whiskers and I smelled the horrible smell of lead.

This is the boldest deed the Yankees ever did. We killed 4 or 5 of them and took 12 prisoners. When the rest of the company came up I joined it, left the wagons, which had thrown out a great many things in the panic, and we were ordered back to try and cut off the retreat of the Yankees for they left as soon as they fired on us. We galloped some 15 miles and were ordered back but did not get them. Our horses had had no corn for 3 days and only a small chance to graze in the woods. After reaching Baldwin we were ordered down on a scout after stragglers and deserters from the army for five days and this is the 3d we have been out. Have heard no news of any kind except reports of fights. I could fill a volume describing them as heard but I only give those *"quorum pars fui."* I am a good deal better and if I could be on this business "scouting" all the time I could keep well.

I have rode now for 3 days at least 30 miles a day, from Baldwin to Moorsville thence to Richmond, Camurge, Okolona west of the R.R. to Houston and on to Pontotoc tomorrow. I don't know when we go back to camp. I have not had on a clean shirt for two weeks and I don't know when I shall get another as [P. P.] Bates has my clothes at Okolona and I had not time yesterday to change them. Our first baggage sent off I don't think we will ever get again. We found when we got to Okolona that Ben Fuller had died the night before. [Thomas J.] Gazaway[4] waited on him and did all in his power for him but of no avail. Typhoid fever, tho he might have recovered if he had not been moved so much, from Corinth to Booneville and thence to Okolona. Poor fellow, he too had a wife and children. Death has entered our ranks and I feel as if it was not the last appearance of the grim monster. I could tell you of heart rending scenes of suffering that would make your blood run cold. You at home can form no ideas of the "Horror of War" as far as sickness is concerned. I think our army is certainly the worst managed in the world and I sometimes doubt whether success ought to attend it owing to its treatment of the sick.

But no more dearest lest I make sadness come over you. Pray that I

[4] This name appears on the muster rolls as Gassaway.

may be preserved from sickness and from death. I hope I may be spared to see you once more. I do so anxiously desire to see our dear children again and to be with you and tell you what I have no time to write. I do not know that this letter will reach you altho the Post Master promised to send it by Little Rock and Helena and I hope you may get it. I love you dearest as much as ever. Write me good long letters and I don't know now where to tell you to direct, but put on "Gen'l Van Dorn's division" at any rate and I'll get it if directed to Baldwin or Guntown.

I don't know hardly what to say for it is rumored that Van Dorn is going back to Ark. I hope so dearest for it will bring me nearer to you. I have heard no news nor seen a paper for 6 days and I hope the next I do see I find some favorable news. There are stirring reports from Va. Stonewall is in Maryland 40 miles north of Washington City, defeated the Yankees, taken a great many prisoners. Joe Johnston has captured 3 entire brigades. It may prove false but is believed in the army.

Good Bye dearest. I send this with a prayer that it may reach you safely and find you in health. May Our Father protect my wife and children that I may see them once more again. Give much love to all. Say to everybody that their friends are well except Jeff Blackmon who has typhoid fever and may die. Most heartily do I wish I could embrace you all. Love to your Mother and the Children. Tell Mother I wish I could get some of her good things but I can buy occasionally on this scout. Do write often. I have got no letters since yours of the 4th of May more than a month. I wrote you on the 27th last now on the 5th but shall not probably write again until I find out what is to be done in the *army*. Good Bye. Kiss our darlings for their loving Father.

Priceville, June 10th, 1862

My own dearest:

I wrote a few days ago from Houston, Miss. and gave you a short and hasty account of the battle at Booneville in which Nat Martin was slightly wounded in the face and I made quite a narrow escape.

That letter was mailed to go by way of Helena, Ark. but I expect it will be a long time before you receive it as the Little Rock letter was so long going.

I did not tell you how hospitably I was treated at Houston. The postmaster kindly gave me a sheet of paper and while I was writing came and gave me a cordial invitation to dinner with him, the first and only invitation I have had to a meal since I left home. I told him I had a partner who was sick (Mr. [J. N.] Murphy, the brother of the young lady whose little Hymn Book you have) and he immediately found him and tried to get him to go up and lie down on a bed but he would not. At dinner time we started up and meeting Loye he was invited to join us. We went to a Mrs. James whose husband was in Virginia in the army, a sister of the postmaster whose name was Lyon. Mrs. James and her Mother and Mr. Lyon's wife met us very cordially and gave us one of the best vegetable dinners—just such a dinner as I would get at home—onions, squashes, beets, cucumbers, Ham & greens, chicken stew &ç, &ç. It was fixed in style too. Oh how I wished I could stay there for a week and recruit for I had been on horseback for ten or twelve days with only one day of rest. We spent two or 3 hours very pleasantly and I told Mrs. James if I should get sick I should come there to stay and was invited to come.

We came out some ten miles from Houston that night and I slept with a rattlesnake all night. Discovered him next morning and killed him, so this time I was preserved from danger. We came through Pontotoc on our way back, there saw some very pretty ladies as also we did in Houston. Both places have large Female Colleges. We got back to camp late Saturday evening and found the Army had dropped back to Tupelo, a Depot on the Mobile and Ohio Railroad some 18 miles from Baldwin.

I found no letters from you and I was sad enough I assure you. On Sunday, however, I was rejoiced when Geo. Monzingo asked me what I would give for a letter and I found yours of the 29th of May. My darling I was so glad. I had almost begun to believe that you had forgotten me for I knew letters did come through by Vicksburg and I could not see why yours did not. I see the reason now you did not mail them. I hope ere this you have got the letters and picture I sent by Mr. Henry. I don't know that Mr. Henry got off for he started the day of the retreat from Corinth and the cars were so crowded with sick that we don't know that he got off tho we hope so.

An army is the hardest place to learn anything that you ever heard of. Nothing is reliable, you hear every rumor imaginable. There is no doubt but France and England have recognized the Confederacy and today we hear that there is an armistice of 60 days on account of it. This latter part we are hardly prepared to believe although it is believed to be probable as a consequence of recognition. I hope it is so for I am tired of the war and an armistice with foreign intervention is a sure prelude to peace. Oh if it is the will of our Heavenly Father I do hope this war will close that I may see you again. There is a great deal of sickness in camps and some of the boys out of camps are dangerously so we learn. Jeff Blackmon and Buck Nelson. [Isaiah] Ratcliffe is quite sick in camp and the Captain is today trying to get off the sick to the country. His Brother, Richard Ratcliffe has come on from Point Coupee Parish and joined us. He is to be Preacher I believe for the Squadron though Capt. Wimberly put him on duty at once and he has been on ever since.[5] I wish I had something interesting to write you my dearest but have nothing save camp rumors which I care not to rehearse. I must tell you that when I came back to camp I pulled off my clothes and wrapped up in my blankets and had them washed. I never had been so dirty before and the branch was so muddy that Rich could not get my clothes clean tho he got off some of the dirt. Just imagine to yourself my dear, your husband riding for ten days in dust so thick that part of the time he could not see the horses before him, and sweating all the time, and you can form some idea of how dirty I did look. You never saw a negro half so dirty before. The rest had no advantage over me tho in it. My last baggage had gone to Okolona and though we went through there, yet my clothes were dirty and I could not change, having only 2 pr. drawers and two shirts. My Iuka baggage I hope to get again—as 3 men from our Co. and 3 from Fuller's started today. It is within the present Yankee Lines but they hope to pop in and get a wagon and bring it out. I hope so for I shall get my other overshirt and soap &ç,

[5] Muster rolls show that Richard Ratcliffe continued to serve as a private in the Minden Rangers at least until the end of February 1864. He may have preached in addition to performing the usual duties of a soldier in the ranks.

&ç. I hope to get my valise also for I have nothing to carry my clothes in but my leggins tho I wrote you for a piece of oil cloth, which I hope you will send. My socks too are most all up there. I may get them and I may not, but I am better off than most of the boys.

In the retreat from Corinth most all our cooking utensils were thrown away and it would amuse you to see the shifts we have to resort to. We are living better than a while back but how long it will last can't say. It is reported (Camp news) that Van Dorn won't allow any more pickled Beef to be issued to his soldiers. I am afraid it is too good. You can't imagine how chary we are about believing good news, the bad almost always proves true. I suppose you know that Ft. Pillow was evacuated and that Memphis has gone under. Little Vicksburg alone holds out but as all our gunboats were sunk at Memphis (6 sunk by the enemy, 2 by ourselves), I am afraid she will not be able to hold out unless our army or a part of it is sent down there. She should be the Capitol of the Confederacy if she holds out and does not succumb. I am afraid tho it will be all over before this letter reaches you, but hope for the best. If this war would only close now I would have gained glory enough to satisfy me.

I am sorry that the boys plague Mr. Jones for I had hoped that they would all behave themselves well and not give him trouble because it will make him think that my boys were not well governed. It is a reproach to me and I want you to tell them so and I hope they will do better. I am sorry that it is necessary for me to doubt the friendship of any *Physician* but I had my own opinions before receiving your letter. I feel sure I can do without him just as well as he can without me. I am not built up by any man though I feel sure I have helped to build up some persons. I begin to think there is no real unalloyed friendship in this world. That everything is selfish I feel fully convinced by my war experience and I find that I am different from most persons for I know my friendship is not interested. 'Tis well I have but few friends.

You know not how sad I felt when at Okolona we rode round by the grave yard and there counted 260 new made graves of soldiers and saw the plain wood coffin of Ben Fuller with the Head Board painted with his name and Co. lying on it not yet let down in the grave. Poor Gilbert Edens too died in camp while we were on the scout, without, as I have learned, any attention whatever and Lieut. Smith had a hole dug and him put in without any coffin or even wrapping him up in a blanket. Poor boy, I did not even know he was sick. 'Twas typhoid fever and total neglect that carried him off. If he had had any attention he might have recovered, so it is said by some of his company. How many pangs. How many hearts will bleed on account of this horrid war. A man's life is not regarded as any more than a dog's, hardly as much. If I should die tomorrow there are none of the Co. who would recollect it for a week. I hope I may never be sick enough to need attention from any one. I shall go at once to the country if I get sick if I have to desert to do it. 'Tis a very hard and difficult process to get out of camps I know.

I thank you for writing me about the steamboats. Why did the people let that Boat go? It was, I presume, the 'Moro' and went directly back to New Orleans for I saw an account of its arrival in Butler's Delta.[6] Why our people don't hang Thomasson, Blackburn, Co. I can't divine for they richly deserve it. I do hope our Independence has been acknowledged for then they are traitors and must be hung.[7] Tho any parish that can endure Bill Blackburn ought to be accursed with just such men.

But my dearest I have nearly covered my sheet and have not said a word about our lambs. I hope dear Will Ed. has his [word omitted] ere this and I hope Thorny has his wagon. He must have it at once. How I wish I could see the little fellow walking about. He would not know me now and that makes me feel sad. Will Ed. will remember me tho so I have that satisfaction at any rate. Oh, Mother, how I want to fly to you and see the dear ones again.

[6] The New Orleans *True Delta* was suspended by Gen. Benjamin F. Butler when the proprietors refused to print the proclamation announcing Federal occupancy of the city on May 1, 1862. Subsequently Butler placed one of his officers, Capt. John Clark, editor of the Boston *Courier,* in charge of the *Delta.* See Robert S. Holzman, *Stormy Ben Butler* (New York, 1954), 67.

[7] The reference is obviously to trade of people in Fay's community with the Federals in New Orleans. Associates of Butler were said to have profited greatly from this trade. Traffic of Southerners with their enemies flourished in all areas adjoining the Federal lines, despite earnest efforts of state and Confederate authorities to prevent it. For a discussion of traffic of Louisiana with the Federals see Jefferson Davis Bragg, *Louisiana in the Confederacy* (Baton Rouge, 1941), 201–207.

We have drawn no money as yet but will in a few days. If I get any I shall send it home I think, tho a man don't know what use he may have for money. His horse may die or get lost and the latter is an easy thing for they steal horses in the army, and then he will have to get another. We lost 3 mules before we left Corinth—Fomy and two others—and could find nothing of them. Luckily two loose ones came to our camp and we harnessed them. We found Fomy at Baldwin in an artillery wagon and got her. We found another under the saddle and claimed it altho the fellow said he paid 165 dollars for it in Confederate money, but he had to give it up. So we got two of them back and have our two strays to boot. Several horses have been lost in the Co. and several have sold their Horses—

I think one or two more will be discharged and that I may get a chance to send this Home by private conveyance. I cannot bear the thought of being cut off from communication with you for your letters are the only solace I have. I do hope my dear that you will write often for you do not know when or how letters may get across the River. They sometimes cross in some manner but I fear the Gunboats will stop everything but skiffs I think.

Tell Will Ed that his "Favy" wants him to say lessons and learn to read but my dear do not keep him so closely confined as to give him a distaste to his books. I wish him to love his books but I fear he will be like his Father and not be overly fond of his books. You know I never was fond of hard study anyway. Don't disgust him with his lessons but try and make him love his books for his father's sake and for yours. Tell him stories and interest him with them. I place my greatest hope in my children. Do take good care of them for my sake. Don't let Will Ed long too much for vacation but let him have it often tho I would advise you to be regular with him. Don't let his lessons be put off for anything except you are sick. Teach him the importance of system and regularity. These are lessons he should learn early and be taught to appreciate the value of them. You must govern him firmly and Thornwell too. Children should be taught to obey as it is a necessary lesson of a soldier. Now my dear I will not seal this tonight for I may add more tomorrow if I find I can send it by private conveyance.

Thursday 12 M. Nat Martin has a furlough for 20 days and will go home if possible as *his wife will be confined* and he will go if he stays over his time. How I wish I could go too my dearest and see you but it would only be an aggravation to stay so short a time with you. I am determined to write Thos. H. Watts, Atty. Gen'l of the Confederate States and see if our re-organization is legal as it was not held within the time prescribed by law, and see if we are not to be discharged at the end of 12 months. Have you thought that I am to be kept here 3 years if I should live that long—I don't think that I can stand it although hitherto I have kept pretty well, but how long it may continue to be so I don't know. I have thought if I should get sick and get a 20 days furlough I would go to Mobile and get on a Boat and go to Selma, Ala. I do wish my dearest that you were on this side of the Miss. River and if it is possible for you to cross the River I think you had better come on with Nat Martin and go to Selma or Montgomery and stay. I leave this entirely with you for I can hardly advise you. I don't think we will ever get across the River until peace is made. If we have to stay 3 years I shall come home on 60 days furlough sometime during the year, but after that I don't expect to see you at all if we stay on this side of the River. Oh Mother if this horrid war would only close and I could come home to my family.

If you can, I presume you had better send me a couple of cottonade pants and I can wear them as pants in summer and drawers in winter. I don't know whether we will get our baggage from Iuka or not, but the boys have been gone 3 days after it and have not returned so I hope they are bringing it with them. The Federals are said to be in force 30,000 at Baldwin, 20 miles north of us, but they cannot stay there as we could not for want of water. I am at an entire loss to know what will be done for I had rather be forty miles from an army to learn news than in it. I just stay in camp all the time.

I want you to be explicit when you write about home matters and tell me about crops &ç, the mill, our hogs, cattle and everything in which I have an interest. Write me long letters for every one I have written you has been long. Your last was two sheets, but there were little items tucked into corners and around the edges, I do so love to see little love messages piled around in the vacant spaces.

There are a good many cases of measles in camps but the weather has been very pleasant for several days and they are all getting along well. I said that Ratcliffe was sick. He is getting better, however, I think. The two Caufields[8] [David W. Caufield and J. M. Canfield?] have furloughs for 20 days and are going into the country. J. Y. Webb has just this moment arrived in camp from Scooba. He is entirely well but left Dr. Patillo down there. He is getting better Webb says and will be back in camp before long. Most of the news I have written has not been confirmed and we fear it is not true. So much uncertainty is really distressing.

Now dearest, I must stop for want of room. I can say but little and I have made a great deal of repetition which I know the eye of love will excuse. I throw myself on your generosity knowing it will not fail me. My love do take good care of yourself and not get sick. Your health is precious in my eyes. I wish I were with you when you have those pains in your head. My love, I always imagine myself coming to bring this letter myself. If I were a dove I would be with you again. You ask me to read my Bible but it is with my clothes and I cannot get it. I read Nat's as he had pockets so he could carry it. I wish I had 3 or four pockets in my coats so I could carry things. My dear you have all my love and I want you to feel that it is precious too. Kiss our lambs for their father and try and train them for a better world than this. Give my love to your Father & Mother & Sisters and kiss the children for me twenty times. Write soon. Write often. God bless and preserve you is the prayer of your affectionate Husband. E. H. Fay.

Be sure to send me a haversack like the one you made me before which I have lost, also a wallet made out of a seamless bag. Sew up the end and cut a slit through both sides so it will fit over the back of the saddle.

Friday Morning June 13, 1862

I wrote in pencil on my letter to have you send me a haversack as I lost mine in the strange gallopade to cut off the Yankees. I want you

[8] Apparently David W. Caufield and J. M. Caufield, privates in the Minden Rangers.

also to make a wallet out of a seamless bag or some strong goods. Sew up the ends and cut a hole through the center through both sides so it will fit over my saddle behind. I can carry my haversack in it. I also want a *hat.* Mine is about worn out sleeping in it and sitting on it. A soft hat 7½ size, but be sure Nat can bring it before you buy it, as it may be that he cannot bring it conveniently. I believe this comprises my list of wants for the present. Though a small bag that will hold 10 or 15 lbs of sugar, another for salt, and another for rice, another for coffee would not prove unacceptable, particularly if "Goodwill" or someone else will mark "Fay" distinctly on them with *good paint.* We have lost almost everything in our various movings. Don't load Nat down but he will bring the articles mentioned if they are fixed up.

Think of the proposition to come to Ala. and write me about it. I could go to you much easier if you were there and you might get to me better. Act for yourself for I don't know what is best to advise. Would I were gifted with prevision, I could then speak *authoritatively.* (See if I can get a substitute and let him come on with Nat. If you have not done it let it alone). Good Bye, Dear one. I will write you again if I can get any paper, *which is doubtful.*

Tupelo, Priceville June 15 1862

My own dear Wife:

A very sultry Sunday evening I seat myself on a small box with a valise in my lap to try and answer your two wifely letters of June 1st and sixth, both of which reached me by the same mail at this place on the 13th inst. You do not know my own dear one how rejoiced I was to get them. I had just returned from Tupelo 3 miles where I had been with Nat Martin to bring back his horse as he started back home on that day. The mail train from Mobile via Meridian had just come in but as the office would not be open for privates for two or 3 hours and the heat and dust were insufferable I came back, particularly as [J. J.] Carter stayed to get the letters. He came in 2 or 3 hours and brought me your 2 letters. Oh how glad, glad I was. The letter through the courtesy of Mr. F. Johnson was mailed me at Monroe the 9th so you see that all of your letters sent by hand are mailed before they cross the river so you need not hesitate to mail anything for fear of not coming as a prayer seems to bring every letter through.

I am very sorry indeed my dear that I pained you by intimating even in a playful way that you did not love me. You know my dear that I have never sincerely doubted your affection for me. I know you love me almost as well as I love you, but my dear you are by no means as demonstrative as some persons, not by any means as much so as I am. I don't think you ever were enough so, and that because you feared you would overdo the matter. You never had sufficient confidence in your husband to let him see how much you did love him but held back for fear he would think you did too much. Your husband should have unreserved confidence. I don't mean that I did not have it, but I am speaking in general terms now. You know that I always made a clean breast of everything, that I never kept anything back. But my dear I'll moralize no more but quit by saying that our married life has always flowed smoothly and on my part very happily.

I wrote you in my letter by Nat that 3 boys had gone on an expedition after our baggage to Iuka. Well they succeeded beyond our expectation for they passed inside the Yankee lines and finding the villains about the place they sent two good men in ox teams to bring it out to them some three or four miles. They pressed the teams to within fifteen miles of this place when I took a wagon and went after them to the Tom Bigbee river. All mine came through safe so I have got my clothes again and Rich has got the old saddle bags and the soap too. I tell you it was quite a treat for we have had no soap given us for several weeks and Rich has bought some hard lye soap for which he paid 30 cts. a lb.

He has made some money and I have $5 of it if you will pay it to Mary for him. If you have not the change convenient, I can send it by Mr. Wimberly and then I'll not have so much money to take care of. He does not do as much as he might for me, but is very idling, yet he has a good deal to do. Has four horses to attend to and do the cooking besides: Bates's who has gone to Okolona ever since we evacuated Corinth to take charge of baggage, Dr. Patillo's who is sick at Capt Webb's at Scooba and Buck Nelson's who is dangerously ill with typhoid fever at Okolona, and Nat's. This in addition to mine keeps him pretty busy.

You ask how my horse gets on. He got over the founder at Memphis and I had his shoes reset there and since he has proved his bottom and good qualities, he has fallen off in flesh but has done all the duty that any of them have done and a little more. He stands it admirably and I would not get off him to get on any horse in the Co. He is perfectly gentle and I shot the Yankee sitting sideways on him without his moving. A better horse never made a track. I forgot to tell you that yesterday after getting to the Bigbee I stripped off and had a fine bath in good clear water and swimming water too. I have seldom enjoyed a greater luxury than that swim. [H. H.] Ward, Bob Thompson and Jim Monzingo from our Co. were in too. This morning we came back and the boys were glad enough to get their baggage I tell you.

You asked me if I got the letters from Mr. Ardis, yes both of them. I think I have every letter you have written unless it is the one sent by Dr. Harper. I sent you a long letter and various scraps by Mabry but understand that he left trunk, Ambrotypes and all at Vicksburg.[9] He had been paid some forty five dollars in all for carrying pictures and letters, he had got the money and little cared he for the rest. I don't think he is the right kind of man anyway. I hope you have got the letter I sent by Mr. Henry. I think he will carry it straight through for he is a mason and did not want money for carrying letters for his company. I do hope the masons will do something for them (Johnson's family) for I know Johnson was a mason and a deserving man as far as the world goes. I am sorry he could not have been prepared for death, for it is a solemn thing to fall into the hands of the living God. How incumbent on us to be always ready with our lamps trimmed and burning. I think I have answered all your questions. I'll look over all your letters again and if there is anything I omitted will put it in.

I thank you for your answer to my question respecting your health. I had no fears but it was not curiosity simply that led me to ask the question. I was thinking that if necessary you could come to Ala. I can get there easily if I get sick, if I can get off before I die. An order

[9] The articles entrusted to Mabry apparently were never found. The picture of Fay that was lost seems to have been the only one that he had made during his army service.

has been passed that no private can get a furlough for even 20 days to go into the country unless he has been pronounced sick by a board of army surgeons and you have to go to them to be examined. It does seem to me that they were trying to kill every man who is sick in camps. They try to drive men to Hospitals where they die worse than sheep with the rot. Every soldier has a horror of the Hospital. Some of our sick have been in them and run away.

Jeff Blackmon died at Okolona Hospital Thursday last at 12 M. He did not wish to die and *hollered* a great deal. A scrap of paper was found in his pockets as follows: "With Miss Mary Kimmons compliments to Mr. Blackmon and with her wishes for his *safte* return." Miserable orthography and chirography. I kept the scrap but have lost it. A Frenchman who was by him took it out and also his money and brought it to Capt. Wimberly. He gave me the scrap and asked if I knew who it was. I told him yes. If she calculated anything on his wealth she made a mistake. His will was made before he left home as he never expected to return from the war. Poor fellow his wealth did not avail him in the day of his extremity. Oh if he had been a christian how happily he might have died and how much good he might have done with his money, how much suffering he might have relieved.

Speaking of suffering you can form no idea of the ravages of an army even in a friendly country. For instance, a wheat field near Corinth of 15 acres ready to cut was used for artillery and cavalry horses. Appraisers valued it at $1320 which Van Dorn paid and the man paid back $350. $500 would have been a large price at $1.50 a bushel. You might think this a money making business but the battery was planted and breastworks thrown up in the fields in front of his house and he was compelled to move everything he had. His meat was all killed and his fences entirely burnt up for fire wood. His garden torn down, his chickens all killed, his fruit trees all gnawed by horses, his well ruined and in fact everything around him destroyed. Money might pay for utter destruction but to bring starvation upon a family money can't pay for it.

I'll suppose you a case, a regiment encamped near your house, the Colonel comes to your house and orders you to get into the kitchen as he wants your bedrooms, his men go into your garden strip every green thing out of it, to your henhouse get every old hen, rooster and eggs and when you complain you are told to make out your bill and you are promptly paid in 100 dollar bills. The country for a radius of 20 miles is in the same condition and what can you get to eat unless luckily your cow has been spared and you live on milk. This is not an overdrawn picture. What signifies it if you have got $2 a piece for all your hens. Can you replace them or can you get any change for your $100 bills. You had better be starved at once. I tried in vain to get a chicken for a sick man and succeeded in getting an old hen that had not weaned her chickens yet, for 50 cts. Pray, pray heartily, earnestly, that no troops may ever be quartered in large bodies anywhere near say 15 miles of Minden.

But enough of this sad subject. You forgot for fear the Yanks would get that letter to tell me what Will Ed said was so smart. I wish you had told it in yours of June 6th. Don't forget it next time. Yanks will not get your letters I hope. They will not as long as we hold Vicksburg for our mails will manage to cross anyway. Our discharged men will go back and probably carry letters. If you do not get the Ambrotypes and your Mr. Hart crosses get him to make enquiries where Mr. Mabry left his trunk and bring it through. Most of the letters and all the Ambrotypes belong near Minden. Get it by all means if our discharged men don't bring it through. We have instructed them to do so for fear the gunboats from above may take the city. I want you to get my picture certain for it cost $8 and I don't like to lose it for it was only because you urged it that I consented to sit for it. I could not refuse it to you my dear but would have done it to any one else. I want you to have it.

For fear you do not get this letter by Mr. Henry I will tell you about the election. Webb was elected unanimously, Watkins got 22 out of 39 votes, Nat Martin was elected over Joe Hamilton for 2d Lieut. and [J. J.] Carter who was not elected first was elected 3rd Lieut. I took no part in the election and protested against it as illegal owing to the legal time having elapsed and so would not allow my name to run for anything. If you have not got my letter by Mr. Henry I will write you fuller about it in my next after learning it. The officers elect have to be examined and are undergoing it tomorrow. I may write you if they pass before I seal this. I fear I shall not be able to write it though.

(Monday morn before sunrise) The examination will not come off I fear today, when it does Webb is ordered to appoint the other officers but he will elect them.[10] But as the office is properly an appointment I shall run for it though I may be beaten as Jim Simmons and Loye will both run against me. I wish Webb had independence enough to do his duty and make the appointment but he is for popularity. I never shrink a duty for the sake of popularity, but enough of this. I leave it all in the hands of God he will do what is right.

About the substitute business now I wish to write explicitly. I will for the sake of my school since Mr. Jones gets along so badly, hire a substitute if possible. Here I can not do it for every one is coming home certain. I must have a sound man, one that will be approved by the surgeons over 35 years of age. I will give him $400 a year during the war, his pay will be $300 more making a sum total of $700 for each year the war continues. This for three years would be $2100 which I think would pay a hearty man very well. He would be entitled to 60 days furlough during this time. I will give him also my horse, saddle and bridle and gun which will according to appraisement be $305 more.

In case I hire a substitute I am exempt from all military duty during the time and there is nothing dishonorable about it that I can see. I will simply be saving my life for my family for I feel well assured I can not stand it 3 years. I think I would try it if the school was flourishing and going on prosperously. I know they need a school in Minden and someone to govern it. I have thought the matter over seriously and if I can hire a substitute I shall do it. I want no man who will not pass the examination before the Board of Surgeons and consequently he had better be examined at Monroe before a board of Surgeons regularly commissioned for I would have to pay expenses for transportation here if not accepted. As only one can be received

[10] By the "other officers" Fay means the noncommissioned group. Captain Webb did appoint these, as he was supposed to do; but when later some of the men who desired to improve their status put pressure on Webb to hold an election of noncommissioned officers, he yielded to their request. See Fay's letter of November 2, 1863.

a month "it were well that what were done were done quickly." Let your father try to get some man he knows there. Men here want $1200 per year, more than I could possibly make at home. The Cavalry service is far preferable to the Infantry for they have nothing but their regular army duties to perform. Let this matter be attended to at once my dear. See the man yourself and tell him the whole matter. I will get a passport from the Capt. of the Co. for him to come on that will admit him within our lines. He had better come on with Nat Martin.

I think Martin Rawls can come through but he cannot bring a horse across. He can easily buy however if he gets here before the 14th of July for the 35 year men will all have horses for sale as they cannot take them back. I hope he will come for I know he can not stand Infantry service. The forced marches would kill him on foot. I hope you may be successful in finding me a substitute but it is essential that he should be sound in frame and limb for they are getting very particular in the army now. I leave it with you and your father hoping and praying that you may be successful in your attempts.

I believe now that this war will never be ended till the North and South are both entirely exhausted with its continuance. Foreign recognition now is the only hope of anything speedier for with commercial relations and an opportunity for trade and supplies from other countries we could continue the war for an indefinite period of time. But a truce to the war subject.

One day our news is favorable and the next day very unfavorable and we can believe nothing. Genl. Price has gone to Richmond and we think it is for the purpose of transferring his command to Missouri.[11] Whether Van Dorn will go too remains to be seen, if he does we go too. I think Van Dorn is better to his men than almost any Genl in service. There is less severity. I don't think him as much Genl. as some.

I will send this letter by Mr. Strange of Bossier or Moore of our Co. I have just seen Strange and he intends going by land so I will send

[11] Sterling Price, a former governor of Missouri, known as "Old Pap" by his soldiers, was transferred to the Trans-Mississippi Department early in 1863. Earl Van Dorn remained east of the Mississippi.

this by Moore, he may get through with it I don't know. I hope it may reach you however in due time to carry to your heart the assurance of my love. I presume you wonder at my practice of inversion or, to use a military cavalry phrase "Right into line by inversion" or in other words write into (between lines by inversion). You are welcome to the pun. It came spontaneously it was not studied. The fact is paper is the scarce article in camps and it cannot be bought in 50 miles and then at $1.50 per quire. Nat Martin's valise came just in time as it had paper in it and I got this huge large sheet hardly thinking I could fill it as full as usual, but I believe I shall. I am troubled when writing to know if you have received all my letters as I want to make references to what I have told before and have no time to rewrite all the circumstances. If you have got my letter by Mr. Henry you have got considerable news, if not you have lost it.

You ask me if you did right to tell Mrs. Wimberly. Yes, you acted very prudently. He got the hardest lick from Thos. Gazaway who came up and said "Capt. all the women about Minden say you should not desert your Co. in the hour of extremity and they are all down on you." The Capt. grew pale and I added that all exempts (35) had to go into the militia and go to N.O. to harass the Yankees. I think Capt. Wimberly wished just then that he had remained Capt. I do hope you got my letter by Mr. Henry for I told you a heap in it. Capt. got a certificate signed by most members that they were willing for him to go if he wanted. You will see it I think when he comes. The last three words "if he wishes" I had added before I would consent to sign it. I thought if he wished to desert the Co. at the time I had no objection.

I have acted wisely I think and hope since I have been in the Co. for I have said nothing about anybody, have kept my own counsel and have talked but little anyway unless socially to tell anecdotes. I really feel but very little friendship for most of the Co. John LeSueur if he was not so vulgar and profane is one of the best men in the Co. An excellent nurse and a very good Physician. Has done the practice for the Co. since Doyle and Patillo have been sick. [J. N.] Murphy, about whom I have spoken before and I are perhaps more intimate than anyone else except it be Capt. Webb.

I have looked over your letters and I find nothing except about the shirts. Don't make them of slazy stuff. You had a great deal better get some of the heaviest Lowells or even such stripes as you made the negroes dresses of just before I left home. I have seen such in camp and they look very well. Something strong is necessary for clothes get very dirty in camp and it takes a great deal of wear and tear to get them clean. I got the letter from Lou all right! I have not time to write or rather paper. If she is a good girl and can keep a secret she may read yours and call them hers. I am so sorry that people will talk so about your father speculating. Every one knows him too well for that. You ask me if I do not attend the prayer meetings? At Grand Junction they held three Baptist prayer meetings but I knew nothing of it. There have been two held since I think, Jim Monzingo officiating. Not interesting but I attended as have every one that I know of when present in camp. I tried to get Sid Killen to hold one last night but it was put off so late that we gave it over till tonight.

I wish I had two more pages for I could write a great deal my dear. Thank Ella for her kind letter and also Lou. I hope your Mother will go over to Texas for she will never have a better time. Why don't you go too, dearest? The trip would do you good. You wouldn't stay long. Tom Nelson is coming home before long, in a day or so and I'll try and write you again by him if not ordered out on duty before it.

Oh dearest I hope you will keep well and take good care of our children. May God protect and preserve you all is the sincere prayer of your husband who loves you devotedly. I have not heard from Mother since May 3rd. I sent you the letter by Mabry and you have not got it. I had not heard that William Henry was at Chicago.[12] They are exchanging prisoners every day or two down here. I hope he will be exchanged before cold weather sets in as I don't think he can stand winter there. Tell your father that *I am anxious* to hire a substitute and if he can make arrangements for less money then the amount named to do so. The government pay will of course be the same. I'd love to keep my horse, saddle and bridle and I'll cross at the mouth of

[12] William Henry Fay, 1st Alabama Regiment, Edwin H. Fay's brother, was at Camp Butler, a Federal Prison located at Springfield, Ill. He was captured at Island No. 10, April 7, 1862, and exchanged five months later.

Red River or somewhere sure. If a substitute could get here by the 1st of July I'd have plenty of company home. I hope he can do it. Kiss the children for me and take good care of them for his Father. Write me often dearest. Do not send my watch for I have no pockets to carry it in nor would I want it if I had for it is a single case and the crystal would not last a day. I hardly know what to say but Good Bye dearest. Direct my mail to Tupelo, Miss. *Your husband*

The Sheet is so large that I have been obliged to fold it in this outlandish manner. Excuse it. Ed.

4

"I Have Satiated My Military Ambition"

Near Hd Qrtrs of Army of the West 18th June [1862]
Camp Priceville near Tupelo Wedndy

My own dearest:

I have a few moments this evening to spare and as I don't know when I shall have another opportunity of writing you I will commence once more a MAMMOTH SHEET of "Nat's"[1] to you although I sent you one fully filled yesterday. It was written several days before, on Sunday and Monday morning I believe. I have nothing new to tell you, darling, and I would not write again just now but Dr. Bush, Dr. Scaife and Nicholson from Homer are here and will return in three or four days.

I am detailed as Provost Marshal of a general court-martial to commence tomorrow at ten A.M. and it may continue for three days or sixty, I don't know. It will depend entirely upon the amount of business and some of it has been put off since the battle of Lexington, Missouri, so I am told.[2] It may hold for three months there is no telling. If you wish to know the duties devolving on me the best I can tell you is that I am to fill the place of Sheriff in a Civil Court. I intend to perform the duty to the best of my ability and if I can secure the good will of the officers I may get an easier berth than private. Yesterday I had it fixed to get the appointment of Adjutant. Webb tended it to me and I learned afterwards from Headquarters ("the only source

[1] I.e., Paper provided by 2nd Lt. Nat Martin, of the Minden Rangers.

[2] The battle of Lexington, Missouri, to which he refers occurred on September 18–20, 1861. In this fight Confederates led by Sterling Price captured a Federal force commanded by James A. Mulligan and occupied the town. See *Battles and Leaders,* I, 307–313.

of light" for they make the Laws) that no man could be appointed except from the commissioned officers of the Squadron and as I hold no Commission of course I cannot come in. We are thinking of forming a battalion and I could easily be elected major of it if I only held a commission of any sort even third lieutenant but again perhaps I am better off for as private I can hire a substitute and as commissioned officer I cannot.

About this "substitute business" I hardly know what to say. I hear of so much having been said about returned or returning volunteers that I do not know whether to brave the stings and taunts of outraged women who do not desire to see any return because forsooth their husbands are not among the number. I tell you it makes a great difference with the women. I venture the prediction that Mrs. Wimberly does not think it contemptible in Mr. Wimberly to come home while I think and so does everyone else both here and there that he has less to call him home than any married man in the Co. (having no children). I took him off the other day and talked to him as a friend for three hours, begged him to accept the major's office and stay with the Co. for twelve or eighteen months at least. I told him what the feeling was in Minden and that he would be sorry if he went back and wish himself back again. He acknowledged the truth and importance of all I said, but yet would not consent to stay, but promised that he would perhaps come back to us which I know he will not do. Unless Mrs. Wimberly has written him something to the point he will come home in a week or two now. He feels now mighty bad about it and will feel worse I think before it is over with. Taking all things into consideration I think Capt. Wimberly has done remarkably well. I grumbled at him once a little when out on Picket and I was taken sick he seemed very unwilling to let me go back to camp. This has passed over however and we are better friends than ever.

"Mais revenons à nos moutons" "the substitute." If the Trustees would invite me to return to the school I would hire a substitute and come. If I thought I could stand the flings and arrows of the outraged women I would come anyhow because if I furnish a soldier to the services as good as myself, that would not otherwise be in it I am in fact actually fighting for my country myself. I think I could serve the country better in the school room than in the field. I try to look at it unselfishly and I do not think there is any self in it but a heap of Mother, Will Ed and Thornwell.

I hope I can stand it and pray that I may and I think that if I never come home it will be Yankee bullets that prevent me from doing so. My health is very good at present and I get along better as we get fresh meat occasionally and when we do not get it I make Rich kill the first pig he sees. Fresh pork has been the only thing that has cured the diarrhoea on me, and strange to say it has done it two or three times.

There is a rumor in the papers now that England, France and Spain have proposed five articles of Agreement Between the Confederate and the United States, to all of which the Confederates have agreed, the U.S. rejecting the last two. You will probably see them in paper ere this reaches you so I will not name them—the last one is an untrammeled vote on the question of Secession in all of the Southern States under the especial surveillance of the aforesaid Powers. I don't believe the report to be correct tho I do think something of the kind is brewing, as Beauregard got back yesterday from Richmond and issued an order for the troops to desist from digging wells or making any arrangement for a permanent camp, and I learned today that he has gone back again. Price has not yet returned to camp tho his Hdqrts. were moved this morning past our Camp. It is said that the army is to be divided into three divisions. Halleck's Army is gone from Corinth and our advanced outposts are said to be stationed there now. I cannot vouch for the truth thereof. I never believe anything unless I see it myself or know someone who has seen it. I take nothing third-handed.

I do hope and trust that this war will soon be over for if it is not settled according to my notions of right I can leave the Country if I see fit. I only hope I may be permitted to come home and see my wife and babies with good health. I feel that I can support and educate them then.

I have given you I think all the "camp news" you must not give it out as positively true tho it is believed here to be so. I believe I wrote you that Buck Nelson of my Mess was dead. It is a mistake as yet and Dr. Scaife who stopped at Okolona saw him and says he will get well if they get him Brandy enough, he drew requisitions for him for three or four days. I do hope he will get well for he is a good man and his family are dependent. They live at Isaac Loftin's old place, go out and see her dearest at once lest she hear the news of his death for I presume it was written by several, and it is a pleasant thing to be the bearer of good news. From what Dr. Scaife said I think he will get well as he has two good nurses, Mat Killen and P. P. Bates, who are with our tents & baggage down there. Ratcliffe has been a little sick and has the "hypo" badly. Send his wife word that he is a good deal better.

We lost a man last night who died from measles settling on his bowels as he had bowel complaint before he took them. He died about nine P.M. last night and I sat up with the corpse a part of last night. Poor fellow he suffered a great deal but died apparently easy. His name was James L. Darby. He had been an excellent soldier and was one of the most quiet and unobtrusive men I ever saw. He will be buried at a church some two miles away tomorrow. We had to send ten miles to Mill to get lumber to make his coffin. Our Co. is thinning out—five men discharged, three dead, and one lost to the enemy, and three unaccounted for. You will have heard the story from Nat as I could never feel like writing you about [J. W.] Neal, [Julius W.] Lancaster and Burt Harper. We have hoped for something to turn up that we might learn their fate but as yet it is uncertain. Martin can tell you all if he has not already done so.

I hear that the gunboats had not yet reached Vicksburg and that the "Whig"[3] which has been whipped since the fall of Columbus, Ky. said boldly the other day that the batteries could keep back the boats and that Vicksburg would never be surrendered—they might batter it down but could never occupy it. Oh if it can only hold out our communications will not be cut off, I can continue to hear from you, my dearest one. Oh darling you don't know how much I love you if you did make "the wool fly" once upon a time nor did I until I came to leave you and our children. I would give all I possess if this horrid war would close satisfactorily and we be permitted to return home in peace. I have satiated my military ambition long since and am willing now to quit. Pray dearest that I may speedily return to you if so be that it is God's will but if so that I die a martyr in my Country's

[3] Probably the Vicksburg *Whig*.

cause remember that yours will be the last name that ever passes my lips and that I will breathe out my life praying for your health and happiness.

But let me anticipate the future. *I* must learn to act in the living present. Hearts within and God overhead. I wish somebody would come right from Minden here. I want to see somebody who has seen you. I presume Nat will be coming back before long. I think I wrote what I wanted you to send by him. I want a haversack and a small bag that will fit in it made of oil cloth or something that will not allow grease to pass through, to carry meat in. If Nat can bring them I want two strong crockery plates as I cannot bear to eat from tin ones. Don't load him down for he don't know that he can get back. See if he can possibly bring them before you put them up. I'll try and find time to finish before those men start so goodbye for this time, my dear.

Friday Morning. Well Dearest one, Dr. Bush will start this morning and I have gone to writing early as I have to attend the general court-martial this morning. The Judge Advocate of it is Captain D. C. Morgan, who you remember addressed one of the literary Societies at the College while A. B. George addressed the other. He is captain in the Third Louisiana Regiment. He treated me very cordially indeed. I record the proceedings of the Court and take down the testimony and yesterday they only finished two cases and have twelve from the same company to try. It may be two months before I get off from it but I will have plenty of time to write you dearest and it is an easy job so I am glad—you have no idea how cold it is this morning. I suffered last night and am shivering now but as I go on duty at nine o'clock I must try and fill this sheet before that time.

It is roll call now and I have just heard Captain Webb read out his appointment for non-commissioned officers and he has appointed me Orderly Sgt. much to my surprise. I stand an opportunity of getting a commission as all vacancies are filled by promotion henceforth. Jim Simmons is mighty mad and declines serving as second sergt. for he calculated to beat me for O. S. in case of an election. You would be surprised dearest, to see *how much my friend* L. B. Watkins has shown himself, altho I almost know he has heard my remarks about him yet in several instances he has put himself to trouble to oblige me.

He has posted himself and will make a good officer I think, not for his kindness but for his knowledge. Don't say anything against him but be silent when he is spoken of if you don't acquire the feeling for him that I have. You know kindness goes a long way with me but flattery don't go down.

I don't remember saying anything, my dearest, about Thornwell being baptized in my last. I am very glad that you have had it done. I only wish I might have been present that I too might have pledged the best of my powers in bringing him up for God. I do want my children instructed in the way of Righteousness and I think one of the foundations is a careful observance of the Sabbath. Do try and interest Will Ed on Sunday by reading or telling him religious stories. Try and teach him that it is wrong to play on the Sabbath. I know I have neglected my duty often and I reproach myself therewith. Try and do yours in my absence. Don't let indifference or a feeling of weariness prevent you for remember you are doing it for the good of your own child and can ease be more pleasant than your child's welfare. I know you will not think so if you reflect upon it.

I presume you have heard of the death of Dr. Doyle. He died at Magnolia. We have just learned tolerably certain that Bert Harper, [Thomas B.] Neal, and [Julius W.] Lancaster were taken prisoners.[4] A negro who hauled them off said that they insisted on going thru Booneville, he was to bring them to the left down to Baldwin inside our lines. They insisted on going thru Booneville and the negro said he drove before he knew it "right into the Feds." and the three sick men were taken prisoners. Poor boys, I am sorry for them but their case is preferable to ours. I think they will at least get better fare and better medical attention.

Tell Mr. Shea that I think that after he lays by his crops he ought to come on and see us anyhow and bring whatever our folks want to send even if he don't stay more than two or three weeks. He might preach to us a few times and if Patillo comes home I think he ought

[4] Harper's name does not appear on extant muster rolls, but a partial roster of the Minden Rangers published in Harris and Hulse, *History of Claiborne Parish,* 236 ff., lists A. G. Harper as 2nd lt.—probably the first one—of that organization. The roll for September–October, 1862, shows that Lancaster and Neal were exchanged and that they returned to duty on October 17, 1862.

to come on and stay with us as chaplain all the time. We need something of the kind. Richard Ratcliff does pretty well but he is mustered in and consequently can not be the chaplain. Someone might come to us every three or four months and bring what little things are necessary.

I want you to write me all the news—as paper is very scarce fill them full as I do. Begin now and save every scrap of blank letter paper and if there is any in town buy a sufficient supply for three years anyhow, for paper is the scarcest commodity in the Confederacy. It sells in Mobile at 2.50 per quire, more than ten cents a sheet. So you see my dear that you had better be economical in the paper line. I don't mean by this that you should shorten your letters at all to me. I'd rather you would write in pencil on a shuck than to shorten your letters any. Don't forget to tell me what it was Will Ed said that you were afraid to write for fear your letter would not go through safe. Tell me all about the children. I love to hear from them everything, my heart is wrapped up in them. I do love my wife and children and I believe better than anyone else could ever love theirs.

I presume your Mother and the children are gone to Texas. I send you this letter as a reward for your love in remaining at home for the purpose of getting it though I believe it would have been pleasant for you to have gone. I know you would have enjoyed it. Give my love to your Mother and Sisters and Bud. I want him to write me all about the school. Don't forget to send me that small pocket testament I wrote for in one of my letters. I cannot carry my Bible for want of pockets. I am thinking of buying a watch here if I can find a double cased one. I shall need some drawers, and when you make them be sure and put some pockets in them like, but larger than watch pockets. I mean in the same place.

But I must close as this must be folded and sent off at once. Goodbye dearest one, may Our Father in Heaven bless and protect and preserve you and our children is the prayer of your husband who loves you devotedly. Direct Camp near Tupelo. General Van Dorn's Division.

at night
Camp Priceville June 23d [1862] 10 oclock

My dearest One:

I got your letter of the 16th inst. this evening by Mr. Hart and you know how glad I was to get it and hear from you once more but at the same time was *greatly pained* to hear you were so unwell. My dear you don't know what a time I had over it, you say you hope I will come home you don't know how you can stand my absence. This pained me dearest for you had told me in one of your letters that you *would not say to me to come.* I thought from this that you too "thought it was contemptible" for any man to come home "just because the law excused him." My dear you know I would not forfeit your good opinion for the world for I esteem it above all else, so I made no farther move towards coming home. I was informed by a little squirt of a Captain of Gen'l Beall's Staff that as I had volunteered I had relinquished my right to claim my exemption as a School teacher. If you think it best write me immediately and I will refer the matter to Headquarters and determine the matter positively. I don't think I could bear the reproaches that would be heaped on me—but if you desire it my dearest one I will come home at any cost for I hold that my first duty is to my family, my country is secondary. I feel sure that I cannot stand a three years service and if this war continues I feel pretty sure in all human probability that you will be a widow. It seems to be the settled policy of our Gen'ls to kill off by their restriction all the sick men in the army so that it can be healthy. I wish I had time to write you more fully about it, but I have not yet told you why I am writing so late at night.

We received orders at Sundown to prepare 3 days rations and report for marching at daylight tomorrow morning. So I had to write tonight if you got a letter by Mr. Hart and I knew that you would be expecting one as you had even written to me while suffering. I intended writing you a long letter tomorrow and would have stayed in camp to do so but our Co. were so small that I thought I would turn out too—there are only 14 men including me that are fit for duty. I did not go out last time as I am Orderly Sergeant and was detailed as clerk of a Court Martial and could not get off. You ask several questions in your last all of which I have answered, but in the letters sent by Mabry and you have not gotten.

A. F. Minchew left Bud's gun down at a Mr. Somebody's in Bossier near his Father's and got another from there. I wrote the name before but I can't remember it now as Minchew is absent on detail some 3 miles from here. I calculated to write also to Lou tomorrow but I can't do it now. I did get Ella's letter and acknowledged it in one 3 or 4 days ago by Dr. Bush which I hope you got. The express man "Hart" charges 50 cents for letters from here back although his printed forms say 25 cents but he has risen since he has seen the walk from Delhi to Vicksburg.[5] I would not pay him such a price or patronize his swindling but I know you will look for a letter and I would not disappoint you for 50 dollars much less 50 cents. I do indeed wish dearest that I had time to write you a long letter.

You speak as if you thought I could come home. I have written explicitly about coming home and if you think I can get a substitute so as not to be called into State service or militia, I will come home. Send the substitute if at all by Nat Martin for Loye has one already here for the present month, and only one a month will be received and I want him before anyone else can come in. Mike Dixon of Bossier Parish pays Weldin and his horse and gun to take his place. This makes for 3 years $4150—pretty good wages for a common man but if I was in his place and had a family I would not rent out my life for four times that sum of money.

I am rejoiced dear to hear such good accounts of my dear children —for they are my care by day and by night. You say you waited to hear if any one spoke of my coming home. You might have known I would not have said a word to anyone if I had not been perfectly sure of coming. I have already learned to *keep my own counsel*—so much for the war.

Dearest it is late. I have to rise before light in the morning to muster the Co. so I must hurry and close. I pray our Heavenly Father

[5] Notices in newspapers of Shreveport and other Trans-Mississippi towns indicate that couriers, some functioning in an official capacity and others operating on their own, carried letters and packages on a fee basis between points east and west of the Mississippi.

that this letter may find you well for if you should continue to be sick, my dearest, I should be almost obliged to come home if I had to run away. I thank you dearest for your scrupulous regard for my wishes. What I have is yours and I beg you will do with it just as you would if I had expressed no wish on the subject. There are none of the Co. dangerously sick I think unless it is Jim Leary who has a severe attack of flux, but I think he is getting better. I hope dearest that Mr. Hart will not be gone before I get back from our 3 days march, if he is not I'll write a great deal more, but good bye for the present time. I'll write by Mr. Wimberly who I think will come in a week or two. God bless and preserve my darlings is the prayer of your husband and their father. I wrote that Jim Leary had the Flux. He is much better now and will doubtless recover in a very few days—I am very sick of the army workings now and I am homesick enough, more so than ever before.

I bought an india rubber oil cloth to put under my bed, of one of the Yankee prisoners and gave him a dollar and a half for it. It has a hole through it so I can wear it as a poncho. I am pretty well provided with clothing at present. My drawers are ripping in the seams but I am going to sew up the rents—I need another pair however, as I have only a change of clothing and it is not always convenient to wash.

I am so rejoiced, my dearest, to think you have taught Thornwell to say papa—I would give a great deal of money to see him and Will Ed. now. Bless his soul. I do pray that I may be spared to see him again—I don't know what my children would do if I should be taken from them—I am glad to hear that Will Ed. has turned inventor. I told his invention to Capt. Webb.

I know you have heard about the election of officers—Not half of the Co. voted at all—Watkins makes a pretty good Lieutenant—better than I expected—and likes to claim that "we" did it if any brave act is done. But my dearest I feel like lying down—you don't begin to know how hot it is here—I am sitting in the door of my tent and sweating almost as much as I ever did in my life.

Tell your father that I am not alarmed at all about old Randall burning our Mill and it would be better for him to talk as little as possible about it—I may come home and he may know that I am interested in the Mill. We have not had any rain of any consequence here since our retreat from Corinth. We had a pretty good season then. I do hope dearest that you will have rain and make good crops for provisions are very scarce here and I don't know when we will get any more. We have had fresh beef but as they issue 10 days rations at a time and we have little or no salt to keep it with and so throw it away.

But my dearest I must close. If Mr. Hart does not come for this letter I shall send it by mail. You might write as often as you can conveniently and mail it for I feel sure the government will keep up a mail across the river. Love to all God bless you darling Your loving husband, Edwin H. Fay.

My suspenders sweat through and get dirty and I want some I can have washed. Get some one to knit them for me. If I could get another cravat I would like it but do not need it at present. I am going to refer my school exemption to Gen'l Price when he comes back and if he does not decide that I am entitled to it I shall get a substitute—If I can get a boy under eighteen years of age he must have the written consent of his parents and must bring it with him—I think it would be easier perhaps to get a boy than a man 35, but it must be done. Loye has not got back. His substitute is here and it will be thirty days after his substitute is accepted before I can have mine but I'll make the next application so as to be in time. If you could send on a man by Mr. Hart next time or the time after it would do—I am going to write for consent to a boy's parents in the 19th Regt. today—I don't know whether I will get it—I don't know the boy's name but believe it is Winfrey from Vienna. Capt Weldon will see him for me before long. If I can get the consent of his parents I'll have him certain. Hart is calling for the letters so I must close. Good bye dearest one. May God bless and protect you and my precious ones is the prayer of your own Ed.

June 27, '62
In Camp, Friday Morning

My own One:

I wrote you a half sheet Tuesday Night in which I told you that we were ordered off on a scout for 3 days after the enemy. We left the next morning at daybreak and marched all day camped and fed two hours and remounted and marched till day began to grow red in the East, when we were accosted by a Yankee sentinel with "Halt! who comes there?" A Capt. in Forrest's Cavalry commanded and was in the advance with Capt. Webb and I was just behind beside Lieut. Watkins. Capt. Coats replied "A Friend" and on being ordered to advance one and give the countersign, began approaching in an oblique direction towards the bushes and I followed him. I could have killed the picket with my shotgun but had no orders. Capt. Coats would have shot him but said his conscience would not let him after telling him a lie by replying "A Friend." The sentinel did not fire but ran off. We had sent a detachment off on another road and at this time they encountered a picket of four men too and fired on them and charged. Sidney Killen reserved his fire and charging up the hill shot one as he got on his horse and broke to run, the ball passing, it is thought, through the small of his back near the spinal column, he instantly fell off and besought him not to shoot again. One of the Forrest men jumped down and got his pistol and gun and cut Sidney out.

We drew up in battle line as soon as we heard the firing, supposing a large force of the enemy and here we found that the far famed Forrest Cavalry could not stand fire very well for we could not get them into line and they would not stand there. Our Squadron held their places and behaved right gallantly. We soon charged on their reserve force and captured 8 prisoners and eleven horses and all accoutrements tho I did not get a shot. Learning that they had a large body, 1500 cavalry and as we had 194 men all told and were some distance above their force (as we had come in on the upper side) we left in a hurry, double quicked it as fast as our horses could come for 12 or 15 minutes before we halted at all.

The most exhausting trip I ever took. We came on and reached camp just after dark having travelled 94 miles in less than 36 hours and fought a skirmish besides. I am thankful that I was so mercifully preserved, though I was in but little danger of being shot—I was never so worn down in all my life in fact I have some fever although I am sweating. I hope I will feel better in a few days—if not I will try and get off in the country for a few days though military regulations are so strict that I really think the Gen'ls intend killing off all the sick men so they may have a healthy army—Such utter disregard of human life you cannot imagine, nor can you short of actual experience gain any idea of military life.

Your letter of the 8th, 9th, 10th, 11th, came last night, the gump you sent it by *"a Schon"* having taken it to the 19th Regt. and there is no telling when I would have gotten it had not Capt. Wimberly been over there and enquired for letters. You speak of "*getting a substitute here.*" It is almost impossible to do so for I know of no one who will be willing to *stay* (in our Co.) I wrote you the other day that Weldin had taken Mike Dixon's place and that a man had come on to take Loye's place. What you do must be done at once. If I can get a substitute I will do so at any price almost, for since I heard of you being sick it seems to me that I cannot stay here. I don't want to desert but I think strong about it sometimes. As for bearing remarks about my course, the remarks of the world have very little effect on me. I have proved by my course already that I am not afraid to go into an engagement with the enemy and never have I shirked a single duty as yet, but I see so much of it done I find it comes very hard on the few who are willing—ten men do all the duty for our entire command. I have just been lying down resting before finishing this sheet for I am tired out and fear my time has come now to be sick but I hope for the best.

I have just re-read your letter of the 12th inst. I believe I told you in a previous one that I had got your 16th by Mr. Hart. You say in your scrap of 12th, Shall I see you soon or not? If I answer truly, I must say dear that I don't think you will ever see me again if this war continues long. My health has been very good up to this time since leaving Corinth. You say substitutes will be as high as $2000. Loye only pays $350 pr. year. In a letter I wrote you I offered $400 pr. year and the governmental pay of 300 for man and horse makes it for 3 years $2100—I will add besides my horse, bridle and saddle which were valued at $275 making it $2375 for the three years. If this is not good wages I don't know it for a man can't begin to make it at home. If I had no family I would not give ten cents for a substitute and I presume I would join a Partisan Ranger band at home even if I did hire a substitute. What is done must be done quickly for only one a month is allowed and Loye's is already here—but he himself is absent. I hope he will come back before long so his papers can be fixed up for June, if they are not I shall have to wait till August before I can be allowed to fix up the papers. I must come home if possible though if I thought the war would be over in the 12 months I would gladly stay my time out. We are ordered to be mustered in on Monday for 3 years or the war—I don't want to swear again, as I have sworn to support the Confederate States for one year and I think that is enough—for the same oath is just as binding as ever.

I talked with the prisoners taken and one man said he volunteered to keep his family from starvation as they got 100 in gold bounty money. They were Michiganders, the Lieut. a student from Ann Arbor. They would lie as fast as a horse could run. The only truthful one I thought was an old one-eyed man, who told me about his family. I talked with only 3 and the other two were strong for the Union. This man acknowledged the war unjust and unholy but alleged starvation as the motive power, as all labor was suspended—Oh may you never taste the horror of war. When scouting we see little cabins filled with women and children but seldom a man is to be seen in the country unless a very old one.

I am very thankful for the socks you sent me for in the hard ride we made trotting my horse wore out a new pair for me entire. I find the bought socks last much better than the knit ones, at least those Miss Mosely knit. They are knitted too loosely and give way at once. I wrote you I had my valise but my clothing is still down at Okolona most of it. I hope I shall get it back before long. I believe I have told you where the army is and how to direct letters "Tupelo, Miss" Van Dorn's Division, Capt. Wimberly's Squadron La. Cavalry. It is known as Wimberly's Squadron so you need not direct to Capt. Webb's care.

I presume Nat Martin has told you all the news—I have nothing to tell, we get papers occasionally from Mobile by paying ten cents apiece for them. The enemy don't know where we are. "They say" in Memphis papers that Beauregard has retreated below Okolona and Gen'l Pope was there, while we were within 6 miles of Gen'l Pope's (Yankee) Headqts up above Booneville some 50 miles above here only a few days ago. Their papers cannot tell the Truth. Capt. Wimberly has just come from Tupelo and brought Minden dates by mail mailed the 18th just as close time as Mr. Hart's express—I have been talking with Dr. Patillo and he says I can hire a substitute under 18 years. If your father can send a good healthy boy under 18 years at this "enrollment" and send him—I think $700 would be quite an inducement besides a good horse, saddle and bridle—You must get one if possible—Dr. Patillo and I presume Capt. Wimberly will come home, start in about a week or more. They are waiting for their money—I would not wait for mine long but would leave it.

My darling I will interline the other half sheet as paper is scarce and I have not enough to last me 3 years. Be sure you read this and the interline of the Blue Sheet last. In reading over your 16th I found several questions—Rich says L. B. Watkins mailed the letter containing the money to Webb Pratt for Mary—I don't know—I am going to ask him about it—You ask me whether Spencer avails himself of the Conscript—he enlisted for the war so he has no exemption—I don't know whether Sam Stoddard is in the same Company or not—I have not heard from Mother or Spencer since May 1st and know nothing—I only learned from you that William Henry was at Chicago—I can hear from no one except you for I think no one else cares anything about me except you—I know you do love me and I never thought you loved me less than Mrs. Caufield—You mistake in thinking I held her up as an example to you—You ought not to be mentioned in the same breath with her for you are not a woman who lives for the approbation of outsiders—

I am very sorry my dearest that I cannot write cheerfully for I see nothing cheerful in our news. Vicksburg stands well yet and the paper of the 25th from Mobile says 24th Richmond, that McClellan has sent for Porter's Mortar fleet to come as the Batteries at Drewry's Bluff must be reduced before he can take Richmond—A telegraphic dispatch has arrived saying that McClellan has been again badly cut up by Gen. Lee—It may be true. Gen. Buell crossed the Tenn. River last Wed. and Thursday a week with 40,000 men—This is true I think. There are but few Yankees below Corinth—on the M and O R.R.—They did occupy Holly Springs but Genl. John C. Breckinridge drove them out a few days ago. They are completely scattered. Where our troops are since our retreat I know not. We lost but very little in our retreat except that the Army became very much scattered—It is getting along very well now—collecting together again.

I send you enclosed a pretty piece of poetry clipped from the Mobile evening News. I think you will like it—It goes home to my heart for I know the reality of it—I think I can tell you some news. (Mrs. Dr. Patillo is in an *interesting* condition). I have looked at the socks and they are so nice—I do thank you and prize them highly for they are the product of your own hands—O my dear I do hope you will when in health learn to spin and weave and do such things as that—It is an honor I think for a woman to clothe her husband by her own handiwork but no more. I know that you will do all that my wife ought to do—I trust you implicity—Give Will Ed and Thorny twenty kisses apiece for their dear Favy—I wish I could keep clean but if I wash twenty times a day, in the dust I get very dirty. You have no idea how much dust a column of 2 or 300 Cavalry can raise. We try and report first altho it is a post of danger—Mr. Hart has just come in and I'll send this by him.

(Sat. Morn) I am feeling a little twinge of Rheumatism this morning but I hope it will not continue long—We had a little shower of rain last night and we are so refreshed—It will do crops good—I think it will rain again tonight as it is very warm. Dr. Patillo will start home before long and I'll write again—I would not be surprised if Mr. Wimberly and Col. Sandidge remained as scouts till cold weather—I surmise this only—Be sure and let me hear from you often. Trust the mails every week. I want to have you send me a pair of cotton suspenders.

Camp Priceville near Tupelo, Miss.
June 29, 1862

My own dear Sarah:

I have written you so much lately that I hardly know what to write you. We have had so many changes lately that everything is in confusion—Were ordered to report to four different Genl's in one day (yesterday) and now find ourselves attached to Gen. [Paul O.] Hébert former Col. of the 3d La. Regt. it is still under his command and the remainder of the Brigade is composed of Texans. I don't like the maneuvre much for I fear it will give us a great deal of duty to do, and also that the Genl. will be very strict. He came over to our Camp today and fearing that he would move us we cleaned up, swept the yard and prepared to receive him with a great deal of ceremony but he came upon us unawares and we let him come. He seemed very pleasant and as I had just made out a "Muster Roll" I asked him if it was right and he complimented me upon it. I dread him however, and as we are the only Cavalry attached to the Brigade we will have the work of a Regt. to do and if there is a fight on hand the 3rd Louisiana will be sure to be in, the Brigade of course and the only Cavalry belonging to the Brigade much more as a matter of course. So you see there is every probability of our having a hard row to hoe.

I expect ere this letter reaches you we may be ordered to Vicksburg or Cumberland Gap. We have heard glorious news from Richmond that Stonewall turned the right flank of the "Young Napoleon" and drove it back on the center while Genl. Johnston attacked the front and he burned his tents and baggage and tried to escape, but they were pressing him so hard there was no chance of escape except by means of boats and he cannot possibly embark under fire.[6] If all we hear is true I have strong hopes of a speedy peace or at least an invasion of northern country—Buell has crossed the Tenn. River with 45000 men towards Cumberland Gap, the Yankee prisoners said, to go to Richmond. They also told us that Charleston was burnt but we

[6] The action to which Fay refers is the first of the Seven Days' battles about Richmond which began with the battle of Mechanicsville, June 26, 1862. He is in error about Joseph E. Johnston's participation, as that leader had been incapacitated by a wound at Seven Pines, May 31, 1862.

see nothing of it in the papers. I will try and send you a late paper when Joe Hamilton and Loye go home—

Loye has a substitute and only gave him 350 dollars. I spoke to Hart to see your father about one for me, told him what I would give. Hart asks me 50 dollars for his services—so I want to know who brings him Hart or your father. Capt. Webb declared today that he would not receive any substitutes but he must do for me what he has done for Loye—Jack Stewart made an application before I did and so I cannot get off before August if at that time—I hope the war will close before I can possibly get a substitute here. If it would we would be happy wouldn't we dearest in our own little home—Is this vision too good to be realized? I hope and trust not.

It is reported here that the British Atlantic fleet captured two transports of the Yankees heavily loaded with provisions—in return for the Bermuda and Circassian captured by the Yankees—If England has commenced the game of retaliation a war will grow out of it quite speedily and that will put an end to this one—I am beginning to think this war game will be played out in the course of twelve months. I hope and pray so. Don't you. I'll try and write more. It is growing dark, but I must tell you that I forgot to send you a Yankee postage stamp taken from his pocket in our skirmish that I wrote you about—

I wish I could write you news of peace that would bring me home. I am homesick but it is my longing for you and my darlings that makes me so—I don't think I am afraid nor do I believe my courage extends to madness or rashness. I believe I am as brave as many of the high officers in command. They don't think it a pleasant thing to be shot at, nor do I—I got a letter from Mother that I will send you to read—She does not write much as you see, says she has written me five times but I have never received but the one, although one was sent by hand—I hope it will come to hand yet. I wrote a long sheet of foolscap to her yesterday which I hope she will get as she did not my letter from Corinth—Ed Leroy McKee is here at Tupelo and I am going to see him tomorrow if possible—I have never been able to find the Prattville Dragoons yet but hope I may some of these days—

Now dearest I must talk again about the children—I am so much rejoiced to hear that they care about their father. Can Thornwell indeed begin to talk—Do you think he remembers anything about his father—I feel sure Will Ed does, but I thank you if you teach Thorn to say "papa"—I hope you will get my Ambrotype for I dislike having it lost after paying so much for it and then it would please Will Ed and Thorn could form some idea of how I look if I could come home—Do write me all about everything there at home—even all little things of minor importance interest me when coming from home. Your letters are very interesting indeed, and I don't think anyone I know can compare with you as a letter writer—I don't think anyone has such a good wife as I—I would not swap with anyone in the world—I will not close this yet for Loye may not start till tomorrow—John Lackey is down at Tupelo detailed as courier with 10 others and is as fat as a beaver—John makes a good soldier and is a first rate fellow, keep him away from opium—We have some cases of measles. Hart who stayed at our house—Send word to Mrs. Nelson at Isaac Loftin's place that her husband is improving slowly.

Camp Priceville July 1st

My dearest:

I have a few, very few moments to drop you a hasty note to put in my letter by Loye. I made out the muster and pay rolls of our Co. yesterday and we are promised pay in a few days. I don't know however if it will ever come. The news from Virginia is even more encouraging than yesterday. McClellan is entirely surrounded and "Lee" has called upon him to surrender to prevent further effusion of blood. He has asked an armistice till 12 o'clock the next day which was granted. His whole army will doubtless surrender prisoners of War. Capt. Wimberly went over to the 19th [Louisiana] regiment yesterday and there learned from a letter received from Virginia that in the battle of Winchester "Will Crichton" was killed, John Monzingo and little Macky, Chaffe's saddler, were also killed from the Minden Blues.[7]

[7] The Minden Blues were Company G, 8th Louisiana Infantry Regiment. Fay apparently confused the battle of Winchester, fought on May 25, 1862, with that of Port Republic fought on June 9, 1862, as Booth's *La. Confed.*

George Miller (Widow Miller's son) and 6 others wounded, so you see dear that our victories were gained at the expense of the lives of some of our friends. I could hear nothing of Jim McKee but hope he came off safe.[8] How happens it that all the representatives of families are taken. Must some families give up their all in this cruel and nefarious war and others suffer nothing—May our Heavenly Father grant that our little family may remain unbroken and be again reunited to live happily.

I got up quite early this morning and called the roll so as to have a good time for writing this letter but an order has just come in to prepare for inspection at 9 A.M. so I have got to drive ahead at Railroad speed or not get it off for Loye starts at 8 o'clock, tho the cars do not leave till 12 M.

Jas. H. Simmons came in last night. He has been in the country waiting on "Alfred Jones" who lived with Wm. Obier at Homer. He died last Saturday 28th some 12 miles from Camp and I fear before many days Jim Leary may die in Camp—Don't alarm his family or friends but Dr. Patillo thinks there is but slight chance for him—His disease is Typhoid dysentery but I think it is flux run into typhoid fever myself. We are losing men, already four—If Nelson recovers it will be an excellent thing—Fuller's Co. have lost 9 men I think, it may not be so many—It is utterly impossible for a man who is very sick to stand any chance of recovery in camps—Conveniences are impossible to be acquired and Medicines are things almost unknown. We were fortunate enough to bring some along but our stock is being wonderfully exhausted—What we will do when they give out I have no idea of judging now—God grant that this war may close soon.

The English have blockaded the ports of St. Augustine, Fla. and taken two Yankee transports, also Wilmington, N. C. I believe—All the ports the Yankees open to themselves England at once closes on

Soldiers, indicates that Crichton was killed, and Miller and Monzingo wounded, the latter mortally, at the Port Republic fight. The 19th Louisiana Regiment, from whom Wimberly obtained reports of the Port Republic fight, was stationed near Tupelo, a part of Mouton's Brigade, Ruggle's Division, Bragg's Corps, Army of Mississippi.

[8] Booth's *La. Confed. Soldiers,* III, pt. 1, 1214, states that James P. McKee, a corporal in the Minden Blues, was killed at Port Republic, June 9, 1862. He was a cousin of Edwin H. Fay.

the ground that a port open to one nation must be to all. I think a war will grow out of it between U.S. and E. Anything to get us out honorably I say, will be gladly welcomed by more than 9/10ths of this army. We hear the Yankees are digging a Canal across the bend opposite Vicksburg on the La side.[9] Now our Monroe troops will have a good opportunity to try their hands with the enemy—I wish some of the swamp rangers would try and pick them off—I would like so much to be there with a good rifle to fight on my own hook. I do not like to be confined here by military authority. The instruction I do not care for for I think I know to obey—I don't care for hard service. I can stand almost everything if I have any heart in the matter.

I hope dearest to hear from you often. If there is no one coming, mail your letters for they do come through but write by every one who comes. I'll write to you when I can. I wish the men about Minden would send us 15 or twenty recruits to take the places of the men who are released by the Conscript Act. I wish too that they would see to it that the Conscript Act is strictly enforced, that none are let off from favoritism or any other cause. Give much love to Will Ed and Thorny for their Father. Why did not your Mother and the children go to Texas?

I hope you have had rain before this. We had a slight shower the other day, and the clouds look very lowering this morning. If you can only make good crops this year of corn I think all will go well. What have you done with our little crop of corn up in the old house. It ought to be taken care of. I hope there is wheat enough made "to bread" you all—Tell your father to raise every hog he possibly can as bacon is going to be the great necessity. He had better commence early and make his salt too for it will be a great item—Collect as many of my accounts as possible and fix up all of my business. You ought to see the money we use here. I sent a silver dollar by Nat Martin to buy you 20 postage stamps—I have none except what are on envelopes and I can get none to send you, but Loye is waiting and I must say good bye. I dislike to do it. My prayers are for you my dearest and my little ones. Truly your affectionate husband,

E. H. Fay

[9] The Federals in June and July, 1862, made the first of several unsuccessful efforts to by-pass the Vicksburg batteries by digging canals. See *Battles and Leaders,* III, 582 ff.

Camp 4 miles from Priceville [July 2, 1862]

Dearest:

I have a few minutes to write you this morning. Capt. Wimberly and Dr. Patillo have taken a sudden notion to leave tomorrow morning and I know dearest you will expect a letter from me by them. There is nothing new since I last wrote by John C. Loye except that we have moved our camp some three or 4 miles from our former camp and are now encamped in a pleasanter place but we fear we will not stay here long as a large portion of the army are moving Northward and they are building a large bridge over the Bigbee at Aberdeen. Gen'l Hardee's Division has moved forward bound for Chattanooga and we learned yesterday that Gen'l Price's forces were going across the Miss River in 7 days. I don't know how true this may be for it is camp rumor. But it seems to be plausible. Of course you have received the news from Richmond of the glorious victory and we heard late yesterday eve that McClellan had *surrendered*. I hope this is true for it will put an end to the war. God grant that it may for I am sure I shall be ruined if it does not readily close.

I am filling the two offices of Orderly and Adjutant and I have more orders than I can possibly attend to. I am almost distracted with confusion. I had much rather keep the Books of a large house than do the duties I have to do. If it does not drive me crazy I shall be glad. I am relieved from duty of going out on picket or scout so shall not be in quite so dangerous position. Since we have been attached to Gen'l Hébert's Brigade we have had orders pouring in on us sometimes as many as 20 in an evening.[10] Today there is to be an inspection of arms and accoutrements, Camps. &ç. I wish sincerely they would get through with us for I am heartily tired of confusion.

I am now occupying the tent with Capt. Webb and when Nat Martin comes back we three will form a mess together. At present Lyman Watkins, Browder Oliver, and 6 or 8 others, Capt. Webb and myself are messing together. Being Orderly too, insures the transportation of my valise since I keep the Co. Books in it. Jos. Hamilton made me a present of a striped shirt—I have sent to Okolona for my drawers and things there, so I am pretty well supplied with cloth-

[10] Brig. Gen. Louis Hébert at this time commanded the 2nd Brigade, Price's Division, of Van Dorn's Army of the West.

ing at present. I don't know what I shall do when I get out—If we get on the west side of the River, you can send me some. John LeSueur says after the 16th of July he will bring on clothing & things to the Co. wherever it is. He is exempt under the Conscript Act being 37 years of age. I am in the greatest confusion imaginable this morning and I don't know hardly what I'm writing. I have a pretty good pair of suspenders now given me by Capt. Wimberly which will do for the present. I am pretty well provided for at present and am so much in hopes that the war will close before 12 mos. pass that I feel as if I did not care about any clothes but I must close.

Oh what would I not give to see you and the dear children this morning, to hear them talk. I have tried to send you some verbal messages by Capt. Wimberly but my voice chokes up so that I cannot. I understand from him on going to the 19th again yesterday that it was Jas. P. McKee that was killed at Winchester instead of Mackey from Chaffe's—I must write to Aunt Olivia about it. Poor Jim, he was a good boy and it has thrown a new grief on me—It seems as if *I* had to suffer in this war if no one else does but I know many hearts besides mine are bleeding deeply. Dearest, pray and invoke all Christians in and around Minden to do so also that this horrid war may be speedily closed. I do believe in the efficacy of prayer as heartily as I do in the Divinity of our Savior. I cannot live as I would wish to in Camp. I find no time for reading and my Bible has been at Okolona with my baggage since the evacuation of Corinth. You will direct your letters as before simply adding 2nd Brigade, Gen'l Hébert, Army of the West. Now dearest do write me often. I shall not need the oil cloth sent for, for I have bought one from a "Yankee" prisoner, "India Rubber" which will do for me. Well darling Good Bye. Kiss the children 40 times for me and talk to them about their Father. Give my kindest love to your father and mother, also Mrs. Simmons and Mrs. Wimberly. Good Bye my darling May heaven's richest blessings rest on you. Your husband, E. H. Fay

3 o'clock—A dispatch this morning comes that McClellan has entrenched himself and we have attacked him three times and been repulsed with heavy loss—Bad news. My horse is quite sick and I fear I may lose him—but hope not as some of the horses in the Co.

have been affected in the same manner and are recovering—I am almost sick from the various excitements but hope I may come out straight—Good Bye my own loved ones. Your affectionate husband and father. E. H. Fay

Camp near Priceville. July 6, 1862

My own dear One:

Again another opportunity offers for sending you a letter and as I can never forgive myself for omitting an opportunity if I am at leisure (which I am this evening), I am seated at a camp table with Capt. Webb opposite me, both of us engaged in the laudable and certainly pleasant occupation of writing to the loved ones at home. I wrote a few days ago by Mr. Wimberly and Dr. Patillo but as Lieut. Frank Smith of the Bossier Cavalry starts tomorrow I will send a line knowing that it will be welcome to you if it comes like a telegraphic dispatch only 2 hrs. later.

I wish, darling, I had some news to give you as indeed I have, since I recollect that I wrote you bad tidings in the Post Script of the last I wrote, that we had attacked the Yankees on their retreat and they had taken a strong position and had repulsed us three times, but by the interposition of a strong and protecting providence old Bankhead Magruder came up and we then routed the whole Yankee army and the despatch came to Gen'l Bragg that "we had captured the bulk of McClellan's army." Only a few escaping and that Stonewall and Bankhead were both pressing on as rapidly as possible to Washington City. An order came for a salute of 13 Guns to be fired in honor of our victory at 12 M and soon the booming of the cannon was heard at Tupelo, Gen'l Bragg's HdQrts. and ere the last reverberation had died in the distance the opening roar from Gen'l Price's HdQrtrs. announced that there too our victory was being celebrated. It was joyful news indeed to the grimly careworn veterans of the Western Department for it seemed as if it might be productive of beneficial results, be the beginning of the end of this War.

The news from Europe is very favorable also, and I sincerely believe that within sixty days there will be an intervention that the North will be obliged to respect—England and France are both satisfied that Seward's promised Cotton Supply is all "bumcombe" and they will trust no longer to the double dealing Yankees. Heaven grant that our Country may be freed from this horrible war. Gen'l Price who now commands the Army of the West said in a speech night before last that he had permission from the President to lead his Army across Miss. to Missouri and if he could not get a fight out of the Yankees before long he would start. On Friday the Division of Gen'l [Jones M.] Withers of Mobile moved up to Ripley, some forty miles above here and engaged a brigade of Yankees and took 1300 prisoners and cut the Yankees all to pieces. They are all moving from this side of the Tenn. River and going back I think to Nashville or Chattanooga.

I told you that we have been attached to Gen'l Hébert's Brigade and I assure you that we have been busy enough since. Orders came flocking in all the time and as I am filling the post of Orderly Serg't and Adjutant both, I have them all to attend to. The Lieutenants do not have much to do. Watkins drills pretty well and makes a better officer than I expected. Carter does very well too, tho he has not much to do. He and Watkins are both complaining a little, nothing serious, however.

I have sad news to communicate, for James C. Leary is dead. He died on the night of July 4th at 10 o'clock and 25 minutes. He had typhoid fever, but we had got him into a house on a comfortable bed and thought him a great deal better. Dr. Patillo thought he might get well when his bowels began to hemorrhage and he discharged enormous quantities of blood. This was checked in some measure by the use of opiates, but he sank under it. Dr. Patillo injured himself I think, with a great many of the company by going off just as he died. Jim was known to be going down to the dark valley but Dr. said there was a chance left for him and then went off. I would have stayed had I been in his place, but he saw fit to go. One day would have decided the matter definitely and would not have made much difference with his getting home. It would have saved him friends here. Every man knows his own business best.

All the men over 35 years have been by order of the War Department retained in the service, till the period of their enrollment, that is, they have to serve their 12 mos. out, also all under 18 yrs. This fell with stunning effect on some of the old men, on Monroe Caufield particularly. I am sorry for David Caufield but am glad Monroe is held on, Kemp too, I am sorry for, but for the others I think a few yrs. ought not to relieve them any more than me. I believe this war will be over before Christmas and I hope under the blessing and protection of a kind Father in Heaven that I may be with you before that time. Pray for it dearest. Every body pray for it. The news from Richmond is still cheering as late as the 4th July. Fighting at Vicksburg continues, but the Yanks make nothing out of it. Their Gun boats get badly smashed up.

We have lost another man, whom we sent to the hospital, a brother-in-law of the late Mr. Hunt who was at our house, his name was Thos. Stanley and died from a relapse of measles. A brave and good soldier. So our ranks have been decimated. Fuller's Co. have already lost 13 and will lose another man tonight or tomorrow, George Hearn of Bossier. We have lost five men ourselves. Fuller, Blackmon, Darby, Leary and Stanley. The insatiate archer is never satisfied.

But dearest, I must talk now about our children, but first let me say I have directed you wrong in regard to mailing letters. Gen'l Van Dorn has been transferred to Vicksburg and we have fallen under Gen'l Price. So your letters should come to Tupelo, Wimberly's Squadron Cavalry, 2d Brigade, Gen'l Hébert, Army of the West. How I would jump for joy to see our dear little lambs, Will Ed's pleasant face and Thorny's ringing laugh. Mother do you keep up his remembrance of his Father by talking to him of me. I hope you do, for the idea of my child's forgetting me is exceedingly painful. Poor child, if he should never see his Father again—

Mother I wrote you about a substitute but an order has been issued that no able bodied man shall procure a substitute, but an unsound man may do it. So every avenue to my return is blocked and you and I must make up our minds to endure it. Let us hope ere the turn of 12 mos. is expired, we may all return in peace to our homes and firesides and all alarms of war may cease. Tell me all the news. I am afraid Nat Martin has been captured by the Yankee pickets opposite Vicksburg—they are spread through the woods.

(Monday Morn) Dearest I have just called the roll and while the boys are feeding their horses I will try and finish this page—I wish dearest one I could write you something interesting—I would send you a newspaper (Mobile) if I thought there was any probability of your getting it, but if letters scarcely go through how can we expect it of papers? I expect Thomas Nuckolls will bring you this letter as Lt. Smith is going to see him across the Miss. River and then go to Ala. I do hope you will get this letter in time for I expect it will be the last letter you will get from me in a month or two—especially if we make the move we contemplate and then I do not know that it will hardly be possible to get letters across the country by horse mails. But God disposes everything for the best and I trust it all in His hands. I know I am not thankful enough to Him for His mercies.

We have had no rain here yet—but the nights are very cool and the days oppressive so there is a good deal of sickness—but none serious now in our company. I think George Hearn will die in the Bossier Co. We learned yesterday that Billy Martin was killed at the same time Jim McKee and Will Crichton, also that Lovick Wren was wounded and going home—if so I presume you will get more information than I can give you. If I could see and talk with you I could remember many things that I have not space to write, but I must close, commending you dearest to the care and protection of our Heavenly Father for He has promised to protect you. Give much love to *all my friends* and my respects to those that are not included in the first class. Kiss the children for me. Train them up for God. Many kind wishes for your Father and Mother though they have been already mentioned. Good Bye dearest, don't forget to share with Lou and Ella. I would write them if I had time but I have not. This is a short letter but it contains my whole heart dearest. Truly your Aff. Husband,

E. H. Fay.

Mr. [P. P.] Bates is now in camp and says please send his wife word that he is doing tolerably well. He is disappointed a little at not coming home.

Camp Maury—July 13, 1862

My Own One:

'Tis Sunday morning and my duties are all done and as I have some spare time I had surely rather devote it to you than to the light conversation going on around camp. In fact you well know dearest that I had rather devote my time to you than to listen to the most philosophical and interesting discussion in the world, and that if it were possible to get the letters to you that I would send you a letter every day—but judging from the infrequency of letters in camp from Minden I fear that mail communication is cut off between us. I accordingly only write when there seems to be some chance of sending by hand. The Bossier company have received letters dated the 29th of June which I believe came through by mail, but our latest dates are the 18th from Minden. I rec'd as already told you, yours of the 16th by Hart's express and the next day there came letters by mail so Mr. Hart did not beat cousin Sally much better that time.

I tell you dearest that it does seem a long long time not to hear from you in a month and to think too that you were so sick when you last wrote dearest if you should die during my absence it would kill me too I do believe. All happiness would be over for me in this world. You dont know how distressed I have been about you for a month and how I dread almost to see a letter come but I hope and pray our Father in Heaven that he will protect and bless the widow and the fatherless during the absence of the husband and Father. Dearest my life is wrapped up in yours and that of my dear children. I only want to live for you. Your happiness is a far greater concern than my own. I could go on and on my dearest telling you of my love but I feel assured that I cannot add anything to your already conviction of the fact for I do think that I have ever proved it to you. If at times I have appeared harsh and severe yet I think I have never given you any occasions to doubt my sincerity or my truth. I know you have every confidence in me, for you have never had any reason to doubt me. But no more on this score.

I wish I had some news to tell you but I have not. I wrote everything I could learn in a letter by Capt. Wimberly and Dr. Patillo and two days thereafter I wrote you again by Lieut. Smith of Bossier Cavalry which letter Thom Nuckolls will bring you I expect, and I think it will reach you before Capt Wimberly does for we heard from him yesterday, date 11th at Scooba at Capt. Webb's brother's where he spoke of remaining several days. It troubles him a great deal because he has gone back, and will more when he learns that all 35 years men have to stay out their 12 mos. It looks as if he had deserted them. Dr. Patillo is glad enough to get off, for between us he did no duty whatever. The first night on picket beyond Farmington was enough for him and he never went out afterward but once—I had no idea he was any worse than I was, *except in one respect* I have by no means the respect for his courage I once had—but it is hard to judge, I may do him injustice, if I do I beg his pardon.

Ben Kemp and J. J. Stewart and Lewis Monzingo have been discharged lately from our Co. Kemp and Monzingo should have had it, but I think Stewart was as well able to stand service, but I may do him wrong, for God only can discern motives. Dr. [James H.] Simmons is trying the same game, but I hope he will fail tho I fear not. He might as well be discharged for all the good he has ever done as he has never yet done any duty of any kind but eating and I assure you he has destroyed as much Govt. provisions as any man in camp if not more.[11] David Caufield got back into camp yesterday, he is not well but I hope he will get better before long, but I fear he will be unable to stand it as a soldier's life is no sinecure. William Nelson that I wrote you about is dead. He died at Okolona, Miss. on the 9th July about 11 A.M. Bates was down there at the time. A letter came for him from his wife next day which I broke open and read. Poor woman I feel sorry indeed for her for she is in a *bad way.* You must go and see her, dearest for blessed are the comforters and she needs consolation I assure you—she hoped to see her husband again but never again on earth poor woman.

Oh to think how many hearts must bleed in this unholy war. The ways of Providence are inscrutable and past finding out. I do indeed feel thankful that a merciful Father has preserved me thus far, and my dearest I do feel that I may in answer to yours and Will Ed's prayers be saved yet to come to you again. I am encouraged too, to believe that this horrid war will close before the termination of our

[11] Simmons was not discharged. See Booth, *La. Confed. Soldiers,* III, pt. 2, 569.

12 mos. I wish it might before cold weather comes for I dread the cold weather as I fear it will affect my health.

I got a letter from Mother of July 5th in answer to mine of June 30th. She tells me that William Henry is at Camp Butler near Springfield, Ill. that she heard from him about the middle of May and he was growing fleshy and was very healthy, two had died from his company. Sister Sarah was not well and expected to spend October at home and perhaps longer. Spencer has been discharged by order of the Sec't of War from Richmond but Gen'l [William H.] Forney objects to it. He got a discharge from the Secretary of War under the Conscript Act as a Teacher of Schools.

If I could get one on like grounds I assure you I would come home again and go on with my school. If they want me to come back to the school someone must get a discharge for me from Richmond then I should come home at once without waiting for any approval of a Gen'l Commanding—I would go home at once if I were in his place but I could do it with better grace than he for I am a native born Southerner—if I knew that there would be an end of this war in 12 mos. I would not care about coming unless my health should fail entirely—but there is not much chance for a sick man to get off, for he has to be in camp till almost dead before he can make application for a furlough or discharge and then he is too weak and sick to get off and they won't discharge a very sick man. They will keep him in camp till he gets better and he often dies before that time comes.

Sam Stoddard has been discharged on account of ill health and Mother says that his health is miserable. Jim McKee, Will Crichton, and Billy Martin were killed in the battle of Port Republic under Jackson. Lovick wounded in the thigh and a prisoner and Will Lewis a prisoner. Dr. Webb and little Joe Collins both taken but both escaped. I wrote to Aunt Lib as soon as I heard of Jim's death but Mother wrote me the particulars so Aunt Lib heard it before I wrote her. There are eight or ten men talking around me and if I make any mistakes you must excuse them.

I would dearest that I could sit by your side with Will Ed on one knee and Thorny on the other and talk to you for two or three hours —I could tell you a great many things that are too insignificant to be written and yet when told by the tongue of love would be very pleasant to hear. I am anxious to hear from Nat Martin as he has been gone 8 or 9 days over his time and I hardly know how to report him on the morning report. I cannot report him a deserter for I know he would not desert for anything. Besides I am very anxious to hear from home and I feel sure he will not come without bringing me some letters. I would give $2.00 for a letter this evening from you and I would increase it to $20.00 rather than be disappointed. Your letters are the green oases of my life and they are in a very dry desert indeed.

"Monday Morning."—A few words more this morning, my own loved one, and I must close this epistle—But first a camp rumor that we have retaken Memphis.[12] It may be or not true. I hope it is as it would be only one more stepping stone to our independence. A rumor yesterday that McClellan was again pushing on Richmond. Not believed though by any means, I am fearful only that he will escape in time to defend Washington City.

Darling Mother, how much I would give to get letters from you today—bless my dear little children, how I do wish to see them. What would I not give to be with you all today to dinner—But we do pretty well now since we get fresh beef, instead of the pickled. We occasionally get some vegetables from the Country. In fact have been living better of late since we left Corinth, though we get no salt and both men and horses are suffering badly for it. A small sack of the article would be very acceptable. Mother writes to know if I want any clothes, as she can have frequent opportunities of sending to me. Am going to write for a couple of undershirts—mine have given out and I am just wearing a linen or cotton shirt and nothing else—I don't dread warm weather but have a horror of cold, though I hope that cold weather will find me at home, the war over—

I suppose you have heard that Gen'l Van Dorn has taken Baton Rouge and 1500 prisoners—This is reliable—and he will take New Orleans in ten or 15 days, he says by telegraph. I do hope he will capture Butler. We also hear that Gen'l Hindman has captured Curtis

[12] This report was false, as were those given in the rest of the letter. Baton Rouge was taken by the Confederates, but not until August 5, 1862; it was re-occupied by the Federals on December 17, 1862. See *Battles and Leaders,* III, 583–586.

and 6000 prisoners. The Yankee papers say that Gen'l Rains is in his rear with 15,000 men and they fear he "may have gone up"—I hope something will occur soon, everything is so still and monotonous—Dispatches from Richmond say that McClellan has been reinforced and that extensive preparations are being made on both sides for a renewal of the conflict—

There was a sale of Jim Leary's and Buck Nelson's effects today and I bid off his horse for $175.00 and a pair of drawers for $2.00—Jack has had the distemper very badly for two or three weeks and I fear if we had to move that I could not ride him as he is now nothing but skin and bones and a fast of four days without any corn is not a fast way to fatten a poor horse—I shall give my note for him and if Jack recovers I shall sell him again—I think I can make twenty-five dollars on him. But dearest I must close—I want no clothing for the pair of drawers I bo't and the undershirt and socks will last me some time. If I can carry all we have got when we start to move I shall be thankful—

Now dearest, do write me by mail often for letters will find their way across before long, they do now. Mssr's Ward and Hart got letters today—18th—from Corny Bluff and there are Minden letters by mail the 22nd instead of the 29th as stated before. But my darling I will not grumble or complain—write me just as often as you can—Give much love to all my friends in Minden and especially to your Father and Mother. I would write especially to them and also to Lou if I did not know that you are all together and one letter suffices for all—We had a good rain yesterday I hope you have had it too—My dear you must excuse my two last letters being written with an infusion of indigo, I had no black ink. Goodbye dearest. May Heaven's richest and choicest blessings be showered upon you. Kiss my darlings for their Father and receive a heart full of love from your own dear husband, Ed.

5

"Your Letters Are Worth More Than Gold"

Camp Maury, July 18, 1862

My own precious One:

Judge my surprise when last night after dark while eating supper without any light Lieut. Carter said "Here is a letter for Mr. Fay." "Orderly Fay" was called all around and although I was very hungry and had eaten but one mouthful I rushed to a smouldering oak fire to devour the contents of the long looked for epistle. How welcome it was you must judge from your own feelings when you have not heard from me in four long weeks, your last date rec'd being the 11th of June. My darling yours of June 30th has not yet come to hand but I hope I will get it in a few days. I cannot afford to lose any of your letters for they are worth more than gold to me at present. Did you not write between the 16th and 30th? Your last (July 5th) was quite unsatisfactory for you did not mention what had been the matter with you altho' you wrote me in June 16th that you were sick in Bed. It distressed me a great deal to think you were sick but I am rejoiced to think you are recovered as I judge you are by your last altho you do not say a word about your health.

I wrote you three days ago, and I sincerely hope you may get it. I sent it by Dr. Scott of Bossier Parish who was discharged as a private to be a surgeon in the Squadron, but as he had killed every case he had anything to do with Capt. Webb dismissed him or rather he resigned and went home. He was a very clever man and I liked him but I could not bear to see men's lives sacrificed to his want of skilfulness. I said above "killed" I should have said lost, for the first is a harsh word and I try not to say them about any one but Picayune Butler.

By the Bye a despatch came yesterday that Pres. Davis had made a formal demand for the person of "Butler" for the murder of "Mumford."[1] I was glad to hear it but I am afraid the threat by which the demand was backed up will be productive of much bloodshed as it will certainly exasperate the Northern mind. He declares if Butler is not surrendered he will hang Gen'l [George A.] McCall who was taken prisoner at Richmond. If it is true I believe the Lincolnites will surrender Butler as McCall is a Maj. Gen'l of the Line while Butler is only a Volunteer, but if they do not and the threat is carried out I am afraid it will lead to an indiscriminate massacre of prisoners on both sides for Buckner would come next and so on down, but we have the advantage of prisoners and can afford to play at the game, but I can't for my Brother is in their power and I don't want to lose him as his life is worth all the Yankees in Lincolndom. I wrote you that I had heard from Mother that he was at Camp Butler near Springfield, Ill. He is getting fat, was very well, tho' two of his company had died.

Of course you have heard the news of the "Ram" Arkansas running the blockade of Lincoln's upper or ironclad fleet, sinking two with her shots, butting the "Benton" with such force as to sink her and setting on fire a fourth that burnt up and arriving safely under the guns of our land batteries having received only two shots one through a port hole opened for air killing five and wounding twenty or 30 others.[2] I suppose too you have heard of the "sure enough" capture of Baton Rouge. Van Dorn has taken it and 1500 prisoners and Commodore Farragut has run off from Vicksburg with his mortar fleet after the insulting proposition that he would draw off his forces and cease the bombardment if they would only permit his upper fleet to pass by unmolested. I would be pleased to see the little "sandy Hornet" Van Dorn's reply to it. He wrote in a private letter to Gen'l [Dabney H.] Maury that he would take New Orleans before the close of July if nothing untoward happened. I do hope he may tho I feel

[1] William B. Mumford, a citizen of New Orleans, was hanged by order of Gen. Benjamin F. Butler on June 7, 1862, for hauling down a United States flag that the Federal forces raised on the U.S. Mint building when they occupied the city. "Picayune" was one of the several disparaging nicknames applied to Butler by Southerners. See *Battles and Leaders,* III, 582.

[2] For the exploits of the Confederate gunboat *Arkansas* in July, 1862, see *Battles and Leaders,* III, 572–580.

sure that Pic. Butler has "skedaddled" as soon as he heard the Ram had passed the "Ironclads." A coward who wars on women and children will not risk any danger.

"A secret." We have through Col. Sandidge made application to be transferred to that command to act as Rangers in the eastern part of Louisiana. I do hope we can be, tho' night before last I thought our cake was all dough for an order came for the Minden Rangers and Bossier Cavalry to be consolidated in one company under one set of officers. All of the officers to be examined before Gen'l [Frank C.] Armstrong and he to select the best from all and appoint them over the consolidated Co. Such mutterings low and deep as you might have heard through the camps. Such a posting up of themselves on Tactics you never saw. I am afraid Capt. Webb will be cut out as Capt. Harrison has been studying hard and is a smart *bad* man tho I hope Capt. Webb's popularity with the Gen'l will secure to him the appointment. Watkins will be the 1st Lieut. now as Geo. Sandidge will not go forward for examination as he wants to go with his father who I think will accept an appointment on Gen'l [Daniel] Ruggles staff. I expect of course all the officers who are not reappointed will be discharged. Oh how I wish now I had run for an office at Corinth. I would not have gone up for an examination and so would have come off with a discharge, my resignation having been accepted. But God does all things right and there is some hidden Providence in it— It may be a sorrowful one. It may be a more pleasant one. "My times, my times are in thy hand Oh Lord."

It seems as if the hand of Providence was in it for yesterday before the time for re-examination came an order to move with all available forces (cavalry) with four days rations, but Gen'l Armstrong says they will not be back before 15 days and perhaps not at all but as soon as our wagons return to be ready to pack up and come on. I don't know where they are going but surmise it is for the purpose of making a recconaisance in and about Huntsville, Ala. as they moved almost due East across the Tombigbee. This postpones the consolidation for an indefinite time and I hope before it arrives we may receive an order transferring us to the quarter above mentioned between Baton Rouge, New Orleans and Ponchartrain. If so it will be glorious and an answer to my prayers. The Companies will not mingle any more than oil and water and if Harrison is appointed he will not prove the potash that will cause them to mingle. What I have written must not get out as it *may* or *may never* come to pass and might create hopes in the minds of some at home that may never be realized. So let it remain with you alone or swear your Father to secrecy.

As regards myself I have invested some lately on a credit, having bought P. P. Bates watch for $35.00 and James Leary's horse for $175.00. The horse I sold yesterday for $225.00, making the watch and $15.00 over and above my investment. I made a clear $50 on the Horse, and I have some $30.00 besides in addition to my gold ($40.00) and silver (2 or 3). Jack has been very bad off with distemper but I hope he will soon improve. If I had full rations of corn I would fatten him, and he will do my riding. I regret very much that I sold the Leary horse for this morning I could not go on the scout. This is the first time I ever failed and the Capt. detailed me to remain at Camp before I sold the Horse so I am not to blame about it.

The first night I had the watch I put it under my head and the hogs coming round after my corn I rose on my elbow to reach my sabre to kill them and put it on the watch and mashed the crystal all to pieces bending the case (it was doubled case). It stopped until I removed all the fragments of glass and then ran on. It does very well indeed but will get dirtier much easier. There is no chance to get any repairs done to watches in Camps.

Tuesday Capt. Webb and I went over to the 19th La. Regt. about four and a half miles beyond Tupelo. We found Parson Scott much better and spent a very pleasant day. I wanted to find the 39th Ala. Col. [Henry D.] Clayton, but found it had moved up to Saltillo so I did not see Edwin LeRoy McKee. Poor Jim and Will. I had heard of their deaths before you did,—but the world says "they fell gloriously." Oh that heart wrapped in ashes that these words are hollow mockery to. What is glory to the bleeding widowed heart? or what renown? I trust and pray my darling that God in his mercy will preserve you from that feeling.

I do believe this war will end before many months and if I am spared to return to you we will be so happy won't we dearest. We'll away to some far distant isle of our own for I cannot afford to live under the tyranny of the Confed. States. I am now in the jaws of the

Lion but I may get out some of these days. I call the consolidation of our two companies a greater act of tyranny than chaining two hound dogs together, not consulting the interests or wishes of over 120 men but throwing them together to save a little expense and yet they will make weekly two or 3 Brig. Gen'ls whose monthly pay will far overbalance the pay of all the commissioned and non-commissioned officers in a single company, so the plea of retrenchment should begin I think among the higher officers where fewer "feelings" would be sacrificed—If the companies are consolidated I shall endeavor to get a transfer to the engineer service and I think I can do it, besides it will reduce me to ranks again and I don't care about going down. However if I could get a substitute it would do me a great deal of good by cold weather. I believe I can stand the warm weather very well but I fear the cold.

I have been very healthy of late. I bought at Leary's sale a pair of Drawers, Socks and an Undershirt. If I had one more good Undershirt I would be fixed but I fear I have more plunder now than I can carry on the *march*. I can put most of it in my valise though. What I can't I can strap on top. But a truce to the Dry Goods business—

I am rejoiced that Will Ed is getting to be a boy but I fear his climbing propensities may be encouraged too far to the breaking of an arm or leg, so I think, Mother dear, you had best limit him somewhat. Bless little red head Thornwell. I do love the child so. Mother take good care of him for you say "he looks like his Father." I wish his Father could look on him this evening. I am sorry my dearest that your dream was not a reality as regards the Ambrotype. I want you to have it but I very much fear that you will never see it until the close of the war if then. I have heard nothing from Spencer save what I wrote you some days ago. He has been discharged by the order of "Sec. of War" and not on his own application. If my friends for instance (Col. Lewis) could have interest enough at Richmond to have me discharged I should come home at once. I think a good school of more importance than the services of *one* man in the Army, at least to the part of the Confederacy called Minden. This must not come from me, that or a substitute with a letter or two will let me out if the war does not close of itself before that time. I only throw out the suggestion if necessary.

As for patriotism that is a fine word for historians, novelists and Big Gen'ls when they have done some fighting and expect to have to do more. There is nothing I have ever seen that has as much humbug in it as military affairs or who make more pretence on little capital than military men. I think my father was right when he always ridiculed Military Schools. It takes a man of business to be a military man and a good one would be a good anything else, lawyer, teacher, mechanic or Ditcher.

But darling if I write all this time I won't have nothing to write next so I must close. Take good care of yourself dearest and of the children. Had you not better wean Thornwell, but no, Mother, let him suck until he is five years old as his father did. I will send this by Thom Swearingen who is again discharged and I hope it will come through safe. Mrs. Carter wrote two full sheets of foolscap to her husband "Miller." You must not let anyone beat you my dear writing to yours, in news or length. I am so sorry you have had such a drought. I am afraid for the corn crop. What have you done with our corn up in the "Ratcliffe House"? You have not said a word about Nat Martin. Did you see him or not? When does he start back? You told me nothing about it. I hope he will come and bring me some news from you for you have told me but little in your last, perhaps it was all in yours of the 30th of June. You must continue to mail letters to me for I think arrangements have been made for a through mail from Texas to cross at Natchez. I hope so for it will take more men than are at present in the Lincoln army to hold the Miss. River but what the wings of love will find means to convey over messages in form of letters to the dear absent ones. If I was foot loose I would like nothing so much as carrying letters back and forth, for then I would indeed be a messenger of glad tidings in both directions and I can imagine nothing more pleasant than to be the bearer of glad tidings.

Swearingen will get off tonight and I have told him to get the latest daily papers he can find and take to you. I would send from here but they are torn up as soon as read in camps. Be sure and write me if Dr. Patillo bro't you any papers. He promised me sacredly that he would do so, but I have not as much confidence in him as I once had. Tell him Mr. Ward paid his trunk a visit 2 or 3 days after he left and got his Instruments, Bible, clothing, powder and everything straight. Be sure you send Mrs Webb word right straight that Capt. Webb was well this morning and would have written but was ordered off at 5 A.M. He was disappointed at not hearing from her by Mr. Miller but supposes she did not hear of it. You ought to get up a club to inform one another of any chance to send letters. It is selfish for anyone to know of a chance and keep it from the rest of the "Cavalry Ladies." You ought to help one another to every opportunity. Now, dearest, I must say that hard word Good Bye. May our God protect and bless and preserve from harm my little family who are so near and dear to me and again reunite us all on earth and more than all permit us all where partings shall be no more is the prayer of your husband. Love to all at home. Rich says tell the negroes Howdy.

Direct your letters by the "Frank" at top only adding "Tupelo, Miss."

5 P.M. I have just written since folding yours to Mother at Prattville according to your suggestion. But perhaps when you next write we will be in some other command. It won't make any difference I reckon as letters will come through anyhow, will follow us up till they find us.

Saturday Evening Aug. 2d, 1862

My own One:

I have finished a letter to Lou and as the day is not quite done and the darkness has not completed its eagle feathered descent I will commence a sheet to you tho I can hardly say when it will be finished. I commence now while the afflatus of Letter writing is on me lest delay might prove dangerous for a soldier knows not at what moment he may be summoned to duty nor can he form any reliable conjecture. You have heard of the exposures and hardships of the negroes on Red River but let me assure you that they are no more to be compared to those of the Confederate Soldiers than living at a first class Hotel is to be compared to living on board a flat boat. I have almost found a different idea of the Creation than the acct. given by Moses for I think the "dust" of which soldiers at least were made must have been comminuted atoms of iron, at least of iron ore. No man whose sinews are not of triple steel and whose frame is not of Brass can stand a 3 yrs. campaign if I judge from my experience. The only thing I know having any comparison is a hunter's life in the Ky. Mountains with this difference (by no means a slight one) that the hunter goes when he wishes, the soldier when he is ordered.

Thus far I have stood it pretty well if I did not have a chill this morning, I felt a good deal like it, could not keep warm with a heavy overcoat on, followed by a little fever, tho I hope it was not a chill for I don't know what I should do with chills in camp. They are not pleasant companions at home when the hand of love is ever ready to bathe one's fevered brow, the bosom of love is by on which to rest one's wearied head, but my dear I hope I didn't have a chill so I beg you will think nothing about it.

I have been writing now most of the evening, have written an answer to Mother's letter sent you yesterday, four long pages, to Lou four short pages and now I am trying to cover this for you. Yes for you, altho your last date rec'd by me was the 5th of July, almost a month. D. W. Caufield got a letter yesterday from Minden the 24th mailed by Geo. Quarles in Vicksburg. Won't they tell you dearest when persons are intending to cross the River? That same "Strange" passed thro' Minden the 23rd (Wednesday) and passed the Mill, too, got here this morning, bro't 3 letters from Minden and none for me. 'Twas provoking but I didn't talk Abner [Abusive?] any, tho I gave him a raking for not calling as he came to Rodney in his buggy and might have brought anything—tho I don't know that I am suffering for anything as yet, an undershirt being really the only thing I need. You once asked me what Hart charged for socks. I'll tell you just here —"Nothing"—He sprung on his letters so much he had not the conscience I reckon—tho I think his is quite an india rubber one.

Writing so often I have nothing new to tell—a cloudy foggy morning Sunday and I am almost as cloudy and foggy as the morning itself. I can see nothing bright in the prospect. I cannot see any end to the War unless by the Intervention of foreign powers. I know not what the Lincolnites or the Confederacy either expect to make of a continuance of the War. The only possible method of settlement I can imagine is to decide by a free and untrammelled vote of the native born population as regards the States of Missouri, Ky. and Maryland. Allow them to choose with which government they will cast their destinies. If it must come to this at last why not now before any farther expenditure of blood and treasure. I would engraft only one more clause, i.e. the Yankees should pay for every negro they have stolen during the War. Such a settlement I think might be brought about right speedily if the proper steps were taken. We certainly don't wish any unwilling territory to belong to our Confederacy for it would always be a source of annoyance to us. I deprecate European intervention and yet I believe it will come sooner or later. All I ask of Europe is to recognize us, make treaties of commerce, and send her vessels into our ports, buy our cotton and send us salt, coffee and other necessaries. Then I have no idea but the Lincoln govt. would give up their idea of subjugation and treat with us on the basis of Independence.

But enough of politics. What has become of that man who was to take charge of the College? and what has become of Mr. Ford. I hope his patriotism has not died out. He might join the army now for I see daily men much older than he battling for their country's rights—I wrote to Father about getting me a substitute but he says it is almost impossible to do it. He advises that the Trustees of the school address a letter to the Sec. of War asking for my discharge if they desire a school there again, and in that case an order will issue for my discharge from Sec. of War, and I will come home at once, tho' I had rather hire a substitute if it were possible.

Did I write you that there was a probability of my being discharged from this service and ordered to join the Engineers Corps—One of our Co. named [John H.] Garrett was a courier for the Dept. and after becoming acquainted with the commander he told him about me and he said if he went to Vicksburg he would take me along but he has been ordered to Chattanooga, but took down my name and command and sent me word that he would see the chief of the department and if the army remained there he would order me there. If I should be ordered there I should want you to come to Ala. as I could frequently come and see you. If this and the Bossier Co. are not consolidated I had rather remain here, if they are I go certain if possible—I am thinking some when Capt. Webb comes back of getting a furlough for ten days and going to Montgomery if I can—I would come to Minden if I could get a twenty days furlough tho that would be only an aggravation. I wish we could get ten or fifteen good recruits to come and join us. They would find it far preferable to the infantry service.

I presume Mr. Wimberly has got home at length—I hope he derives much glory and honor from his short but brilliant campaign. He might raise some recruits for us if he would but I presume he has some ambition for he figured hard for a Colonelcy while in service. If he had not done it we might have joined Thom Scott and formed a legion. But such is life and such is ambition too. I don't approve of Mr. Wimberly's action. I don't think he ought to be called "Capt" for he did not serve long enough to acquire the title tho' he did very well while he remained. I don't think he ought to be recognized as a military character—But no more on this score.

Now dearest I have made out a good long letter to you again and I do wish I could get one from you this evening. Oh a month is a long time not to hear from you. How I wish our command could be transferred across the River into our own state—I would then see you sometimes. At least hear from you. I hope dear little Will Ed is well. How I do want to see the child and hear him talk. If some were passing now, you could get the Daguerreotypes in Mabry's trunk. I wish you could find out where he left the trunk, as then I could have it carried across. Now I don't know where it is and consequently could not get anyone to take it if I had an opportunity—

Tuesday morning 11 o'clock. A messenger has just handed me your letters of the 10,18,22d., my heart is bursting Mother, I cannot be reconciled to the death of my eldest born—I dreaded something hence my warnings in every letter to take care of my children. Could not God have afflicted us in some other way. He took our little daughter, must he take our eldest born too. Thornwell will go next, then you, my dearest and I be left an outcast. My heart is bursting. I almost fear I shall go crazy—I don't see how I can stand it. It would not have been so hard to give him up if I could have been there and heard his last words and seen his last breath, held him in my arms. My heart bleeds for you dearest though you have some consolation and friends around you, I have nothing but my sorrow. Oh God why didst thou thus afflict me. Could I not have been punished in some other way if need be. Must I give up by first born after giving up my little daughter? Strange are thy ways and past finding out Oh my God. When our little daughter died I could become reconciled because I had seen her suffer so much but to lose my Will Ed whom I left in blooming health, my misery is greater than I can bear.

Oh Mother he ran out of doors too much and ate too much fruit. If I could have been with him I could have kept him from doing so—I do not blame you Mother I sympathize deeply with you, but woe to the Yankee that ever falls into my power from henceforth — their accursed villainy took me away from my family who was their natural protector and now I pronounce a double woe—I have not enough to live for if all my children should be taken away but I love you dearest of anything yet. Oh, I believe I am crazy—Your letter did not reach me till August 5th. It was mailed in Mobile, Ala. Aug 2d. Only yesterday I was out in the country and talking all day about my little Will Ed and today I know he was dead. Oh God, hast thou no compassion on me—I left my boy and came away. I curse myself for doing it. I was exempt—I might have been at home to see him die—I dreamed of you last night and of killing three rattlesnakes. My brain is burning now—'Twere better for me were I too dead if it were not for you. Would I could be with you now, dearest, you might relieve my brain. God is so cruel to us. My child is in heaven but I had rather he were where I could see him again.

Oh, darling, take care of our last one, do not let it die. I must come home—I cannot stand it here—I shall desert or do something worse—I cannot stand it. I cannot write—My heart is broken—I don't deserve or crave to live—Oh Mother what shall I do—How could you write me those cruel words our little Willie is dead. I shall send your letters to Mother at once. I cannot write her. Farewell dearest Mother. My heart is bursting, my brain on fire. E. H. Fay

3 o'clock. Darling *I do love you.* I will pay $1000 for a substitute just as soon as he is accepted and sworn to. I can use Spencer's money. May God give you strength to bear our loss my dear. I know you suffer as much as I—I am afraid I shall be sick as I have shed tears all day since I got yours. I cannot stand it I don't believe. But cheer up

my darling—our eldest born is in heaven happier than we. God gave and shall he not take away. Try and say with me "blessed be his name." If it is possible dearest I must get out of this and come home. I cannot be away from you under these circumstances and keep my right mind.

Camp Maury Aug. 9th 1862

My dearest One:

Again I have an opportunity of sending you a few lines from my pen and I shall send also a few late papers by that man "Strange" who starts tomorrow for Minden via Rodney, Miss. altho he could cross now with ease at Vicksburg. Thos. Fuller will go too I reckon. Well I have no news to tell you dearest one for the news is, to express it in Army phrase "about played out." I send you all I have in the papers save a little individual or rather Company news. The Command came back this morning and we are ordered to hold ourselves in readiness to move at a moment's warning but where we do not know, perhaps two or 3 miles and perhaps into Ohio, as I have just returned from Hdqrtrs where I have been copying orders for Gen'l Armstrong. Gen'l Price says in Gen'l Orders that every true patriot or Good soldier will not hesitate to respond cheerfully, quickly, and boldly to gain the glory of assisting in driving the Invaders from the Soil of Miss. into and beyond the Ohio. An advance movement is at hand and I rejoice at it thus far, my only drawback is that my horse is not in as good order as I would like. I will buy me another if Jack gives out.

The Boys are very glad that they have been actors in the glorious expedition from which they have just returned and are loud in their praises of Gen'l Armstrong and of the Ladies of Ala.[3] They praise my native state and I am proud to hear it. I think the next move we will make will be into Tennessee. I am very anxious to bring this War to

[3] Brig. Gen. Frank C. Armstrong led a successful cavalry raid from Tupelo into North Alabama in late July, 1862. His decisive victory over a force of Federals at Courtland, Alabama, on July 25, won the commendation of Price and Bragg. See *O.R.*, XVI, pt. 1, 826–829.

a close for I think it can only be done by our own strong arms. I am angry with Europe and I don't ask for her aid now. I hope now that necessity will compel them to propose conditions to us. I would be willing to grant easy ones. These I have previously stated. I will try and write you soon as to our possible destination. I cannot divine it at present.

Oh my dearest my heart is sore and broken and I cannot write what I would to you. You know how I feel by questioning your own heart and you can never know how I suffer until I see you and pour out into your loving ears my tale of sorrow and grief. Oh my dear I can never tell you how much I realized the horrors of War when I am held away from you so now. I would give anything to come to you for only 60 days. I would give as much as $500 for a furlough for two months. I feel as if I could not live and not see you. Oh Mother I must see you. I will try and get a substitute here if I can but have no hopes of it, for we shall be on the move all the time. I am in good spirits as regards our trip and I believe I shall live to get through it and come to you again.

I must see the grave of my eldest born my own little Will Ed, my noble, precious boy. Oh God? Why did you deprive me of my treasure. Oh Mother can none of our children arrive at maturity? Must we lose them all in infancy? Oh my son, my noble, brave, beautiful boy. He did not lose to the last that look so much resembling Murillo's Infant Saviour. His prayer to make him a "good boy so that when I die I may go to Heaven and live with my darling sister Feeda" has been answered. He is now singing the praises of the Redeemer & the Lamb. I wonder if all the Angels of Heaven singing around the Throne were ever on Earth as lovely beings as our loved and lost ones. Are there grades of Angels? If so I know our darlings are in the first ranks around the Throne. Will not God grant that the Parents may both meet their children in Heaven. I had formed many plans for the future respecting the education of my eldest born. He was my darling and my pride. Why must he be taken of all others? My heart will question all the time tho my reason and religion both teach me that my child is happier singing the praises of the Redeemer than buffeting the cares and sorrows of this wicked and troublesome world. My child is gone, but oh the bitterness to me. I felt when Our Thera died that I could not possibly stand it if it had been our noble boy and in my heart I blessed God that he spared my first born and I thought he would continue to be merciful and spare him.

I must close now, dearest, as the order has come to move at daylight and the shades of evening are settling down now, so I can no longer see—Mother do take care of my remaining child. Love to all and may God preserve and bless all for my sake. E. H. Fay

We go to Guntown 20 miles North on M & O R.R.

Camp Louisiana Aug. 13th 1862

My own darling:

Again amid the scenes of War and Camp I find a few moments to devote on paper to you. (My thoughts are devoted to you the greater part of the time.) I wish I could write you cheerfully but such are not my feelings. I fear I can never feel right cheerful again. It appears as if sorrows multiplied for us my dear. First our little daughter was taken from us. It seemed to me that the very "sunshine" of my life was taken away. I feared I could never get over it but time if it has not produced forgetfulness has at least dimmed the poignancy of my grief. The wound had not healed over only scarred when it was opened afresh by the untimely plucking of my eldest "flower." Yes, his life was truly among the flowers. Oh my dear you cannot imagine what I calculated on for my eldest boy, the pride of my heart. I was anxious that he might learn to read and then I determined to study carefully his tastes and the bent of his disposition and educate him accordingly. I was proud of my boy and it did not seem possible that my healthy eldest boy could die. I had only one fear and that was that he might eat fruit and trash and get his bowels out of order, hence my oft repeated entreaties to you to watch over my children and take care of them. I knew, too, how careless Laura was and I feared Thornwell might get hurt at any time.

Oh my God! how could it be that my eldest born, my beautiful child could be taken away just as he began to know and remember his Father. It is a sad thought to me that if I am spared to go home I shall find only one child and even he, my beautiful red headed boy will be a stranger to his Father, will not know me, will shrink from me on my return, that my precious, noble boy who wondered where his father was will not be there to throw his arms around my neck and say "I am so glad my Favy has come back, ain't we Muvy." Oh Mother, I feel as if I could not stand it, as if I could never be reconciled to his loss. I know God does all things well but I would be glad, glad indeed to know why he took my boy? Why did he not wish me to train him? I could have made a good boy of him, I think. I would have taught him to despise evil just as I do. I would have taught him to read about Jesus and love the angels. But it is all useless my beautiful, noble boy is gone. He can never come to me again but I can go to him, but he will not be my child then. But Mother I must leave this sad theme and turn to something else, for if I dwell on it my brain is on fire and I shall go mad. I am obliged to keep actively employed all the time to keep my mind away from matters and things. I do not lie down in the day time for sleep and I try to weary myself so that I can sleep at night and not let my thoughts run riot.

I have as I before stated the duties of three men to do. Adjutant's, Lieutenant's, and Sergeant's. I want very much to come home but as I volunteered for 12 mos. I feel as if I ought to stay out my time, tho I would come home if I could get a sound healthy man for a substitute tho I hardly believe Capt. Webb would accept anyone in my place. I could go into the Department of Engineers if I should try but as long as the companies remain unconsolidated I dislike to leave him. He needs another Lieutenant and I think I shall take the place as it will be done by promotion. I wish we could get a good many recruits for our Co. Mart Rawls has acted very disgracefully I think, and I do not like the way Martin is acting. He—at least I should be mighty anxious to get back to knowing as I do that Dr. Harper is not a surgeon in the C.S.A. and the consequences are his certificates are not good for anything.[4] I want Nat Martin to come back for I don't want him to get into trouble.

We were just leaving our old Camp when I last wrote you. I sat up nearly all night and we started by daylight the next morning and came two miles above Guntown where we encamped in a woods lot,

[4] He returned, and existing records do not show him absent without leave. Booth, *La. Confed. Soldiers,* III, pt. 2, 896.

a hickory grove, one of the most pleasant places I ever saw if it was not for the dust which is oppressive and it is right on the Roadside. We have not had much rain in a week or more and it is terribly dusty —I think when it rains the Cavalry will move across the Tenn. River. We are to cut down to one wagon and no tents at all, all baggage that cannot be carried on horseback is to be sent off or burned. My valise will have to go tho I will have to throw away some of my clothing. I have been wearing my plain cloth breeches all this hot weather. They are not much account now but not torn at all. I had a watch pocket put into them and also into my green breeches. A widow Lady (grass) put them in for me. Her husband had gone off and left her & after trying to steal her child from her she heard from him six yrs. ago in Texas. Others have their sorrows as well as we.

Oh if this war would only close! I hope from the signs of the times that the war will close by Christmas at any rate. If it does not I must come home at any rate. I am anxious to serve my country if I can do so—for there is an offer in the gift of the President that I desire, "a mission to Chile" and I shall work to that point. I have an influence in Richmond but I don't want to use it only as a last extremity. If the trustees of the Academy call me at Christmas I will come. I want to come now dearest and be with you my own darling one. You know not, for words will not measure the height and depth nor length nor breadth of my love for you. I once thought and said *that I loved another,* but my own one, I knew not the depth of my affection until after we were married and you were a Mother. Then my dearest my whole heart went out to yours and you possessed the entirety of a full grown man's love, not the boyish love a man feels for his first love. Oh how happy we might have been had our little darlings been spared to us and we had been permitted to live together in our own little home. But God willed it otherwise.

I was rejoiced yesterday to get two letters from you, one mailed at Monroe Augst 1st, the other Minden 2d but in the same package came one to Caufield Aug 7 at Minden. My dearest do let my letters come as often as any ones. They were a sad sorrowful pleasure to me. I am glad you told me about our loved one's sickness and death. Oh cruel fatality that took me away from the death bed of my child. Oh if I could have been there and held his aching head and cooled his fevered brow I believe I could have charmed him back away from the grim monster and kept my child. I am sorry indeed for poor Mrs. Simmons—but she knew her child grown up to man's estate and had enjoyed the pleasure of his society for many years, while our noble boy had just begun to be interesting. Did you think dearest that we have had the pains and trouble of raising three children and now have only our little Thornwell left.

But my dearest I must hasten to close as I want this letter to go on the cars this evening. I have seen no news not having seen any papers for several days. The latest was the capture of the Federal Army in East Tenn. and the probable surrender of Buell's army in North Alabama their whole artery of supplies being cut off—Our men at Courtland cut off one of his sources. They were greatly pleased as you have doubtless heard with their trip and had improved in health and spirits in a great measure.

My health has been quite good, in fact I don't know that I was ever in better health. I weighed the other day and only 187 lbs with woolen clothes on, and I think I am 30 lbs. heavier than I was when I left Corinth. My clothing is quite good. If you have not sent the pants you had better not do it I reckon as I have no way of carrying any more clothing than I have. If I get out I can supply myself at QrMasters department. Everything I have lasts well. I told you of buying some clothing at the sale. Jim Leary's drawers & undershirt. I am wearing the socks you sent me dearest and they fit me fine. I have never seen but one better pair, and they were double *heels* and *toes too* and looked as if they would last forever.

Lt. Carter is waiting for this to take to the office and I must say good bye. Do take care of my precious baby. Love to all and may God bless and preserve my own dear ones is the prayer of your loving husband and Father. E. H. Fay

Camp Louisiana Aug 16/62

My dearest:

I have a few moments this morning which I will devote to you as I understand Monroe Caufield goes home this morning having procured a substitute for the remainder of the 12 months, being over age. He paid "Strange" a negro boy to get him one and "Strange" paid a small boy $300 and Caufield's horse &ç to take his place. He, "Strange," has made four thousand dollars speculating on substitutes but has left very suddenly.[5] Robt. Hart's wife has also sent in a substitute to him so if I had one I could not muster him in until the middle of September. I believe I can stand it very well till Christmas.

I commenced this this morning but have had to stop to make out a pay roll for the first two months service. That is done and I assure you it is no fool of a job either. I have been at work at it all the time since soon this morning and now at 12 M have just completed it. I shall draw pay my whole time as private $86.00 and now my pay will be even larger as Orderly. But money is no object with me for it is hardly more than the paper it is printed on. I have but little use for money and I wish you had some of it but have not time to send it now. I hope I may be able to send some of it to you if I have a good chance.

I wrote you a long letter and sent it by mail a few days ago. I had just received two sad and mournful letters from you and oh, dearest, it makes my heart run over to read of the death of my precious boy. I cannot become reconciled to it. I hope dearest you can make some arrangement to have me discharged by substitute or otherwise for we are now thrown into a Regt. composed of miscellaneous companies from Tennessee, Ky. and Miss. & (La. when we go in). I want to leave for we will be ordered about by some fool of a Colonel who will not do anything for our favor. I am sick of it now but had determined before this happened to stick to the Co. all the way through, but as soon as the order came I sat down and wrote Col. Sandidge who is on Gen'l Ruggles staff to try and get me detailed on the Engineers Corps there. You spoke of coming to see me. I do wish you would if you could only bring a substitute with you. If you could I would then go with you to Ala. and we would stay there for some time. Oh Mother I cannot bear the idea of coming back to Minden where

[5] Speculation in substitutes, such as that described by Fay, enhanced opposition to the system. Substitution was finally abolished on December 28, 1863. See A. B. Moore, *Conscription and Conflict in the Confederacy* (New York, 1924), 27–51.

there is nothing I desire save the graves of my two darling ones. I am anxious to stand over them once again and then I am willing to leave Minden forever.

I cannot write dearest for I have been so busy and the whole Co. are standing around by me and talking so I can hardly hear myself think. I am very well at present but don't know how long I shall continue so. If I had a substitute I would pay him one thousand dollars "cash" to take my place, but would have to borrow Spencer's money to do it. I am welcome to use it. I have heard nothing from Mother since I wrote you and since I sent your letter to her. I am anxious to hear for I know that she suffers when we do. But J. M. Caufield is going I must close. Do mail me letters often, at least once a week until you hear that the communication is cut off at Vicksburg. Love to all. Kiss our *only* little one for his Father and you know you have my whole heart.

Camp Louisiana near Guntown
Aug 19th 1862

My own dearest Wife:

I have a few minutes again today which I will try and devote to you, tho I have nothing new to tell you. It is very dry and dusty and food and forage scarce but here we are yet, with the Yankees 8 or 9 miles above us just destroying everything, stealing negroes, cutting down all the standing corn, ransacking houses, bursting open bureaus and wardrobes and ordering the negro members who are with them to clothe themselves in the best, and tearing in pieces the remainder, carrying off mules, horse, wagon and harness, in fact leaving the country almost a wilderness. Cursing and insulting the men and sometimes proceeding to even greater lengths with the women, and we, tied down here by an imperative order "not to press the lines here" until the fate of Buell at Huntsville had been sealed.

I think that his fate will be sealed in a few days for Bragg can easily move from Chattanooga and attack his rear or front as pleases him. A special dispatch came to Gen'l Armstrong this morning that Morgan had taken Gallatin, Tenn. and blowed up the R.R. and captured a train of cars, destroyed a large amount of property. This was Buell's only source of supplies and in fact the Tenn. River is so low that Nashville is in a precarious position. In fact Morgan telegraphed the Mayor that as he had failed for office in the Confederacy and had gone over to the Lincolnites that he (Morgan) would call on him at an early day. A few days ago there was a fight at Corinth among the Yanks about the negroes and 100 of the foremen killed each other and at the same time killed, some reports say, 200 of the negroes. At Iuka an Illinois Regiment rose and drove out the negroes from their camps and had a general row about it. They swear they will not fight for negro freedom.

Of course you have seen that ole Abe has called for 300,000 vols. and a like number of "Melish," an artful dodge to secure his quota of Vols. He cannot support an additional expenditure of two millions per day to the four millions already expended. I wish they would quit their nonsense and go home and let us alone. I want an end to this cruel and fast-getting-to-be-barbarous-uncivilized war. I have no idea that there will be many prisoners taken by this division of the army. Jennison's Kansas Jay Hawkers are in the neighborhood of Iuka.[6] They are regarded as outlaws by all the Missourians of Price's army.

I wrote you by Monroe Caufield a short note a few days ago and believe I told you that our Squadron had been attached to five companies of Forrest's old Regiment and formed into a Battalion. Yesterday we elected a Lieut. Col., Major [Robert M.] Balch, the old major, and a young man Adjutant of the Regmt. [Edward B.] Trezevant was elected Major. L. B. Watkins ran for Major and came pretty near an election. A major was promised our Squadron but Linn was beaten badly for they acted in bad faith towards him. They promised him a warm support but after we had helped them elect their Lt. Colonel they flukered. However, Capt. Webb & Watkins recommended me to Lt. Col. Balch for appointment as Adjutant. I have no idea that I will receive it though, for as they have five companies they will take not only the Lion's share but all the offices. If Linn had been elected I would have been 1st Lieut. probably by appointment of

[6] The reference is to the 15th Kansas Cavalry Regiment, commanded by Col. J. R. Jennison.

Gen'l Armstrong, but not a word of this to any one, for I learn you had already told Mrs. Webb what I wrote about the consolidation of the two companies and Mrs. Webb began to look for her husband home.

Oh dearest do not tell anything I write you. I have no objection, however, to your telling Mrs. Webb for the Capt. and I are as intimate as two brothers and have but few secrets. He is an excellent man and is quite popular. I am glad we are going into a Battalion for I wish to dissolve all connection with Fuller's Co. under Harrison. The command was out on picket for 3 or 4 days and Harrison remained in command of Camp and he could do none of the business but called me for everything. There is not a man in the Co. save young Sandidge who can make out a morning report, for he (S) and Harrison both tried it one morning and I had it to do at last. But no more.

If I cannot get a substitute I shall try and get a Lieutenancy and will resign if the Trustees wish me to come back to the schoolroom. If I can get a transfer to the Engineer Corps I shall accept it and if there is a probability of remaining on this side the River shall come after you and take you to Ala. Oh Mother I often think that if you had only consented to go to Ala. before I went off our darling Will Ed might now be living, but I try not to think of it. I keep my mind off the matter as much as possible. In fact I am so much occupied as a general thing, by my duties that I have but little time to brood over my sorrow. Tomorrow will be a month since we lost our eldest darling. Oh God! why was it necessary for us to give up our eldest boy? Could we not have been afflicted in some other way. Must our first born be taken away from us when we had only two. How are my hopes frustrated! How my fond aspirations are dashed to earth. I had looked forward to the time when my children around my fireside would be a joy and delight to their parents. But now my boy, my precious, beautiful boy has gone, gone and his little sister too. That it is a consolation to believe they are indulging in the enjoyments of Heaven I admit but that does not dull the stings or blunt the pain of their loss. I had begun to feel that I could be reconciled to the loss of our little daughter and thought that our little boys would be our delight in the early part of our married life and our support in declining years should God see fit to grant us length of days. But now all my earthly hopes and expectations are dashed to earth and I feel as did Jacob of old that I am "orbum liberis" deprived of my children. Mother do take care of our only child and watch over him that no accident may befall him. Do not let him get far away from your sight and keep him near you.

Oh my dearest do take care of yourself and not get sick. I know how fond you are of fruit and trash. Please for my sake do not eat it this fall—Chinkapins nor Muscadines. Do not eat such trash for it may give you the same disease our first born died with. Remember Mother that you hold in your hand not only your own life but mine also, for I am afraid I could not live and lose you. You don't know how my whole soul is wrapped up in you my dearest.

I hope you will remember and get the cutting of that Scuppernong old Mr. Loftin promised you and have it set out in our yard or garden. We will have to begin housekeeping anew if I should live to get home and I wish you would go about and get some fruit trees and such things, strawberries etc. and have them set out. It would help the sale of our place in a great measure. I expect we will have to live in our house for years after the war is over to get our money back paid in building it. But if I live to come home it will be with a ready hand and a willing mind that I will work for you and our little one. I will try to keep you from suffering. Do you need any money my dear. If so I will try and send you some. I have now more than I want, and if I had any safe way would send you fifty dollars for I think Jack is getting strong enough to carry me and if I can get him fat would not give him for anybody's horse. He is pretty low in flesh now but is improving rapidly. If he does not go off on a trip in a week or two he will get in good order.

I commenced this letter thinking I would send it by Milton Smith who is discharged but I learn he will not get off in a day or two, so will mail it as letters go or rather come in five days from Minden here. A large lot of letters came yesterday mailed in Minden the 11th and 12th but I noticed very clearly that I did not get any from my wife though other husbands got two. Do you forget to write or are you waiting to send by hand. Do as I do, send by hand every chance and write by mail regularly, too. If I don't get them do your duty at least.

Mrs. Webb wrote the 11th but my last date from you is the 3rd, I believe, no the 1st. You beg me not to feel hurt. Could you expect me to do otherwise under the circumstances, tho I do not feel hurt but rather think you will give me a good reason in your next.

How did your Mother like her visit over to Texas? and did she see all her friends. Tell me all about it in your next or let Lou tell me. I send you Mother's two letters received yesterday. You will see what is in them. Now dearest do write me often and give me all the news. How does the mill get on?

I send you a scrap from a paper which you may have seen, but lest you have not I send it. It shows what a gallant woman may do at times—I wish every woman in the South would learn the use of the Pistol for I believe they will have need for them if this war does not close. I can form now no idea of the duration of it. I hope and pray though that it may not be long.

If you will answer this immediately on its receipt I shall get it by the first of September. It has turned quite cool for the last few days and I have worn my coat the greater part of the time. All the morning I have been fixing up the payrolls and as I had to look over those of both companies it has been no fool of a job, to fix the accounts of men am'ting to $9000 nearly but I have got it right at last and they will go up this evening—if anything strange or new happens I will write you in a few days. Have you ever got any of the newspapers I sent you? I hope you have tho they are old when you get them. Give much love to all for me. Kiss Thornwell a dozen times for his Father and remember there is one who loves you very much and that one is your Husband.

Camp Louisiana, Aug. 21st, 1862

My darling:

Again I am seated to write you as John Lesueur is going home and I cannot omit the opportunity of sending if but a word. I know it is a pleasure to you to get even a scrap from me and as you know, I am always anxious to give you any pleasure in my power. I therefore write even though it is but a line to tell you that I am still well and would give almost anything for a letter from you for we are ordered out with ten days rations and in light marching order and tho' I have no means of knowing where we are going yet I would not be surprised if we did not go into Tennessee or Ky. before we returned. I hope we may go safely and that I may be permitted to come off unharmed for my life is now supported by the idea of seeing you again. But I have but little time now to write so I will say in a few words what I want.

First and foremost I want a pair of Boots made at Ditmer's by *that crooked legged "Dutchman"* Fred. I want him to make them especially for me. He knows me and will make them right. I want them made large in the Leg and a regular cavalry Boot. Ditmer must not charge too much for them, though I want the best he can possibly make for this winter. My old boots are tolerably good yet, and my shoes too, but I don't know when I can get another pair so I'll send now for fear.

I hope you will write me what is doing in regard to the school. I hope I can come home for Christmas for I am afraid I shall not be able to stand the cold weather especially as we shall in all probability be much farther North than at present. Do try and see what you can do, for I have no chance now to do anything. I believe I have made myself necessary to the Co. and therefore I cannot conveniently leave without seeming to abandon them, or to coin a word "Wimberlyize." I wish I could come home for a few days and see you, and if I get back safely from our present trip I shall try and get a 20 days leave of absence and come and see you if possible. If I cannot get one for so long I will try for a shorter time and go to Montgomery and see our Father and Mother there. If you can send me anything that John Lesueur can bring make an effort to do so, tho' I know of nothing exactly that I stand in need of. I cannot carry what I have got, so I have nothing to say about what you send unless it is a substitute and that, not without a petition from the Trustees. I fear else I would not be received.

A month today, my loved one, since our noble boy was taken from us and today my heart bleeds afresh to feel, to know that my darling is no more, that I can never see him again, that he can never again climb upon my knees and throw his arms about my neck and show me how much he loved me. Oh Mother I cannot stand it, Why did my child die? Oh could you not have saved him. You should have sent for every doctor in the country. Why did you not send for Dr. Webb? I hope the Conscript will get Dr. Patillo because he fooled along and did not get home waiting for John Maples. If he had shown half the friendship for members of his own Co. that he did for John Maples he would have had many more friends. But my sheet is full and I can only say Good Bye. My love to all. Kiss my darling for his father and know that you have a heart full of love from your own dear Husband,

Ed.

At Mrs. Blackburn's 7ms. East of
Holly Springs. Tuesday eve 3 o'clock
Aug. 26, '62

My own dear One:

My week has rolled round and I find or rather have made an opportunity of writing you a few lines and I presume you would like to know how I have made it and I will accordingly tell you.

I expect you will have rec'd my note by John Lesueur and if so will feel anxious to know what had become of me. I wrote you we were ordered off and that I knew not whereto but presumed it was Westward. Everybody said eastward but me. Well we started last Friday morning at 3 o'clock and kept a Southern course till we reached Saltillo, thence due West and here we are or at least I am here, but I have not told you how I made the opportunity.[7]

Last night after camping, I went with Capt. Webb to a house to get our supper and coming back passed a blacksmith shop. It occurred

[7] This was the beginning of a raid from northern Mississippi into western Tennessee by some 2,700 Confederates led by Brig. Gen. Frank C. Armstrong. Proceeding northward from Baldwyn through Holly Springs, Armstrong on August 30, 1862, attacked a force of Federals near Bolivar, drove them back, and took 73 prisoners. He skirted Bolivar and moved on toward Jackson to Medon, destroying railway trestles and bridges. Reports that strong Union forces were at Jackson caused him to fall back toward Denmark, near which town another sharp fight occurred on September 1. After this engagement, in which 75 Federals were killed or wounded and 213 captured, Armstrong returned to Baldwyn. His exploits were highly praised by Price. See *O.R.*, XVII, pt. 1, 51–52, 120.

to me that Jack needed a pair of shoes. So I engaged to be at the Shop at daybreak and have them on. I saw Col. Balch and got permission (the only possible thing that could have obtained it except sickness) and staid. The Command (a whole Brigade) passed me and Sim Gray and I went to the Shop. It was 11 A.M. before our horses were fixed and we have not yet caught up, having stopped to get our dinners and to get a letter written to you. I will state by way of parenthesis that Jack could have gone a week longer without being shod, but your letter could not as I do not know when I will get another opportunity of writing ("Confound the ink, 'tis as thick as mud") so you need not be alarmed if you do not hear from me for several weeks tho' I will write as often as I can find a chance, but as I brought no clothing except a change, shirt, drawers and socks, I could bring no paper and I assure you it is a scarce article throughout the country. A pretty young lady gave me this but where the envelope is to come from I know not as I neglected to direct any and bring them in my memorandum book. But I'll trust to Providence and you shall have your letter at any rate.

Of course you will be anxious to know where I am going and also of course a non-commissioned officer does not know anything or at least is so supposed but to obey orders, nevertheless I have a head of my own and I think we are going to make a demonstration on Memphis (Ink all dried up) if not to take it. We may be going up into Tenn. to take [Fort] Pillow and Columbus, for Jack Morgan so the rumor goes, has taken Donelson and Henry also Clarksville—I could give you reasons for these surmises but hardly have room here. I believe the Yanks will give up the Ship soon for I feel sure that on land they are easily conquered. Bragg, I suppose you have heard, is going from Chattanooga to Nashville and has—000 men. Can't say how many. Enough however. We have ———well, how many Cavalry do you reckon. Just as many as you please & we have not been marching already five days for nothing. You'll hear from us before long and I hope and believe all safe. I don't think there will be much fighting though there may be, God only knows.

We are all keen for the onward movement tho' we have thirty men all told. Several are taken suddenly sick when a march is to be made. You will probably learn who are in Camp by letters from Camp. All are well who are on the mach. Our trip thus far is very pleasant except the dust which is terrible, four or five thousand horses raise no small amount of dust. We start at 3 o'clock in the morning and travel till 10 A.M. when we generally camp for the night. It takes all the rest of the time for the wagons to come up and get us corn. We all cook and eat at the same table, viz., Mother Earth and quite a family our 30 make. Some time we go to a house and get a meal but not often, but today I am in the rear and can do as I please. We suffer for water as no man is allowed to leave ranks save for "a call of nature." Yesterday I had bowel complaint but did not stop but once. Today I feel very well.

The heat is oppressive and I am in low spirits thinking of our loss of our noble brave little boy. Oh Mother, my grief increases daily. I don't believe I can stand it, but I try to feel resigned, keeping my thoughts busy on something else. I believe I wrote you all were well. Capt. Webb and I ride in advance but the dust is oppressive as some days we are in the rear of the Column and some in the rear of the Battallion. Once we have been the advance guard, yesterday the rear guard, today I am not posted, but presume the center. I do not know how to fill this as I fear I shall not find an envelope. I'll fold it as there are none here but will put in all I can.

I regret so much I did not get a letter from you. Others have had as late as Aug. 16 but Aug. 5th were my latest dates before leaving Camp—I expect I have letters at camp by this time or will have when I get back. Give much love to your Father & Mother, Sisters & Brother. Kiss my only darling for me and know how well your husband loves you. I am very dirty riding in the dust, you would hardly know me but I guess I'll get clean some of these days if my life is spared. Once more kiss dear little Thornwell for me a hundred times and let me beg you to take good care of him and also of your own sweet self. From your husband who loves you. God preserve and bless you all is my prayer. I'll try and write again before long but don't be uneasy yourself nor let Mrs. Webb be uneasy if you do not hear from us for four or six weeks. I think we will all come out straight before long—Do write me often and direct as before, for I want a pile of letters when I get back—My horse has done finely so far and I hope will continue to do so.

6

"Our Co. Led the Charge Gallantly"

Friday Sep 5th 1862
La Grange Tenn. Camp
on Wolf River

My own dear One:

I dropped you a hasty note from Holly Springs a week ago and told you that we were on a Scout. I wrote at Mrs. Blackburn's 7 miles East of Holly Springs. I overtook the Command at dusk that evening camped in the yard of a Gin Factory at the latter place. I tell you Southern Soldiery met a hearty welcome at Holly Springs. The entire Battalion was invited out to supper as they had been to dinner. Although not hungry, having eaten dinner late I determined to go to supper for the purpose of forming the acquaintance of persons there so followed after the greater part of our Co. had gone some distance to a nice looking mansion. Found the boys just through supper so I had just what I wanted, a seat with the family. After "tea" we adjourned to the parlor where I spent a pleasant evening listening to music and pleasant conversation till 9 P.M. when I returned to our Gin Land and spread my shawl on a plank pile and went to sleep expecting an order to march at 3 A.M.

The order did not come, however, and at sunrise I got up, put on some clean clothes, sent dirty ones to wash and was starting back to Mr. Long's to breakfast but finding all the boys had gone there and not wishing to impose on their kindness the Capt. and I went to the Magnolia House the principal Hotel. About ten o'clock came the order to march and as our wagons had been sent off I had to tie my dirty clothes to my saddle. We struck out northward and camped 6 miles south of La Grange, Tenn., riding till 12 at night, rested the next day and night and next morning took up line of march for La Grange, passed through Gd. Junction and struck due north for Bolivar, Tenn. Camped within 7 or 8 miles of Bol. and within 3 ms. of Middleburg. The next morning at 10 started and near Middleburg found two Regs. of Infantry and one of Cavalry sent out from Bolivar to attack a small band of Guerillas. Gen'l Armstrong marshalled his forces and a regular pitched battle ensued.

Two skeleton Regiments of ours attacked the Yanks, entrenched behind an embankment of the R. Road and charged over it, whipped the yankees killed twenty-five, wounded a hundred. Our Battallion was ordered forward but the Yanks had run so far there was no showing of our overtaking them. [Col. Robert] McCulloch's Regt.[1] charged and killed four Yankee Colonels, took 76 prisoners, lost one man killed, Capt. Champion, a champion indeed, the bravest of the brave shot through the head. The Yanks fired on us with a Battery of Artillery and threw shell all around but did no damage, then ran back into Bolivar. We had five men wounded, two shot themselves after the battle was over, accidentally. We remained on the field waiting for them to renew the attack but they did not see fit to do it.

We then struck out south six or seven miles turned west and north rested and fed one hour from 10 to 11 and moved on and next morning attacked a R.R. Station where were encamped some Regt. of Yanks but they had heard us and fled. Burned some trestles & bridges, scouted round, found scattered detachments of Yanks killed a good many, took 86 prisoners. Marched to Medon a station some 6 miles above, but am too fast. Heard a train coming ambushed it and if the goose in command had only torn up the track behind would have burned it but he only fired on it as it stopped to land reenforcements and a great many jumped back and the train ran back. At Medon about sunset found some four hundred entrenched behind Cotton Bales on the R.R. platform. Skirmished with them till dark when they were reinforced, stayed there that night and the next morning at light we moved back, crossed the R.R. and not having had any rest or food

[1] McCulloch commanded the 2nd Missouri Cavalry Regiment. At the Bolivar fight on August 30, he engaged Lt. Col. Harvey Hogg in hand-to-hand conflict; Hogg was killed by one of McCulloch's soldiers. *O.R.,* XVII, pt. 1, 44.

for three days, Gen. Armstrong passed and said to our Battallion that he would give us some rest that day and something to eat.

This was Monday the first of September 1862 and a terrible Monday it was as you will see by the sequel. We marched some five or six miles and the Gen'l had just stopped at a house for his dinner and the command was going on to a creek. McCulloch's Reg. at the head, our Batt. next and our Co. at the head of the batt. when the news came that 2 Regs. of Inftry, one Cavalry and a section of Artillery was only 3 ms. ahead. We halted at once and had hardly stopped before their pickets fired on our advance guard. Hardly had the first half dozen shots been fired when a cannon opened on us with grape and canister. The Yanks were ambushed for us and the accursed Union Tories had let us rush right into it. Gen'l Armstrong came galloping up and ordered McCulloch and Col. Balch to take that Battery. Mc to go first, we to support. We started and as the battery was in a corn field had to let down the fence. I jumped down being at the head of our Column and tore down the fence, and before I could get to my horse again the Command charge was given. Jack rushed by me at the head of the Column and I charged forward on foot after him to within 20 or 30 yds of the battery, but my horse being obscured in a cloud of dust and no chance to catch him with a hundred of being trampled to dust by our own men, I rushed back to the fence. Our Co. led the charge gallantly being four times repulsed although at the 2nd charge the Enemy abandoned their guns entirely, but as they were supported by a whole Regt. of Infantry they were obliged to fall back. The fifth time they drove back the infantry and Pinson's regt. sent in some men and hauled out the cannon claiming the capture of the Battery. Our Batt. would have carried it at the 2d charge but they had moved it outside the fence and across a deep gully which horses could not cross.

Oh such carnage you never saw or heard of. It is said never to have been equalled except at Donelson. Col. Balch says Shiloh was nothing to compare with it. Suffice it to say, their Battery was ours, we took a hundred and fifty prisoners, burned their wagon train loaded with drugs, clothing, commissary stores. They had 22 wagons. The battle lasted 2 hours and a half from the firing of the first cannon, and as reinforcements could have been sent from both Jackson and Bolivar double quick in that time, Gen'l Armstrong withdrew. We burned the captured arms, the two cannon and struck out for Jackson. Only one of our Co. was wounded, Hudson from Bossier Parish. John Bennet and Simeon Gray had their horses killed under them, the first & 2d charges. I found my horse at the fourth charge but I did not get into the fight at all on account of losing him. It may have been a merciful interposition of Providence and probably was but I am sorry it happened as it looks as if I had kept out of danger. My conscience is clear on the subject however and whatever may be said will not affect either you or me. I know however I shall not let down another fence preparatory to a charge but shall be at the head of it certain.

Fuller's Co. lost two killed outright. Two Cooks, no relation, one Big Cook by a canister shot through the back, the other shot through the head with a minnie ball. Such a terrible battle I hope I may never again be in. We left the field toward Jackson but being worn out and having nothing to eat for 3 or 4 days, our horses being broken down from forced marches, Gen'l Armstrong started back. Detachments were posted in ambush on all roads but by travelling through swamps and corn fields we avoided them all and reached La Grange yesterday. Have been here all night and Capt. Harrison sends home a wounded man after clothing for his Co., we get a chance to write.

The Yankees report a loss in Monday's battle (of Denmark) of 500 killed and wounded, ours was 9 killed and 30 or 40 wounded. We have marched some 300 miles in less than ten days, fought two battles and 3 skirmishes, taken 350 or 400 prisoners, have had one meal in five days, ashcake and raw bacon, which was greedily devoured. I lost one of my blue linen shirts and the pair of drawers I b'ot of Jim Leary's estate and a pair of socks together with my gun on the battlefield. I wish I had another shirt and an undershirt of Lowells if no net ones can be had, also a pair of drawers. I found a pair of saddlebags on the field full of clothing but not such as I will wear, and this half quire of paper which has proved very acceptable, also a pocket inkstand. If you make me shirts, make them fuller in front so they won't gape open when buttoned, though I have fallen off so these do pretty well now. I do not weigh over 165 lbs now I think. Intend to weigh if we go to Holly Springs this evening or tomorrow if possible. I do not know where we will go from here as everything is dark. Gen'l Lee has dispatched to Pres. Davis that he has annihilated McClellan and Burnside and taken "30,000" prisoners. News from Memphis says that we have recaptured New Orleans. I hope true.

Now dearest I will close this hasty note. I've been through a great deal since I last wrote you and suffered a great deal but mostly feeling a deep grief for our loss. Hardly a night no matter how worn out I may have been but my pillow (my saddle) has been wet with my tears. I cannot be reconciled to the thought of not seeing my loved one again. I cannot endure the thought, and it is no use trying to banish it for it hangs like an incubus upon me. I would give all I possess if I could come home now if only for a short time. Once I supported and cheered you in affliction and now I feel that I need in an especial manner your consolation and support. I cannot get on alone here. I have no one to sympathize with me and it seems as if the burden of sorrow locked up in my heart would burst it. Love to all from me, Father, Mother, Brother and Sisters. Kiss Thornwell a hundred times for me and oh take care of him. God bless you my dearest. Your loving husband.

We captured a Yankee drummer about ten years old, a beautiful little fellow but I presumed hardened in sin as all boys in camps are. We paroled the privates. I do hope I shall get a great many letters from you when I get into camp. No one can imagine the cloud of dust in which we had to march, it was perfectly suffocating and would betray us to the Yankees when within five or six miles. After marching we can only recognize each other by our horses and clothing, our faces are a quarter of an inch thick. Good Bye, I have written this sitting on the ground under a beech tree on the bank of the Wolf River ¾ mile south of La Grange, Tenn. Do write me often my dearest one.

In Camp at Baldwin Miss
Wednesday Morning
Sep 11th 1862

My own darling One:

I have got back again Sep. 11th, 1862 to camp, if camp it can be called with all of our tents taken away and an order to pack up everything and all sick and well to move this evening at 3 o'clock somewhere, Corinth I suppose as Buell has ordered Rosecrans to join him with all possible dispatch. I have no doubt but we will march to near Nashville without firing a gun. God grant it for I have seen enough of fighting for some time at least. We were ordered soon after I wrote you by Dr. Bright at La Grange to prepare to march to Bolivar that eve at 6 o'clock and that we would take it at daylight, but at 5 P.M. we were ordered back to the Mobile & Ohio Road and accordingly came back to Baldwin and are now ordered to leave at 3 P.M. for somewhere as I said above.

You don't know my dearest one, my noble wife, how glad I was to get 3 long letters from you, 2 by Nat and one by Sligh mailed at Jackson Sept. 1st. I had hardly got through reading them when the mail came in bringing me yours dated Aug. 30th, mailed in Minden Sep. 2d. This is the latest from Minden as yet. God bless you *my noble wife* for your self-sacrificing devotion to your country and your husband. How often does my heart swell with gratitude to think that I was led to marry you. I thought that I had been afflicted but I am so thankful for it. I have long been so my dearest but could never fix it up to tell you so. Yes, my darling, know that you possess the entire heart, the warm, entirely manly (not boyish) love of your husband.

But my darling I am very anxious to see you, but I fear it will be impossible for me to come home on furlough as I have just read that Gen'l Bragg has announced to his army that he is candidate for the Governor of Ohio. Our armies are pressing forward and darling, I believe we will conquer a peace before long. Your last letter was gloomy in the extreme and I am sorry you feel so for I think a brighter dawn is breaking on our Confederacy. I think we will conquer a peace. My darling packing time has come and I must close. I wish I could be with you my dearest to weep over our darlings' graves for my heart is very full of sorrow. I wrote dear Mother a hasty note and enclosed one of your letters, the 14th, I believe.

You say the Trustees met and held up the school for me. If they wish me to take the school they must petition the Sec. of War at Richmond to order my discharge. If he does it, why I can come home and none can gainsay it. If they do I don't care. I feel I could do as much good in the schoolroom as I can here in the army, and if they want me I will come anyhow, no matter what may be said. I know I will not be liable to conscription nor militia for they have made a law to 45 and that will do away with militia so I can stay if I come.[2] I am sorry there seems to be that Union feeling as opposed to Secession. It will be productive of bloodshed after the war I fear. I am obliged to stop. Good Bye darling and may God's richest blessings be showered upon you. Your husband.

I'll write more if I can get time before sending this, if not, in a few days when we stop. I do love my noble, heroic wife and hope she will write me often. Love to Lou, and Mother & Father. Consult with them and tell them your fears. Does the school still go on. I wrote you a long letter by John Lesueur and told Bill to give it to you. I am sorry you did not get it for I wrote particularly about some things I needed, a pair of Cavalry boots. I do hope you will get it and believe you will. Pack Bates sends a paper of the 8th and if you will send it to Mrs. Bates you can borrow it I reckon. A thousand kisses to you my dearest one. Farewell, au revoir, Your affectionate husband.

Iuka, Miss. Sep. 18th, 1862.

My own darling wife:

You will see by the date of this letter that I am at Iuka which place we entered last Sunday morning the Yanks having evacuated during the Night.[3] Gen'l Armstrong attacked it Sat. morning and captured the picket post, our company doing it, and a forage wagon when the Infantry and Artillery opened on him and they fell back some four or five miles. Gen'l Price came up with his Infantry and the next morning Armstrong entered the place and found the birds flown. They escaped towards Corinth. He took 25 prisoners on Sat. morn and as I had been detailed with the train they were bro't down and turned over to my charge. I ordered out a guard and kept them all night and the next morning about 12 M I marched them with the train into Iuka.

[2] An act extending the conscription age up to 45 years had been introduced in the Confederate Congress; it was not finally approved until September 27, 1862. See *O.R.*, Ser. 4, III, 160.

[3] This was the beginning of a series of skirmishes culminating in the battle of Iuka, September 19, 1862, as a result of which Price yielded the town to Rosecrans. For Price's report of the campaign see *O.R.*, XVII, pt. 1, 119–124.

There were 2 Lieuts. 7 Illinois Cavalry and some from Michigan. I have a list of their names that I will send you at some time if not now.

I am in a great hurry as a man is going to Jackson, Miss and that is my only chance to mail this. We captured over half a million worth of stores of various kinds. Corn, flour, 100 bbls. whiskey, fine wines and brandy and some 8 6-mule wagon loads of preserved fruits, some 2000 boxes Crackers. But the poor privates get nothing of it but bacon & crackers, the good things are reserved for the officers. Salt in sacks and in bbls. but the Yanks cut the hoops on the bbls. and tried to destroy it but we got most of it. We captured a travelling bake-oven that is made of corrugated galvanized iron, a perfect wagon and yet to bake while travelling along the road. Truly a Yankee invention. We have skirmished with them for two days, they having gone out as far as Burnsville on the road towards Corinth, Miss. They say that it was only a squad of Cavalry that took their stores and they intend to have them back but they will find Gen'l Price here and they have fortified it to the utmost extent so I don't think they will quite take it and —000 men of the Army of the West.

God has been very merciful to me and I am preserved as yet in good health and strength though I slept last night in the mud and rain (we have no tents) and had been wet all day too as yesterday was as blustering and stormy a day as I most ever saw. I am hardly dry now altho' it has been sunshiny all day. I made out payrolls again today for 3 mos. and got some $75.00 which I wish, dearest, you had as I have no use for it now. We are paid up to the 1st of September now. The report has just come in that the Yanks have left Burnsville and gone back to Corinth. If so we shall have a pretty severe fight for it, as they have improved our breastworks there. But Breckinridge & Van Dorn and [John B.] Villipigue have gone up Tenn. to Bolivar and will stop the Mobile & Ohio R.R., and Memphis is said to be evacuated. I don't know where the Yankees will get their supplies as they are surrounded if they stay there. I had hoped we were going across the Tenn. River but now I don't know. I hope they will for I have seen blood and carnage enough already and I would gladly settle this without further expenditure of life.

I am in hopes something will happen that will bring about a peace. I have seen no papers since we left Baldwin and I know nothing of news outside our camp in the town. I have had the Blues badly since yesterday for when riding along coming in from picket in conversation with Capt. Webb about pickles I mentioned Martinoes and told him what our darling called them. This called him to mind and my eyes have hardly been free from tears since. I forget sometimes that he is dead and am lively but if anything calls him back to mind again I am miserable for days. If I could only come home for a single week I could bear it better for I could then fully realize my loss.

Oh Mother, I believe I shall go crazy if I don't come and I don't know how I can come for I don't suppose it possible to get leave of absence, though some do. If we do not make a forward movement in a few weeks I shall try and get leave from Gen'l Armstrong and come back though my time will necessarily be short. Darling if I could only hear from you how much good it would do me but don't know when I shall as we have no mails here, our letters may come up from Tupelo but I know not when. I hope long ere this you have got my letters from La Grange by Dr. & Mrs. Bright and they have told you all about me. How glad I would be to see some one who had seen you and talked with you, but dear Mother I don't think I shall ever see you again tho I hope to. As regards my coming home I have this to say, that if they wish me to come they must petition the Sec. of War in Richmond to have me discharged from the service. The Trustees can say that I volunteered for one year and for one year they could give me up but as I was exempt under the Conscript Act & they needed a school now, that the Sec. of War would confer a favor by discharging me. I have no doubt but it would be done at once. I leave this entirely with you dearest as I have no time to attend to it. If it can be done I should be glad to have it done as soon as possible before very cold weather comes on for I don't think I can stand the cold weather this winter. However, you must proceed cautiously as I don't want to be known as directing the matter. I want to lay it all on you, for you know you used to say I laid everything on you.

No, dearest, I don't mean what I say. You are my best beloved and you well know that you have my entire heart. My dearest, if I should ever live to come home I have learned something that will be of advantage to me and tho' I have lived far more happily than I deserve, yet I think we shall be much happier than we have ever been. I think our capacities for enjoyment will be enlarged by the suffering we have undergone. I know I shall appreciate you far more highly than I have ever done before—

I hope you did get the letter by John Lesueur for I wrote for a pair of Boots and I hope you will send them for I shall need them before long. My shoes are pretty good but my Boots are nearly worn out. I need cavalry boots with legs that will come above the knees so as to keep them dry. I did hope to finish this sheet tonight but it is getting dark now and I must make preparations for supper, as we may be called off before morning. There is no telling what may happen to a soldier for he belongs to his officers much more strictly than a negro does to his master. Our field officers in this Battallion are not such men as one would wish to have control over them, and consequently our situation is not as pleasant as it has been heretofore—I do hope we get out of it for it is a most unpleasant company to be in and I want to get out of it.

I must close now dearest. Much love to all, Father, Mother, Sisters and Johnny too. Do take the strictest care of my darling spared Lamb and know dearest that the burden of my prayers after my own salvation is that you, my darlings may be preserved in health and happiness. Good Bye, my dearest,

Your loving husband who prizes his wife,

Do write me soon and often Ed. H. Fay

Wednesday
Baldwin Miss Sep 25th

My darling One:

I wrote you a few days since from Iuka Springs, Miss. on the Memphis & Charleston R.R. and I hope dearest you have got it. If you have not I will briefly recapitulate that we left Baldwin Thursday 11th inst. and marched to Iuka. Gen'l Armstrong approached the place Sat. Morn. and not supposing there were any Feds. there gave orders to Balch's Battallion to ride leisurely into town. Capt. Webb started, captured their pickets and rode within 50 yds of their breastworks and found them filled with Federal soldiers. They were then obliged to fall back and wait for Gen'l Price who came up that night and the next morning Gen'l Armstrong marched into town, found the birds gone but they had left nearly a million of stores there which we got and bro't off. We remained there a week and on Friday the enemy moved out from Corinth, Memphis and Columbus, Ky. A severe battle was fought Friday eve and Gen'l Hébert with his brigade drove back about 6000 of the enemy. The 3rd La. Reg. was cut all to pieces but took the 11 Ohio Battery which has been 11 times charged before but never taken. This 12 charge, the 3rd. killed every man of the Battery, none escaping, they fought with such desperation, and out of 156 horses only six were left alive. You see by this with what desperation the Feds. fought.

The day before Gen'l Price had been ordered back and I learn today that he meets Van Dorn at Holly Springs and uniting the two armies they move together through West Tenn. We drew all forces from there to Iuka, thought we were going across the Tenn. River but now I think Gen'l Price is going to Missouri. I wish we could be detached and ordered to La. for I don't want to go North. We have no tents and riding all day and sleeping at night in the rain on wet blankets I fear will not improve my health. I only weigh 172 lbs. now.

We brought off most of the stores from Iuka. The Yankees had everything there and I know most of their troops live better in the army than they do at home. They have mixed vegetables pressed and hermetically sealed so you have only to put on water and break off a cake and throw in & you have excellent soup.[4] Coffee, concentrated milk and sugar in the same way, only put a small piece into a coffee pot with water and you have Coffee ready for drinking. Imagination can hardly conceive how well *their armies* are supplied and how poorly *ours*.

God will surely smile on our efforts, tho at times I fear for the cause, there is so much profanity, so little regard for religion. I wrote you for a pocket Testament long time ago that I might carry it in my pocket, but my dear you forget my requests, or neglect them. My bible is so large I cannot carry it in my pocket and I want a pocket

[4] Billy Yanks did not give the desiccated vegetables—called "desecrated" vegetables by the soldiers—as high a rating as did Fay. For discussion of processed foods used by the Federals, see Wiley, *Life of Billy Yank,* 241–242.

tuck Testament. Don't neglect it this time, but send me one for I would give five dollars for one rather than not have it. I could tell you a great many incidents of our retreat from Iuka if I had time and space, but as I have neither will delay it, till I see you face to face if possible, if God in his Providence so orders it. But my dearest I sometimes fear I shall never see you again. I feel sadly when others get letters even up in Iuka mailed Minden Sept. 12th and here on my return Sep. 16th and my latest before leaving here Sep. 2d. My dear I do not doubt your love but I fear out of sight, out of mind and that you don't write me regularly. My letters ought to come when Bates' & Carter's come regularly. I have but very little time and yet I never fail if it is possible to mail you a letter once a week. I wrote from Iuka and again now and I know my dear I put myself to much trouble that you may get letters. I almost hoped I might be wounded at Iuka that I might come home. I am almost crazy when I think that my loved, noble Will Ed. is dead. I cannot stand it, any remembrance brings tears I cannot restrain. Oh, Mother if I could only see you and realize it I might bear it better. I often think of home and he invariably rises in the foreground of the picture. Oh, my God why would'st thou so afflict me.

What are the Trustees doing about the school. I see the Military school at Alexandria is in operation. Cannot I get the professorship of Mathematics in it? All this I leave in your hands, trusting to your judgment *entirely* in the matter.

Do write me often and tell me all about everything. As for directing your letters. It is said we go to Holly Springs. A letter would reach me sooner if I knew *certain* that we were going there but you had better direct to Guntown or Tupelo or Baldwin as before. I shall probably get it if it is sent even if some days later. I want a letter as soon as possible. Love, much of it to all from me. A hundred kisses for both yourself and Thornwell. He wont know me when I come home. Oh dear, I cannot stand the idea. God bless you.

I thought dearest that I could only write one small sheet as I wanted to send you a paper of the 22d or some pieces cut out from it but as I have some more time I will try and fill out one more sheet. Our Wagon train came out from Iuka in an Easterly direction and have not yet arrived here. It has been reported that they were entirely cut off by the enemy, but we have since heard from them and they will be in in the morning. I hope so for Rich is with them and all my baggage. I have nothing with me except the clothing I have on, my uniform pants and brown coat and my shawl, blue linen shirt, undershirt & drawers. I told you I believe that I lost drawers shirts and socks on the battlefield at Denmark, I got a pair of drawers (drilling) good stuff from the Quartermaster at 1.00, quite as cheap as you could make them at home. I am glad indeed to get them for I need three pairs. I lost the pair I bo't of Jim Leary's Est. as before mentioned. The two pairs you made me I have yet tho one is ripped a little but I intend to mend them the first time I get a chance. When that will be I do not know as a soldier never knows where he will be three hours after.

I wish we could have two or 3 weeks rest now for my horse's sake as he is quite poor, having never recovered from the severe attack of camp fever he had at Pound's Spring where Wimberly & Patillo left us. By the way Patillo wrote Capt. Webb that he was coming back to the Co. I hope he will try for I think they will stop him in Monroe and put him where he belongs into the ranks as a *Conscript Private.* He certainly is no better than many others. As far as his friendship for me is concerned he never possessed any and I knew long ago, but I tried to make him my friend because I liked him, but he feared me, I think, and therefore did not like me. But I bear him no malice. The world is wide enough for us both and he can go his way. As for Mr. Wimberly, he never cared about me nor I about him since his stand in the school matter. He knows nothing about military matters for he never got into any service but picket service. He never has been in a skirmish and knows nothing of military service actually. I am glad he has a clear conscience. I bear him no ill will. I only admire his [in]consistency. He promised in the rock house that he would go for twelve months or *12 years* if necessary and when some one spoke of business, he impatiently said: "Don't talk of business keeping a man. What business or property has any man if he has no country." I quote his very words. "But Brutus is an honorable man."

As far as coming home is concerned I am willing to stay my 12 mos. out, but am not at present willing to enter Confederate Service again till I see some different men as Generals & high Officers, or their conduct closely scrutinized. We had nothing but a military despotism at

Corinth and also here till lately. Bragg shot whom and when he pleased without even the form of a court Martial. I learn his conduct is to be inquired into. If I could come home once in a while I could stay but I know I can do the Country as much good in my sphere at home as here, and more, tho' I don't believe I would be satisfied for some time at home.

I think this war will be over by the first of April as we have glorious news again from Va. not Maryland !!! glorious Maryland !!! Oh if these lines could only be pressed here and we again be masters of Tenn. & Ky. what glorious times we would have. It would not astonish me if Price went to Va. and the cavalry left to guard these Rail Roads in Miss. A few weeks will develop the plan of the new Campaign. But war matters aside.

I have lived the last five days on Pilot Bread. You have seen the deck hands on Steamboats eat it—a hard kind of cracker, a little bacon which I ate raw and some fresh Beef which I warmed stuck on a stick over the fire, and yet God has mercifully preserved my health & life and I feel quite well tho tired almost to death as I am acting Commissary for the Battallion and am kept going all the time. I shall get out of it when the train wagon comes up. Nat Martin wont have his Lieut'cy as he wishes to procure a substitute, as officer he cannot. I want Capt. Webb to appoint me and I'll get some position in Quartermaster or Commissary Dept., being Commissioned Officer. I can be discharged just as well as now. Keep my letters to yourself. The Co. is generally well tho a good many men shirk duty.

I hope dearest you will take good care of yourself and not get sick, also of Thornwell. Does he seem to miss his Brother any. Oh darling why am I kept from you by this horrid war. I must see you and the grave of my child or go crazy. God bless and preserve you dearest. Love to your Father & Mother, brother & sisters from me and know that my heart beats for you alone. Your husband who loves you, Ed.

Tupelo, Miss. Sep. 26th, 1862 10 A.M.

My own dear Sarah:

I mailed you a letter in pencil day before yesterday and I am sorry

I sent it my dear though you may be glad for if I had not complained so much of not getting letters from you, I should not now be writing this. I had got no letters since yours mailed Sep. 2d. and I assure you my heart was full very full of disappointment. I cannot bear to have others get letters and I not get any. I became almost frantic and getting a *pass* (for a white man)! I came down to this place, Tupelo, knowing that there must be letters from you. One dated August 7th, sent by hand, the others mailed Sep. 11th and Sep. 16th (mailed). You don't know my dearest loved one how glad I was to learn that you were well and how sorry I was that I had written complainingly about not getting letters. I hope you will forgive my impatience dearest for you know it is one of my besetting sins to be impatient. I try to overcome it but find it very hard to do so, the evil is present with me ever and the good it is hard to do.

You would perhaps be glad to know where I am writing and I can tell you in a Telegraph office at this place on a dining table while the news is rattling over the wires of victories again of Stonewall Jackson over Burnside killing and capturing his whole army save 2000. Gen'l Lee is certainly a Napoleon, for his retreat across the Potomac caused Burnside to attempt to follow him when Stonewall was ordered to fall on Burnside while crossing and rumor says he dammed up the River with the slain. A confirmation comes this morning of all the glorious news and they are anxiously awaiting to hear of Bragg crossing the Ohio with his victorious legions.

Again rumors come from Richmond that Pres. Davis intends making proposals for "Peace" before entering on the Northern Soil. It is said that a company of Pennsylvanians joined Jackson all armed and equipped, their own officers elected &ç saying that they would be drafted to fight for Abolitionism and they preferred the Confederacy. It is expected that the peace propositions of Pres. Davis if not accepted by the Lincoln dynasty will entirely divide the North, there being no doubt a large peace party there. I do hope and confidently believe that the dawn of peace is beginning to break. I have no idea that the Western States will stand the Abolition scheme of Mr. Lincoln. Oh Mother! if it will only close we may be so happy, so happy yet. Pray God that it may be so.

We are going to Holly Springs and will probably overtake our command there. I know not where we will go from there but you had better direct your next letters either to that place, Grand Junction or here. I don't know how to tell you. Van Dorn is moving trains through to Gd. Junction now up the Miss. Central road. I learn too that the road is completed via Meridian to Selma, Ala. I am glad to hear it indeed and if you were only here, I mean there, I could see you in three days. However all things are for the Best I believe tho it is hard to feel it in the case of our darling little Willie.

But this morning after reading your letter I feel more resigned. God had need of him and has taken him. He gave and shall he not take back his own, yet notwithstanding all this it is hard, very hard to give him up on whom all my hopes were so centered. It did not seem to me that he could die. If I expected to see anyone it was him on my return, but now my house is left desolate. You ask my advice about a paling around the graveyard. Have it by all means my darling, if you desire, only have a nice one. If I live I shall have it enclosed with a cast iron railing as soon as possible after the war.

I am exempt under the Conscript Law after the first of April or at least 90 days thereafter and I think now if I live I shall claim it. You wrote me nothing about the school or matters there. What are the Trustees doing? Are they having any school at all? They could get me at any time by a proper petition to the Sec. of War, I presume. As regards clothing—I do not need any nor do I think many of the company do. Yet I will show your letter to Capt. Webb and if anyone comes I hope it will be me. Mr. Wimberly wrote Capt. Webb to know if *independents* would be allowed? and Dr. Patillo wrote that he was coming to rejoin our Company.

As far as Mr. Wimberly's story about Rich was concerned I knew it before. I wish I had Henry and Rich was back on the Farm, for he is as trifling a negro as I know. You know, I always thought Cynthia was too. If you could sell or swap her do so if you choose. Anything you do dearest will be perfectly satisfactory to me. I have great confidence in your judgment. As regards undershirts I have found a most excellent one, and now have two that will do me. As for the gray Jeans, I am wearing my uniform pants now and my green ones are almost as good as new. Jones has my measure for Coat & pants somewhere on his books. He can cut the coat and pants too, if you desire to make them. As for woolen socks I shall not need them. The Boots and Testament are all I need at present. I am released under the Conscript Act as teacher of schools and at the end of the 12 mos. I intend to come home anyhow. So my dear be of good cheer, God may have happiness in store for us yet.

And now dearest I will close my letter as I wish to write a few lines to Mother as I also got a letter from her here. Write regularly, my dearest, and I will promise not to grumble if I do not get it, but will believe that it is on the road. Give much love to everyone for me. You did not say whether you got the letter by John Lesueur. I suppose Milt Smith had not reached you when you wrote. As for weaning Thornwell do just what you think best. You had better persevere when you commence. Good Bye, dearest, the train from Mobile has just arrived and I must get off to rejoin our Command. A thousand kisses to you and little Thornwell. I love you both oh how dearly. I will enclose Mother's letter in this so you can hear from her too. The news you get in the "Whig" so I'll not send you a newspaper this time. Your loving and devoted husband. Ed H. Fay.

All *your requests shall* be complied with.

2½ miles from Ripley, Miss.
Oct. 7th 1862

My own dear Sarah:

I wrote the "2½ miles" some four or five days ago and I am at the same place now having been marched to Corinth since that time and retreated back having driven the Yankees back through entrenchment after entrenchment until Price's army went quite into Corinth but we had not men enough to hold it and were obliged to fall back.[5] The Yankees in the meanwhile largely reinforced from Bolivar down on our rear and in our Retreat we were obliged to cut our way out again through them to save our wagon train. We also lost some of our

[5] After the battle of Iuka on September 19, 1862, Van Dorn and Price joined forces for an attack on Corinth. In a brief but bloody battle on October 3–4, 1862, the Confederates were defeated by Rosecrans' defending forces. See *Battles and Leaders,* II, 737–760.

wagons on the road and lots of ammunition. The principal cause of our having to leave was the impossibility of getting water. We fought them for a day and a half and the troops were worn out for water and could stand it no longer. Corinth can never be taken unless in Winter Season when there is plenty of water and it will also take a plenty of men. The Yankees killed a great many of our men and "we piled the ground with Moslem slain." Our retreat was conducted with the greatest confusion and Van Dorn was drunk all the time and Villipigue too and I expect Price too. Everybody was commander and Price did the fighting. We lost half of Price's army killed and *straggling*. Such demoralization was never seen in an army before.

I think the cause of the Confederacy is lost in this West. I think that the army will fall back to Jackson, Miss. first to Holly Springs then I fear to Jackson. I am almost in despair as regards our cause. Price, I never considered a General, and I do not think now Van Dorn and [Mansfield] Lovell are for we were led into a trap. I could see the want of Generalship but could say nothing for I am not an *officer* you know. I tell you Sarah that I am whipped now. I wish you could have seen the Battle I don't believe such fighting was ever done. We (the Cavalry) were not much exposed but were preventing them from turning our left flank. For 4 days and nights our saddles had not been off our horses and since I commenced writing we have been ordered to saddle up. I do wish I could see you dearest, I could tell you so many things I cannot write. I could give you some idea of the Battle which I believe to have been the most terrific in the world. Oh if we had only 15 or 20,000 more men we could have held the place.

God has most mercifully preserved me, tho I am worn completely out and am sick and sore. Another all night march or picket right before us. If our army was not so badly confused I should have some hope, but so it is. These troops will never fight again under Van Dorn or Lovell. I am sick at heart at seeing such a panic prevail, for there is no necessity for it. A retreat should always be in good order.

But darling I have said nothing about ourselves. I do so want to see you and if possible I will come and do so as soon as we stop. But do not put any confidence in seeing me for I am at the caprice of officers you know. Col. Sandidge is just here from Richmond and says the Yanks are reinforcing at New Orleans very largely, and bro't despatches for Van dorn. I hope we will get back as far as Vicksburg. I mean our Cavalry. I tell you the times look much darker than I ever expected to see them, but I still trust in God that He will bring order out of all the confusion. But the wagons are moving and I must close. Good Bye my dearest. My love to all.

Truly your devoted Husband, E. H. Fay.

Cold Water 4½ miles North of Holly Springs
3 oclock
Sunday Oct 12th 1862

My own darling Wife:

It is with feelings of intense disappointment that I write you, for yesterday morning I expected before this time to have been in Vicksburg on my way home. Capt. Webb detailed me to go home after clothing and Col. Balch signed the pass very readily but when I presented it to Gen'l Armstrong his reply was: "It cannot be granted now." I asked no question for he is in the habit of cursing men and if he should curse me without a cause I should be tempted to shoot him. Capt. Webb also asked him for leave of absence, and he said that a fight was impending here, but if we went into camps he would grant it. I think we will probably go into camp here for the enemy are not pursuing us now and the cold rainy season has set in and I think Infantry will go into winter Quarters. Cavalry you know have no winter Quarters to go into. In fact I have not seen, to say, sleep or step inside a tent for more than three months.

But I presume you will want to hear of the grand battle at Corinth. I last wrote you by Col. Sandidge a hasty note from Ripley and told you we were defeated at Corinth. We stopped a short time at Ripley but learning that we were being pursued put out again and a panic again seized the train. Again we were ordered as rear guard and were on duty all night. The train got off and the next morning we were ordered back to within 5 ms. of Ripley to stay till we were driven in by the Yankees. We went back and waited and sent some scouts to Ripley and the reported 20,000 Yankees turned out to be a fiction. Lt. Watkins went clear into Ripley and there had been none there.

We waited on post and concluding that the train had got far enough in advance at one P.M. having had nothing to eat for 2 days we put out without orders.

We came on the Road to this place and camped 7 miles below Holly Springs, but hearing the Yankees were coming down by Gd. Junction we were ordered out in the hardest coldest rain and marched some ten miles and when we stopped I was almost frozen to death. However, we soon had a rousing fire and were at last thawed out. It quit raining before bedtime and I slept by the fire, a little coldly it is true, but I slept. I have caught a pretty severe cold but with that exception I am pretty well tho the trip to and from Corinth was very severe. The saddles were not off our horses for five days and nights and for nearly three days and nights we were hardly off our horses, but I have lived through it. I wanted a letter from you so much this morning. Was in town yesterday but the office was not open so I went in this morning myself and went to the P.O. and looked over some 2000 letters but found none for me. I feel confident however that I have some at Tupelo and I hope they will come here in a day or two. But if I can come home I shall be off without waiting.

This is Sunday evening but little like a Sunday has it been to me, and little like Sabbath have any Sundays been. I do hope this war will end. I went and called on the Jackson Grays[6] who were captured at Huntsville, Ala. on their way to Va. They were at Sandusky City on an Island in Lake Erie and were doing well enough. Have been exchanged. Learned that Wm. Henry was ordered with his Regiment to the mouth of Red River, La. I wrote him this morning a hasty note and told him to go see you.

I have a strong notion of going into the heavy Artillery service if I cannot get into the Engineers Corps. I shall try and do it if possible if the Trustees of the school do not have me discharged to come home. I had rather, however, claim my exemption under the Conscript Act and come back and stay on La. soil. I think I could fight better there than anywhere else. I would try it on my own hook if I could and I know that I could do more damage with my own rifle than any gun in the service. I did think my dearest that this war would close soon but I

[6] The Jackson Grays were Company K, 9th Louisiana Infantry Regiment, from Claiborne Parish, Louisiana.

can see no hope now for it unless by foreign intervention (and I don't expect it now) until the term of old Lincoln has expired unless God in his righteous Providence should strike down the old villain by the arrow of Death. Many a valuable life will be sacrificed ere its close and you my own darling wife may be a widow, but God does what is right tho' I can't always see it, nor can I feel it in his late dispensation.

No, Mother, I don't believe I can ever become reconciled to the death of my first born. My heart bleeds Mother and I am most crazy. The thought of him never rises in my mind but my eyes are filled with tears and I can now scarcely see a letter I make. I have no one to sympathize with me in my grief and I must bear it alone. Oh, if I could come home and see you once more, I could bear it better.

What have you ever done about having our house painted. It had better be done as the paint is wasting and the house will be preserved thereby. But do just as you think best. I shall probably bring Rich home with me and if he will do better work on the farm than Henry, bring him back and leave Rich. He has been driving our private wagon for some time back and consequently not of much service to me unless I had a mule for him to ride. Mother you are entitled to fifty dollars bounty from Claiborne Parish so I learn and as our property will be taxed to pay for it, I think you had better draw it and use it if you need.[7] But this matter I leave entirely at your discretion trusting to your judgment in the matter. But these matters I will discuss when I come home and have more time. I hope you have had that grave yard fence put up for I know you dote on it, but I don't think you ought to pay for all of it if you have it made large enough for both families. But you and your father can arrange the matter between you. What has become of our hogs? My poor boy can't take care of them now as he promised me when coming away. Oh why did God take my boy away from me. I will try and come home before Christmas if possible. I will not need anything I think unless I could get a nice Uniform which I will do if I can get a situation in the Engineer Corps, but I have no chance to do anything tied down here as I am, so I must get out. But I hope all things will be ordered for the best.

Have just heard in an Appeal that Bragg is firing very heavily on

[7] Bounties were offered by both Confederate and local authorities to stimulate volunteering.

Louisville. I hope he will capture it. Tom Randle and Abe Monzingo are sitting down by me chatting like blackbirds. They are both well and Tom Randle has dates from home of Oct. 5th but my latest are Sep. 16th but I don't blame you for I know I have letters on the way. It is getting so dark I cannot see.

Monday morning—I closed last night but will add a few words this morning. I expect we will start this morning to La Grange on a scout towards Bolivar again. Don't know however. Have heard that there is a probability of our being dismounted. Col. Thos Scott is trying to get us Gen'l Villipigue's body guard. I hope we will succeed for then there is no danger of being dismounted. Soldiers are badly treated by the authorities, contrary to Military or civil Law. But they are simply soldiers and have no method of redress. I think some one ought to look into these matters.

But I close, dearest—I don't know what will be done but I do know I want to come home mighty bad, and I think I will stay when I do come, too. We are expecting good news from Ky. Bragg has mustered 50 Regiments of Ky's and Kirby Smith almost as many. This war is fast approaching a war of extermination and if not settled before January 1st will come to that certain. You will see by the papers the late acts of Congress relative to Lincoln's emancipation proclamation.[8] Now my dearest write often and direct to Holly Spgs. for I think we will stay on this road for some time. Give much love to all for me, Father, Mother, Brother & Sisters. Ask Gen'l Simmons if he will give me a place on his Staff if I am exempt under the Conscript Act as I will not have to drill with militia. Do write often my dearest, at present to Balch's Battallion Armstrong's Brigade care of J. Y. Webb. God bless my darlings. E. H. Fay

[8] Issuance of Lincoln's preliminary emancipation proclamation on September 22, 1862, caused the introduction of angry resolutions in the Confederate Congress. But no laws were passed to implement the threats to raise the black flag. See E. M. Coulter, *The Confederate States of America, 1861–1865* (Baton Rouge, 1950), 264–266.

Camp near Salem, Miss.
Oct. 18th 1862

My own dear Wife:

I wrote you some days since when encamped near Cold Water 6 miles north of Holly Springs and as nearly a week has elapsed since writing I will try and compose my mind enough to write you a hasty note. We have moved our Camp out near Salem some 12 or 15 miles north east of Holly Springs and are encamped in the woods the only resting time we have had for nearly three mos. Of news I have very little to tell for this army is in a transition period both as regards Infantry and Cavalry, for Van Dorn has been superceded and Pemberton of S. C. assigned to command though not yet assumed it. Gen'l Armstrong has resigned and a Col. [William H.] Jackson of Jackson's Cavalry assigned in command of all Cavalry. Everything is in a mess and we are trying to get our Squadron transferred to Maj. Gen'l Dick Taylor. I don't know whether we will succeed or not but intend trying our best and not giving up until everything has been exhausted. This must not be spoken at home unless someone there can have some influence with Gen'l Taylor. I am determined to get out from this Tenn. assignment if possible. If I can't do it in one way I can in another I presume. So much for military matters right here, now for other news.

We have just received dispatches from both sides announcing the fact the Bragg had whipped Buell and the Louisville Journal acknowledges a loss of killed, wounded and prisoners from between 25 & 28,000 men while our dispatches say that Bragg took 22,000 Prisoners alone. Anyhow Ky. is redeemed from Northern despotism.[9] I again feel confident that this war will close before March 1st, '63 and right here I want to say to your father to try and get Cotton at 10 cts. if he can for all our notes and accounts. If the war closes as I believe it will it will be worth 50 cts. per pound and if it is burned the Govt. will pay us the ruling price at the end of the War. It will be a safe investment anyway and we cannot lose and may make a great deal. If I had time

[9] Like most early reports of military actions that circulated in places far removed, this version of Bragg's achievements in Kentucky given by Fay was grossly distorted. After the battle of Perryville on October 8, 1862, Bragg withdrew from Kentucky and his poorly conducted campaign was generally adjudged a failure. See Horn, *Army of Tennessee,* 162–189.

I would write explicitly to him. I would like much to hear from him at any rate. The Black Flag will be hoisted after Jan'y 1st '63 and the soldiers of the North will pause ere they covet a resting place under its folds. So much for the other Military Matters.

Well night before last John Lesueur came in and the boxes and trunks from Minden. I got all my things and have on the clothing, all of it except pants, undershirts and socks. They all fit very well but are full large as I weigh now only 170 lbs. I have the striped shirt next my skin and the debage over it. The drawers are soft and nice and I am very thankful for them though I stood in no need of them as my valise is already full of clothing. I have worn my overshirts but very little since I left home and had plenty of clothes. My pants are all good except the plain cloth and I shall now give them away. My uniform pants are good and I have worn them a great deal. My green ones will do good service yet, so I am well supplied. I had rather have had handkerchiefs for I loaned my red one to Linn and he lost it, tho' I have two very good ones yet. My boots fitted me very well and I was glad to get them but why did Ditmer charge me $25.00 while Capt. Webb's and Linn's only cost $22.00. I want your father to let Mr. Ditmer pay three dollars more per hundred for flour than any one else. Please say to Mr. Wimberly that *"I am very well I thank you"* (on the bottom of my boots he wrote "How dye do"). The Testament I am very thankful for, but I had got one only the day before I got it. I have but little time for reading it and I confess to not much inclination. Camp life with its vexations is not conducive to religious improvement.

I wonder if it is true that the Trustees have sent up a petition for my discharge. I shall write the Hon. Thomas H. Watts to see if I am not exempt under the Conscript Act.[10] If I have waived my right by the fact of having volunteered as some would contend, I have seen so much injustice and fraud committed by commanders that I am perfectly disgusted with the Military Gov't of the Confederate States and if I and mine were safely in some South American country I would care little what became of them. If abuses could or were likely to be regulated, I might fight with some degree of patriotism but now I

[10] Thomas H. Watts of Alabama was attorney general of the Confederacy from March 18, 1862, to September 30, 1863.

have but little and I am free to confess it. If I had not been in service and knew what I know now, I would not go into it unless drafted, though I would not object to fighting if we were properly treated—

Ben Neal and Julius Lancaster joined us this morning and they give quite amusing accounts of their captivity. They look very hearty but will have to be climatized before they are fit for much service. The nights are very cold and the days very warm, but the health of the Company is very good. Rich'd Ratcliffe, [J. W.] Plunkett and Giles Monzingo being the only sick ones in Camp now, though eight are in Hospital. George Monzingo, [John A.] Clinton, [Stephen] Darby, Bill Jones, Mat Killen, Nacy Meeks, [S. G.] McKamie & (Hart's substitute) "Ellen" [Alkana]. Several have lost their horses and will have to get them others. Neal & Lancaster will have to do so too.

What did Mrs. Dr. Bright tell you about me? Anything? Both the grown daughters were at Mr. Slack's in Monroe when I met their parents in La Grange. Say to Dr. Bright for me that if his sons enter service we would be pleased to have them join our Company as we are all from Minden. Mother—I could not imagine the night I got your last letter by Taylor who you meant when you said "her teacher." I could not make head or tail of it until the next morning. Her teacher will next turn up in a Hospital as a 2nd Florence Nightingale or as a Lunatic in some Asylum. I don't think her mind well balanced and the fact that the "War does not concern her in the least" shows it. I think she is disappointed in love, ha! ha! what think you. Did your Mother see her in Texas? and if so what did she think of her—

I am afraid you have not got some of my letters. Did you get the ones from Iuka and Tupelo. It is not my fault, *my own loved one* that you were three weeks without a letter, though I would have been a whole month if yours had been one day later. Your last directed to Tupelo I have not yet got, but I learn they are coming through by land by some of our boys. I don't want to lose one. What makes you so tired directing letters to Tupelo? You may change now to Holly Springs if you wish. I was right in having them directed to Tupelo for I have lost less letters than any one. As regards your placing your affections on Thornwell. I don't think you act right. Love him as hard as you please for he will not die because you love him. As for me I have *become perfectly hardened.* If I have got to lose all my children let them go. I care for nothing now. My boy is gone. My punishment is greater than I can bear.

You ask me if I know anything of John Lackey. I saw him on our return from Iuka. He stayed with me all night. He is killing himself on opium and I would not be surprised if he was dismissed in disgrace. I hope not. Don't mention this for I may be mistaken. I don't know where he is—I think 3d Arks., Moore's Brigade. If I can see any chance I will send him the bundle. Nat brot him some letters and told him but he has not come after them.

I am sorry for your sake, dearest, that you cannot have that fence built. You must try and have it done, if not, have the ground staked off and my name put on a board in the center of the plot. I intend to have an iron railing round it, if ever I am able, which I hope some day to be, if I live. If I do not, it will not make much matter, as you will not always live in Minden I reckon. This is a mighty hard sheet to fill out but I reckon I'll succeed. I want you to go about more and see more of the people so you can write me some of the news. You give me so little in your letters. I am mighty sorry they did not hang Jasper Blackburn. He richly deserves it and I do hope the call will be made for the 45 yrs. conscripts so as to get him. I would rather he would be hung though, any other death is too honorable for him. I collected 45 dollars hire for Rich at Hd Qrtrs. the other day. I believe I wrote you that I hired him for a dollar a day, that will almost pay for Lizzy. I want you to send Mrs. Hughes $25 when you send Laura home Christmas. That is what and all I agreed to pay for her. If I can possibly come home I intend to do so before Christmas, but in case I do not I write this. Will you need Laura another year? I am very sorry the thrush compelled you to wean Thornwell for I sucked until I was five years old and he might have done the same. I have not heard from Mother since mine from Tupelo. I don't know what can be the reason. I wrote you that William Henry was at the mouth of Red River, the 1st Ala. prisoners having been sent there to man Heavy artillery. I presume the rest of the Reg't will go there. Your last was written on the day we were fighting so at Corinth, Oct. 4th—I think Slack sent Dr. Bright to Chaffe to strengthen the anti-Ford party in the College.

There will always be division in the school now. Have you collected any of my school accts? You must try and do so if you need funds. I would send you money if I had any way. I have over $200 now.

Give much love to your Father & Mother and the children one and all for me. Tell Lou Rector Smith was at Corinth when we were there in May last. He left Columbia with our army. He was a true Southern man. Write often dearest one. My only pleasures are your letters. Goodbye, my dearest. Your loving husband, E. H. Fay.

I have just written a letter to the Hon. Thos. Watts asking his opinion whether I was exempt under the Conscription Act or had waived my right. I directed him to address me at Holly Springs and duplicate letter to your father at Minden, La. so you will know whether I am exempt or not.

Camp North of Tupelo, Miss.
Nov. 29th 1862

My own dear Sarah:

A week elapsed since I wrote you and I have looked a little, a very little for a letter from you.[11] I hardly dared hope that you would write until you heard from me but did not know but some impulse of love might move you to a pleasant surprise and that you might write me a few days after I left, particularly as you were not very well and knew that I would feel very anxious, but, my dear, I have been only a little disappointed for I did not calculate very strongly on a letter till you heard from me. I wrote you hurriedly last Sunday and gave you the most interesting events of my trip but I fear my letter was not interesting as a whole for I wrote in the greatest haste imaginable to get my letter off. I hope ere this you have gotten it. Capt. Webb gave me two letters from you the first day I got back into camp and yesterday in looking over his trunk found two more. One by Mr. Stinson and the other Oct. 20th. They did not answer quite as well as new ones but were much better than none at all.

Oh, my darling, you do not know how much I miss you and I had

[11] Fay was home on furlough from October 26 to November 18. The letter of Sunday, November 22, to which he refers was evidently lost.

rather be with you than to be Gen'ls. Pemberton or Lee. I am like the Psalmist and can exclaim. A day in *thy* courts is better than a thousand with the highest honors of the land spent apart from you. You are my light and my life. I love you better every day of our lives and regret that I am compelled to be away from you. It pains me greatly that any clouds should ever arize upon our horizon and darling if I should ever live to come to you again, we must try and prevent any ever rising again, on my part by being more thoughtful of your feelings when I speak fretfully and you by being a little less sensitive and passing things *not intended* over.

But I must hasten for I hear cannonading in front and learn that the 1st Brigade under command of Col. Thos. M. Scott is ordered to have rations cooked for three days. I cannot believe the enemy intend advancing upon us here for we are strongly fortified and can hold this point against any of the Abolition Hordes. Lt. Gen'l Pemberton reviewed the troops a few days ago and was received by a salute of 15 Guns. No military moves that I can hear of. It is the gen'l impression that we, as I have said before, are going into Winter Quarters here. I hope so for the weather has been and is very cold. But we have a few refused tents into which the boys crawl at night. I have slept very warmly for we have gathered a lot of grass and made a very good bed. John Lesueur and I sleep together. We heard last night that Tom Lesueur was dead but I am inclined to disbelieve it. It may be so however. The Company are in good health, our Frenchman, Theophile [Duffard] has a slight attack of pneumonia. All the rest of the Company are in camp now but [J. W.] Plunkett and [John W.] Hudson and John C. Wimberly. (Cannonading continuing and growing heavier every moment) I expect the enemy are reconnoitering in force.

Have just received a Memphis Appeal of the 28th but there is no news. No fighting in Virginia yet. The enemy under Burnside are evidently striving to find a weak side and it argues well for our cause there. I do hope this wicked war will soon close and I believe it must before long for I cannot feel that the Yankee Abolitionists can carry it on much longer. "Cannonading continuing heavy." I hope we shall not be ordered out for my horse is nearly dead and I have no money to buy another with at present. He had camp fever and received but very little attention from J. W. Lancaster to whom I had loaned him. His back was hurt very badly but is about well now. I have had a very severe cold since I got back but as it continues loose I do not mind it much. It troubles me by keeping my nose sore.

Smallpox is in Camps in Lovell's and Price's Divisions, but none in ours yet. John Lesueur has vaccinated a good many in the Squadron and also in the 12th La. Regt. I have been vaccinated again but hardly think it will take in my arm. Bert Neal bro't the Matter from Illinois as they had it in the Alton Penitentiary. I hope it will take in somebody's arm so we can know the matter is good. It was in Monroe, La. when I came through there, and Alonzo Johnson & Bill Hadley were boarding at a house where a child had it. I did not feel alarmed about it for I was on the streets most of the time. Besides when we know we cannot escape danger we do not dread it near as much and there is no running from it in the army. Rich had a present of a pair of old boots which he swapped for a very good pair and I think he is provided for this winter if he will take care of them but he is very inattentive and may not do it.

2 P.M. The cannonading in front has ceased and as we have received no orders yet to move I presume we are to be stationary. I see in the "Appeal" I have just laid down an advertisement of John L. Barrington as a deserter from Co. "A" 12th La. Regt. I expect he went to the Yankees at Corinth. I presume you have seen another speech from John Van Buren.[12] Everything tends to show a peaceable disposition of the Democracy North. "Firing again in front." Heavy skirmishing in front. Will hear before long I hope as Capt. Webb has gone to see Acting Brig. Gen'l Thos Scott and he will tell him I reckon. A dozen from the 12th Regt. have just come down to be vaccinated. I learn it is taking finely in the 12th now. I hope it will not take on me. Firing has retired almost beyond hearing. Enemy falling back. Hope they may be driven effectually back.

But my darling I don't expect war news interests you much. I sent

[12] John Van Buren, New York lawyer and Democratic politician, son of Martin Van Buren, made numerous speeches during the war in which he criticized conscription, suspension of the writ of habeas corpus, recruiting of Negroes, and other war measures sponsored by the Lincoln Administration. He was a strong supporter of Seymour and McClellan.

off my last letter in a hurry and did not enclose Mother's letter as I intended. I will do it in this. I wrote her the next day after yours and also to Wm Henry. Will send their letters if they contain any interesting matter. I am sorry now that I did not bring all the eatables as they would have proved very acceptable and I had so little trouble with my things. It did not cost me anything to bring Rich from Vicksburg as he could not ride with me and I forgot him. I do hope Lou is quite well and that all are well at home. Wish you would go and see Mrs. Webb. Poor Nat I feel so sorry for him. He heard of the death of his other child the other day. He takes it very hardly. I can sympathize with him in his great suffering.

I feel dearest that this letter is very incomplete but you cannot appreciate the circumstances under which it is written. If we should go into Winter Qrtrs. and I should send for you would you come? Col. Scott wants Capt. Webb's wife to come with his and Capt. Webb wants you to come too. But I hardly think it is best. Orders have come to cook 3 days rations. I will close with much love to all. Your own husband,

Ed. H. Fay

7

"Gen'l Tilghman Said I Ought To Be a Colonel"

Camp 3 miles East of Grenada
Tuesday Dec. 9th 1862

My Own Loved One:

I wrote you a little more than a week ago but my dearest I fear you will fail to get it as the army was in the way of falling back and I believe the post office was already removed, if so I know you will not get it. But I will renew my description of our retreat. Sunday eve about an hour by sun I received an order to report at once in person to Gen'l [Albert] Rust's HdQrtrs. which I did and he informed me that he wished me to take command of a Pioneer Corps and open an old road out two miles and a half into the big road which I completed about 11 P.M. in the hardest rain I almost ever saw fall. On my return to Camp I found the tents and all the Baggage sent off and laid down in the Rain and slept in wet clothes all night. At sunrise next morning came an order to move. We had previously packed our surplus baggage in those big trunks and sent down to the Rail Road at Abbeville to be sent off on the cars. These were all burnt as well as new clothing, shoes, Hats &ç for the whole Division. Thousands upon thousands of dollars worth I put in the trunks, my uniform Coat, my green pants, leggings, old boots, net Jacket, soap, towells &ç all of which are lost. Also the Company Books and Muster & Pay Rolls. Everything was lost, my pillow and two or three other small things I don't recollect.

When we reached Gen'l Rust's HdQrtrs the next morning I was ordered forward with 10 men to fix the roads again. I found Roads horribly cut up and trains stalled and bogged down almost every hundred yards but I got them all out and crosswayed the places. Gen'l [Lloyd] Tighlman [sic] came on and payed me quite a compliment, said I ought to be Col. of a Regt. instead of O.S. I told him I desired no promotion, was not an aspirant for any favors—I also got well acquainted with Gen'l [Mansfield] Lovell who was yesterday relieved of his command and Van Dorn appointed in his place. It seems that Van Dorn has had no command since Pembertons command. By the By, I saw Pemberton and he is the most insignificant "puke" I ever saw and will be very unpopular as soon as known. His head cannot contain sense enought to command a Regt. much less a Corps. Oh what will our Country come to, when we are cursed with such worthless Commanders. Gen'l Rust is a gentleman & a soldier and a *humane* man. He treats his soldiers as if they were men, as far as he can.

We are well situated at present as long as there is no fighting to be done for we have no picketing to do or duty of any kind. I am afraid our lot is too good to last however & fear we may be sent back sometime or other to that infamous battalion. I went ahead as I was sent and passed through Oxford. There they burnt 50,000 lbs Bacon and how much flour I don't know but a large lot. We were pursued by three or four thousand Abolition Cavalry or rather Mounted Infantry and this is what caused such destruction. Another force of 2500 landed opposite Helena, Ark. and came overland to tear up the R Road. This force was variously magnified to 75 and 80,000 men & as they were on our flank it behooved us to get away. [Col. John W.] Whitfield's Legion of not over 200 men met and drove them back and they put spurs for Helena. Jackson's Cavalry could have captured both forces if he had been any account but he runs first and his Cavalry are well drilled to follow their leader. He is not worth shucks. But he is a West Point graduate and therefore must be born to command.

I tell you Dearest our Country is gone up unless God interposes by taking away Jeff Davis and let some other than a West Pointer hold the reins of Gov't. I have begun almost to despair there is so much mismanagement. I am almost tempted to desert and go to Mexico.

If you my dearest were safely out of this country I would come to you as soon as possible.

I did not find the Command until we got to Coffeeville and then just as they were going into a fight as the Yankees dogged our steps.[1] There Gen'l Rust turned back and the 6th Ark. and Col. Scott's Brigade drove them back hustling. Two of the 12th Louisiana were taken prisoners and paroled and they said we killed over a hundred of them. They sent in a flag of truce and demanded if we had taken their Gen'l Prisoner, as he could not be found. He was killed we think. Gen'l Tighlman [*sic*] recognized one and had him brought in. He soon died and Gen'l Rust had him buried. I printed Abolitionist on an Oak Board and stuck it at his head for the Yanks to see if they should come after we had left. He was a Kansas Jayhawker. We suffered some on the Retreat from hunger, but as I was with them but a little part of the way, I escaped some of the hardships. We reached Grenada Sunday afternoon some 50 miles South of Abbeville. The worst Roads, you can form no idea of a wet, muddy road after an army train and Artillery has passed over it. So I will not attempt a description.

I was rejoiced when overtaking the command at Grenada to find Capt. Webb handing me your letter of the 24th inst. Oh my darling, how my heart swells up with love for you whenever I get one of your letters. My darling you are truly the light of my life. So kind of you to write me when you had no letter from me. I would have written you from Monroe if I had had time. Do not blame me. I got along all straight and much sooner than I calculated on. But my first letter told you all this. I will not repeat it even if you did not get my second one. I am very glad to find out that *"we were mistaken"* but at the same time my dear shall feel much more uneasy in regard to your health. Women are generally much more healthy when they are *"not mistaken"* but my dear I leave you in God's hands and I pray that he may preserve my darling alive and in health for me if I should live to come back. You can tell Mrs. Hughes that your husband does

[1] The fight at Coffeeville referred to in this and the next letter took place on December 5, 1862. For Gen. Lloyd Tilghman's report of the engagement, see *O.R.*, XVII, pt. 1, 503–507.

not always "play the mischief." If I should come home I would be sorry but as my coming is doubtful I am glad.

I wrote to Dr. Quarles and told him the position I was offered and told him I had refused for the sake of the Trustees and people of Minden and I wanted them to decide at once in regard to the matter so that if another occasion should offer I might accept. I will probably hear from him before long in regard to the matter, and then I shall know what to depend on. If I come home I shall teach one year and then make preparation to leave the Confederacy, for I have lost confidence in it under the present management.

I do not know what is going on in the world as I have seen no papers for more than a week. The Memphis Appeal is removed from Grenada and consequently I fear we will not make a stand here.[2] Col. [Thomas M.] Scott says we will not (he thinks) remain here for many days. I think we will. If we do not I think we will go to Vicksburg or Jackson. My old coat is the only one I have. If you could get some Jeans and that old man could cut and make me a coat, you might perhaps find some opportunity of sending it to me though I can get along very well without it I reckon for some time yet. It has been very cold for the last few days and the ground is hard frozen every night but I have slept very warm in the open air and have not suffered from cold except my feet. I borrowed a pair of woolen socks but cannot see any difference. I can wear them if I had them but it makes no matter. I wish you would learn to knit me some undershirts of cotton. Try and do so if you can.

Would you believe it I have on now the same clothes that I put on the morning I left home. It was so cold on the Tallahatchie that I put off changing until we started and we have been more than a week on the Road. One reason was I was vaccinated and I feared to take cold in my arm. It took well and made me quite sick for several days

[2] To avoid capture by the Federals the Memphis *Appeal* changed location so many times during the conflict that it came to be known as the "Moving *Appeal.*" It was published successively in Grenada, Jackson, Meridian, Atlanta, and Montgomery, and at the end of the war was overtaken by the Union forces at Columbus, Georgia. See R. A. Halley, "A Rebel Newspaper's War Story: Being a Narrative of the War History of the Memphis *Appeal,*" *American Historical Magazine* (Nashville), VIII (1903), 124–153.

but I had to keep travelling though I should have laid up if I had been at home. I may send a scab in this letter to Dr. Patillo to vaccinate the family with if you wish it. I think it had better be done as the small pox is in Monroe certain although the Drs. say it is not.

James Newcomb heard in a letter that they were provisioning Vicksburg to stand a siege of 8 mos. The Rail Road is done through to Selma, Ala. so if you wish you can come on and spend the summer there.[3] My parents are anxious to have you with them and I would be glad to have you there too. If I can ever get off again I shall go see them as Mother writes me that Father is failing fast. I have not heard from William Henry since I was at home but have written to him and am looking for a letter from him daily. Hope I may get it today as also one from Mother. I sent hers to you in my last which I fear you will not get.

I am so sorry for poor Mrs. Simmons. Give her my kind regards as well as my sympathy. I love her and believe she is one of the best women in the world. Your letter I have read and re-read. As regards the spelling of the word Abbeville you see how it is spelled. Carter cannot spell and "long hungry" David Caufield neither. I am sorry that his poor circumstance abused me that I didn't bring his honey &ç. I had almost as soon have her ill will as good, for I think there is less woman about her than any body I know. I respect her less after what she said than before if it is possible. As regards Mrs. Kennon, my darling I should never notice her at all. She is unworthy the notice of any sensible woman. I feel sure I shall never teach any of her children so she need not fret herself about it. As far as Walter's substitute is concerned I don't care anything about it.

My paper is greasy and I take my pencil. I still think this war will close next spring for I don't see how we are to carry it on. We have nothing now to eat but beef & coarse corn meal though they can burn up bacon by the 50,000 lbs and flour too. The beef is so poor it can

[3] The gap in the rail line from Monroe, Louisiana, to Selma, Alabama, that had just been completed, was between Demopolis and Meridian. However, the Tombigbee River was not bridged and cars had to be ferried across that stream as well as across the Mississippi. See Robert Black, *Railroads of the Confederacy* (Chapel Hill, 1952), 153–158.

hardly make a march. Tell the Johnsons I saw their brother day before yesterday, he was very well and standing it finely. All our company is now present some left sick on the Road. Caufield's substitute and John Garrett and our frenchman Tofield [Duffard] who was left on the retreat sick. [John W.] Hudson has bro't old Ben Walker but I don't think Capt. Webb will receive him. Plunkett and John Wimberly all are very well except John Dunn who has gone to the Hospital this morning. George Monzingo was limping around with Rheumatism and was sent to the Cars but when our baggage was brought and he found out he would have to march, he told the boys to come on and if they would not carry their baggage he would and beat them all walking to Oxford, beat the Yankees all to pieces, so his Rheumatism is at last proved. He had rather give it up than be a prisoner. Our Company are pretty well pleased with their position, though our papers for transfer were all approved through up to Gen'l Pemberton. If Gen'l Taylor would ask him for us we would be sent over the River. I hope Col. Lewis will not relax his efforts. Please tell him so. A Louisiana Co. in Slemmens Ark. Regt. wants to come too.[4] But I must go wash and put on clean clothes. Good Bye darling. Love to all, every one. Many kisses to you and Thornwell. I wish I could write more but cannot. God bless my darlings. E. H. Fay

I have just got your letter of the 30th of November, but as this is ready to seal I cannot reply to it. Good Bye. I think my next may be mailed at Vicksburg or Jackson and our army be there too. Your loving husband, Ed.

Camp. Rust, Dec. 14th 1862,
3 ms. East Grenada.

My own dear Wife:

You don't know how sorry I was yesterday when getting your letter mailed last Sunday a week from today, to find that you had had no letter from me. I assure you my own one that it was no fault of mine. I did not have time to write while in Monroe nor in Vicksburg but I

[4] The 2nd Arkansas Cavalry Regiment, commanded by Col. W. F. Slemons.

embraced the first opportunity after getting to camp. I wrote you on the 23rd of Nov.[5] the same day that P. P. Bates wrote and why my letter did not come through too is more than I can imagine. The mail carrier of the 12th Regiment took our mail out and put it in for us and I fear he lost my letters and did not put them in. A fool for luck I have always heard is an adage and that is the reason I think Pack [Bates] and [W. A.] Davis's letters got through, so my Darling I don't blame you for feeling badly about not getting letters from me for I know what it is to be disappointed as far as letters are concerned and I regret that I ever complain to you, for you take it so patiently and me complainingly that it is quite a rebuke to me.

My own darling, I do wish I could bear things as well as you do but I am not half so good as you are nor do I ever think I can be. You are my own noble wife and if I am spared to come home alive I know that I shall appreciate you more than ever. I feel as if I should live to come home to you again and that there is much happiness yet in store for us.

But I must tell you of the circumstances attending the reception of your kind letter. Yesterday morning we were ordered out by Gen'l Rust to accompany him to a grand Review of all the Troops of Van Dorn's Corps. It came off in an old field South of Grenada. As escort we accompanied the Gen'l on the Field. After Review by Van Dorn we marched in Review through town before Gen'l Pemberton at the Hotel. By the By, on the march from Abbeville I had an opportunity of seeing Gen'l Pemberton and he has the most unintellectual *pukish* countenance of any man in the army. You must rest assured he is not worth shucks. He has not sense enough to command a company, judging by his looks. Our army is disgracefully treated by being put under such commanders as Pemberton and Van Dorn. It was rumored yesterday that Pres. Davis and Gen'l Joe Johnston were to be present but they were not. You have doubtless seen accounts of our skirmish at Coffeeville. The Yanks threw away guns & everything and did not stop running for twenty miles. Gen'l Rust fixed for them but they did not come his way. Although a lot of stragglers from the 12th [Louisiana] pitched in with an Ark. Regt. and fought like tigers—six were wounded.

[5] This letter was lost.

I am sorry everything looks so gloomy to you my darling. It is brighter here in Camps. I know not for what reason. Yet it is so. I don't think this war can possibly last longer than the 1st of April, for I think the abolition Govt. will fall to pieces before that time. I have just read extracts from [Clement L.] Vallandingham's speech at Cambridge City, Indiana in the Vicksburg Whig of the 12th instant and if he does not intend peace I do not understand language.[6] He seems to have no doubt that we will voluntarily, through the ballot box, return to the Union. I have fears myself of a growing spirit throughout the South in favor of a *reconstruction*. John Carter said yesterday that he for one was very willing to go back but this is between ourselves.

I asked him about that Caufield matter and he gave David fits about it. Said his wife told him about it at the time. Said David was mad because I ordered him up to Saltillo on duty and because he would not excuse him, when he was ordered to send every man fit for duty. This was the whole matter. David has rendered himself the most contemptible man in the Company. We are quite uneasy about a general order from the Sec. of War allowing only twenty men for a body guard. We are very afraid we may be ordered back to the Battalion *again*. Gen'l Rust seems anxious to keep us. I expect Fuller's Co. will have to go back. We have secured such an influence in higher quarters I think that we can probably be transferred over the River to Chambliss' Batt. and form a Regt.[7] I do hope we may get on the other side. If we were going to be on this side all the time I would like so much my dear one to have you over at my Father's. I got a letter from Mother saying she had been looking for you or had hoped that I would bring you over with me. I will send it to you if I don't forget it.

My darling you don't know how sad it makes me feel to think that you are having chills. I am almost sorry *"we were mistaken"* for in that event I think your health would have been much better. You

[6] For a discussion of Clement L. Vallandigham's peace campaign see Eugene H. Roseboom, *The Civil War Era, 1850–1873,* (Columbus, Ohio, 1944), 405 ff. Roseboom's book, which is Volume IV of *The History of the State of Ohio,* edited by Carl Wittke, will be cited hereafter as *The Civil War Era.*

[7] Probably the 13th Battalion, Louisiana Partisan Rangers, commanded by Lt. Col. Samuel L. Chambliss.

must leave no means untried to break up those chills. I wish you would drink Porter regularly as it is such an excellent tonic. You must take something regularly and get fat for if I should come home to you again, I would hate to see you so wan and lean. You know my darling my happiness is wrapped up in you and it is your duty as you value my love to take care of yourself and guard your health jealously. Oh my dear, when I think if you should be taken from me how desolate I would be it brings a feeling of sadness I cannot resist. Do take good care of your health for my sake, for you and Thornwell are all I have left and Our Father will certainly spare you to me. A bruised reed he will not break.

We are very pleasantly situated as far as duties are concerned and Quarters. Col. Scott has given Capt. Webb a Sibley tent (one of these conical ones) large enough for 15 men, almost as warm as a house, a perfect protection against rain. We have floored it with hay, pulled from a corn field, about 6 in. deep and sleep quite comfortably even the coldest nights. The men lost their tents on the retreat from Abbeville but they have stripped off bark and made booths which are quite comfortable. A good many sleep in our tent.

About hiring Laura, my darling, you know very well that I am perfectly willing that you should do just as you please. If you need her, hire her by all means. I want you to have every comfort my means can possibly supply you. If you need her, and I believe you do, hire her, but don't pay enormous prices for her. As far as selling meat as your father does on consignment, all I have to say is, that I have to pay such high prices and even higher and that it takes all my wages to feed me. The Govt. gives us little and I am obliged in self defense to ask such prices too. Don't sell any of mine except for the highest market price. As far as extortion is concerned I think it's one's duty to play for even. We pay 30 & 40 cents for pork that if we didn't buy, the Yankees would take. All we get is a little Beef and corn meal and old Pickled Pork Salt from the Govt. and hardly enough of that. We live hard and if I sell anything I want to be paid as much as anybody. I think your Father did right to let Mrs. Ratcliffe have meat cheap for it is being charitable to the widow, but wrong to let Mr. May or Dr. Quarles have for less than 20 cts. But his are his own and he can do what he pleases.

I have not seen a dust of flour since I left home. I wish I had a blanket more for while I was gone they lost everything I had. My surcingle, saddles, blankets, Saddle Straps, Sabre, and belt Holsters etc., so I have no arms save my pistols now. I need a saddle blanket or a good comfort and then I would take one of my blankets for my saddle. I told you in my letter last Tuesday of the loss of my clothing burned at Abbeville. I wish now I had a Coat though I can get along without it. If we remain as escort we are going to get a Uniform and then I shant need a Coat.

But my darling, I have covered this sheet pretty well over. I love to write letters to you if I had any conveniences therefor but have only my knee to write on and consequently get very tired but when I do I lie flat on my b——y or stomach and write till I am tired of that posture & resume a sitting one again. So I have to wade through letters. I tell you it don't take me half as long to read a letter as it does to write one and it is far more pleasant to read. I suppose it is to you too, and that is the reason I love to write you. I never fail to write every week and frequently oftener. If you don't get letters my darling blame the mails for I write them and generally on Sunday for I have less to do. Yes, my darling, I am glad indeed to hear that you were at work before breakfast. You, my dear, if you had a little more energy, could do a great deal of work and I prefer it to be the active exercise of Spinning or weaving than that very debilitating one of sewing.

I want you to knit or have knitted for me a pair of cotton undershirts as much like store shirts as possible. John Lesueur has some like the Rust Road stockings but I don't like them. I had rather have a crocheted one. Do not confine yourself closely. Get around among your friends—I insist on your visiting right shortly Mrs. Webb and also Nat Martin's wife. Do go and see them soon. I sent you some vaccine matter in my last letter and will send you some more in this for fear that miscarried. It comes from my own arm. Give it to Dr. Patillo and be vaccinated yourself, have all the family, Thorny too, vaccinated and tell him to vaccinate Mrs Webb and her children too. Be sure you do it at once for it is important. The small pox is in the army but it creates no sensation. A good deal of Pneumonia prevails, too, but I hope you and yours my darling wife may be spared for me. You can leave Thornwell at home while you go visiting. You must go for it will be beneficial to your health and it will not hurt Thornwell to be weaned from you. Be sure now darling, to go. Do anything for your health. 'Tis your husband who requests it of you and you know he loves you.

Be sure you write me good long letters as I do you. I can read them even if they are crossed and then one sheet contains as much as two. But my own loved one I must close this and send it to the Office as I hear the Cars just come in and the train just goes out after coming in, but this will be too late to start till tomorrow (Monday). I don't think the Yankee gunboats will stop communication with Louisiana for the Batteries can play on them across the point now the timber is cut down. I got your last letter in six days, marked Sunday at Minden, and I got it Sat. at Noon. Now my darling one do write me often and tell me all the news, tell me all about yourself. Tell me all about your *health*, may *you* not be mistaken and not *we* about certain things.

I am glad you have taken cutting lessons for I think it will be of great advantage to you in cutting your dresses and in saving corsets, too. You can perhaps make me a *corset* for my stomach when I come home. But I must close. Give my love to all my friends. The Trustees must act quickly if they wish me to take the school for I shall accept a position on some Gen'l's Staff if it is offered me and then I wont come home if I am discharged. So what they do, they must do quickly. I am not going to be their plaything. Remember to give my love to Mother Shields and tell Lou she must write me. Love to all and a shower of kisses for yourself and Thornwell. God bless my darlings. Your loving husband, E. H. Fay.

Tell Dr. Patillo to vaccinate Mrs. Nat Martin & Family too.

Camp "Rust" 3 ms. East Grenada
Dec. 16, 1862

My own darling:

I have a few moments now before dark and will devote them to you for I think from the signs of the times that we may be again on the retrograde in a few days and I don't know when I shall have time to write again. If this army does fall back it will be to Jackson, Miss. and then I hold that the cause of the Confederacy is indeed "gone up." So you need not be surprised if you should see me at home before long for when I despair of the Republic I shall come home and lose my life trying to protect you from insult.

Desertions are multiplying so fast in this army that almost one third of it is gone, I think it is indeed a gloomy prospect ahead of us and it is only foreign intervention or Democracy of the North that can now save us. Everything seems to be going amiss tho' Lovell has been removed and Van Dorn appointed to Command of all Cavalry and has this morning gone out 6000 strong to feel the position of the Enemy. Some say it is gone over on the Mobile & Ohio Rail Road to try and check the advances of the Abolitionists down that way and protect Columbus, Miss. where the money and arms manufactories of the Confederate States are. I do not know what we are to do, for I think it is a poor chance for us. I think we shall leave this place before three days are past but this news is contraband and you must keep it. But no matter for it will be known to the world before you get this letter. We will fall back forever it seems.

You need not be surprised if you do not hear from me in two weeks and I don't know when you will hear again but I will write you my darling whenever I have the opportunity. Do not feel badly if you do not get letters from me dearest for you may be sure I will write you whenever it is possible. You know dearest that I love you devotedly and my thoughts turn always to you. I wish you were on this side of the river and I could see you oftener perhaps but perhaps not. The fate of war no one knows but I am now making no calculations on living in the Confederacy even if we gain our Independence. I don't think the government will ever be good for anything at all and I cannot endure the idea of a Reconstruction of the Union on any terms. Consequently let it result as it may we must look us out another home and where dearest do you wish it to be? for I want to consult you. Oh, had we some sweet little isle of our own far out on the dark blue Sea there in the society of each other we could live far from the tumults and noise of the world. But this is the time for stern realities and not for castle building. Oh when will God give us release from all our troubles. I wish the Trustees would act in that matter for I do want to come home now worse than ever and if the Abolitionists should come to Minden I should come home certain. Rats desert a sinking ship and are accounted prudent and I shall desert a country for which I have very little regard. I am sorry I have to acknowledge this but it is lamentably true.

I have not been very well for several days this sore on my arm makes me sick all over but it is healing up and itches terribly. I have sent two scabs from it to you to have Dr. Patillo vaccinate you all. I hope you may get them safely and thereby escape the Small Pox. We have but little fear of it here though it is in all parts of the army. I mailed Mother a long letter this morning. Have heard nothing from William Henry yet am looking anxiously for a letter from him. It is said that Banks is landing a Column at Ponchatoula above New Orleans to fall in our rear and it would not surprise me if our whole army did not go to Vicksburg & stand a siege, they are provisioning it for 8 mos. for a large force.

But my paper is almost covered and I must close. Tell Lou to write me. A heartful of love to you and our left darling and as much as you can spare of it to all the rest. To the God of the Widow and Orphan I commend my darlings. Write often, direct as heretofore to Grenada. I'll get in Jackson if there. Truly your loving husband, Edwin

Thursday 18 Dec. '62

My own dear One:

I sent you a hasty note yesterday by Mail but learning that [John P.] "Cahill" is going home I write again fearing that Mail Communication may be cut off, and I want you to send me some little things.

I want four old knives and forks. Don't care how old or mismatched they may be so they are knives & forks. Also four plates of crockery ware if Cahill can possibly bring. I want also a thick Comfort if you can spare it for I sleep cold some of these freezy nights. If Cahill can bring it, pack Jim McKee's trunk full of things for *"me and Capt. Webb."* I don't care how much butter & Sausage meat you send nor pepper sauce either. If he will bring the trunk you can pack it with whatever you please. Have your Father see Cahill immediately before he promises to bring too much for others. But I hope the Trustees have made that application for me before Cahill gets there and that I may be discharged if so I shall not need anything. I want a saddle blanket if there is an old blanket anywhere on the place also. I shall have to buy me another horse for Jack has about gone up with camp fever, but he may recover yet and I don't want to buy another if I am coming home but I don't make much calculation on coming for I think that Jake Lewis does not want me about Minden and I am afraid Simmons don't either. If I can write home before Cahill leaves and can think of anything else I need I will write for it. I do hope dearest you can send me the trunk. If you can let Mrs. Webb know and you two can fill the trunk with something.

I am not very well, my arm has not got well yet. My love to all every one. All the boys are well. Do write dearest often. Your affectionate & loving husband, E. H. Fay

In camp at Grenada
Dec. 21st, '62

My own dear Wife:

Sam Monzingo has just come from the Office and I hailed him and asked him for my letter, but hardly dared hope he had one, but I was mistaken. He handed me one and I was so glad to hear that you had at last heard from me. You don't know, my dearest, how grieved I was to hear that you got none of my letters as I wrote three from Abbeville and have written you three or four from Camp Rust. Capt. Webb's letters written at the same time as my letters, Mrs. Webb did not get, though Caufield's, Carter's and other letters did go on the same days. I cannot account for it and still hope you may yet get the letters as I wrote you several things of interest that I do not remember to rewrite. I don't know what I wrote you in my letter mailed the 10th but will briefly recapitulate.

I reached Camps on Sat. Morning 22 after leaving you, having stayed overnight at Monroe and Tallula Station but hardly had time in Vicksburg to get my transportation. Van Dorn's Adjt. Gen'l objected to my pass and ordered me to Jackson's HdQrtrs., but I met the Company at Tallahatchie River coming over to act as escort for Gen. Rust of Ark. who is Comdg. the 2d Division 1st Corps, Acting Maj. Gen'l and will in all probability be Maj. Gen'l or ought to be even if not a West Pointer. He is a man of good hard sense and a perfect gentleman, as brave as a Lion.[8] But an order from the Sec. of War allows Maj. Gen'ls only 20 men as Escort and we fear we will have to return to the Battallion. Col. Scott who is Act. Brig. is doing all he can for us and he has great influence in Official Circles. While I was at home the petition to be transferred to Trans. Miss. Dist. was approved by Gen'l Price, forwarded to Van Dorn, approved and forwarded to Gen'l Pemberton and by him disapproved on the ground that we were needed where we were. If we cannot remain as Escort, we intend to apply to the Sec. of War for the transfer if Lt. Col. Chambliss would make the application for us and let us know it and we would send up our approved petition. I have no doubt but it would be granted as the 6th, 3rd and 9th Texas Regts. together with Whitfield's Texas Legion have all been unmounted since our refusal, but we do not think it will do to renew the application to Gen'l Pemberton, so here we are.

I went to see Lt. Watkins yesterday who is 12 miles in the Country sick with Yellow Jaundice and if we had a respectable petition from the citizens of Bossier & Claiborne Parishes we would have a better chance of success. Speaking of petitions, if the patrons of my School would petition me to claim my right to discharge under the Conscription Act, I believe I could get the discharge through right here in the Army. If Mr. McDonald would start it and send it to me I think I could be discharged and commence school in six weeks after my reception of it. Your Father could approach McDonald on the subject as both are interested in the School. Let the Trustees sign it as Trustees and patrons as patrons. If the proper effort was made I know I could be discharged and I would come home at once. Capt. Webb would not sign an application for discharge unless I would

[8] Fay's very high estimate of Rust was not shared by Col. Thomas L. Snead, of Missouri, who wrote after the War: "Rust though a very successful politician was one of the most incompetent of all 'political generals'." *Battles and Leaders,* III, 445.

show him a petition from Citizens of Minden desiring me to ask it. I would then send up to Gen'l Rust the application and Gen'l Rust would sign it I know and here I would come. I would write to Dr. Quarles about it but you dissuaded me in your last letter so I leave the matter now to be brought before the people by who will do it. If you are consulted you can suggest the way a Petition to the Sec. of War, of which I gave Dr. Quarles a draft, would answer all purposes, however, should the petition come to me it should state that the time of my original enlistment was not out until the 4th of April but the necessities of the people were so urgent they were induced to make it earlier.

But no more on this subject for there is every reason to believe the war will close before the 1st of April next but you see the papers. Gov. of Michigan states in his proclamation to the Legislature that if the war is not ended and peace made by the 1st of Jan'y next he will recall all Michigan troops.[9] The Yankees have fallen back to Holly Springs and there is no prospect of a fight here soon. It will be almost entirely a Cavalry war this winter and woe be to us if we have to return to the Cavalry. Our Mess is fairly well now for we have a tent given us by Col. Thos. Scott, but the other boys have hard times tho they erected tents while at Camp Rust but ever since we moved into town they have had a hard time. Bates says you told his wife that the Company had all their clothing burnt. I hope you did not for it was not so. Our Mess had some surplus clothing, and so had some of the others, while some lost nothing, not having sent it to the Cars. Never tell Mrs. Bates or Mrs. Caufield anything and be careful how you tell Mrs. Carter. I hear everything here in Camps.

I'm so glad you got the scab sent in my letter. Hope Dr. Patillo will use it. He ought not to charge you anything as you furnished the matter, and will not I presume. Be sure and tell him to vaccinate Mrs. Webb & Martin as I promised to tell you. There is a good deal of small pox in the army and it is in all the Hospitals, but I don't think there is much fatality. If there is I don't hear it, but of course the Surgeons are very anxious to get matter and I have promised this

[9] The governor of Michigan at this time was Austin Blair, but the report of his issuing a "peace" proclamation to the legislature was erroneous. He strongly supported a vigorous prosecution of the war.

scab when it comes off. I do hope the small pox will not rage for I believe if the Yankees gain nothing this Winter they will give it up in the Spring. The Holydays are almost here and Miss. is not conquered yet. I think trouble is brewing in camps. But my darling my hand is so cramped that I'll finish in the morning.

Monday Morning. I have just finished my breakfast of 30 cts. pork and corn Bread and now I resume my pen, tho I feel little like writing this morning for I walked through the Grenada graveyard and saw so many graves of children that reminded me so forcibly of our buried treasures that tears would come from my eyes. Oh my darling I can never become reconciled to the loss of our eldest born. It almost kills me to think of him. Our affliction is greater than I can bear. But I must banish the thought or I cannot write and this letter must go to you today.

About that Albertson & Douglass matter. I don't recollect. I think you will find a schedule of it in the Hole marked "*Invoices.*" The amount was $1530.00. I remember that. Write me what your Father wants to know for. Tell him not to pay it, for we *may not have it to do yet.* It is not certain. Tell him to get gold if he pays two for one and come here and buy negroes for likely negro men are selling for $150.00 in gold and they can be bought for that. Every one is fleeing from the Yankees and the negroes are running to the Yankees. So your Father can act on his judgment about it. I'm so sorry that you hear so many rumors of small pox for it frightens the people without doing any good. Am glad Thornwell improves so rapidly. Hope he may be spared us many years.

I have been compelled to buy another horse. Have a fine black mare which cost me $250.00. I think of sending Rich home on Jack to get him fat as I have but little use for Rich and I hate to sacrifice Jack and am not allowed to keep two. So you need not be surprised to see him at home before long. I wrote you a day or two ago by [John P.] Cahill for what things I want. As far as woolen socks are concerned I do not think I shall need them as I find cotton ones much warmer. I only need a good coat tho I might use perhaps a pair of pants if I had them. I sent word for my overcoat but I expect I shall need it more after I get home, if I ever do. I hope I will get that petition and if I do I may get home before long. I am sorry for Mrs. Patillo and more so for Mrs. Quarles. Will she never get through. Poor woman, a hard life is hers. Why did you say anything to me about an amusing incident of yours, then not tell me about it. If a thing is not worth telling me for Heaven's sake never mention it again in a letter to me. Always tell me if you think of anything.

The position I was offered on Gen'l Rust's Staff was "Chief of Engineers" and if he had been a full Major General I would have accepted it regardless of Trustees but I learned from Col. Scott that Gen'l Rust had no right to raise my rank and I would only draw an Orderly's pay and I would not take the responsibility. I had rather be under some good Engineer a few months before I assumed the responsibility of Chief. I'll bide my time and perhaps it will all be for the best. I think the Trustees and patrons of the School are due me something for the fact that I gave up so much for them. If they don't act I shall never teach in Minden again. I can live without teaching there, I reckon. I'll try and live through this war and I'll bet I never get into another one.

If paper is scarce in your Camp do as I do and write all over a sheet of paper. I tell you my dear to write me long letters. I do so love your letters and they do me so much good, only they are not half long enough.

I wrote you we were going to fall back from here but all the baggage and troops have been ordered back and it is now the determination to hold this place. We were on the point of moving when I wrote. So I was not at fault but the Commanders changed their notions. The enemy have fallen back to Memphis and Holly Springs and here we stay quiet. I think this war is at its culminating point and is being fought out at the North. God in his wisdom will bring order out of this chaos. I got a letter from William Henry which I will send you. He writes very confidently about being able to repel any attack on Port Hudson. I have not felt very well lately though I keep up all the time. I fear I am taking Yellow Jaundice. If I do I shall try to be sent to a hospital in Selma, Alabama for there is no small pox there. If so, you must come on and spend the winter there. I am so sorry you get low spirited for I think there is happiness in store for us yet.

If this war closes negroes will bear fabulous prices and I want to buy now while they are low. I want your father to turn all his accts. and notes into Cotton or Confederate Bonds as I see that Mr. C. G. Memminger proposes to reduce the interest on the Bonds and Richmond is thronged with European Capitalists purchasing them all up and offering to loan the Government any quantity of money. While Lincoln cannot raise a dollar in Europe. It would not surprise me if he did not evacuate Washington some night and sail for Europe before the 1st of March next. His impeachment is almost certain. Wish I could send you the Memphis Appeal as it contains a great deal of interesting matter, but you get the Whig. I see the Gunboats have gone back up the River from Vicksburg. So I hope our communications will not be cut off for some time.

But now my own darling one write me long letters and write often. I can get them in five days, at least your last letter came in that time. Minden dates of the 7th instant came by the same mail so I think the Monroe Road must be running daily again. Give my love to your Mother and Father and all the children. Tell Lou she must write to me and I'll answer her letters if I have time. Tell Cynthia if she does not have a *young one* or is not in a fair way for one that I intend to whip her almost to death. She shall have children. I hope my dearest you have broken your chills before this and will continue well. Kiss Thornwell a dozen times for his Father, and Mother, know that you have a heart full of love from your affectionate Husband. God bless and preserve my darlings. E. H. Fay

Grenada, Miss. Jan'y 1st, 1863

A happy New Year to you my dearest Wife. I wish this pleasant sunny morning after one of the coldest frosty nights of winter, and with a desire to make you and myself both as happy as possible under existing circumstances of war and pestilence I devote my time and pen to you. My thoughts are yours all the time.

I have just returned late last night from an eight day trip after deserters. Have travelled almost 200 miles and captured and "*scared in*" together nearly thirty deserters from the 15th Miss. Regt. One after running him some 800 yards and repeatedly ordering him to stop, I shot but as I afterwards learned did not hit him but frightened him so that he *besmeared* himself all over and started next morning back for camp. He had repeatedly bragged that he would never go back to the army and that no Cavalry could catch him. I visited while absent a factory village somewhat resembling Prattville named Bankston.[10] They run a Cotton Factory of some 1000 spindles and also a wool Factory, use some 300 or more bales of cotton a year and are making jeans and plain cloth (linseys), I believe they call it, for the Govt. I could have got a bunch or two of Factory thread as a special favor if I had had any way to bring it or send it home. I also engaged a Barrell of Irish Potatoes if I can find any way to send them back.

I suppose from what you write I shall not be petitioned to come back and take the school and if I am not I assure you that I shall never teach in Minden again. I have upheld Gen'l Simmons against many attacks, but now believing him to be my enemy I shall let him go. He is not the man I bargained for. I like Mrs. Simmons and shall always love her for her kindness to our darling "Dody," but as for him we are *enemies forever.*

You know not how much I rejoiced to get your loving *wifely* letter, but my darling, the writing was most miserable, by far the worst I ever *saw from your pen.* You must certainly get a new pen. I was so sorry that it had been gotten from the Office during my absence and the *direction* seen by other eyes than my own. My love for you can hide all defects even spelling (two Whigs) *too* Whigs. Don't think me too critical for it is my excessive love for my wife which makes me mention trifles, but when she is writing to her husband she should remember to appear better in his eyes if writing for all the world. But I am criticizing yours and my own looks as if a spider had

[10] Prattville was a pioneer manufacturing center of Alabama. It was named for Daniel Pratt, a New Hampshire native who migrated to Georgia in 1821 and to Alabama in 1833. In the period 1840–1860 he established various industries in Prattville, including a grist mill, a lumber mill, a gin plant, a cotton mill, a foundry, a woolen mill, a carriage factory, a tin shop, and a merchandising establishment. In 1858 his Prattville property was capitalized at more than a half million dollars. See Allen Johnson and Dumas Malone, eds., *Dictionary of American Biography* (22 vols., New York, 1928), XV, 170. To be cited hereafter as *DAB.*

crawled in ink and over my paper rather than my pen but I have been riding 8 days and my "vaccined" arm is inflamed and swolen so that I can hardly write at all. Besides I have no conveniences and am writing on my knee the way most of my letters have been written. My thoughts are awfully confused and I never felt so little like writing in my life. I can only think how much I love you and if I wrote the burden of my thoughts it would be like some bank bills you have seen with only the word *love* written in microscopic characters all over the sheet. But I know you have confidence in my love dearest and assurances could not strengthen it. You have my heart and feel *now* that you have so I will try and cover this sheet with something "new."

Of our late great successes I presume you are already partially apprized. Van Dorn captured Holly Springs and paroled 1861 prisoners and destroyed fully $5,000,000 worth of Quartermasters' Company Stores, Cars, Engines, etc.[11] He went as far as Bolivar, Tenn. and has forced Grant and his army to fall back to Gd. Junction. Our glorious victory at Fredericksburg and the one we are now gaining at Nashville, as Bragg we hear is driving Rosecranz into the River at that "place," having cut off all his supplies and forced him to fight. At Vicksburg too we have driven back the Ruthless invader in an attempt to storm our Batteries, and captured 400 of them & 5 stands of colors. I am anxiously expecting the evening mail to bring us further particulars.

I have just finished my dinner of poor beef and pure corn bread, it being our only rations but we seem to thrive under it as the boys look fatter and healthier than ever before. *It is hard on* me however for I don't like cornbread anyhow. I got some biscuit one night while I was out, but they savored too strongly of *rats in the wheat* to be palatable

[11] Van Dorn's spectacular and destructive raid on Grant's base at Holly Springs, December 20, 1862, compelled Grant to abandon his projected campaign against Vicksburg from the northeast. See *Battles and Leaders,* III, 475. Lee won a decisive victory over Burnside at Fredericksburg on December 13, 1862, and the Confederates at Vicksburg successfully repelled an attack led by Sherman on Chickasaw Bayou, December 28–29. But Bragg failed to follow up an initial advantage gained at Murfreesboro on December 31 and three days later, after a bloody and futile assault, yielded the field to Rosecrans.

to me. I met at the Factory some acquaintances of Jno. C. Blackmon et freres, also of Lang & Felix Lewis. The agent, Mr. Hallam, I found a very pleasant and affable man. I also stayed one night at Mrs. Doffin's whose husband was in Bragg's army. I found her a graduate of the Judson Institute, Marion, Ala. Quite intelligent, a very good performer on the Piano, married two months after graduation in /53, your year I believe. I spoke to her of you and she said she wished she knew you. Richard Ratcliffe was with me. I had 7 men all the trip but that night he alone was along. I could tell you a great many amusing incidents of the trip if I could see you but they don't read well on paper so I will defer them till I see you, which from all the signs of the times I hope will not be long, as the N.Y. Herald and Greely's Tribune are now clamorous for peace on *any terms* and I believe Old Lincoln's Abolition Congress will be anxious before long to recognize the Confederacy for the purpose of defeating and provoking the Democrats. I believe it will be done before March 4th if they are signally repulsed at Vicksburg & Port Hudson as I have no doubt they will be and then we can all come home and our happiness will be as complete as it can now be on earth.

I do hope you can have our graveyard paled in as you desire, but if you cannot and the war should end as I believe, I intend to surround it with an iron railing that will endure when we are laid by their side if such be our lot. Oh, darling how I wish I could come to you. I shall send this via Rodney as the Yankees have the Vicksburg, Shreveport and Texas Railroad. You speak dearest of not hearing from me often. I assure you I have written you quite as often as you have me. I cannot imagine why you have not rec'd the letters from Abbeville. I expect they are lost. I have written every week and sometimes twice except this last, it has now been 9 days. Do not blame your husband dearest but trust *his love*. It will never fail you. Some ladies are close here now who have come 70 miles to see their husbands and *they* left Vicksburg 3 days ago. It is a sad disappointment for them I know. I rejoice it is not you, tho I would give a great deal if you were on this side the river now. I could get sick and go to see you. I expect we will stay here in Grenada this winter and if you were only here you could board in town and I stay with you. But all is for the best I reckon. I got a letter from Father and Mother yesterday will send you Father's to read. You must go and see our parents whenever you can cross at Vicksburg. The road is open through to Selma now.

The night you were writing (19) I was lying quietly in my tent asleep, I reckon, for we go to bed early, dreaming of you and also the war. I wrote you I had bought a fine mare, $250, and intended to send Rich home on Jack. I now think it is not best for I fear she is with foal and if so I'll send her home to raise from. If the war closes I would not take 300 for her as stock will be scarce in La. and if we go to Texas I will want half a dozen of the same kind. Dearest Mother I asked you several questions in some of my letters that you have not answered. Some in regard to your *health*. I hope you will write me freely. Will Fay has lost his little girl, you remember her when we were there with our eldest born. She was about his age. She died in November and his youngest was sick also. Others suffer too but I don't believe they loved their child as we do ours but perhaps they do. I'll send you Mother's letter too and you can see all about it.

But I must close this for the mail as I wish it to go off in the morning so that you may get it as early as possible. Tell Lou to write me and give me all the news. Tell Martha Moseley I saw her brother a few days ago. All are well in their Company I believe at present. Love to Mother Shields and tell her for me I hope she has got *over fretting* and particularly not to board *Henderson,* the Methodist preacher. I know him better than any of you. He is no preacher and not much of a man. If he boards there I want you to move home when I come certainly. If your Mother wants to enjoy preaching, tell her not to board the preacher. (I don't like him at all) but this between me and you. The Vaccine matter was taken from my own *arm*. I am glad it has taken so well. Kiss our darling child for his father and a hundred kisses for yourself, my darling. Love to all. I am with my own loved one in my dreams constantly. May the God of the widow and fatherless protect my defenseless family. Truly your husband. Ed. H. Fay

Grenada Miss Dec [Jan.] 4/63

My own darling Wife:

I wrote you a letter three days ago and sent it to Jackson to be mailed via Rodney hoping that it could find its way across to you bearing its missives of love, but as I have an opportunity of sending tomorrow (Monday) morning I will write again hoping that should the mail fail at least you will hear from me consequently I have seated myself this beautiful sunshiny morning (Sunday) to try and fill out a sheet to my noblest dearest and best of wives. I wrote you New Years day as the fittest offering I could make you my dearest and had intended making you a Christmas gift of the same kind but was unexpectedly called off to go after deserters the day before and was gone eight days during which time I found no opportunity at all of writing you but I devoted the first day of my return to you. If you are fortunate enough to get it you will find it dull and quite uninteresting as I never felt so little like writing in my life. I felt very much like talking to you and I could talk all day this morning too.

You know not how much I want to see you this first Sabbath of the New Year. My heart is full to overflowing and I find no sympathy here in camp. I find none that can even temporarily fill your place. I could live it seems to me in the midst of a desert with you and be perfectly happy, without you a palace is miserable. On my return from the trip spoken of above I was rejoiced to find your letter of Dec. 19th and also found one from Mother and Father, both of which I enclosed to you in mine of the 1st. I do hope you will get them for I want you to see Father's letter. He speaks so affectionately of you and now that communication is partially even interrupted I wish more than ever you were on this side of the River. But wishes avail little in these times of war.

Night before last it commenced raining about 8 P.M. and continued without interruption till 10 P.M. last night. Our tent was some protection the first night but the rain drove in at the door and flooded the straw on which we were lying and when I waked I was lying in a puddle of water. There was no help for it so I turned over and went to sleep again. Last night I slept on a bedstead I cobbled up yesterday but my blankets were wet, but I slept soundly. Dreamed of being with you at Father's. This morning I am drying my blankets in the bright sunshine. You would think it hard to sleep in wet bedclothes but it is not so bad after all. I am so glad my darling that you are vaccinated and that it has taken on our dear little Thornwell. The matter came from my own arm and it is by no means well now. I vaccinated a great many while I was out after deserters.

I am glad you got the latest advices once, for you have had few enough from me though I have *written regularly*. As far as the woolen socks are concerned I shall not need them but the undershirts I will and if this war closes as I believe it will you can always knit them for me. It will be good work for odd times. As to hiring Laura. I wrote you before. If you want her, *hire her by all means* but I should not pay much for her if I was there, as her clothing is worth her wages during these times. I wrote you to tell Mother Shields by all means not to board Mr. Henderson. I know him and don't like him much either. You were right in believing him to be not much of a preacher. But you will get that letter I hope. I sent you a letter or two by Cahill which I hope you have received before this. I wrote what things I needed and thought you could send them all in Jim McKee's trunk. I fear now that you cannot send them. If you can I want a comfort, but know you cannot send it so no matter. Mother says she will send me one if she can find an opportunity.

I hope you have got all the good news that we have, how Bragg has completely demolished Rosecranz near Murfreesboro and Morgan and Forrest between him and Nashville with 15,000 Cavalry. We have completely defeated them also at Vicksburg and presume, yes feel very confident that they will find nothing but destruction at Port Hudson. I believe now that in desperation the Abolition govt. itself will recognize the Confederacy before the 1st of March for the purpose of thwarting the Democrats. Oh that we might have a speedy peace. I am getting worse tired of the war than ever as it approaches its close. I fear a six months armistice and we be kept in Camps and drilled all the time. I want to come to my wife and child.

You must be looking out for something for me to do when I return for I am determined not to teach in Minden again if I can help it, but I must do something for a living, for I do not expect we will have anything left when this war is over and I must do something for the support of those I love. This may all be premature though, my love. I expect if I do not go to Texas to stock farming I shall go back and take care of my Father & Mother for they are old & some of their children must do it and it seems to devolve on me. Father is most 70 years old and Mother says is failing fast. I hope his life will yet be prolonged many years.

I wish you would fill your letters fuller of writing. If paper is scarce you can write as I do between the lines. Do write me long, long letters. Tell me everything that happens about home. I do not expect you to write it all in one night, but you can write a little every day and by that time I shall have full letters. It is a task for me to write in Camps for we have but little news and the incidents and details of Camp life quite monotonous. Occasionally a *woman* passes camp and it is a three days wonder. But women only serve to remind me of you and our separation and I don't care to see them. I do not have the *bad thoughts* about them that some do. The only woman I care to see is you my *loved one*. I hope you have broken those chills and that they have not returned on you again. Write me all about your *health*. There is no danger of your letters being seen as I burn them almost always after they are reread.

Tell Lou I shall expect a long letter from her, also tell Mary I hope she is growing more ladylike and losing some of her rough ways. Ella I hope is improving fast in her studies. She must learn now a great deal as she too will soon be grown to the station of a young lady. My kindest regards to your Mother and Father. Mail me letters my dearest, if you have opportunity of private conveyance do not neglect it. But my dearest I still hope I may be allowed to come to you again. If an armistice should take place I shall apply at once for a discharge under Conscription Act. Many kisses to you my own darling and a goodly lot for our *only remaining child*. My heart still bleeds my dearest and I cannot feel reconciled. May God bless you my best loved one and preserve you in health and restore me again to you.

Your husband, Ed.

Camp in Grenada Jan'y 5/63

My own dear Sallie:

Today a whole package of letters came through and I had the *mournful satisfaction* of learning through the courtesy of Lieut. Carter who got two letters from his wife that you were making me a coat. So far so good but no letters came for me although latest dates from Minden in camp are the 26th of Dec. I will not complain but when I saw the bunch had no yellow Envelope in it I felt sure there was no joy for me in that package. I judge from the haste those letters have made that the Yankees have abandoned Vicksburg for they must have come through that way, nevertheless I shall send this to you by hand but who by I do not know. I am only aware of the opportunity and I don't want my darling to experience the feelings I had this evening, notwithstanding. I sent you a letter this morning. I write this too to go tomorrow on a sheet of paper that Mother enclosed to me to write her on.

I have no news to tell you but the same story of my love for you and remembering my experience with Miss Abby Rudulph I am almost afraid that the reiteration of it may pall on your appetite. It has always been a philosophical question in my mind if even one called by the beloved and enduring name of wife could not be loved too much for one's happiness that is if the lover permitted his wife to know it. Whether love was not in one point of view like sweetmeats and when taken to satiety palls on the appetite? Am I right? I imagine I hear you reply, Yankee like, by asking another question, viz. Do you believe I could be loved too much. I'll answer your question should I ever live to return to you. If I love you too much you may bestow the excess on our darling little Thornwell. I know it will not hurt him yet awhile. But badinage aside I would give all my old clothes to see you this evening.

Would you like to know what I have been doing today. Yes! Well then I have been making out a written report of our trip after deserters, Capt. Webb having got in last night. Since then John Lesueur and I have been playing "whist" with Lieut. Watkins and his partner and beating them most unmercifully. As Escort we have but little to do and we have to amuse ourselves as best we can, playing ball, cards, checkers, etc. Today is an unusually dull day as we get no daily paper, they not being printed on Sunday at Jackson.

I intend sending you two latest Memphis Appeals tho there is not much news and you will probably get later news from Vicksburg. As to our future, I believe that the Abolitionists in their mad phrensy to spite the democrats will when they find the sceptre departing from them acknowledge the Confederacy and since I advanced the opinion I find some of our leading officers incline to it. Oh that it may be so and I be returned to the bosom of my little family is my daily prayer. Have you gone up to see Mrs. Webb yet. If not do so by all means. If Banks Lesueur sends for a couple of our guinea stock of pigs tell your father to let him have them for I have swapped a couple for some of his large stock with John Lesueur. My dear I must tell you a good joke on myself. I have scratched my vaccine sore and then scratched my "sitting down place" and am vaccinated on both sides so I can with difficulty sit down at all. Don't say anything about it to any body. Why did you torture me in one of your letters about something good that happened in connexion with Mrs. Murrell. Be sure to tell me all about it and about everything I have asked in my other letters. Write me as often as you can find time and good long letters too. Take two or 3 days for it.

But I must close as we are camped right on side of Rail Road and the cars make so much fuss that I can hardly write. I am going to make out the pay rolls tomorrow and hope we will get some money soon. I shall send Rich home with my horse. What think you about it. Does your Father want him. Where is Mr. Wimberly now, I expect he is a Conscript now. I hope Mrs Wimberly will get well again. Perhaps you had better not sell our house tho I leave that with you entirely. I hope you will have our cattle got up from Jim Tookes if possible and try and take care of what we have got. Learn them and look often at them it will only be good exercise but you will soon take an interest in it. Let Thornwell write "letter papa" as much as he pleases. Tell Mrs. Johnson I saw her brother today. He is fatter than ever in his life he says—Love to all and a kiss all round. Two to Thornwell and a hundred for yourself my darling. Yours truly, Ed H. Fay

I heard the other day from your relatives in Columbus, Miss. All the men folks are in the army here somewhere but I don't know their names. Can you tell me. If so I may find them. Good Bye. To our God I commend you, *Faithfully* yours Fay.

Grenada, Miss. Jany. 13th, 1863

My own dear Wife:

Again the time for writing you has come round and as I learn from Col. Sandidge's eldest son, 1st Lt. in the "Bossier Cavalry"[12] that the Col. will be up on this evening's train and after spending one day, is going across the River, I seat myself to write you a letter. I do this with very little spirit I assure you for there has been two mails from the Trans Mississippi Dept. and some members of the Company have got letters of Jany 1st while my latest dates from you are Dec. 19th. I do not attribute this to want of affection on your part but I do to fear that your letters would not reach me since the interruption of communication. While if you had written I would have got my letters when the others did. I do not complain. I trust you my best beloved implicitly—

I feel right anxious about you as I hear nothing from you though I did hear through Lt. Carter's letter that you were making me a coat. If the war does not end soon, I shall need it for my old one is most gone though I fix it up when it gets ragged and it does tolerably well. We are going to get a uniform for the Company if nothing happens as the Govt. will allow us nothing for clothing but requires us to draw it from the Quartermaster Dept. which of course contains little or nothing. Soldiers less patriotic than those of the Confederacy would rebel against any Government that treated them as wretchedly as our Soldiers are treated. Nothing but poor Beef and what meal can be sifted out of hominy and a little salt. Sugar, Molasses, Flour, Coffee, Vinegar all gone, nothing left but beef and Bread. I am sorry that I did not bring those good things that they wished to send, for now I wish I had some similar bonbons—

I hope you got my letter by Cahill and will send me the things sent for though the Comfort I shall not need as John Lesueur has bought

[12] This was Lt. George M. Sandidge, Company C, 6th Louisiana Cavalry.

a woven worsted quilt and that makes us cover enough at present and warmer weather will come with the spring. The cars are coming I must get a paper.

I got the paper for 25 cts. (the usual price) but not much news in it, would send it to you if there was anything good in it, but as there is not will not do it. All the indications are of a speedy settlement of our national troubles. For my own part I would not be at all surprised if the Abolition congress in the impotence of their rage did not as a climax of their foolish doings recognize the independence of the Confederacy just to spite the Democrats. I feel satisfied they will do this if they think there is the most distant hope of a reconstruction—

I believe I have not told you that the whole company had gone out after deserters who have organized themselves into a band and defied the Confederate and state authorities to arrest them. I would have gone but have three or four bad sores broken out on my behind or "down sitter" so I can with only the greatest difficulty sit down on anything much less on a saddle. They are vaccine sores and were made by my scratching my arm at night and then scratching there. The matter was transferred in that manner. So you see I am quite thoroughly vaccinated. The small pox still prevails to a limited extent in some parts of this army but the greatest care is taken and the best sanitary regulations adopted and I do not think it will prevail to any great extent though there are cases in the Hospitals at Jackson & Canton. The sores I spoke of look just like the small pox and if I had been exposed to it I should think it the Varioloid, that is if I did not know whence they originated.

Lieut. Carter and I are again left in charge of the Camp four or five men only being retained as guard. We are having a good time even if David, alias "lean hungry" does write back to his "ducky dear" that Carter & Fay don't get along well. He wrote his wife that Carter's Coat was the laughing stock of the whole company which was as false as his deceitful tongue. Everyone wanted to buy it, Capt. Webb offered him $50 and a good overcoat for it. So much for such a story.

It is raining and has been for almost all the time since last night at dark but it has been a very warm rain so far but the wind is now whipping around to the North and I look for it to be very cold indeed.

We have had a great deal of cold weather and for the last month a great deal of rainy weather. The roads are horrid and our times would be too, for we have no tents yet except ours which Col. Scott gave us. There is an old house with a stove in which the rest of the boys stay and keep quite comfortable. The negroes of our mess have a fly which they picked up on the retreat and it does them tolerably well. But it is awful weather on our horses, having to stand tied up to a tree all the time. It would not be so bad on them if they were in a lot where they could run about. They have to stand and take it. A perfect Norther has set in and the rain comes driving in the tent but still we manage by shifting to keep dry, yet this life though it has some pleasures is by no means as pleasant as if I were at home with you my loved one.

But I hope and pray that the time may speedily come when I can fold you to my breast and feel that I am not again to be separated from you till death do us part. We will be *comparatively* happy then my dearest, wont we? But never will we be as happy as when our darling Will Ed was alive. No child we may ever have can ever fill his place even should we ever have any more children which I don't *now believe will ever be the case.* Do you?

But I fear I shall fill this letter and not tell you why I am writing it. I bought you some papers of needles which I will send in this letter. I send two papers of No. 1 "Sharps" and several papers of smaller sizes. Rich sends some for "Mary." You may let her have one dozen of the larger size or a whole paper if you wish, tho' a dozen will do her if you need any more. The other papers I will mark so you will know them. I paid one dollar per paper for the large size and 50 cts. pr. paper for the others. If you want any little things that I can send in letters write me and I will try and send them. If you will write me what things you need I may have opportunities of sending by hand. I don't know what may turn up.

Well the Cars have again come in and I have got a paper which I will send you as Col. Sandidge goes down in the morning having come up on the evening train. All reports from the north go to show that a spirit of discontent is arising among them such as they have never exhibited before. They cry peace, peace and it is reported that a *lady* has come through as an envoy from the Govs. of Ill., Ind., Ohio & Iowa proposing an alliance with the Confederate States, but you can see from the paper I send you that the feeling is growing there. The money market is a pretty sure index of events and Gold in N.Y. has gone up to 136 and the "Herald" says that in 2 weeks gold will be as high as 160, but you will see it in the papers. I will quit speculating on the war.

If you have an opportunity of sending me you had better send me a pair of drawers as those I drew from the Government would not fit any body in the world. I have worn them once and can do so again on a pinch. My two pairs of Lowells do very well and are by no means worn out. Will last me for a long time, but for a change I need another pair. You need not feel uneasy about my clothing for if I need anything at any time very badly I will send Rich home after it. I can do it at any time, and if I do not get some letters soon I shall send him home after them.

It is now Wednesday Jany. 14th and I have had nothing from you since the 19th Dec. I always take none for good news and consequently do not feel very uneasy about you but I hate to get out of the habit of receiving letters for they are certainly a great source of enjoyment to me, but it is getting so dark I cannot see so must close. I'll light a candle after supper, a Confederate candle which we made in our mess, the best tallow candles I ever saw. It is still raining hard and our camp ground is all afloat.

I have eaten supper and seated myself again. The rain continues and it is almost such a night as the last Sunday night I spent with you. The River at this point is very high and rising faster. At the depot this evening I met Gen'l Price and his daughter, who stays with him most of the time. She is a beautiful blonde, I do not mean that she is very pretty but has very fair skin and is almost as fat as Penny George. I saw also a very pretty young lady, accompanied by a red headed Lieut., her Brother I judge from the family resemblance. There are quite a number of fine looking ladies in Grenada, but there is only one lady that I care to see and she is in La. far, far from me. I am but a soldier and I by no means seek the acquaintance of Ladies. I met one I believe I wrote you about while after deserters—an educated intelligent woman. Such I should be pleased to meet often, but simpering Misses were always my detestation.

I wrote Mother a long letter the other day and am looking soon for a letter from her. I hope you got the one I wrote you inclosing hers and Father's as they were quite interesting. I have received only one letter from William Henry and am looking daily for another. Others can get letters from all directions but me. My luck seems to be bad in that line. If I don't hear from you tomorrow I shall be *hugely* disappointed. You must learn when Col. Sandidge returns and send letters by him as the Mails evidently don't bring your letters. The thought has just flashed across my brain. What if you should be dead? and renders me just now most miserable, but you know I never borrow trouble and so shall dismiss this.

Oh, my darling! what would I not give to be with you tonight. I wonder what you would give. I expect you are knitting by the fire or perhaps reading before going upstairs. Do you find anything to read nowadays. I do not and the only way of passing off time I have is playing "whist." You know that is a game I am very fond of. If I had a set of Chess then I would play chess a great part of my time as it would be very improving to the mind. Whist strengthens the memory only, while chess improves all the mental processes to a greater or less degree. I have read over what I have written and it is decidedly the most ungrammatical, uninteresting and almost nonsensical letter I ever wrote. The fact is my tent has been filled with the boys chattering away so I could not write at all. If you will forgive me for this letter I will promise not to inflict another such an one on you. It seems to me as if it consisted of nothing but "its" and "buts" though I believe there is one "b[ehin]d" in it.

I must close and go to bed for I am tired, sick, homesick, weary and worn out doing nothing. Give much love to your Father & Mother from me and to all the children. Lou must write me for she can tell me lots of news as she goes to school, the center of village news always. I will add a kiss for you and Thornwell in the morning if nothing happens. Goodnight.

I found my silver spoon the other day, which I had not seen since June last. Aren't you glad. It is sleeting now as hard as you ever saw it and the mud knee deep. Good Bye. The Cars are getting ready. Ed.

The most awful night I ever witnessed last night. Our tent blew over. I had to go out in the storm to stake it down.

Grenada Sunday Morning
before Sunrise 18 Jany 1863

Well I have just got up and am sitting by the fire to write you a short note, having learned after going to bed last night that Parson Clampit was going across the River and altho I wrote you *Tuesday* (and not Teusday as you spelt it) by Col. J. M. Sandidge still I will write just a note to let you know that I never neglect an opportunity of sending you a note whenever it is possible. Capt. Winfrey Scott came across the River the other day and mailed letters at Vicksburg but none came for me. It is cold enough this morning to freeze the hair off a cast Iron dog & my ink is ice and my fingers here in the open are not far short of it.

The morning Col. Sandidge started I was taken very sick vomiting and running off at the bowels. I went to a house near by and went to bed, ate nothing all day and got up the next evening. Yesterday morn I came back to camp and am getting on smoothly now, feel very well indeed. The day I wrote it sleeted and snowed all day and the snow is not all off the ground yet. We are camped now in town and of course can get no wood but what we haul two miles and our wagons are kept going most of the time after corn & fodder and we almost freeze. I slept all night very comfortably doubling blankets with News Murphy as John Lesueur has gone with the Capt. after deserters.

This is Sunday & I am going to the Presbyterian Church if I can get in. It is usually filled to overflowing. The second day of my sickness I got two letters from you dated 25th mailed 30th Dec. & 31st mailed Jany 1st. There are letters from Comi Bluff as late as Jany 5th and I do hope I may get one from you by this evening's mail. We are believing more and more strongly every day that we will have peace by the first of March. Col. [Thomas M.] Scott told the 12th La. that they were now in their last camp. A lady, wife of Ex-Gov. of Ill. came through last Monday from Memphis with despatches from Ohio, Ill.,

Indiana & Iowa that if the navigation of the Miss. was guaranteed to them they would withdraw from Lincoln's dynasty and form an alliance offensive & defensive with the Confederate States. This is a reliable fact. Gen. Price accompanied her to Gen'l Johnston at Jackson and she has gone on to Richmond. Col. Sandidge thinks the whole thing is almost over and I believe as I have frequently written you before.

I wish I could write you some interesting news but have had no papers for two days. I take a daily paper at 12½ cents pr. day. I understood yesterday that we were not going to be paid off till March as they believed they could disband us at that time. This is rumor and I do not vouch for it. We have had no pay since Sept. 1st and the boys are needing money. Don't be in haste about Selling our house & lot. We can get three thousand dollars as easy as not for it. I do not intend to live in Minden long after my return so don't be uneasy, but you will not want to leave will you? Count the cost before you consent. Love to all, the cars are whistling now and I must close. Good Bye. truly your loving husband, Ed.

8

"My Almost Broken Heart"

Grenada, Miss. Jany 24, 1863

My own darling wife:

The rain is falling in torrents and as I have no other place I have withdrawn into the inmost recesses of our Sibley tent (a cone of cloth some 20 ft. in diameter at base) and after sundry manipulations around my valise I have exhumed from its very bottom a ¼ of a quire of this wide ruled blue foolscap. I have often wondered why letter paper of a certain size was so called and having never found a reasonable solution of the fact have concluded it was because (before the invention of the copy book) it was used for the pot hooks and hangers of new beginners in the art of quill driving. This solution has at least one recommendation, simplicity, and the same cannot be said of military matters with which I have been far more conversant than the initiatory efforts of tyro's. But *seriously* as you say, about the male school, I have wasted a large surface of paper that I sincerely wish was covered with more interesting matter on your account, yet, "a little nonsense now and then is relished by the best of (w*o*)-*men*" (yourself of course).

I received your letter of the 8th inst. Wednesday while yours of the 1st inst. by Parson Scott did not reach me till last evening's train. You can only imagine, my dearest one what pleasure your letters give me. You have no standard of comparison for you are at home among friends and my letters are not near as necessary to your comfort as are yours to mine. You see the point I wish to make so I need not amplify. Well! to take your questions *seriatim*.

I think you would undertake a very large job if you should undertake the male school (in one of your letters you spelled it mail), not that I doubt your capability of teaching any boys around Minden, but there are a great many considerations connected with it. Of course you would teach in the Academy. How would you climb the fence twice or three times a day or would you call to your aid those accomplishments you learned when extremely small and "you used to ride the fences and hurrah for Henry Clay & all the Whigs." What would you do for fires and who would go to and from school with you. Where would you go when you *wanted to go out?*[1] How would you keep your school house cleaned out, or in fact manage the bad boys, tho I have but little fears of the latter. I ask you these questions, if you can answer them satisfactorily to yourself, I have not the slightest objections that you should try it, but remember that the trial must not[?] be made for a whole session and not a shorter time. The proposal in your last letter would seem at first glance to be the better one tho I presume there would not be so much money in it. If the Trustees of the Academy would give you a salary of say 800 a year and you obligate yourself not to keep in school an insolent or disobedient boy perhaps the first would be the better plan. But is it necessary for my own loved wife to descend to the unthankful occupation of teaching? and if you commence can you hold out? will not your new born energy fail? All these are questions which arise in my own mind and I use them only as suggestions. I admire your resolution to do something and indeed regard you, my dearest, as a helpmeet indeed. You might have known at once what my decision in the matter would be. Suit yourself dearest in my absence always and you will best suit me. I have this much confidence in your judgment and reasoning powers. If you wish to teach it meets my approbation and if you wish to spin it does also. But you can do both and you need some active exercise to make you eat hearty and grow fat for I hope to find you fatter than the last time I met you.

I regret very much to find your Father has sold his house and lot and *our* Mill for so small a sum as $6000. I would not have sold the Engine and Mills for that price alone. The Engine would bring four

[1] That is, go to toilet. Rural folk of earlier times, dependent as they were on outside sanitary facilities, when required to meet a call of nature commonly said that they had "to go out." A boys' academy normally would have no toilet facilities for women.

thousand dollars in these flush times by itself and my interest in it I do not like to have sacrificed. I am unwilling to ratify the Mill part of the trade and if Chaffe buys it, *I shall put him to trouble about it.* I find that even when peace is made an exceedingly high tariff will be placed upon all foreign productions, especially on manufactured products and Machinery will bear a very high price. To replace the Mills and Engine would cost near $4000 after the War, and I don't *know what* your Father is to do for Bread and biscuits till its close. I thought at first that the sale included my place also but as it does not I have nothing to say except about the Engine & Mills. Tell your Father that every man who lives anywhere near laments it and say they cannot stand to have Chaffe control the Flour Market of the country. I almost believe the men in this company would subscribe $6000 rather than have Chaffe own that Mill. I do not know how much your Father values his house and land but I do know he values the whole *at less than half* in mine and in the opinion of all this company who have known anything of it—I do not consent to sell my share as I now understand it and want you to tell your Father so. I shall certainly sue Chaffe for the recovery of my interest when I come home. If the war closes as I do most sincerely believe I will be willing to sell out and go to a stock farm if he wishes but I don't think it [good] policy to sell the Mill during the War as flour will be scarce and corn too.

I suppose you get papers from Vicksburg and if you do you see the dissatisfaction of the western troops in the Yankee army. I can but feel that this war is bound to close by the first of March. The news from Europe is that the Question of Mediation is one of days not even of months and that early in February the Emperor Napoleon will interfere in this struggle. John Van Buren proposes calling a Convention and so amending the Constitution of the U.S. as to acknowledge in plain, unmistakable terms the right of separate State Secession, this right not to be exercised before 1869 or '73 allowing two or three more Presidential terms. This would give the North their Reconstruction and the South their Secession, but he ignores the fact that it takes two to make a bargain. I regard our Independence as certain and not far off—

I would not be surprised if our Company was sent across the Miss.

River and if it is I would give all my old shoes for I have outwitted Gen'l Pemberton, if we are ordered across. Let no intimation be given of this to any one as it is not known even by the company. Gen'l Rust goes to Richmond and has promised to work it for us. He recommends the communication and says on the back of it that it is the best Company in the Confederate service. We already have more influence at Hd Quarters than any Regt. in Service I know of. But this does not bring me home by any means tho I feel that I shall not be separated from you again as long as I have been. If you can get a situation in the College I shall be very glad to take the Male school. I hardly know what I shall do for a living after it is over unless I get a position as Engineer on Vicksburg, Shreveport and Texas Railroad. I intend to try and do that if possible or on some other R.R. or go on to a stock farm or back again to the hated employment of teaching. If I could see you and consult with you, I could determine on something.

One thing I wish you to do is to take a deed for that land of ours and I want the line, the extension of Wade's line close down by the Shop to the branch and down the section line on the East to the branch. *Be sure to have your Father make out the Deed,* continuing *the line between Wade & our place down to the Branch* instead of down that hollow between the shop and our house. Have this attended to at once before your father makes a deed to Chaffe. You can have it made in your own name if you prefer. You can sell our house and lot, too, if you wish for not less than $3000, for it will bring that. If you all move over there, have a paling put up around it if you think it is best. It will help sell it, and have the yard cleaned up and put in order. I have not written half I want to and must get another sheet of thin paper. You wont object.

(You will of course read all of the first sheet upside down before turning to this one)

I don't wonder that your Mother objects to selling out her home and I can't imagine why your Father took such a notion. I thought he was afraid of Confederate paper and did not know what to do with what he had. I wish I could collect my money and buy a negro girl. Tell your Father to take Spencer's money and buy a negro girl for a nurse if possible. Most of the Bills are the Hoyer & Ludwig plates and if they are not spent soon will be worthless to Spencer as all of that issue are called in. I would be doing Spencer a kindness and myself too. I had much rather pay $800 for a little girl now than to pay 40 a year for Laura. Forty dollars is the interest on $500 and that would almost buy such a negro as Laura. If you can buy two likely negro girls with Spencer's money, do it by all means. I can make it good to him when he wants it. Buy the negroes at once if possible for they are going to be worth 2 & 3000 a piece when this war is over. Besides we ought to make some provision for our child if he should live. These negro girls in all probability would increase before many years.

Now while in this connection tell Cynthia that if she does not begin to show some signs that way when I come home that I'll whip her most to death or sell her to the meanest man I can find on Red River. Be sure you tell her so for I am not going to be fooled with by her any longer. I bought her to breed and I know no good reason why she should not do it and she shall or I won't own her long. Don't raise the objections I fear you will but be governed by me in this thing, for as Phoebe says "niggers will be niggers." You know she is not virtuous and she adds to it now that other thing you regard as sinful. I have no objection to her having a husband but she has got to have children. If she was a virtuous negro I would never say a word my dear you know.

We have decided to purchase a Uniform for the Company with the company fund and if the papers go through, Ben Neal will start to Atlanta in a day or two. I shall write to Mother to send me some good things by him on his return. I shall have me a very fine coat made, except the chevrons on the sleeves & bars on the collar, a Captain's coat. I need a nice coat and military will be all the go when the war is over. It will cost $80 or $100 but the company voted to have a uniform and I am not going to have a *jacket* and a pair of breeches, would not wear it no how, so am going to have a uniform coat like the officers, tho not one. I may get a Staff appointment. Since I last wrote you Gen'l Rust has been sent back to his brigade, or rather his Division has been converted into a brigade. I think he goes to Richmond to try and get the appointment of Maj. Gen'l. If he does I will accept a position on his staff if he offers it to me and I want a uniform to suit. I shall not wear it in the company.

I made out the Pay Roll and we got our money up to Jany 1st. I received $128.00, 4 months pay for self and horse but paid it out again in 10 minutes. I got (& all the Company) our pay in $5 bills. I paid Capt. Webb $250 for my mare. Have found a name for her "La Lis" how do you like it? It is a pretty name for a girl. Don't you think so? I find considerable fault that you never answer my letters. You write but don't reply to my letters. I sometimes ask questions and you never heed them. The consequence is I don't know what letters you have received and what ones you have not.

Last night I got your letter of Sep. 21st directed to Tupelo. You spoke of our darling's death and I had a hearty cry. I thought I had steeled my feelings against giving away anymore, but I can never think of our noble boy's death without my eyes overflowing. I try to banish all thoughts as he has gone from us never to return, and tears are powerless, for good. My sufferings are greater than I can bear, I can never be reconciled. My first born just when he had become most interesting, to be taken. I see no love, no mercy in it. I can never forget that last evening he went hunting with me. He was more manly and sensible then than I had ever seen him. But I cannot bear it. I am sorry you feel so in regard to Thornwell. Our loving him wont kill him and let us center on him our whole affections. It wont do him any harm. I do hope you are teaching him to mind. Be particular to make him stop fretting and crying when anything displeases him. Put a stop to it at once and it will never trouble you afterwards. Don't let anyone talk baby-talk to him, teach him to speak plainly at once. I wish I could be at home now to train him as I think he is inclined to be headstrong. Do not allow the children to tease him and try and prevent his disposition being soured by every means in your power. I want to make him all Will Ed was if possible.

Since I last wrote you I have received a letter from William Henry. He writes from Port Hudson but gives me no news. Says his company has charge of erecting a Battery of a 30 pdr Parrott gun—a splendid piece according to his description. He writes very patriotically indeed, but I presume you have heard from him by this time. I am sorry you do not get mails regularly. I shall send this by way of Rodney or Natchez. I hope you will see Cahill and he promised to bring that small trunk for me. If he comes by way of the River, as he will do, he can bring it very handily. I do hope you can send me some nice things. The quilt or comfort you need not mind about, for the worst part of the winter is over I think and I may not need them. I am glad you have learned how to make shoes. I could give you some lessons if I was with you. I can make almost as nice a pair of Ladies shoes as Ditmar could. What has become of him? How many of my letters have you received lately? Have you got one by Col. Sandidge & one by Mr. Clampit? Did you get the papers I sent you? Answer all my letters, my dearest, for there are a great many inquiries in them. Don't write in such haste as most of your letters are written. You need not write all at a single sitting.

I met a man at a boarding house who used to live in Greenville. He knew all the folks there and told me a great deal about them. I sent a great many messages to my friends there. I believe I wrote you about it before. I have seen him since then. I have not been very well for a week, in fact have done no duty since last Monday but the pay rolls. Will report for duty tomorrow if I feel no worse. I was quite sick for two or 3 days though. If I had continued would have gone to the hospital in Selma if I could have got there. If you were only on this side of the river now I might see you again. Am glad you are pleased with Mr. and Mrs. Henderson. They will be some company for you. he will be gone a good part of the time won't he? My kind regards to Dr. & Mrs. Bright when you see them. He is a pretty good preacher is he not? I am sorry you think of moving in town, don't do it. As far as my coat is concerned you might have left the buttons off for I can get buttons here for $18.00 a dozen and I'll have them put on. I hope Cahill will bring it though. I don't kneed it very much. I wish I had written you to send me the drawers I left at home as I shall need them.

Write often to me dearest and tell me all the news. I think I have made this quite a news letter and I know you cannot object to the length of it as it is written very close and holds a great deal. Give much love to all for me. I hear they are fighting at Vicksburg but don't know how strong yet as the papers have not come yet. I want you to pay Mary for Rich $5.00. I would send it but it might be lost and I need the money. Just pay her for him. I had to make him send it. He don't care much for her I think but don't tell her so. He does tolerably well now. I would send him home with my horse if I had a good opportunity, but the Mill is sold there is no bran to fatten him on. Tell Thornwell he must write to his papa and you must not fail to have his "guggen" fixed. Don't fail now I charge you, let it cost what it may he must have his wagon. My love to your Mother & Sisters. Kiss our darling a dozen times. A heart full for yourself. Ed.

Tuesday 1 P.M. [Jan.] 27th '63

My own darling One:

I sent you a letter by yesterday morning's train, a long, long one and this evening I am sorry to have to be compelled to write you again, not that I don't love to write you but I am sorry to have to report to you the bad news which has befallen us.

Yesterday morning we received orders to report at once to Gen'l Van Dorn at Coffeeville. The River was so high we could only go up on a train and all the trains are engaged in transporting troops to Jackson for Vicksburg or Port Hudson. I don't know which. We are today ordered to report at Okolona on the Mobile & Ohio Road as soon as possible. Van Dorn goes from there up through North Alabama to Murfreesboro or near there and with Wheeler, Morgan & Forrest will probably go across the Ohio River so it is said. I fear we may have to go with him and if we do I know I cannot stand the cold weather. It may be possible however that Col. Starke to whom we are ordered to report, may be left there, if so you may anyhow venture one letter to Okolona and I may get it. Write me there to care of Capt. Webb, Minden Rangers, Van Dorn's Corps of Cavalry. I will write you again as soon as possible if I find where we are going and what we are to do. If I go on this trip up there, I am going to send Rich home on "Jack" as he cannot go with me. I would not pain you dearest, but you had better be prepared not to hear from me again under two or three months. Pray earnestly my dearest that I may be spared to return to you once again if God so wills it.

Today I got your letter of the 14th inst. which came up on yesterday's train making 12 days, pretty well that. I was so glad to hear that the Mill trade was broken up and so were the company generally almost as much rejoiced as I. I am so sorry to hear of Mrs. Wimberly's sufferings. Give her my most heartfelt sympathy. I feared your Mother would get her foot in it boarding a Preacher's family. I wish she had taken my advice but I fear it reached her too late.

I am distressed about the way we have been treated and are yet to be treated. We have sent on our petition to the Sec. of War, through Senator [Thomas J.] Semmes & Henry Marshall to be transferred to Col. [J. Frank] Pargoud's Regt. (3d) La. Cav.[2] It is to be sent directly back to Col. Scott care of Gen'l Rust. I do sincerely hope it may go through before we get up North. I do dread going on that scout but I reckon I can stand it if anyone can. If I get sick I shall stop, that is all. A powerful effort is to be made to uproot Rosecranz army, and I think we are to watch the Tennessee River to prevent supplies coming up that to him. Capt. Webb is looking for his wife to come with Mrs. Col. Scott and he is in a quandary too. A sad looking sett we all are now I assure you. I expect we will be put back in that same old Battallion again but hope not, we may do worse however.

Do not feel badly my dearest for God disposes of even the minor matters of Earth. He may bring me back safe again to you and if he does all these hardships will only make me love you the more, if not, and I should never again see you, you will know that I died breathing your name. But I will not anticipate evil for I don't think it a good plan to cross a bridge before getting to it. I have just heard it said that we may perhaps stay in Okolona some two or three weeks. So write me there anyhow once. I will write you when I find out where we are going. So cheer up my dearest for we shall whip the Yankees most terribly at Vicksburg if we can fight them there. I am afraid they will cut through their canal and get their transports through. But God will certainly aid us if we trust in him.

Take good care of Thornwell and if I should never get home again try and raise him to obey you implicitly. This can only be done by commencing now and never relaxing your efforts. Be of good cheer

[2] Semmes and Marshall represented Louisiana in the Senate and House, respectively, of the First Confederate Congress, February 18, 1862–February 17, 1864. Semmes also served in the Second Congress (May 2, 1864–March 18, 1865) but Marshall was not re-elected. See *Executive and Congressional Directory of the Confederate States, 1861–1865* (Washington, 1899).

my dearest I have felt much blue-er since I have been out. A hundred kisses to darling Thornwell and my whole heart to *my darling.*

Okolona, Miss. Feb. 12, 1863

My Own dear Wife:

You will doubtless be surprised at the date of this letter if you received my last letter from Grenada sent by hand across the River. I did not then expect you would have an opportunity of hearing from me in some time. The Command has been gone nearly a week and as I am now well enough to ride I shall start tomorrow or next day to rejoin it for you must know my own dear Wife that I have been sick for nearly a week, having been attacked with a congestive (I think) chill. My fever lasted me some 36 hours and as I deemed it imprudent longer to remain lying on damp ground, I came out to this place and have received the utmost kindness from all members of this most amiable family consisting of Mr. & Mrs. Madry and their two daughters, Misses Martha and Addis. The old folks are very plain & uneducated but the girls are very *pretty, refined, intelligent* and have the warmest, kindest, hearts in the world. They live in style in the black prairie and I want you to write them and return your warmest thanks for their kindness to me for they wont receive any pay and Miss Mattie said she wished she knew you she would correspond with you. So do write her one of those interesting letters you so well know how to write. Do this for my sake for they have been very kind to me. I came here on Monday eve and tomorrow, Saturday, I am calculating to start to Tuscumbia, Ala., whither the command has gone. I feel "quite" well only nervous, so much so that I can scarcely write at all.

Don't worry about me for I have been appointed Quartermaster of the Battallion and if I had not been sick should have already executed the Bond ($20,000) and been exercising my office. I rank as Captain and get his pay besides *not being allowed* to go into battle. John Lesueur has been attending on me and will go with me tomorrow. I do hope I will not lose the appointment but God does everything for the best and, dearest, in an argument the other day with John & Capt. Webb, I had occasion to refer to my testament and I found there the doctrine of the final perseverance of the Saints so fully expressed that I am really encouraged to believe that I once had well grounded hope of Salvation through the atoning blood of a sacrificed Redeemer and that I shall be spared to come back into the Fold. These feelings came over me before I was taken sick. I leave it all in God's hand and have strong faith that I shall see you before the summer is over to remain with you.

Day before yesterday I got your two letters dated 12th and 21st Jany. also one from Mother. You know not dearest, how glad I am to get letters from you, to hear of your welfare, but I do not by any means like that way of having chills you have got. you must stop that. I am so glad that our only remaining child is improving so rapidly in talking and writing. I have been quite homesick since I got your letters, for I do want to see you all so anxiously. Oh could I clasp you dearest to my breast and feel that I was going to remain with you to be separated from you no more it appears the summit of happiness here below. I am so sorry to hear of Mrs. Wimberly's continued ill health. I am afraid she is not long destined for this world. Poor woman.

(After Supper) 10 o'clock. I have spent a pleasant evening in the parlor and now I will try and finish this scrawl. When I was called away from my letter, it was to go and read the latest "Mobile Evening News," 12th inst. I learn that still greater dissatisfaction exists in the Northern army and I do not believe Western troops can be prevailed upon to fight even if brought into battle now. Lincoln's Congress has passed the bill arming 150,000 negro recruits into the field and I know it will not go down in the army.

But why do *I write you* such things. I had rather my letters were brim full of the love I bear for you, and it is because I have hopes of being with you ere long that I write it. You say in reply to our invitation to come and spend the winter with us in our winter quarters that you are not going to be caught in a *"snap."* I am sure I stayed three weeks at home and you were not caught in any *"snap."* I don't see why *you* need fear. If you were *"snapped"* your health might be better and you would not have so many chills.

I am sorry to hear that there are any who oppose the Militia Law.

I am sure if men won't fight for their own homes they ought not to have any. Maybe their patriotism will improve when they learn that peace is near at hand. John L. Bannister is a deserter and ought to be arrested and sent back to his command. I wish I could send Rich back home and if it were possible I would do so, but am afraid now to do it lest he might be captured by the Yankees. If I sent him it would be impossible to send any Irish potatoes as he would come on old Jack. In fact to get Jack back would be my only reason for doing so. I expect I shall keep him for if I go into Quartermaster Dept. I shall need him there.

My greatest regret in going on this trip is that I shall be so far away from mail communication that I cannot hear from you. If you could get a good chance to come over this side the River do try and do so as Mother begs me to urge you and I might have an opportunity of seeing you again. Mr. Hayes mailed your letter at Brookhaven, Miss. Feby. 2nd. Mother says Spencer was in the battle at Murfreesboro and escaped unhurt. Ed Le Roy was wounded in the leg but fought on all day, but I'll send her letter if this is not too heavy. I am sorry, indeed, that Cahill has not got here with my coat. I need it very much as the coat I have is quite ragged but perhaps when I get into Tenn. I can get me one there. I have no idea I shall ever see that coat, but even *trivial* things happen for the best. Not a sparrow falls to the ground, without our Father's notice. I do not wish you to worry about me at all for when I am sick I don't expect to travel. I shall stop, so give yourself no uneasiness my own loved one.

I am going to do this morning what I hate to do, viz., burn all your letters. I have between 30 & 40 and shall burn them as I may never see my valise again and your letters are far too sacred to me for other eyes than mine own. Who the other partner in that game of whist I don't remember but it was most probably Ben West. I only omitted the name for economy of space. My *wife* would not certainly entertain the thought that I would play with anyone that I would hesitate to name to her. I feel my dearest I possess your confidence too entirely for that. Do I not? I trust you implicitly. I hope you have received my letter by Col. Sandidge but I fear not as I forgot to frank it, or pay postage and he went up Red River probably to Shreveport. I am afraid now that I shall render this unintelligible but you must try and decipher it the best you can. I enclose two scraps clipped from a newspaper. Please preserve the Jewish one, the other you will admire for its purity and force of language and Bud will commit for the purpose of spouting around as it affords fine opportunity for oratorical display.

You have never acknowledged the receipt of anything from me but I presume it is an oversight on your part. Do you find the Memphis Appeal interesting? You write me but do not answer my letters, and now since I have commenced fault finding you spelled the word in one of your letters *maneuvres.* Look in the dictionary and you will find the terminal ending *ers?* My wife is so near perfection in my eyes that I want it attained completely.

But now I am without having said a word about our darlings. Willy's memory is as fresh and green as ever in my almost broken heart. I cannot trust myself to speak of him to any one for the tears will come unbidden. You cannot imagine how Thornwell's childish sayings interest me. You must begin to teach him his letters as soon as he can talk distinctly. I don't wish him confined to his book by any means, but he can learn his letters as a past time.

It is raining this morning and I don't know that I will start today. If I do not I'll try and scribble over the other side. I wish I could write you interesting letters, but that I cannot do. I have been reading while sick "My Novel" by Bulwer. It is a fine thing. I think you read it in Harper's Magazine. Give my love to all the family, Father, Mother, Brother, & Sisters. Lou has not written me that letter yet. Tell Cousin Mary I am sorry to hear a bad report of her old Teacher. She professed to me that her Bible was her all in all, but at the same time acknowledged that she did not think dancing sinful at all. I think to say the very least that dancing at the present juncture of affairs is in very *bad taste.* But you, darling, were the iconoclast who destroyed my idol long, long since. The wind of her folly has even driven away the dust. I have been disappointed once but I feel secure in my affections now. I feel that my love is returned in its full measure, only not in its intensity. (Hey?) I am going to write to Mother and William Henry today if I do not start and the weather is at any rate unfavorable. Yesterday I wasted and today must make it up.

But I must close as my paper is almost covered and I must close for want of something else to say. I dreamed I was with you last night and you can imagine my happiness for while the dream lasted. You must take the best care of your health for you are not now living for yourself alone, and for my sake be prudent. Take care of my own darling boy Mother, do not neglect him. Watch him closely both as regards his health and his disposition and temper. Govern him yourself and let no one interfere in the least with your government. Don't let him fret, but you know dearest what I want better than I can write it. Do everything, the knowledge of which would give your Husband pleasure. Pray for me dearest and believe me yours most devotedly, Ed. H. Fay.

Okolona, Miss. Feby. 22d/63

My own dear Wife:

I did not expect when I last wrote you that I would be able to write you another letter from this place but such were the designs of Providence and our God overrules all things for the best. I wrote you that I intended leaving Mr. Madry's Saturday Morning but it commenced raining so we put it off until the next day. Sunday morning Mrs. Madry came to me and begged me not to start till next day. I consented and John L. and I spent the day in reading the Bible and discussing the doctrine of foreordination and falling from grace. I find the doctrine more and more fully and clearly set forth everytime that I examine it. Monday morning Mrs. Madry bade me goodbye with tears in her eyes and we started, came into Okolona and called on Capt. Harrison who told us that the Abolitionists were picking up the stragglers in rear of Van Dorn and that we had better wait till he (Capt. Harrison) started the first of March. I was glad for I wanted to hear from you again and am in hopes Cahill will come and I will get my coat as my old one is worn completely out. But warm weather is coming on and I shall not need a coat then. Thursday Eve we went out to Mr. Madry's again and on the way back I lost my memorandum book containing $300 belonging to the company fund. I did not discover the loss until the next night when I took off my coat to lie down. It had been the only clear and pretty day we have had for a month and I thought the next morning I would go and look for it. The next morning it was raining but John & I had our horses saddled and started. I had prayed earnestly the night before that I might find it and I felt sure that my prayer would be answered. I rode some three &½ miles and sure enough I found it all right. I returned a fervent thanksgiving to God for his mercy and I do feel that God is my Friend. Oh that I could love him as I ought!

Today we are invited out to Mr. Madry's to dinner and I expect we will go. The whole country is black prairie and the mud is belly deep to a horse; it is almost impossible to ride through it and is so full of Lime that it takes the hair off the legs of our horses as it would off a cow's hide. This is the anniversary of the Confederate States and the death [birth] of Gen'l Washington and oh that it might be the anniversary of Peace among nations.

We are flattered up here with the idea of a revolt of the Northwestern States: Ill. & Ind. & Ohio. The question is discussed in the Richmond Congress as to their admission in the Confederacy. I have hardly yet formed an idea as to the expediency of admitting them. I await further developments. It is also rumored here that Rosecranz is falling back to Bowling Green. I hope this latter may be true for it demoralizes his army worse than a defeat and he will never be able to reorganize it. The Resolutions of the Ky. Legislature are a weak and wishy washy affair. They have not the manliness to grasp the Bull by the horns and declare at once that they will not submit to Abe Lincoln's domination. I am looking for Seward or Lincoln to make a famous coup d'état about the 4th March. The papers say that today is the day set apart for the grand attack upon Charleston. I presume Beauregard is prepared for them. I hope so. Our papers of the 20th from Mobile give an account of the capture of the Queen of the West at Gordon's Ldg. on Red River.[3] I know you are all much rejoiced in Minden at the news, so are we. Peace will, I think, dawn upon us by the 1st of May.

[3] The *Queen of the West,* of Admiral David D. Porter's Mississippi River fleet, was captured by the Confederates on February 14, 1863, after a spectacular expedition down the Mississippi past Vicksburg, up the Red River, down the Atchafalaya and back again to the Red River. See *Battles and Leaders,* III, 564–565.

Tell Lou that the company are in Columbia, Tenn. I presume before this. One Brigade is we know but not whose. We are in [George B.] Cosby's Brigade, a Gen'l imported from Va. whose forehead is about the width of your two little fingers, and doesn't look as over twenty two years of age. Men are commanded in this army by insignificant boys. I expect I will lose the appointment of Quartermaster as I will be so long overtaking the Command. But all things are for the best. I wish your Father would get Mr. McDonald to get up a petition to Pres. Davis for my discharge for when this thing is settled it will be a long time before I can get home and I am anxious to get there as soon as possible. I am determined when I do come home not to stay in Minden. I intend to go somewhere either to Western Texas or to the Southern part of Louisiana. I will not stay in Minden any longer than I can help. Mother intimates that some of her children ought to live with their parents and take care of them and I intend to do it. We may go back to Alabama to live. How would you like it? I wish you could come across the River. If you were in Selma now I could fix up a trick to see you. As perhaps our Command is at Chattanooga and I would go through to Selma to go there and stop some days on the way. But you, my dearest, are not there and I cannot go there for less than your society. I wish I could see you for a few days now. I could say so much more than I can write. 'Tis so cold writing that I can't feel my pen scarcely.

I hoped I would have got a letter from you before this but none have come. The one by Mr. Hayes being the last. Hope you have got my letter that I sent home by Murphy's negro but I fear that it distressed you very much. I hope you will not cease to write me to this place as often as you can. I may not get your letters if I go away from here but it may be they will be sent through by couriers to me. We may be retained here perhaps till the Command comes back from Ky. nothing is certain in the army. As to my health, it is very good at present. I have had no return of chills as yet and I hope I will not.

How I wish I could see my dear little Thornwell now. Yesterday I stopped out of the rain and saw a little boy 2 yrs. old 13 April, one month younger than Thornwell. He could talk quite plainly and his Mother dressed him in a military suit. He looked finely I tell you though I don't think he was as pretty a child as ours. It made me quite homesick and I feel as if I should almost fly to you today. But I'll bide my time and it will all result for the best some of these days. I wonder what you are doing today. I presume you have been to church and are now about returning home. There is no church here and I have spent the day so far writing to the one I love best upon the earth. Do you ever think of me during the day when engaged at your work? Do you ever wake up in the night and think of me?

You don't know what a terrible time we have had. Snow & ice and rain, never four days in succession of fair weather since Christmas. Enough to kill any kind of men, but so far we have got along pretty well. I wish I had something interesting to tell you. I know my letters are dry enough. I do not feel like writing this dry letter. Do my own darling one take care of your health and of our darling little one, too. My only hopes of happiness in this world all center in you and I believe and pray God will preserve you from all danger and harm.

Give much love to your Father & Mother for me also to the girls. As for Bud, make him write me letters. It will be improving to him and interesting to me. I want your father to buy me two negro girls if possible with that money lying idle in Mr. Wimberly's safe. It will be doing Spencer a favor. We will not go to Mr. Madry's to dinner as Lieutenant Carter objects, giving as a reason that the others have got no where to go to dinner. He is the most supremely selfish man I ever saw. I bear with him however, but make him feel bad by rebuking selfishness in others. The envellope I send you is one lost in my book with the money. I think it will carry this letter safe to you. It has again turned very cold. I do indeed wish this winter weather over and I believe with the Spring comes the dawn of peace. You wrote me that Joe Bays had written me. If you write him tell him I have never received any of his letters and I would write him but don't know his address. My best and kindest wishes to him when you write and write him if he writes you. I'll go and mail this letter as I can get no paper. I hear that Mrs. Webb is on this side of the River and Capt. Webb is in Tenn. Good Bye dearest. A dozen kisses to Thornwell and a heart full of love for you. Your affectionate Husband,

Ed. H. Fay

In Camp. Okolona, Miss. Feby. 27/63

My own dear One:

I have still an opportunity of writing you one more letter from this place and you will no doubt be surprised if you have not previously received the one I mailed you some 3 or 4 days ago. In that I told you that Capt. Harrison has detained us here till the first of March, and indeed I am so glad for yesterday Mr. [Henry H.] Ward whom Capt. Webb had left with Col. Scott to bring his wife to his Brothers at Scooba, came up and bro't me your letters and best of all my coat. I was needing it sadly. It fits me very well being a little too small across the stomach, but that doesn't matter. It is a splendid coat & I appreciate it as the gift of my dearly beloved wife.

Three letters. Oh, how much good they did me. Your last, Feby. 9th directed by Dr. Patillo, Ward bro't in his pocket and in it you spoke of a long one with sundry additions and as he saw Lovick Wren and did not bring it, I concluded that Wren did not bring it or lost it. A sack containing some clothing proved also to contain a package of letters & among them two for me, one containing Mrs. Henderson's letter to her sister which I will be careful to mail if I get inside Yankee lines or send by some paroled prisoner if I have an opportunity. I'll use my best endeavors to get it to her. I got your letters just at dark but a Confederate candle was soon procured and sticking [it?] in a junk bottle I managed to read your very well written letter.

My dear, I am very sorry you misunderstood my corrections of your mistakes. As far as your handwriting is concerned you can improve it by practice if you will. I gave you some lessons once which if you will practice you can improve in a short time. My darling I did not mean to say I was ashamed of your writing. I might perhaps have expressed my meaning better by saying that I regretted it was not written better. However, my dearest, always do the best you can and I will be satisfied. You know not my dear how proud I am of you and I wish you perfect in everything. You are almost perfection I think, anyway but I must not praise you too much. I am so glad that you answered all my questions even if you did have to reread my uninteresting letters. I have written you quite regularly except the week I was sick at Mr. Madry's, then 9 days I think elapsed. I have visited Mr. Madry's several times since I came into town and may go again tomorrow night as John L. and I are invited. I want you to be sure to write to Misses Martha & Addis care of Mr. E. C. Madry, Okolona, Miss. They have been very kind indeed to your husband. A kinder or more pleasant family it has rarely been my lot to become acquainted with.

There are very few excitements in this region of the Earth except the daily arrival of papers which bring us the news. I have attended the Lodge and Chapter in this place two or three times and have made some pleasant acquaintances. The boys are all talking so I cannot write so I will stop for a while.

(Saturday Morning) They are still talking around me but as I am anxious to get this letter off I will try and finish out this sheet anyhow. I expect I will start to the command the forepart of next week, if no orders come to prevent. I have not heard a word from Van Dorn's army since it left, though one of his Staff wrote his wife who is in this place to direct her letters to Tullahoma, Tenn. Our Brigade may be ordered somewhere else and I don't know how to advise you to direct. Carter will remain here with the Baggage and will take care of the letters so that I will get them sometime, if I live. I do hope that we may be ordered to remain here for I do not fancy the trip into Ky. at all, at least until spring opens. My times are in the hands of the Lord and he will preserve me if such are his designs. My ways are in his Hands.

There is one thing about which you have studiously avoided giving me any information, that is about "King and his Arkansas trip." Did he return you that "Pistol" I loaned him & did he collect those certified accounts? A great many things of that kind you forget to tell me, though your last letter gives me a good deal of news. About that School Matter, I care but very little although I intended to apply for a discharge under the Conscript Act as a Teacher of Schools, which I cannot now do if that school goes on. I have no idea he will teach two months for I believe the boys will turn him out before that time. I don't presume to dictate to your Father about sending your Brother to school, but I make it an invariable rule better not send to school at all than a poor one. It will do your Brother far more harm than good to go if that old man is such a Teacher as I have heard he was. But this is no concern of mine. As far as being under any obligation to the people of Minden is concerned even had they sent up that petition and procured my discharge I should not have taught in Minden. There are many places where they need a school just as much as they do in Minden and I should have found such a place.

I do not intend living in Minden at all after this War is over, in fact if you were on this side the River I think it altogether probable that I should not return to Minden at all. If Father is living at the close of the War, I shall probably go and attend to his affairs for him. If not, I shall take care of my Mother. I would not be surprised if I lived in Ala. I still intend to apply for a consulship to Chili when commercial relations are established and I think I can obtain it. My desires about living in South America have been kept down, never extinguished, and nothing would give me so much pleasure as to live there, though in all my plans for life when this war is over, your tastes and wishes shall be my guide.

As to the Gin business I never expect to have any more to do with it, except it may be to save a little from the wreck. I may have to do that for your father is too old to ride over so much country collecting. I am willing to do all I can towards settling it up and will do so if I can. I am combatting the natural bent of my inclinations when I give up mechanical operations but anything my dear to please you, I will willingly do. Something I must do to make a living though, that is certain for I cannot live without work. The professorship at Alexandria is a matter of *official* patronage & gift and I can never condescend to supplicate favors from anyone. Besides, the professorships at Alexandria will all be filled before I get out of this War. There will be plenty of stay-at-home patriots to fill all such stations and I can assure you that a soldier will stand a very poor chance for anything unless they take matters into their own hands.

The indications at present from the Northern States are that there is more probability of a recognition from the Radical Abolitionists than from any movement on the part of the Conservatives. I distrust the whole Northern Crew. "Timao Danaos et dona ferentes," since you are reading Virgil.

What has become of your *"school projects."* You said nothing about them so I fear you did not read over *all my letters* for I wrote

Edwin H. Fay
(*about 1880*)

you a long one from Grenada in regard to them and you said nothing about it. I wish you had taken the Male School. No I don't either. I want them to lament in "sackcloth and ashes" the patriotic plans of Brig. Gen'l Simmons and Jake Lewis. For the sake of education I am very sorry two such men should have influence, for my own sake I am glad they did. My time is not now but my revenge is sure and certain. I dislike to think of these things. I am only sorry that your father sent Bud to school and I am sure there is a motive in his doing so. If our places had been reversed I would have been very clear of sending my Son under the circumstances. Col. Lewis' influence must be quite potent over him yet.

What did you put 3 postage stamps on for, 15 cents will not pay any postage in the Confederacy. If it had weighed over ½ oz. it would have required 20 cents to pay it. I took off all the stamps however and will use them as they have never been cancelled. I am very much obliged to Lou for her letter and will answer it some of these long summer days if I get a good opportunity. You talk of rain & cold & sleet and snow but you have seen nothing of it yet I think. It has rained almost every day since we have been in Okolona and we have never had two bright days at once since we came. They say they have had such a wet spring and farmers are very backward with their crops. I fear it will be another dry year this year and that there will be very little made.

The Confederacy is pretty nearly "played out," to use a military phrase, in the eating line on this side the River tho' I hope you will feed the Port Hudson and Vicksburg boys well from that side particularly as you have taken both Gunboats—Queen of the West & Indianola, the capture of the latter being announced in yesterday's papers.[4] It caused quite a rejoicing here, I assure you. I am glad the fights are coming off at Vicksburg and Port Hudson for I am sanguine of success to the Confederate arms and I believe a victory, a complete one at either place would precipitate a peace almost by electricity. The Lincoln Govt. will give it up as gracefully as possible. I don't

[4] The Union ironclad steamer, *Indianola,* under Lt.-Commander George Brown, was rammed and captured below Vicksburg February 24, 1863, by Confederate vessels, among them the *Queen of the West,* which the Southerners had repaired and adapted to their own use. See *Battles and Leaders,* III, 565.

think there is any doubt but the army at Murfreesboro has been largely reinforced from our Va. army but I have no idea there will be any fighting there till Spring shall have dried up the mud. Before that time I hope the contest will be decided at Vicksburg & Pt. Hudson—I have no idea they will attack Charleston till after those battles are terminated and would not be surprised if Mobile did not have their respects paid to before either of them. The 12th La. and in fact all of Gen'l Rust's Brigade has been ordered across the River opposite Port Hudson so Mr. Ward says and he came from Jackson only a few days ago. Gen'l Bragg supercedes Pemberton so it is said. Longstreet's & Hood's corps & divisions from Fredericksburg reinforce Johnston at Tullahoma. I think there is a mistake about Kirby Smith in La., tho it may be true. So much for military matters till the papers come tonight when I may have more news to communicate.

I am sure you have now received all my letters from Grenada. I hope you have before this time and will act on the suggestions and follow the directions contained therein. I am sorry that Laura is so she cannot attend to Thornwell. He should always be allowed to have a "pensser to ite to papa," but not to trouble his Mother. I am glad he is learning to talk. Do you think he remembers me or is it only the name *papa* he remembers. Oh Mother it almost kills me when I think of our darling Will Ed. I can never be reconciled to give him up. It almost breaks my heart when I think how he cried when I took him in my arms and bade him goodbye. Why was he not spared to us is a question coming up at all times—I try to forget him, entirely forget that we ever had such a precious, noble boy. I intend to have a fine iron paling put around and his name inscribed on the reverse of little "Dody's" tomb—'Tis all I can do for him now.

I suppose Mrs. Mitchell is occupying our house and lot. You have not told me what rent she pays or anything about it. I am afraid you are not a *shrewd business woman.* You ought to cultivate that branch. It might stand you in hand some day when I am dead and gone and even during my absence. You have not told me how much meat we had put up nor anything about my affairs. Do you never think that meat and bread are necessary to sustain life? Have you commenced learning to spin yet and can you weave. These are accomplishments that will recommend the future housewives of the Confederacy. You told me you were going to review Virgil, of which I was very glad, but I hope not to the exclusion of the two accomplishments above mentioned. I prefer the former and I know it will be far more beneficial to you unless you intend taking a part in Mrs. Bryan's book, but dearest you can do both if you only will. But let me entreat that during my absence you will become as domestic as you can possibly be, and literature will find its proper place between times—I want you to spin and make me a Partridge net by the time I come home. Lou can make that while you spin and weave me a suit of Osnaburgs or Jeans. But enough about working. I know you will do all you can. You remember Penelope, the wife of Ulysses while her husband was absent in the war.

I want you to take constant and watchful care over Thornwell. Laura may have small pox, you cannot be too careful. I do hope you will both be preserved to me if I should be so fortunate as to return from the War unharmed. God grant that my Wife and child may be preserved, they being the only hopes in life that I have—I hope that in God's providence we may be permitted to live together again in peace after the war is over. I was sorry to hear of the tragedy at Bob McClendon's. I stayed there through the night my horse was so badly foundered. His wife is quite a heroine. I wish I knew that you had so much self possession. That pistol I want you to have loaded and keep it where you can put your hand on it at any time if it is necessary. You may at some time have use for it, and it is better to be prepared. I wish you would practice shooting anyway. It can do you no harm if no good. The fortune of War may bring the Yankees into your Country yet.

We have just heard here that there are some Yankee Gunboats at Florence Ala. and that they were now occupying Tuscumbia. I can imagine no reason for their being there unless it is to bring a force in the rear of Johnston's Army. They have moved their army from Fredericksburg and may have sent them up the Tenn. River. I want to have the fights come off and settle this matter as soon as possible for if I am to come home and live with you again I want to do it, if not there is no matter how soon the matter is over with me. I get to thinking about coming home sometimes and it seems to me I can hardly stand it, but that I must come to you right away at once. I am glad to hear you have broken the chills and am glad too that you feel so well, you say as well as you were before you were married. Have you not had just as good health since your marriage as before? I am glad you have been so fortunate and I hope now you don't regret any *longer my coming home*. I thought *sometimes that you did*.

I heard that Mr. Wimberly had gone to the Hot Springs with his wife. He can stay with his wife but if you were sick I could not come to you. Our Confederate Laws do not operate equally upon all men. Some favored few can occupy places of ease and emolument while others must bear all the suffering. If it is right I can't see it. I am sorry for poor Mrs. Wimberly and I don't blame him for staying with her if he can. I only wish I had his chance, I would improve it. I don't blame any one for staying from the war for I know I would if I could, but as I cannot I submit with as little murmurings as possible. If every one would come out and if our Gen'ls drew a little less pay I think the War would be a little sooner closed. It is to their interest it should continue. I know but one in the Confederacy that I would trust far and that is Gen'l Rust. He is one of my favorites. He would fight if he only drew a private's pay, and he is a fighter, too. I do wish we could have been retained in his command. We could now have been over on your side of the River and I could have had *you come to see me*. Capt. [William] Harrison's Wife has been with him for some two weeks or more. I wish you had come over on this side of the River with Mrs. Webb. You could then have gone on to Ala., but it is perhaps all for the best. As for your Mother's fretting, tell her I was only joking. I do not know that she frets more than other housekeepers with boarders.

I must close as it is getting nearly time for the Mail to come in and as I want to get down town will stop with this sheet. I know it is not a full return for your interesting and long letter but such as it is I give unto thee. I am glad you have commenced the undershirts, hope you will finish them so I can have them this summer. I do not need them much at present though the knitted one I have is all coming to pieces. My coat is very heavy so much more than my old one that it seems very oppressive, but I'll get used to it before long I reckon. I am thinking of paying $18.00 for 24 large and 6 small buttons (Confederate) but don't know whether I will do it or not. They are very pretty & will show off my coat very prettily but I don't care much for show.

Give my love to your Father & Mother, to the girls and all *my friends*. I know they are few but so much the better. Write me to this place at least until further communication and I will get them sometime. I have a faint hope of getting one more letter from you before I leave, if I do I'll write you again, if not I may not write from this place any more. Dearest do take care of yourself and of Thornwell and be sure to write me. Good Bye, dearest. I pray God that I may be permitted to see you once again. Good Bye Dearest and may God in his infinite mercy bless and preserve you. Your affectionate Husband, E. H. Fay

Okolona, Miss Mar 9th

My own dear loved Wife:

Mat Killen says he is going home and although it is almost dark and I can get no candle I will write what I can to you while I can see. Oh how I wish my own dearest that you had come over the River with me I could now see you again. I start tomorrow morning for Montgomery, Ala. to accompany Mrs. Harrison that far on her way to Ga. She has been staying in Okolona for 4 weeks and as Capt. Harrison is ordered off on a scout he has detailed me to go to Montgomery with her. I shall see Father & Mother and come back by Selma, be gone 10 days. I am quite well now, spent a pleasant day yesterday at Mr. Madry's. I call it my Miss. home. I will write you again from Home when I get there. You must write me a series of letters when Killen comes back. I have had none from you later than 9th of Feby. I do so want to see you. I would give $500 if you were on this side of the River so I could see you once more. I presume as Killen goes horseback you will have heard of Van Dorn's fight at Franklin, Tenn. 'Tis so dark I will finish in the morning.

In the Mason's Lodge, 6 A.M. I was up at a meeting of the Lodge till nearly twelve last night and will devote the few minutes I have before breakfast and ere the Cars start (8 A.M.) to filling out this sheet. I am afraid you will not call this a letter, only a note but if you knew how my heart goes out toward you in its pages you would certainly esteem it a letter. My own darling I do love you so much that tongue much less pencil or pen will never express it. You are the burden of my thoughts by day and my dreams by night. Col. Sandidge is coming this morning so I understand and I hope he has got a letter for me, but as it has rained all night and every hollow is swimming I fear he will not get here till I am off on the Cars. Oh my blessed one I do want to see you. I am almost crazy.

As to the Termination of the War I am fearful that the Northern States have so far thrown away their liberties that now they will not be able to recover them again. If four weeks does not exhibit in the distance a termination of this war, I fear it will last two years longer. God will do right even though it will be very painful to us. I am thinking of applying for my discharge under the Exemption Act and coming home and joining the State forces at Alexandria. What think you. I wish you could see Col. Lewis and get him to use his influence to get me an appointment in the Engineers Corps of the State. I can then get a discharge very readily to come into that service and be nearer you. I don't care about leaving the service I only want a position my talents render me capable of filling, and I know I can do more good on that side of the River than I can on this.

But it is time for breakfast and I must close. Do take the best care of yourself dearest and also of our little Thornwell. Bless him. How Father wants to see him. Give him a score of kisses and a hundred loves for yourself. Do dearest one write me often and continue yet awhile to direct to Okolona. I may get them though I expect when I get back from Montgomery to start to overtake the Command if possible. The Yanks may get me but I hope not. My own loved one you must think of me and pray for me. I am very wicked though I try to be better but camp is a hard place for even a Christian to live right much less one who is not. I trust and pray that this war may soon be over and I be permitted to see you and our little darling again. Give much love to your Father and mother for me also to Lou and Cousin Mary. They must both be good girls. I will write Lou the first opportunity I get. Write me all the news and accept a heart full of love from your husband who truly loves you. Good Bye dearest, Good Bye. Ed.

Montgomery, Mar 15/63
Exchange Hotel
Sunday Morn 6 A.M.

My own darling:

You will see that I am in Montgomery on my way home. I came up the River on the "H. J. King." If you have received my note from Okolona you have already become apprized of my visit to bring Mrs. Capt. Harrison & Sister this far on their way to Ga. Reached here just at daylight this morning one minute too late for the Cars. I am going to see Mr. Hastings and get him to put the Ladies on the Cars this evening and I am going to foot it home this morning. I travelled up the River with Lt. Col. [Trevanion D.] Lewis of the 8th La. Regt. on his way to Richmond and he told me all about the Minden Blues. I would tell you but haven't time. I stopped a couple of hours in Selma. Uncle Lloyd did not know me. They were all very glad to see me.

I have just met John Wimberly who was discharged from our Co. and as he is going right across the River I send this by him. I am well. Sarah has a pretty baby, but oh, my own darling how it distressed me to see her boys running around and think our darling had been taken from us. Grandma mentioned him with tears. Oh my darling, my heart is too full. Wimberly is in haste so I must close this. I'll try and write you by mail from Father's. I shall stay there over my birthday. Oh dearest if I was only going to meet you there. But God wills it otherwise. Kiss dear Thornwell a hundred times for his "dear Favy" and accept a heart full for yourself. Good Bye my own darling one and may God's choicest blessings fall upon you and protect you and your husband and bring him back to you. Truly and ever yours, Ed. H. Fay. Love to all.

Rocky Mount Thursday
March 20th 1863

My own dear Sarah:

According to promises made you in Montgomery the other morning I seat myself in the old sitting room to fulfill the same. Mother is writing to Selma on my left and Mrs Sayre is sewing on my right, while your own dear Husband is seated in Father's rocking chair with the ironing board in my lap scribbling away a few lines to the light of my life, to use an Oriental phrase. Oh my own loved one what would I not give to have you with me now.

After giving my letter to John C. Wimberly in Montgomery, I went up to Mrs. Hastings to see the folks and as they had not breakfasted I stayed and ate with them. Eddy is almost a grown man while Kate is "quite old and ugly," and the baby when we were there is now quite a large boy. Did not see Mr. Hastings as it was Sunday Morn and he was not up and was also complaining of not being very well. Mrs. H. and Mrs Reid were both quite well and enquired very particularly after you. Expressed themselves as very much pleased with you what little they had seen and wished they might become better acquainted at some future time. A horse, a horse could not be obtained even tho my kingdom had been offered for one, so I took up my line of march for the ferry but found the River so high they no longer ferried over. I wandered along up the bank and found and resumed my line of march for the Mount. Got out to the mill two negroes going across in a skiff and accordingly secured passage about 8 miles and found Gus on a horse which I pressed and rode the remainder of the way. Folks all gone to church and house locked up, but small boy (negro) soon started to Prattville to carry the news of the arrival of Mâss[5] Ed. and the carriage in due time came rattling home.

Meantime Mâss Ed had opened a window and got into the house and was making himself quite comfortable. Folks all mighty glad to see Mâss Ed, quite unexpected pleasure, quite disappointed that Miss Sallie was not along too and I assure you they could not have regretted it more than I did. Oh why did I not bring you across the River when I came. But it is useless to lament now. The deed is done. Monday went with Mrs. Sayre and Mother to Prattville and spent a couple of hours. Saw Will and Hattie and Nellie Fay just a few minutes. Will came up after supper and stayed all night with me and is going to Selma with me tonight. Hattie has two children and Nellie

[5] Perversion of the term, master. Slaves normally addressed all male members of their owner's household as master.

one, a little boy. It makes me sad indeed to see others with their children playing around and feel that Thornwell is all we "have left now, our darling and our pride." It may be and doubtless is for the best, but it is hard to school the heart to say sincerely "Thy will be done." If our child could only have been spared I could have suffered almost everything else, but why do we mourn our eldest, we have our little daughter also in Heaven. Oh what a joy she would have been to you now in my absence. I shall go down to Selma tonight on a boat. Dunham goes down to go into a Saddler's Shop to keep out of the Army. He is little fitted for the army, but it would make a man of him. He is nothing but a child now not 8 yrs. old at that. It makes me sad to see how he has been spoiled by undue indulgence and kindness that was the greatest unkindness. He is much more helpless than a woman. But no more, if he should have to go in the army he would go to William Henry and not come to me.

A letter from Will came last night, he is enjoying his campaign at Port Hudson wonderfully. The papers bring news of a bombardment there on Sat. night last in which two steamers passed the batteries and one was lost, burned or sunk, supposed to be the "Mississippi."[6] The two that passed I hope will soon be captured by her Majesty "Queen of the West" who has certainly acknowledged our Independence. Will sent your letter to Mother and I got a chance to read it but it was dated Feby. 2nd so it is not as late as mine of the 9th Feby. How I do wish I had a letter from you. I feel so anxious. More than a month has elapsed since I heard from all that are dearest to me on this earth. If I did not feel that I would get letters from you when I got back to Okolona I believe I should desert and come to you once more. I do hope I shall see you before long—tho I hardly dare hope it as my plans may not work out. I shall start back from Selma Monday morning and will go right on to Van Dorn from there. I presume Capt. Harrison and the rest have gone ere this but he

[6] The naval engagement to which Fay alludes was the battle of Port Hudson, March 14, 1863, in which a portion of Farragut's Union fleet successfully ran past the batteries of the fort. The Union gunboat *Mississippi* was lost in this battle and the *Lancaster* a short time later. The Federals destroyed the Confederate *Queen of the West* on April 14. These naval victories gave to the Federals dominance of the Mississippi below Vicksburg. See *Battles and Leaders,* III, 566, 590, 592.

promised he would leave John Lesueur to go with me. Will go up by Huntsville, Ala.

I do not feel quite so hopeful concerning a termination of the War but feel sure that four or six weeks will settle matters as far as whether it will be long or short. I hope the people will not submit to Lincoln's Dictatorship, but I feel that reason is fled to brutish beasts and they are bounden slaves forever. If there is any manhood left among them they will necessarily be compelled to show it before long now. If we cannot see distinctly a close by the 1st May there is no hope for a close till Lincoln's term closes and not then if his coup d'état goes unresisted till that time. I hope, however, his arms will meet with such repulses ere that time that he will be compelled to sue for peace. Our times are in the hand of the Lord, let him do what seemeth good unto him.

Mrs. Sayre says: Present my kindest regards to your wife and tell her I am so anxious to know her. I have heard so much of her. Mother says: Tell Sallie to embrace the first opportunity afforded her of company and come here and stay till the war is over. I do not know what to say about your coming but I will determine and if I cannot come across the River I shall want you on this side. If I go back I will want you where you are. I bought me some cloth at Prattville and am going to have me a pair of pants made. Sister Sarah will make them for me. Uncle Lloyd will cut them. Grandma does not look any older than she did when you saw her, but Mother has lost her teeth and looks even older than Grandma except the gray hair. Mother's hair is still the color of a raven's wing. Father is a little more gray but has grown no older. You don't know how much he *feels* and *expresses* for me and *mine*. He thinks you are the *greatest woman in the world* and you are his standard of comparison. I tease Mother about looking old and she don't like it much. Dunham is as tall as I am and being slim looks even taller. Aunt Add is the same old sixpence and expresses as much *holy horror* of my teasing Grandma as ever. She is as usual very kind to me and expresses a great deal of love for you. Sister Sarah is growing old, looks broken, but is the same good affectionate Sister. She loves you very dearly and says she is going to see you just as soon as the War closes. I hope we may make some arrangements by which we can live nearer each other and see more of one another. Cousin Will, too, says he wants to live nearer me and he will make arrangements after war closes to get me into business with him. What say you? But sufficient unto the day is the evil thereof.

I do not know where to tell you to direct your letters but will try and write you and let you know when I get to Van Dorn where to direct. I have been talking all the morning while I have been writing and I expect I have a very disconnected mess of it. Mother, Father and Mrs. Sayre all send a heap of love to you and Thornwell while his father sends a dozen kisses to his Mother and to him too. Your ever loving Husband, Ed.

Monday Morning, March 23rd '63
in Sister Sarah's Room, Selma, Ala.

My own dearly beloved:

I bro't my letter down with me from Rocky Mount, thinking it would go sooner via Meridian than by Mobile and have neglected mailing it until now. This morn have broken it open to add a few words. I came down from Washington on the "Southern Republic," a two story boat having a double cabin for both Ladies & Gents., a beautiful boat & calculated to leave this morning for the Coosa, but as Sister Sarah could not get my pants done (I bought some Prattville goods at $2.00 per yd. and she is making them for me), I waited over a day longer. Shall go tomorrow via Demopolis in company with this letter which I hope will soon reach you.

Oh, darling, I feel miserable this morning. I waked up thinking of our *lost ones* and I cannot drive my mind from the subject. It comes with double force upon me when I see Sister Sarah's children running around enjoying such perfect health. Her baby reminds me of our little Dody. She had it baptized yesterday tho Sam had to be absent being carried off to Mobile on the Gunboat to paint it. Mr. Small, their minister, I heard preach twice yesterday—at night a very interesting and practical sermon. He seems quite fitted for the position he occupies and will I think do good.

You would be surprised to see the number of men in Selma &

Montgomery and Mobile that are not in the Army tho I am informed they are employed on the Govt. works going on at these places. Selma is a Confederate States Navy Yard and Depot.[7] 3 Gunboats have been built here and one is on the stocks at Montgomery. All machine shops, foundries, etc. of Govt. are located here, moved from Columbus, Miss., Jackson and New Orleans. The N.O. powder mills are here too. This river is fortified beyond the possibility of a doubt. I wish I could get a position here in the Machine Shops till the close of the War and if I thought you would like it, I would try, but I know you are so much opposed to anything of the kind that I will go back and shoulder my gun if I cannot be discharged. Yet if I was here I could have you and my own dear Thornwell with me, but no such good fortune is for the favored few to be with their families and friends not exposed to dangers on the untented fields.

I came down by Prattville and found "Esther Ticknor," you remember her, Mary Hagen's Mother (what for the last 10 years I have believed) *drunk as a fool.* Poor woman, she learned to love it when a girl. This though must be kept between us. I did not see Cousin Eliza at all. Sister Sarah is very well but grandma is troubled with erysipelas in her leg tho I think it is nothing serious at present. Uncle Lloyd is growing old fast. Dunham came down to go to work in a government shop at the saddle and harness business. He has improved some and I hope that now since he has got away he will appear much better and become quite a man. Selma has improved so much you would hardly recognize it now. A Rail Road to Pollard is nearly done and the one leading to Montgomery is said to be progressing.

But all this doesn't bring the war any nearer to a close and consequently my return to you. Oh, Mother! I feel badly this morning, blue you may call it and I fear if I write further I shall make you so too. Tell Lou that when Van Dorn was in Columbia, Tenn. Mr. Smith and his wife & daughters vied in showing attention to them. I read a long account of it in the Mobile paper and tried to get it to

[7] For a description of war production activities in Selma during the Confederacy see Frank Vandiver, *Ploughshares into Swords: Josiah Gorgas and Confederate Ordnance* (Austin, Texas, 1952) 107, 123, 148, 169–171, 219; also Walter M. Jackson, *The Story of Selma* (Birmingham, 1954), 197–219.

send her but could not. I'll write to her if I get a chance before I leave for Tennessee. Sister Sarah sends a great deal of love and says you owe her a letter which you must make haste and pay.

The papers this morning give an account of the passage of the Hartford & Monongahela past the batteries at Warrenton below Vicksburg as also of the defeat at Tallahatchie by Gen'l [William W.] Loring and their driving the Yankees back to Yazoo Pass. Rumors of increasing dissatisfaction in the Northwest but on the other hand the Conscript Act is being enforced and gold is falling in Yankeedom which are signs I don't like. Tho Rosecranz has retreated from Murfreesboro and Grant is said to be leaving Vicksburg. Oh when will it close, will it be while I am yet alive or will it be when you, my dearest one are a widow and my child an orphan. God alone can tell. I told Father & Mother of your promise to live with them and bring up Thornwell in case I should be taken away and they were very much rejoiced, indeed. That promise must be fulfilled by all means.

About our lot, stock and property: you had better dispose of it if you can tho you had better be governed by your Father's judgment in regard to it. I feel sure I shall not settle in Minden should I outlive this War. Will Fay is anxious to have me go into business with him and I may do it, but I do want to see an end of the War even in the dim distance before I adopt any plans. My predilections are for a stock farm in Texas.

Oh dearest more than a month has elapsed since I have heard a word from you, tho I expect letters, one or more, are awaiting me at Okolona. If I should be disappointed it would be a very severe disappointment indeed. But you know I am hopeful and it supports me even now. I will try and get time to write you from Miss. again before I leave for Tenn. and then if you do not hear from me in four months don't feel uneasy, I beseech you, for I feel as if I should come to you again. How to direct me I do not know at present how to tell you, but you must write heretofore and the letters will perhaps find me and now dearest once more I will close, sending you all the love of all your acquaintances in Selma and all the fond affection of your husband's heart with a multitudinous package of kisses for dear little Thornwell from his father. Ed. H. Fay

Camp Cosby, Spring Hill, Tenn. April 11, 1863

My own darling:

We have just this morning moved back to the rear from advance 3 ms. in front of this place where Gen'l Cosby's Brigade has been encamped for the last three weeks. Yesterday as you will doubtless have heard before this reaches you we advanced on Franklin some 10 miles from our camp and drove in their pickets, and [Col. Peter B.] Starke's Miss. Regt. charged clear into town around the Court House Square and the dastardly Yankees that threw up their hands in token of surrender as our forces rushed in recovered their guns and got in the houses and cross fired upon them as they were coming out.[8] Franklin is situated on the South side of the Harpeth River in the valley while mountains rise abruptly from the water's edge on the other side upon which mountains the enemy have breastworks and heavy guns mounted. We drove them, the greater part at least, across the River and then they opened on us with their big guns which fortunately did us no harm though they killed and wounded 75 or 100 men in our Brigade. Forrest & Armstrong were on the Right wing and I have no idea of their loss. Have heard that his (Forrest's) Artillery was captured by the enemy but that he made a desperate effort and retook it. I know he has it now. Our Co. acting as escort to Brig. Gen'l Cosby was not engaged in firing but was *hotly* engaged in pulling down Stonewall Fences of posts, rails and boards as warm work as I ever did. We were then detailed as Scouts on the left to watch the approach of the enemy should they endeavor to flank us. So much for the battle.

We drew off in the evening having gained as Gen'l Van Dorn said all he intended. If we made anything I certainly did not discover it unless to harrass the enemy, as greatly to our advantage. We lost a great deal I know. This morn. we were ordered to be saddled up by daybreak expecting the enemy would come out and attack us, but although we learned that he had been reinforced by two regiments of Cavalry he did not see fit to follow us up. So we moved quietly back to the rear and another Brigade took our places. Our Co. went into the outskirts of Franklin and stayed nearly all day.

[8] Starke's regiment was the 28th Mississippi Cavalry. For reports of the engagement at Franklin on April 10, 1863, see *O.R.*, XXIII, pt. 1, 222–239.

But to resume our history of the war as seen by the author. I wrote you last Sunday was one week ago and was then calculating to start to Tenn. on Monday but it rained and snowed so hard all day that I did not start. Tuesday morning the waters were so high we concluded not to start till Wednesday. It was a bright clear day and the roads dried up amazingly, which I assure you was no small item in that Prairie Country. Accordingly next morning John Lesueur, the Frenchman (Rivinac) and your dear Husband set out accompanied by Rich who had Jack loaded down with provisions put up by the good kind provident and motherly old lady, Mrs. Madry. A Ham, a turkey, biscuits, cakes and a pone of cornbread almost as large as a Washtub. We made the trip in 8 days and brought some of our provisions into camp with us. We had a very pleasant trip of it as the weather was as clear as a bell and we came on quite rapidly as it took Capt. Webb two weeks to make the same trip. We passed through Aberdeen, Miss., Millville, "Pikeville, Ala.", Moulton, Decatur, where we crossed the Tenn. River then through Athens and across the Tenn. Line to Elkton, thence to Pulaski and Columbia where we got a pass from the Provost Marshal and crossed Duck River, came on to Spring Hill & found the Company at Gen'l Cosby's Hd. Qtrs.

Tell Lou that I intended to call on Rector Smith and would have done so but I did not know how long it would take to find the Company, and I did not like to be straggling. I think I shall go down there in a day or two and try and get the Young Ladies to make us a Battle Flag for our Body Guard. If I don't go I shall write to him on the strength of your acquaintance and ask him to have it made for us. Oliver Butler stayed the other night with Mr. Henly, the old man you used to go out to see. He inquired particularly after Treeby Chaffe and you, so Oliver said. He does not live more than two or three miles from our Camp. I shall try and see him if possible before we leave here so I can write you about it if I ever get another chance to write. Our chances are not very good to get off letters, Columbia being distant some 12 miles and that is our nearest Post Office.

The Adjutant, "Capt. Bullock" of Gen'l Cosby's Staff is sitting right in front of the Tent and talking about yesterday's fight. He says there were 14 killed in our Brigade, 37 wounded and 17 missing, some of whom are supposed to have been killed. He says our move was only a forced reconnaisance to find what their strength was. I suppose they must have at least 15,000 men, and they are so strongly posted we shall not attack them again soon. I would not be surprised if we did not surround the place and go on to the Ohio River. If so we shall probably come back here and you may therefore continue to direct your letters to Columbia, Tenn. Tell Lou she can write now to the Rector and Mrs. Smith. There is so much talking in front that I hardly know what I am writing.

We heard here day before yesterday that the enemy had attacked Charleston and after losing two or three of their Monitors had been forced to withdraw and also that Savannah had repulsed a simultaneous attack. We have also heard that the enemy have abandoned Vicksburg and that the Hartford had been captured. We see no papers here and of course know nothing except what has leaked out from Hd. Qrtrs. and Gen'ls in advance do not often make many disclosures of any sort. I hope I shall get some papers before long for I am getting hungry for news. I shall rust out if I do not.

Oh, my darling if this war would only close now and permit me to come home once again to you how happy I would be. I dreamed last night that I had been wounded and had gone home to Ala. and my Mother met me bathed in tears and said that Father had just started across the river to bring you there. Oh how rejoiced I felt to think I was going to see you, again once more. My darling, you don't know how I long to see you, but I presume it will yet be three months or more before I can do so. I was glad to see Bob Thompson for he had seen you and could tell me about my dear little Thornwell. Oh Mother can I ever stand it even if I am not killed, till I see you again. I wish I could get a position on Gov. Moore's staff or Engineer Corps and then I would get a discharge and come into service on that side the River.

I am sorry that we are here though this is one of the prettiest countries on Earth, but provisions are getting scarce and to tell the truth I have not had a meal for two days. We get plenty of corn for our horses and there are nice clover fields where our horses graze. We have sent out in the country to try and get something for our mess this evening, and I hope we may succeed. I am anxious to go somewhere where we can get plenty to eat and enough for our horses & as little

Sarah Shields Fay
(*about 1912*)

fighting as possible. I wish the enemy would fall back to Louisville as it is believed here that Rosecranz will probably be compelled to do as Col. [Thomas G.] Woodward holds the Cumberland and sunk two gunboats and one transport below the mouth of the Harpeth River. The Cumberland is going down and he has no other source of supplies. I wish I could write you something besides War News but I have nought else.

All the Company are here now except Ratcliffe, Roane, and Van McKamie who are detailed as guard at Okolona, being dismounted, that is having no horses—& Mr. Ward who is sick in Miss. somewhere. We have had several recruits lately and have now a fine company. Browder Oliver has been transferred to the 30th Regt. of which his Brother Bill is Quarter Master and he will be assistant. Some folks are born to luck. Our Battallion has been broken up and Harrison's Company is attached to Woodward's Ky. Regt.[9] Our Co. is assigned to it too, but will in all probability never report to it.

My dear I have heard a report that makes me heart sick. A young lady who lives near Homer that I always thought was the pink of perfection has been delivered of a bastard and a *black one* at that. I shall call no names but her Mother was your Mother's friend. I don't know when I have heard anything that has shocked me more. But it has come by two different sources and I cannot help believing it. What is this world coming to. Have you heard it before? It is said that another woman will have one before long. I don't know who that is. Heaven grant it is no one who is my friend. Illegitimacy I fear will not be the least curse of this War. Be sure to write me everything you hear for I have no confidents and anything you may say will be as if you whispered in my ear.

I have not written what I wanted to in this letter. I have written in such haste that I might get a letter off to you, as I know your anxiety to hear from me. I shall write whenever I can and you must not be disappointed if you do not get letters from me regularly. Didn't Johnson Cox and others go to Mexico on some trading expedition instead of avoiding the Conscript. They know they can never live in Louisiana when the War is over if avoiding military duty is their object. Give

[9] Col. Thomas G. Woodward at this time commanded the 2nd Kentucky Cavalry Regiment.

much love to your Father and Mother, Sisters and Brother. I will write Lou some of these days. Remember me to Cousin Mary and to Anna, if she is with you. Tell Mrs. Mitchell & Miss Mary that John is well and doing well. Remember me to them when you see them. Tell your Father I would like from him the news in and around the farm & Mill & Minden. Good Bye dearest one and may God in his infinite mercy preserve and bless you and permit us to meet again when this war is over. Kiss dear little Thornwell a dozen times for his father and a hundred for yourself, Lovingly, your own "Edwin."

9

"A Soldier Only Knows What He Sees"

Camp near Spring Hill, Tenn.
Monday Apr. 20th 1863

My own dear Sarah:

Another week has rolled around and the time has again come for me to write you and I must fulfill this duty though I feel sure there is very little chance of your ever getting it. The mails are so uncertain and letters have such a long way around to go though I hope now since the Abolition scoundrels have left Vicksburg our mail facilities may become somewhat expedited. But the Abolitionists have come to Memphis with some design on our rear I am afraid. I feel sure that there is some important move on foot in our Army too and long before this letter reaches you I believe our Cavalry Corps will be in Ky. I believe in the Rear of Rosecranz or else we will have fallen back across the Tenn. River. We hear conflicting rumors respecting the movements of Bragg's Army that he has advanced & is entrenching 15 miles north of Tullahoma and again that he is fortifying heavily south of the Tenn. River. One thing is certain that he has issued orders to keep 7 days cooked provisions on hand all the time. We hear nothing but rumors here getting no papers through. I did get an "Atlanta Intelligencer" of the 14th day before yesterday that contained some news, a description of the Charleston fight and Telegrams. The news from Abolition papers was quite favorable. The New York Democracy are clamorous for peace. Gold in Wall St. 98¼ & Rumor from the front says that two Ky. Regts. threw down their arms at Franklin 10 miles in advance of us and deliberately marched out, disbanded and went home. It is believed, though Dame Rumor is a deceitful jade.

I believe I have told all the news except one little piece that may be good or bad to you. I hardly know which. I have sent up my petition for a discharge under the "Conscription Act" having faithfully served out my term of original enlistment. It has gone up to Gen'l Van Dorn and I presume to Bragg & Johnston having been gone now three days. I think it will be granted for it cannot be lawfully refused. If it is, I shall send it up to Hon. John Perkins[1] or Henry Marshall and get them to lay it before Pres. Davis and Congress. I am determined to test the validity of civil over military law. Do not count too certainly on my coming home for it may take a long time, especially if I have to send it up to Richmond. If it comes back granted in a few days, I could beat this letter home but want to go by Port Hudson and see William Henry which will probably detain me a week longer. I don't know my dearest that I ought to have told you this but I can never keep anything from you. You may count too strongly on my coming and I may be in a dozen battles before I get the papers back but I hope for the best. I shall still be liable for State service and I am going straight to Gov. Moore & ask for a position in the State service, either in the Corps of Engineers or in some state Cavalry. If our Co. could have been transferred across the River I would not have applied for my discharge but as it is I cannot afford to be so far separated from you my best beloved. If I come home I will examine your class in Algebra with a great deal of pleasure.

I believe I have rec'd yours of March 15th since I last wrote you. [Richard] Ratcliffe sent it through from Okolona by hand. I did not expect it at all and you don't know how rejoiced I was to get it. I was glad to know of your continued good health and that you were in such good spirits. Labor is not such a curse after all when it keeps our minds employed that we brood not over sorrow past and is it not a plan of Divine Providence that the curse pronounced upon ancestral "Adam" may prove a blessing disguised? I regret much to hear that Thornwell stutters, be very careful you do not confirm him in it by your attempts to break him. If you have not succeeded in doing it, put a small pebble in his mouth when he tries to speak and that will break him I think. You made many excuses about the greasy scraps of paper. They need not have been made to your husband for he realizes the scarcity of paper daily, therefore it is very easy to excuse you, but

[1] John Perkins, Jr., represented Louisiana in all three Confederate Congresses.

there was an error in your spelling, the pronoun their instead of the adverb there. But the best scholars are apt to make mistakes sometimes, for you say I have made them. Do not think me hypercritical dearest. I am so proud of my wife that I want her perfect.

This is a most beautiful region of country through here but I am sorry I cannot say much for the morals of it from the way I hear the boys speaking of going out to see women. I fear the standard of virtue is not very high though a mountainous country is historical for easy virtue, a "mountain girl" being the synonym for one of bad character. Of my own knowledge I know nothing except that the presence of a large army is very demoralizing to any section of country. The man you ask me about getting married was John A. Garrett, a relative of John Garrett above Homer. He was paroled by the Yankees being left sick in our retreat from Abbeville. I do not know about it having [neither] seen nor heard anything from him since he left Grenada. He intended to marry and may have done so for all I know. I don't think he was much force anyway.

I wrote Lou a long letter on Friday which I hope she got as I told her about Mother Smith and the Athenaeum. I wrote the news for you. The same day I wrote a letter back to Okolona to our kind friends there. I do not have much time to write and paper is remarkably scarce, in fact none to be had. If I get my discharge I shall go back to Okolona after my clothing. I left my valise there and though I cannot bring it on horseback I can fill my saddlebags. I bought or rather swapped a pair with Parson Ratcliffe yesterday. Gave him $5.00 difference. I had the old pair Rich bro't soap in when I left home first time. I got a very nice pair, patent leather, and I can now carry all my clothes. My horses are both improving. Old Jack is getting fat again on this grass and I have been offered $400 for my mare. I could get $600 for her I think.

Capt. Webb did not like to approve my application for discharge for he dont want me to leave him but I told him I had promised you I should make it and I should keep my promise. I also told him I had no idea of teaching school until the war was over. He hates it very much that he missed seeing Mrs. Webb and so do I. I think he ought to be allowed to go home. He is sick at present and has gone today into the country to try and get well. I feel lost without him for Nat Martin

& Carter are the only officers and neither has got sense enough to lead a blind jackass to water. I'll have some rich things to tell you when I come home if I ever do, and I hope that God may speedily open the way, for I do want to see you so bad, though I get along better than I thought I should before I left you. Some members of the Company are so much enchanted with this country that they say they dont want to go back over the River, but their influence is not much. I believe I wrote you while at Grenada that we had sent a petition to the Sec. of War through Senator Thos. J. Semmes of La. We heard from him Feby. 7th saying that he had received it and would lay it before the War Depart. the next Monday (the 9th). We have heard nothing further from it since and I sent a letter this morning asking in regard to it. I hope it will be granted and that the Co. may come over again.

But I still feel cheerful about the close of the War. I learn that the Northern Conscription Act is pronounced a failure and their troops say they won't stay after their time is out, so I hope the 1st of May will bring about important changes respecting the end of the War. I think their Charleston experience will not tend to render them anxious to continue the War. But God rules over nations as well as individuals and if Christians would pray more sincerely I think an end would sometime come.

This is a poor letter my dearest for I feel unusually dull this evening, very little like letter writing. I haven't your letter by me and consequently cannot tell if I have answered all your questions. I know you did not answer mine if you had gotten all my letters. You must do so in reply to this. I believe I did not tell you that we had a Grand Review of this Cavalry Corps today and several of the boys prophesy a fight soon because we had a Review the next day after I got here from Okolona and the day following we dashed into Franklin. The Inspector Gen'l of Bragg's Army was here today and I do not apprehend a fight very soon. It may be tomorrow though. A soldier only knows what he sees. He never hears anything but orders and these he is expected to obey. But I solace myself with the words of Aeneas "forsitan *etiam haec* olim meminisse Juvabit." The war cannot last always, that is certain but it may be always to many a poor fellow as far as life is concerned, ere it closes.

My darling, now that you are in school do not neglect Thornwell and leave him entirely to Laura's care. You had better take him to school with you if he will not be too much trouble. I know your Mother will be as careful of him as anyone can be but Laura may steal him off some times and he may get hurt. He is our only pet lamb and we cannot be too careful of him. Lou might begin to teach him his letters and that might be a good way to prevent his stammering. Bless him and it does seem at times as if I would leave any how and come home but I wish to leave a good name to our child if we never have any more. But we will have a little daughter if we live, won't we? Tell your Father we ought to have our wheat mill up here. There is a field of 275 acres of the prettiest wheat just beside our Camp. They have no mills worth anything near here. I hope there will be a good wheat crop made in La. this season. We buy wheat here for $200 a bushel and get it ground and have been eating biscuits most of the time since I got here. Beef of the very best though high, our Commissary having paid $190 for a yoke of oxen the other day for beef. The Yankees have ruined a great part of this country along the Pike having totally destroyed fences for miles thereby preventing the planting of crops. I hope however they will never get it again. We are now in a last summer's Yankee Camp.

Say to Mrs. Mitchell that John Lesueur is well, he has taken Sandy to a shop in the country to shoe some horses today. Now, darling, I have written you a long letter. It is most time for roll call and must close. Write me long letters even if I do come home I'll have them burned when they reach camp and if they do not they will prove a source of great pleasure to your husband who loves you devotedly. Give my best love to your Mother & Father, also to Lou and the other girls. Tell Bud he is getting too old to act badly and I want him to improve. Remember me kindly to Dr. & Mrs. Bright also to the Ladies (teachers) at the College. Kiss dear Thornwell a hundred times for his Father and know that you possess my whole heart. Ed.

April 23d 63

[*Editor's Note:* Fay began his letter of April 23 by copying for his wife's information correspondence with General Van Dorn and Congressman John Perkins concerning his unsuccessful effort to obtain release from the army.]

Camp near Spring Hill, Tenn. Apr. 17/63

To Maj. Gen'l Van Dorn

The undersigned born in the State of Alabama and thirty-one years of age was enlisted in Capt. J. Y. Webb's Co. Escort of Brig. Gen'l Cosby and mustered into service of the C.S.A. April 4th 1862 to serve for the term of one year and now prays to be discharged from said service for the following reasons, viz., Having been engaged Principal of an Academy for the past eleven years he is not liable to a longer period of service under either Act of Confederate Congress relating to Conscription. He gave up a school of 50 pupils with the reluctant consent of his patrons, most of his scholars being between the ages of 12 & 18 yrs. and consequently their opportunities of acquiring an education, should the war continue, are extremely limited; that this request is preferred at the instance of his Patrons & Board of Trustees.

Respectfully

Edwin H. Fay

Approved:
(Signed) J. Y. Webb, Capt. Comdg
Gen'l Cosby's Escort

It was undersigned as follows

Hdqrs. 1st Brig. April 17, 1863
The exemption act repealing act, approved 21st April 1863 is by Genl Order A & I Genls Office ordered to be "construed *prospectively* and does not authorize the discharge of any one enlisted or in service prior to 11 day of October 1863." Mr. Fay is not therefore in my opinion entitled to discharge under provisions of the Exemption Act, unless entitled to discharge & subject to re-enrollment at the expiration of his enlistment 4th April '63 in which case he is clearly exempted by the Act above quoted.

Respy forwarded
(Signed) G. B. Cosby, Brig. Gen'l

Genl Van Dorn endorses
Hdqrtrs 1st Cavly Corps Respy forwarded, disapproved
Earl Van Dorn, Maj. Genl.
Hdqrtrs Army Tenn. Apr. 20/63

Genl Bragg's A.A.G. endorses as follows:

Disapproved Brig. Genl Cosby's endorsement approved. The Exemption Act does not apply to anyone in service. By command of Genl Bragg—Kinloch Falconer, A.A. Gen'l.

It came back to me last night and this morning I wrote Hon. John Perkins of Catahoula Parish, at Richmond, Va. as follows.

Believing Dear Sir that you are one of those who are opposed to a *complete* triumph of the Military over the Civil power of the Confed. States, I make bold to address you, the representative of the People of La. tho not from my own District, and to urge you as such representative, to give your attention to the enclosed petition. The right of petition is the only right which a conscientious soldier can use, and as such I sent up the enclosed as directed in the Army Regulations through the intermediate Commanders. But I most *positively* object to the *Military* construction of a plain, as I think, law as shown in the endorsement of Brig. Genl Cosby on the enclosed. I cannot yet be persuaded to believe that the Confed. Congress enacted a law bearing alike on all, yet conferring far greater privilege on men who remained at home and were forced out by act of Conscription, than it does upon those who stepped forward at the time of our Country's greatest peril.

Whether Genl. Cosby, endorsed by Genl Bragg's A.A.G. construes the Act *prospectively* or *retrospectively,* one thing is certain that if I had not volunteered in the Service of my Country Apr. 4th '62 neither nor all the Acts of Congress relating to Conscription passed and published to the world would have included me had I remained in my Schoolroom as my patrons and the Trustees desired me to do. I would not have been forced into Service & cannot see how my volunteering and serving my country faithfully for the period of my enlistment should debar me now from claiming the privileges plainly granted me. Had I not volunteered—I was told by an Officer ranking high in Confed. Service some months since when respectfully protesting against a clear illegality, that "the (I give his very words) Will of the Commanding Genl. and military necessity override all law of Congress," and I am sorry to be compelled in truth to admit that the Officer's assertion has been verified too, in my own experience.

I sent up the petition enclosed as stated in the face of it, at the earnest request of my patrons who are anxious for me to resume my school not that I am anxious to leave the Cause of our Independence as I was one of the earliest Asserters and one of the Candidates on the Secession Ticket in my Parish (Claiborne) but since the petition has been "Disapproved" on what I consider illegal grounds I consider it my duty to use every effort in my power to obtain the expression of the opinions of those better versed in Military Jurisprudence than Brig. Genl Cosby or Genl. Bragg's A.A.G.

I am aware it is the province of a Soldier to obey and for the proper discharge of my duty in that respect I appeal to the testimony of my immediate officers—but to surrender all of even a private's rights without protest I think is the first step towards a Military Despotism and the right of appeal or protest I am unwilling to surrender. Feeling thus, may I, an admirer of your course since the birth of our Young Republic, request that you lay this letter before the War Depart. I would not have troubled you, dear Sir, but would have addressed this directly to Pres. Davis but thought I might possibly not reach his eye, and the knowledge that you have ever been the soldier's as well as the people's friend, is my only excuse. As to my character and standing I take pleasure in referring you to my fellow townsman Col. John L. Lewis of Minden, La. also to two of my former friends and acquaintances, Hon. Wm. L. Yancey[2] & Hon. Thos. H. Watts—Hoping that I may hear from you at your earliest convenience, I am sir, Most respectfully yours &c.

Such my own darling One are the efforts made to come home to you and you see how far I have succeeded. I have but little hope now as everything goes by favoritism in Military matters and I have no political influence through which to pull the strings but as I have now appealed to the highest authority I shall have to be content with that decision. But I have learned to expect nothing and shall not consequently be disappointed should it meet a similar fate at the pinnacle of power. I am determined to assert my rights whether I obtain them or not. But enough of this.

I was greatly surprised last night to get a letter from you so late as March 30th sent across the River by Mr. Smith at Meridian but in the same package came letters mailed in Minden Aprl. 6th & 3rd so you see my dearest that the mails prove faithful too—They were directed to Columbia while yours was sent through Okolona by hand.

[2] William L. Yancey, "fire-eating" secessionist leader of Alabama, was at this time a prominent member of the Confederate Senate. He died July 27, 1863.

I was so sorry my dearest to hear that you were having chills again. Cannot you break them up? Leave no effort untried to do so and spare no expense for your health is dearer to me than all the world besides. But while speaking of it: Have you ever had the Wagon repaired for Thornwell? If not, dearest, do do it at once for his papa will have him 'A aggie' and he may haul 'ood lots with Ben & Black. Mary too. Bless him, his father loves him and would dream of him every night only the nights are too short and he is too tired to dream except of Mother *some times,* not often and then as if she was separated from him and he could not come to her.

You spoke dearest of going out to Dr. Bacon's but did not tell me how you happened to go, nor how long you were sick. Chills are a bad beginning for a teacher. You had better hitch up the buggy and take Bud and go to Texas and that trip will cure you of chills particularly if you will camp out soldier fashion. Maybe a sight of my old *sweet heart* would cure the chills on you. It would bring them on me if she was what I last saw her—such a heroine.

I have written you a long letter only a few days ago and cannot more than fill this sheet now. I am sorry, truly sorry dearest one that my criticisms have caused you to think so many excuses necessary when writing me. Your every fault even when mentioned has been previously excused. You will avoid all mistakes by reading over your letters after having written them. You used to be an excellent hand at correcting school girls compositions. I remember that and sometimes even discovered those my eyes had overlooked. My dearest if I did not love you so much I would not be so anxious that you do everything right. You know that. You say I find fault with you for not writing often. Well perhaps I do but you can't imagine the pain it is to have "Letters" cried out in Camp and see others getting them and yourself doomed to disappointment. But I will try and not complain more because I know you have written me when sick in bed and unable to do it but I shall begin to complain again if you don't tell me the news more thoroughly and answer my questions more particularly. In some of my last I have asked a great many and I do not know whether or not you have received them as you certainly have not *answered them.*

This morning when we went out to drill we were met by a courier from Genl. Cosby who told us that he (the Genl.) wanted us at his HdQrtrs. and accordingly we wended our way thither and drew up in line in front when Mrs. Cosby presented us with a flag of pink silk with an Italian Cross in blue in the Center and 13 stars in white above the arms of it on either side. Together with Lieuts. Watkins, Martin & Carter and John Lesueur I was appointed on a Committee to draft a series of Resolutions expressive of our sentiments and present them to Mrs. Gen'l Cosby but I was writing this letter to you and I would not stop to make Resolves to Mrs. Cosby when I was complaining of the tyranny of Gen'l in disapproving my petition for Discharge. No one in the Co. knows anything about the application except R. E. Thompson, [John A.] Lesueur, Watkins & Capt. Webb and only Watkins & John that it was disapproved and I do not intend anyone else to know it. You need not say anything about it at home except to your Father and Mother. It must not go outside the family and the children are not cautious you know.

I hear thro' Mrs. Bates & Carter that Alonzo Johnson, Cox, Reid et omnes ejusdem have been drafted in the Militia of the State. The lot has justly fallen on Jonah this time. But to War news here. I wrote you in my last some 3 days ago that we had been ordered to keep 2 days rations of provisions in our haversacks. Well we have not moved yet but I think will in a few days North of the Cumberland in Rear of Roseranz while Bragg makes a vigorous attack in front. I think we shall whip Old Rosey this time but I don't like the idea of going where I cannot get your letters or you mine. But such is the fate of the War and a man can't die but once and it is only a question of time if one can't be discharged when one wants to.

By the By I saw a letter from Parson Henderson and he speaks flatteringly of his boarding house. He did not dream I reckon I would ever see the letter. Lou seems quite charmed with Mr. Smith. I knew his two elder Bros. and they were both very handsome men. One a real Bill Harris. This one I don't think I ever saw. Lou had better look out how she fancies young gentlemen. I have given her away and she may not catch the young gent she once said she had set her cap for. Lou must weave a suit of gray jeans before she thinks of young gents. That is to be the test when the War is over.

I think it will be some days before we move from here and I hope I shall get a letter from you directed to Columbia before we do. Write as often as you can dearest but never trouble yourself again to write when you are too unwell to sit up for I had rather forego the pleasure of a letter than have you put to so much trouble. I have been sitting down with a valise in my lap since 12M and the sun is almost down so I'll begin to draw to a close. Give much love for me to your Mother & Father, the children one and all. Remember me to Mr. & Mrs. Henderson. If we go into Ky. as I think, I will deliver her letter which I still have in possession. Kiss Thornwell a hundred times for his Father. Be particular with him Mother. I am glad to find he has stopped stuttering. Take care of your own health dearest for what would the world be to me without you. Write and tell your father to write. As for paper the Margin of a Newspaper or a leaf from a blank book will do. A hundred kisses and my whole heart to you my love. Ed. H. Fay

Camp Spring Hill, Tenn. May 9th '63

My own dear Wife:

I have just heard this moment that a Col. Griffith[3] of Texas Legion is going to start across the River today at 12 M. and as I fear from the fact that not hearing from you since the 30th March that letters do not really cross the Miss. I avail myself of this opportunity of sending you a hasty note in pencil for my pen is being used by Oliver Butler in copying duplicate payroll that I made out this morn, and as my head was aching badly I got him to copy the other two. My precious wife, you know not how uneasy I feel at not hearing from you and I would do anything to get out of Tenn. so I could get news from home, though we are very well situated as Escort of Gen'l Cosby.

Yesterday Van Dorn was buried in Columbia having been shot by a Dr. Peters whose wife he had been too intimate with. He went into his room about 10 A.M. and shot him through the back of the Head, the Ball lodging in his brain though he lived till 2 P.M. but insensible. It may be a great gain to the Confederacy. I do not think it was a

[3] Probably Lt. Col. John S. Griffith, 6th Texas Cavalry Regiment.

great loss. Peters made his escape and went to the Federal lines through a good southern man.[4] This Cav. Corps paid him the last tribute of respect yesterday morning. Jackson takes command for the time being and Cosby commands Division. There has been no fighting lately.

I wrote you some weeks ago and sent it to Mobile to be mailed. I do hope you will get it for I told you of the success of my application for Discharge as teacher of schools. It was disapproved but I sent up a protest to Jeff Davis through Hon. Jno. Perkins of La. and I believe it will be *approved* by the highest authority, though I have made up my mind to remain during the war.

I saw a paper of May 6th containing a dispatch from Gen. Lee that he had thoroughly beaten Joe Hooker on the Rappahanock, Stonewall having crossed and got in his rear but it is a serious loss to us as he had his left arm shot off close to his shoulder. A. P. Hill and Henry Heth were both slightly wounded.[5] Forrest who left us some two weeks since captured 1200 Yanks at Moulton, Ala. and cut off 1600 more who escaped into the mountains and were making their way towards Rome, Ga. when the Citizens took up arms and drove the advance guard from the city and held them till Forrest came up behind and they surrendered without firing a gun. 1600 good horses, arms, wagons, mules &c and 2800 prisoners with 300 killed. Our loss was 10 killed and 20 wounded.[6] You have probably gotten this news if your Eastern mail is not cut off. I hope our successes will bring the Yanks to their senses and that they will make peace. The New Orleans true Delta says the U.S. are on the eve of war with England & France. God in his mercy grant that this War may speedily close.

I got a letter from Spencer a few days ago which I will send you. Poor Chum, he has suffered as *we* darling have. I sent your last letter

[4] For an account of Van Dorn's death, by one of his officers, see G. A. Hanson, *Minor Incidents of the Late War* (Bartow, Florida, 1887), 32–33. Contemporary reports of the incident may be found in the *Richmond Daily Dispatch,* May 13 and May 25, 1863.

[5] The reference is to the battle of Chancellorsville, May 1–3, 1863.

[6] Fay alludes here to Gen. N. B. Forrest's pursuit and capture of Brig. Gen. Abel D. Streight and his entire force of about 1,500 Union Cavalrymen, May 3, 1863, near Cedar Bluffs, Alabama. See Horn, *The Army of Tennessee,* 234, and *Battles and Leaders,* IV, 414.

to Mother as I was writing her, not having heard a word from her since I left there and I wanted her to see how our youngest darling could talk notwithstanding you wrote her at the same time. Did I tell you that Will Fay wants me to take his place in the Office of the Factory after the War if I live and will do so. What think you of it? It will be a very laborious task but labor no matter how constant will be sweet when performed for you my own precious one and when I can be encouraged by your approving glance daily. I presume ere this you have seen Mrs. Webb. I am sorry for her poor woman missed seeing her husband. What would I not give to see you dearest this bright day of May. I have dreamed of you for several nights and saw you last night ride into camp.

I am saving Jack for a saddle horse for you when I come back. He has proved himself a war horse and shall do no more menial office than to carry my lady love should I live to bring him back. Was offered $200 for him last night and have been $600 for La Lis. She was appraised $250. I am fearful you cannot read this pencil interlining but I have only four sheets left and can therefore only afford this half sheet, but if you can only make out my scribbling it is all I care for. I know only you see my letters. You recollect hearing me speak of Eliza Withers. Her husband W. H. Ewing died last week in Franklin from effects of whiskey. The Yanks hold Franklin or I would go and see Mrs. Withers, her mother. I always liked her Mother, but not herself. I feel sorry for her though for he was her husband.

I expect to write you a good long letter in a few days and send by David Caufield and Thos. Geren, the latter of whom has been discharged and David will probably be, being over 40 yrs. Thos. Geren was under 18 yrs. when enlisted. He is waiting for David's papers to come through and then intends starting. I hope you will send me something by Ratcliffe and Van McKamie who I learn are at home. Carter is going to take these letters over to the Texas Legion so must close now. Much love to your Father & Mother and all the children. John Lesueur is well tell Mrs. Mitchell. Write me long letters dearest. I don't care how close or how much interlined if paper is scarce. I have never I believe told you who my messmates were. Capt. Webb, Watkins, LeSueur and myself. We have Rich and Sandy, John's boy to cook for us. Rich, tell Mary, does very well, is a good cook and is a better boy than formerly, tho I gave him a good whipping the other day. I wish you would send me another shirt, domestic, if you have a chance. Kiss Thornwell a hundred times. A heartful of love to you dearest. Your loving Husband

Camp Spring Hill, May 20, 1863

My own dear, dear Sarah:

You do not know how much rejoiced I was last Wednesday while up at Wartrace to get from the 19th Regt. your long, interesting, beautifully written and truly wifely letter sent by Capt. Kennedy and you know not how much my heart warmed towards you for writing me so long a letter. You were really one time egotistical and that is how I want your letters to be (grammar?). This time, too, I was proud of the hand writing for there was unmistakable evidence of an effort to improve it, all words were spelled correctly but some were left out, for instance, I could not find out from whom you got the large sheet of foolscap, but presume it was Cousin Mary or Mrs. Henderson. You know, my dear, I take great interest in your inner everyday life but you were a little selfish not to mention that Mrs. Capt. Webb got back, when he was so anxious to hear it, as he has heard nothing from her since she left Natchez April 9th and he calculated of course you would say something about her return. I feel sure she had reached home in safety but he is quite despondent. I hope he will hear from her soon as letters have reached camp mailed the 20th Apr. in Minden.

But you will be anxious to know how I came to be at Wartrace 60 miles east by South from here. Gen'l Cosby ordering a detail to go there from the Escort and knowing Spencer was there I detailed myself as one of the Couriers, Gus Minchew, the other. It took us a day & a half to reach Wartrace and there I found Chum [Spencer] and Robt. & John Nall with their Battery on the outskirts of town encamped in a beautiful grove.[7] I hardly recognized Spencer he looked

[7] As previously noted, Spencer was in Semple's Battery of Bragg's Army. This unit, to which Robert and John Nall, presumably Fay's friends of Prattville days, also belonged, was then stationed at Wartrace, Tennessee, near Shelby-

so fat and hearty. His health was excellent though considerably bronzed by exposure. Gus went to the 19th and bro't me your good letter, while I remained with Spencer 2 days & 3 nights. Poor Chum, he was sad indeed, he, too, having lost his first born, though he was more calm and collected than I expected, could control his feelings far better than I could do when speaking of our darling's death. We talked over old times and it was pleasant and refreshing. He expressed a great deal of affection for you, and wants us to live together when the war is over if we do live till that time. He wishes your Father to invest his money left in Wimberly's safe, in seven per cent bonds of the Confederacy. Please get your Father to attend to it at once as it has to be done before the first of August if at all. If you had gotten my letters it might have been done before the 22nd April and at 8 pr. cent. Be sure and have it done. I read a letter he received from Jennie May 6th and I assure you it was a most beautiful and loving letter. She loves him devotedly and I rejoice that I was instrumental in bringing it about. I know Spencer thanks me in his inmost heart. He wished me to give you his love when I wrote and I accordingly do so.

I was pleased with Robt. Nall. He is a nice young man I was told as unmoved amid the hottest fire as at ordinary drill in Camps. John is a boy yet but as brave as needs be. So much for my visit to Wartrace. On my return I found a letter from Mother of Apr. 24th, a long time reaching here. I had despaired of hearing and had written her only a few days before. It was lucky that Hyder bro't my letter through for if it had been mailed in Okolona I would never have received it I fear for the Yanks have been there and my letter would have been captured or run off and when I would have gotten it there is no telling. I wrote Miss Addie & Mat Madry after coming up here but have heard nothing from them yet.

But to the answer to your letter. I agree with you my own dear wife that Dr. Bayliss has no business with the Prophecies. He had better be prophesying when the war will close by adding his effort in that direction. It is strange how evanescent the patriotism of some of the early volunteers was. In fact I think it is the only time we have

---

ville. Visiting friends and relatives in other organizations was a favorite diversion of Johnny Rebs.

seriously needed men. I think as does Spencer that the present summer will witness the closing scenes of this war and now we need every man to assist us in making our victory as complete as possible. I fear, however, that the North is entirely enslaved as they have allowed Vallandigham to be arrested, tried by a court Martial and be sentenced by Burnside to banishment to the Tortugas for two years, which sentence the Gorilla King has commuted by "being sent South out of our lines, penalty death for re-entering them."[8] Thus the famous baboon gets rid of the only man who has the courage to denounce his usurpation of power and the unholy war which is being waged against us. If they submit to V[allandigham's] banishment, Abe's Govt. is certainly supreme.

We have various accounts of our successes but the news that especially cheers us is that Kirby Smith has whipped out Banks, but no particulars are given. We also hear that a portion of Grant's Army's 15,000 occupied Jackson, Miss. for two hours driving out our 4000, which being reinforced to 10,000 drove the flying and discomfited enemy back towards the Miss. River. We only now and then get a paper and never hear the confirmation or particulars of anything. I brought about 20 papers from Wartrace and our Camp has been quite a reading community for two or three days. The boys who went out with a flag of truce yesterday got a Cincinnati Gazette & also a Commercial but they are filled with falsehoods which serve in an astonishing manner to bolster up the courage of their troops. If Kirby Smith can only capture Banks' whole army, or Grant be captured, a decisive battle anywhere I believe would be in our favor greatly. We learn that 14 "Alabamas" have left the English coast and that they are doing everything they can to fortify New York & Boston. But I presume you get news too in the papers. If you have any on that side of the River be sure to write it for we can hear nothing reliable except through private sources.

I feel sure you have failed to receive several of my letters and I fear the direction, Okolona, has caused several of yours to miscarry. If you

[8] Tortugas, commonly known as "Dry Tortugas," was a notorious prison maintained by the Federals off the Southwest coast of Florida. Fay errs in stating that Vallandigham was ordered to Tortugas; he was to be imprisoned at Fort Warren in Boston. See Roseboom, *The Civil War Era,* 412.

direct to Cosby's Escort, Van Dorn's Corps you will always send them through if no post office is mentioned though now, Columbia, Tenn. is the place. I have written you punctually every 6 or 8 days since I have been here but fear you have failed to get any of my letters though others letters go thro' by mail both ways. I wrote a long letter in pencil and sent by hand just previous to going to Wartrace which I hope you will get as I gave you a detailed account of Van Dorn's death. My letters have all contained more or less news. Some I dislike very much your not getting, as they contained some important information.

We heard yesterday from Senator Semmes, and he says his application at the War Dept. for the transfer of our Company was unsuccessful, that they would transfer no troops across the River. Now I believe if Col. Lewis and McDonald would through Gov. Moore exert themselves with Kirby Smith we might still be brought over there. Will not Minden people try what they can do? I would write Col. Lewis on the subject if I had another sheet of paper, but it is so scarce, only worth $600 a quire. Your father can talk with him just as well.

But I commenced once to answer your letter, and got as far as the Prophecies & Dr. Bayliss & led off. I have always wanted to read Armageddon, not because I had any confidence in his explanation of Prophesy but as a matter of curiosity. I do not think those things revealed to man, but you need not to have waded out for I am sure my wife could wade in any water of learning that Dr. Bayliss could. The sketch of your instructress' life was interesting though not diversified and suggested the questions if *rations* are short at the College that Misses Nettie &c share yours and Lou's. The next decision I have to make is relative to Dr. & Mrs. Bright's bed. I decide on summing up the evidence and weighing the testimony that the matrimonial bed belongs to the party who *does not* wear the *breeches.* They (the Breeches) having a right there only by sufferance, The Court finds accordingly—I am sorry Mrs. Bright dislikes Mrs. F——Do you know the cause thereof. The reception of the Coat question has been frequently decided and entered so upon the docket but as an appeal has been taken this Court decides and affirms the Coat is a decided success and reflects much credit upon the sewer. It will be a fine next winter coat. I thought I wrote about Mrs. Sayre putting on three more pockets. Did I not? The soap, Drawers, wool socks &c came too and were thankfully received and gratefully acknowledged. Rich can wear the socks next winter if I get back to Okolona to get my baggage. I left it all there save a change. Gladly will I receive the cottonade Pants, if I can get them. I can make drawers of them in winter. I need another pair—I wrote you some things in my other letter and presume as it went through by hand you will get it. Send me 50 Wm Shields & Co. envellopes by 1st opportunity. I am about out. I left plenty of paper at Okolona only brought one quire with me. I wish I had another now. Have four sheets left now, and will save them for you. Perhaps I may come across some more some of these days.

I don't think there will be a battle here in Middle Tenn., Bragg nor Rosecranz being willing to make the attack. There is some move on foot, it may be to turn the left flank of old Rosey. We are ordered to keep 4 days rations constantly on hand but don't think we will move. I learned last night that the 12th La. Col. Scott has been mounted. I am inclined to think this will turn out a Cavalry war after all. But I hope my old "sweetheart" will be successful in her efforts to make peace, while I assure you I shall never regret not being Mrs. Fay's Husband. I read that to Capt. Webb and he says you are yet jealous of that woman. Is it so, dearest. You told me when at home that you would never feel so any more. Do you ever? Tell me truly? I told him he had more the advantage as his wife was jealous of his old sweetheart and he acknowledged the case. I wish you would write me freely all your feelings. But I cannot believe that you ever doubt for one moment that your husband's heart is all your own. But if so tell me truly for a frank confession is the quickest remedy for wrong. I think with you that it would be far more consistent with the Christian modesty which so much becomes the female character to pray in secret and the Lord who heareth in secret will perhaps reward openly. That longing for notoriety has ruined her in my eyes forever. The charm was completely banished last October. Her interest now does not tally well with a remark you wrote me and I questioned her about. She had no interest in this war and did not want her friends even to mention it in their letters to her. It did not concern her in the least. Ah, fickleness thy name is woman. If she will agree to make peace and fulfill it you will love her, won't you my dearest. But I have devoted already too much of this space to her and her vagaries. "Let them rest in obscurity and peace till other times and other men can do justice to her character." I think she is somewhat crazy, and told her so when I last saw her.

As regards the letter by Mr. Gregg, it has not yet come to hand nor do I think it will soon for Mr. Gregg was a deserter and I fear he will not come across the River again.[9] I presume you have seen [Richard] Ratcliffe, [S. G.] McKamie & [J. M.] Pearce, they having, as we have heard, gone home. I hope you will have gotten several of my letters before they leave as I want you to answer several in the ones you send by them. You must tell me what is going on in your little world of Minden as you are at the College, the HdQrtrs of news. You'll do better next time, won't you?

We are camped now on a high hill ¾ mile from Spring Hill overlooking the town and have a beautiful vista of 12 or 15 miles in every direction except the rear. It would be a favorite camp if there was level land enough on which to make a pallet, but we came near rolling down hill and if an oven or pot gets tipped over it does not stop under 100 yds. A field of wheat of 275 acres lies between us and the village and while speaking of wheat I must add that the whole country is covered with wheat which is now most of it in full bloom. An abundant crop will be harvested in 4 or 5 weeks, the largest by far ever made in this country. Oh if it were not for this desolating war this country would be a Paradise. But let us hope for the best. There are numbers of Union tories in this part of the country.

I am glad you stuck it out in regard to the Presbyterians worshipping in the Methodist Church. Does Dr. Bright preach at the Baptist Church in the forenoon? Why not there at 3 P.M.? You say "I felt really unhappy last night and began to regret taking Music lessons." Now dearest, is that right? Did you know what a pleasure the knowledge of it gave your husband, you would never regret it again. You

[9] Probably Private John J. Gregg, Company C, 6th Louisiana Cavalry, a resident of Bossier Parish. Muster rolls for January and February, 1863, show him absent without leave. He was paroled at Shreveport, June 21, 1865. Booth, *La. Confed. Soldiers,* III, pt. 1, 98.

knew he would not think you *vain* and *frivolous.* You have done just to suit your husband and if you prize his approval know that you have it. Banish such thoughts as you hint at and never again let them annoy you. I have the utmost confidence in you my own darling one and am sure you will prove worthy of it. I think your Music will be much more of a benefit now than ever before. It is not one's duty to be always sad, because we have experienced a great sorrow.

You say you are going to spinning when you quit teaching. I would like you to be like Penelope, a very domestic woman, that you might instruct your handmaids in all kinds of work. In other words I would be pleased to have you able at a fair to exhibit the finest piece of cloth at the same time that you could adjourn to the parlor and surpass all the others on the Piano. Your only fault, if fault it be, is apathy. You must encourage and cultivate by every means in your power, energy. Bud is more like you in that respect than any of the children and you see how it seems in him. Do not think I am finding fault in the least degree. I only mean to exhort you to increased diligence in conquering your only fault if it is a fault. I fain would have her whom I hold dearest on earth come quite up to my ideal of perfection and she can do it too I feel sure. Be Queen of domestic affairs and I know dearest you will be a fairy queen of music too. Be both dearest if either. You will still be my dearest beloved if neither. Dearest my pen will not express nor this paper contain my feelings which flow out towards you. Do they elicit a response from your heart or do you fashionably love me just because you are my wife and cannot therefore love another. Tell me, Tell me truly dearest, e'en tho the truth would kill.

I am not surprised that Cornick is deposed, I only wonder he ruled so long. A petition from the Trustees and patrons now would restore me to your arms. Are you too Patriotic? It can be done now, if mooted. The Sec. of War could grant it for he has done the like. I do not wish ever to teach again in Minden but would do so to be with you, tho not one day longer than the close of this war. I think we may live in Ala. Will Fay has agreed to stay where he is if I will consent to take his place at the close of the War and $4000 is more than I can make in the school room.

I am glad Aunt Ann is going to send you a homespun dress, don't let pride keep you from wearing it, dearest. I may keep this letter for some days as I fear to trust it to the mail. I may write more. If they are discharged I shall send this by David Caufield and Thom. Geren. I want you to have it. Your "please forward" was not inappropriate by any means for Hyder obeyed your instructions and sent it by Gus. I read it to Spencer. After writing so far on Monday I washed and changed clothes, came back to camp where we found orders to be prepared to move at a moments notice. We fixed up tho' I was convinced we would not move that night. (Read Mother's letter now).[10] So did not hurry. The next morning we were ordered to be ready by 11 A.M. We got off about 2 P.M. and are now in camp 3 ms. south of Columbia on our way as I prophesied 6 days ago to Miss. Will move southward again today towards Huntsville, Ala. I believe Rosecranz is sending all his Army to reinforce Grant in Miss. and I know a part of Bragg's has gone there.

Just before starting from our Hill Camp yesterday Caufield got his discharge all right and will start home as soon as we reach Miss. I shall send this letter by him but will continue to write as long as I can find any paper to write on. Capt. Webb got two letters from Mrs. Webb yesterday and was relieved of a load of anxiety I assure you. He is not very well this morning. Tell Mrs. Henderson that three weeks ago, despairing of getting to Ky. I sent her letter by a cousin of Lt. Watkins who lives within 25 miles of Elkton, Ky. and who promised to deliver in person her letter to her sister. I thought it was the best I could do, tho I assure her I should have been pleased with an opportunity to deliver it myself.

In Columbia we heard that Grant had been defeated at Jackson and we had captured 10,000 prisoners. I believe the great battle will be fought in the Valley of the Miss. and that state too, and will be the decisive one of the War. If we go to Columbus, Miss. I can get my valise and some more paper. David Caufield can tell you my address. I expect it will be Columbus, Miss. You know the rest. But "Boots & Saddles" are sounded. I'll write at next encampment. A loving kiss for you dearest.

[10] The rest of this letter, and the first part of the one beginning on May 24, were written between the lines of his mother's letter to him, dated April 24, 1863.

Sunday 24th, Decatur, Ala. May '63

My last was written 3 ms. south Columbia. That evening we started at 4 P.M. and travelled 25 miles camping about 12 o'clock. The next day Watkins and I left the Command and went to see Robt. Thompson who was sick at Maj. Marks some miles in the country and overtook the command at Decatur. We had a pleasant time. I meant to have written you every day but have not been able to do it. This letter [Note: Written between lines on one from his mother. Ed.] I have torn, it having stuck to the envellope when I pulled off the stamps. I had written this far when Col. Pinson, Comd'r Brigade, came along and we had to saddle up and come on. We are now 3 miles from Courtland, Ala. having reached our camp last night after dark. I slept under the shade of a large oak and dreamed of you, my *best beloved* but only waked to find that you *were not* lying upon my arm and it was not your well remembered arm lying so affectionately upon my breast. No, it was only a dream. No wife, no Thornwell near but Lieut Watkins snoring on the other side. Such a dream. I wonder if in the silent watches of the night you ever think of your husband lying under the broad canopy of heaven upon the damp ground. If you ever do be sure his spirit is holding communion with yours through the medium of silver winged dreams. But to the incidents of the morning, for the above reflections make me very homesick.

Well, first on waking up, Lieut. Watkins' horse was stolen and cannot be found, so Rich has to ride in the wagon and let him have "Dandy Jack" but the bugle sounds Boots & Saddles so I must close abruptly. Good Bye. Au Revoir.

Tuesday Morn Sunrise. We remained at Courtland till 4 o'clock and then marched 20 miles in dust so thick that you could cut it with a knife. Got to camp on this creek at 1 o'clock in the night. Have had no rations for two days. Went supperless to bed and this morning ate a little raw bacon and a slice of unsifted bread made of yellow meal. It is said we move 40 miles today, 30 of it without water. We got glorious news from Vicksburg yesterday. That the enemy had attacked it several times and had been repulsed with a heavy loss. That Beauregard was on one side and Johnston on the other and they would probably get all of Grant's Army. That Price had taken Helena, Ark. etc. But the Bugle sounds Saddle up.

Thursday, May 28, Moscow, Ala. We started at sunrise and marched 40 miles yesterday. Did not stop till after dark. I intended writing yesterday noon but had to sleep + as we did not get into Camp till 12 o'clock the evening before.

24 Miles N.E. Columbus, Miss. I wrote as far as the cross in the line above at Moscow when we had to move on and now in this creek swamp on my knee I will resume my letter as I got a good night's sleep last night and can do without today, but I have nothing new or interesting to tell you. I am the dirtiest, dustiest mortal you ever saw I reckon. I had the domestic shirt and drawers you made for me stolen 2 ms. south of Columbia, Tenn. They were taken out of my saddle bags. No it was the old pair of drawers I bro't from home with me that were stolen. I'll borrow clothes while I have mine washed and then I won't have so much to carry. I hope I'll have a chance to go to Okolona and get my valise. Watkins and John Lesueur dropped out yesterday and I presume will go by that way. I expect we will go from Columbus to Jackson & Vicksburg. I do hope we will not get up in North Miss. again. I believe I forgot to reply to your query as to whether I wanted those cottonade pants. Yes, I do, for those Sister Sarah made me are all worn out in front rubbing against my saddle. I am going to try and have them mended.

It is very dry and dusty not having rained here for three weeks. I do hope it will rain before we have to march any more. Oh if I could only go home with [David] Caufield & [John] Clinton and see you again and if all the good news is true I hope I can before long. I'll take another half sheet. I'll take this *half* sheet of Confederate paper, dearest as I expect it will contain all I have to write though I could write you daily forever but expect will have a chance to send it off soon, can't tell. I have written all this letter on my Memorandum book, lying on my knee. Oh dearest what would I not give to be with you today. I do so want to see our little Thornwell. If Cavalry was ever stationary I would have you come to me. I understand we are going clear to Columbus so I will stop writing now, and sleep some so I won't fall off my horse tonight. I love you and you only my own dear one. Au Revoir.

Columbus 30th. Well dearest, I spent last night with ex-Governor Whitfield and his daughter, your Cousin Julia.[11] The circumstances were as follows. Rich went up town and enquired and told them whom he belonged to and Mrs. H. came to camp in her carriage and Mr. Whitfield came on horseback and invited me to stay to supper and all night to which I readily consented, as it looked very much like raining. I left this morning after breakfast. But I have skipped lines. I'll try and do better. Your Cousin George is Quartermaster at Jackson, Henry is on Baldwin's Staff and Antony is in Commissary Dept. on Baldwin's Staff. Your Cousin Sarah Morton is married. They told me several other things that in the hurry and bustle of moving I do not remember. We are moving and I'll stop till we stop again. Your uncle sent much love to your Mother & self. He was at your Grandpa's in Jany. and left him quite well he says. He (Gov.) has just returned from Richmond. I was kindly treated but they did not talk enough about your Mother and yourself to suit me. They live in style. Columbus is a pretty place and I had a fine time bathing in the River.

If I only had some clothes to put on. I tried to get a pass this morning to go by Okolona but Col. Starke would not sign it, as he is in Command of the Brigade, ranking Col. Pinson, who has had command since Gen'l Cosby left. I have a pr. of drawers in my valise there. It is good enough for me though for I should have gone yesterday to Col. Pinson who would have granted it.[12] Old Starke told me a lie and I came off. Every one in his own Regt. despises him. However, it is all for the best somehow or it would not have been so. We expect to go from here to Canton and thence rumor says to Yazoo City but I believe we will go to Jackson and below Vicksburg in the rear of the enemy. I hope we will do something soon. I wish I knew how matters stand at Vicksburg for I learned this morning that our

[11] James Whitfield, by virtue of his position as President of the Mississippi Senate, became Governor of Mississippi in November, 1851, and continued in the office until January, 1852.

[12] Col. R. A. Pinson commanded the 1st Mississippi Cavalry Regiment.

batteries at Snyder's Bluff had been abandoned and that the enemy were getting their supplies by way of Yazoo River. It is said we are going to Yazoo City which is feared the enemy hold. I do not know when this will reach you as there is no telling when Caufield will get off. But I'll stop now. Goodbye my own dearest one.

3 ms. East of Louisville, Miss. June 1st, Monday Morn. Six months & 13 days since I left you my dearest one and how my heart yearns towards you and my home, but I know not when I shall ever see them again. We have saddled up ready to start and are on the road the Yanks under Grierson travelled.[13] I do not know what County unless it is Oktibbaha, for we have travelled so much in the night that I have lost my geographical reckoning. I have breakfasted *most sumptuously* on raw ham, cold unsifted cornbread and a raw onion. Is not your mouth watering for some of it? Just step in and breakfast with me. We heard yesterday that the enemy had attacked Vicksburg with greater fury than ever and had been twice repulsed with the slaughter of 40,000 and loss of 10,000 prisoners, but I have lost confidence in Telegraphic dispatches in a great measure.[14] While in Columbus I mailed a letter to Mother and enclosed in the envelope your last long dear one rec'd at Wartrace. Oh darling if you were only on this side the River so I could hear from you regularly I could stand it better. I take great pleasure in feeling that this will be almost certain to reach you as it goes by hand. Will you love me half as well when reading it as I do you when writing? Yes, six months have passed since I have seen you and I do not believe if God spares my life that it will be six months longer before I see you again. I cannot believe this war will last another half year. But I will not fill out my sheet now for fear I may have something more to write at a future day. Mon coeur est le votre's.

[13] For an excellent account of Col. Benjamin H. Grierson's spectacular 600-mile raid, with some 1,700 Union cavalry, from LaGrange, Tennessee, down through Mississippi to Baton Rouge, Louisiana, April 17–May 2, 1863, see D. Alexander Brown, *Grierson's Raid* (Urbana, Illinois, 1954).

[14] Grant made two assaults on Vicksburg, May 19 and 22, before settling down to the siege that led to capture of the city and its defenders on July 4, 1863. Grant's total casualties in the two assaults were probably less than 4,000. See K. P. Williams, *Lincoln Finds a General* (New York, 1949——) IV, 386–390.

Tuesday 12 M On the Road south of Kosciusko. Nothing to tell you dearest today. Heard yesterday through Mr. Ward at Louisville of Ratcliffe's coming on this side the River. He was at Dr. Webb's in Scooba. I do hope he has a package of letters for me for I have done nothing but think of you since I heard it. Oh if I could only see you. When, oh, when will this war close. I do wish the trustees would write to Jeff Davis. He had a teacher discharged the other day upon such an application. Why cannot I be. If I could only get an appointment to some service under Gov. Moore I could then be discharged *by promotion.* Anything to get across the River. I'll send you my pass from Okolona to Tenn.[15] I don't expect I can write much longer today for old Starke is saddled up to go right now. Expect we will reach Canton tomorrow for we have been now 17 days on the way and I am tired of travelling. "To horse" is sounded. I must mount.

Wednesday morning 8 A.M. 25 miles from Canton. Well this far on our march, now the 20th day & the most dusty disagreeable time I assure you. Our Co. went off the Road last night to a house to get corn and camped there. I ate supper and breakfast and paid a dollar for fat middling and cornbread, but had butter and molasses, the latter being something that we have not seen in a long time nor sugar either, but you know I seldom grumble about eating matters so I get enough. After stopping last light I went to the Spring and found a tub and dipped up a tub of cold water and had a fine bath and if I had only had some clean clothes I would have felt very well but I have no drawers, having been wearing these all the way from Spring Hill. But I'll send up to Okolona and get my baggage if we ever go into camp again for a few days.

We have now moved about a mile away from a weed which is said to kill horses and I'll now resume my scribbling. If you are ever able to make it out I'll be glad. There are a thousand rumors afloat

[15] The pass enclosed in the letter stated: "E. H. Fay. My dear Sir: Today we leave Okolona for Columbia via Pikeville, Moulton, Decatur unless circumstances render a change necessary. If so, you will follow on our track as best you can. Come on as rapidly as possible showing this to all guards and pickets as permit for this. . . . [On back of sheet] Pass Bearer & 1 Man Gen. Cosby's Com'd. I. L. Bullock, Prov. Marshall."

about our successes at and around Vicksburg. I do not believe them to be very reliable. Expect we will have some very heavy fighting there but of our own success I am not doubtful and I really hope that our Southern land has been sufficiently punished for its sins and we be relieved in some way of God's own appointment of our sufferings in this War. If it (the war) would only close now there might be some happiness in store for us, a happiness all the more refined for our sufferings.

I was thinking of our darlings last night both living and dead and I remembered that I wanted to tell you not to forget as soon as our little Thornwell could speak sufficiently plainly to kneel with him every night and teach him the little prayers our darling used to repeat. Teach him the little verses Will Ed used to say and teach him to sing as his darling elder brother used to. Oh darling make him just as much like our noble boy as it is possible to do. Do this my dearest for my sake and it will be the most acceptable surprise you can offer me. I have already told you how glad I was about your taking Music Lessons. I wish you had time to take lessons in drawing also. You know I am proud of my wife and everything she can do to improve herself only makes me the more proud. Have you ever had that wagon fixed up as I requested for Thornwell, if not, do have it fixed before you write me again as I want him to know his "papa" does want him to "haul 'ood & Ben & old Black Mary too." Bless him. What would not his Father give to see him now.

Thursday Morn, June 4th, 3 miles East Canton, Miss. The Company have all gone out on Inspection with the Division to be Inspected by Gen'l Johnston and I, not feeling very well did not go out but have written to Dr. Bush to try and get me an appointment from Gov. [Thomas O.] Moore to some position in State service so I could get a transfer to your side of the River. I may enclose it in this letter and in case I do you must seal it and put on a stamp and mail it at once to him as I am anxious for it to go through by express. We heard yesterday that the enemy had been disastrously defeated at Port Hudson and Sherman killed.[16] Would it not seem an act of retributive

[16] The report was untrue. From October, 1859, to January, 1861, W. T. Sherman was superintendent of the Louisiana Military Academy at Alexan-

justice if he should be killed at last on La. soil whence he fled after feasting on her fruitings and instructing her youth in the art of War.

I don't know what I have written in all my sheets & soon will have to stop a while and re-read what I have written. But it is such a job I believe I'll run the risk of sundry repetitions rather than do it. If Dr. Quarles would only have a meeting of the Trustees now I believe they would be anxious to send up that petition for my discharge to the War. Dept. But if there is any other way I don't want to come to teach though that a hundred times rather than not come at all. Oh, have I any friends in Louisiana that will do anything for me at this juncture? But a shout is rising adown the line of Cosby's Brigade and I look up and see Gen'l Joe Johnston riding up and down the lines. I recognize him at once having seen him in Mobile last spring. I hope we shall get some papers this evening and that Capt. Webb will come through from Scooba and bring me some letters from you my dearest and best beloved.

Friday Morn 6 o'clock. Order to cook two days rations and take 3 uncooked and move to the front. I think to Edwards Depot on the Jackson & Vicksburg railroad. We heard heavy cannonading yesterday in the direction of Vicksburg but have no news from there. Capt. Webb has not come from Scooba and David Caufield talks of starting tomorrow and try and make it across the River. Mr. [Henry] Ward started up his papers yesterday and I will have the opportunity of writing again by him I hope. What would I not give to get a letter from you before he goes. Thos. Geren has just come up and says David intends starting this morning, so I must hurry up and finish my letter. But Sandy says breakfast is ready.

Well, I have broken by fast on fritters & molasses and fried ham and now will resume and first let me repeat that Mr. Spencer wants your father to take that money of his and invest it all in 7 pr. cent bonds of the Confederacy. I presume there is a depository in Shreveport. Please get your father to attend to it right away. I did reread all I had written yesterday and I fear you will find it very difficult to make out but if so the letter will be all the better like a conundrum

---

dria. See Walter L. Fleming, *General W. T. Sherman as College President* (Cleveland, Ohio, 1912), 45–346.

for the intricacy. The letter to Dr. Bush I want forwarded to him at once. He is Maj. of the Militia and may be out in the field for all I know, if so I want the letter forwarded to him at once. I am determined to leave no stone unturned that lies in my power, but what I will get on the other side of the River and if my friends there will help me I will be able to do it I believe.

I wish this infernal war would close but must confess that I see no end to it any way. We can get no news of any kind here, the Rail Road being torn up at Jackson. Gen'l Cosby got back last night and I tell you we were glad enough as it sends old Starke back to his regiment. Everything is in a state of excitement this morning. The 12th La. Regt. and the 19th are both here in fact I think that Johnston has a very large army already organized and Grant will have to leave Miss. I think or be captured. We go to the front as I have already told you and I presume the Yankee wagon train will suffer. I do hope something will be done speedily so that this war will be brought to a close in some way or other and I sometimes think that I don't care much which way, but that is only momentary. I see so much flagrant injustice done that it cools my patriotism worse than an ice bath. I have not very much fear anyway, perhaps it will improve with our successes. I have never in my experience during the war been at so great a loss to understand the relative positions of the two armies. I do not know where Grant is but I think Johnston will find him out if our Cavalry does not.

But darling I must now think of closing my letter and it is almost as hard to do that as it would be to part with your very self. I would caution you once more to be very careful of your own health and to be very watchful over our remaining pet lamb. Do be very careful of both dearest for if I should survive this war and you not be spared me I should be miserable indeed. Life would not be worth living deprived of you. But dearest my heart tells me that there is still happiness in store for us yet and I am hopeful.

Rich is with me and is a pretty good boy, at least is so skillful in framing excuses that I can find but little fault with him. He told me that when Cynthia was sick it was from the effect of medicine she had taken to procure abortion. Have you ever told her what I told you to tell her. If she does not have children I will not keep her for the work she does herself. How I wish I was at your Mother's to get some vegetables now. A year ago tomorrow I wrote you a letter from Houston, Miss. and you did not get it till just before I got home. That day I ate some vegetables at Mrs. James'. I believe I did not tell you that the ladies of Columbus, Miss. gave our Cavalry a cooked dinner—a most excellent and abundant one.

Now dearest write me regularly and mail your letters, they will find their way through to me in some way. Don't fail to mail me a letter and if you find a private conveyance you and I make that much. Direct your letters to Jackson or Canton to Gen'l Cosby's Escort, Jackson's Cavalry Corps and even if no Post Office is mentioned it will come straight while we are in Miss. Give my best love to your Mother and Father, also Lou, Ella & Bud & Al. Has Anna Thompson commenced boarding with you yet? Be sure and tell me. Love to Cousin Mary and all my friends. Kind regards to Mrs. Copeley when you see her and Dr. & Mrs. Bright. What has become of Mr. Wimberly and who were drafted in the militia? Tell me all the outside news. Has your father lost any hogs with cholera? Tell me all news of every kind. Write me good *long* letters for they have to last a long time they come so scattering. Give a hundred kisses to Thornwell for his papa and do not let him forget me, talk to him of me a great deal. Dearest do you love me as much as I do you. Good Bye and God grant we may speedily meet again. Your Edwin.

June 13, 1863

'Tis Sunday Morn my own darling one and as I cannot play chess today I will devote a part of it to interlining Mother's and Aunt Liv's letters tho I assure you I have nothing interesting. But as I mentioned chess I presume you would want to know how we got the chess men to play with. I have in vain endeavored to purchase a set in every town we have been in since I started out almost so day before yesterday, the time hanging heavily on our hands, Capt. Webb and I determined we would make some so took our knives and got some sassafras wood and did whittle ourselves out a very pretty set and played with them yesterday. It is a relief indeed to the monotony of camp and cards cannot be had for less than five or ten dollars per pk. I expect we could get $10 in a minute for our chess men if we would sell them. I colored the black ones with my ink so when I sat down to write on this sheet I found a dry inkstand but sent up to HdQrtrs and the Adjt. Gen'l Capt. Bullock, sent me an inkstand full. The Staff at Head Qrtrs are very kind and friendly to this Company, very familiar and make our soldiers life as pleasant as possible and that is not pleasant I assure you when I am separated so far from my darling one.

I have been thinking a great deal of you this morning. The Bugle rêveille waked me from a dream of you. I thought you were lying in my arms your head resting on my shoulder and my hands in their *accustomed place* and we were talking of our former happy life. It was too hard to be awaked to war's stern, sad realities.

It was reported that Gen'l Johnston had offered a thousand dollars and a discharge to any man who would carry a dispatch into Vicksburg.[17] I sent up word that I would undertake it on those terms but last night two couriers came out having left there on Sunday night last and brought out despatches to Gen'l Johnston. They return this evening. I talked with one this morning and he knows all the country and people around and he met an acquaintance who told him that Commodore Porter told him that Grant had lost over *25,000* killed in his attacks on the place. Perhaps you don't know the situation of the forces. The yankees hold from the mouth of the Yazoo clear round to Warrenton below Vicksburg and are reported to have 150,000 men. They are entrenched within 300 to 400 yards of our entrenchments. Nine times they have essayed to storm our works by making their men drunk and they have been mowed down as it were by the breath of a tempest, our boys taunting them with the ten-pin alley expression of "set up your pins again," a "ten-strike" etc.[18] The Yankee dead were piled 3 & four deep around our breastworks for 3 & 400 yds. and lay unburied for 6 days. On the 7th we sent a flag of truce and gave them permis-

[17] Couriers carried several communications between Johnston and Pemberton during the siege, though some were intercepted by Grant. See Horn, *The Army of Tennessee,* 217, and *O.R.,* XXIV, pt. 1, 39–40.

[18] Soldiers on both sides often alleged that opponents who participated in desperate assaults, such as those made by the Federals at Vicksburg on May 19 and 22, 1863, were filled with liquor before they went into the attack. These allegations appear to have had no foundation of fact.

sion to bury their dead, who were rotten almost. I was told they were black in the face and they put four shovels under them and rolled them in pits dug out. They were too rotten to be moved by hand. They say they intended to starve the city into a surrender. They know they cannot take it but I think Gen'l Johnston will attend to their case before long. They are well fortified but our troops believe it is the decisive battle of the war and will fight desperately.

Yankee deserters are going into Vicksburg daily—some (Missourians) are joining our army, others are paroled and set across the River to go home. Lincoln says he expects to hear good news from his army but is prepared for the worst. We are quite confident of success and every one has or seems to have the utmost confidence in Gen'l Joseph E. [Johnston]. We heard that Bragg's entire army would be here in a few days. I expect a very large part of it will be, but not all. I think the greater part of Rosecranz's army is here. They have plenty of ammunition and provision to last four months in Vicksburg. Some two weeks ago they sent their best Iron Clad, the Cincinnati, down to silence our Batteries and the 3d shot disabled her so that she raised the white flag and turned back but when she was ordered to our side, kept on when they riddled her, sinking her just above the city.[19] They caught some of the crew who were floating off on Bales of Hay and they report 100 killed on her. The heavy firing spoken of in my other sheet were the mortars shelling from behind the point again, for two days now they have ceased entirely and accordingly the impression has got out among these milk and water Miss'ians that we had surrounded the place or more strictly in military parlance "that it had gone up."

Oh if our own people were only true there would be but very little danger of encouragement to the Yankees. But our folks, the Union Party, who joined the army to recover the power feared to be lost, are very tired of this war. Lieut. Carter is now as he has ever been a reconstructionist and I believe would like to see the Confederacy overthrown that he might be a true prophet. Other wise he is a very clever man in his subordinate position. I like him when he does not have

[19] The *Cincinnati,* commanded by Lt. George M. Bache, was sunk by Confederate guns at Ft. Hill, just above Vicksburg, May 26, 1863. See *Battles and Leaders,* III, 569.

command. The most perfect dunce is the doughty Lieut. Nat Martin. He has the reputation of being a clever man so he is when he has his own way and where he expects to be tickled in turn & that fact stamps him as anything but agreeable to me. This is between us however. I could tell you so many things if I could only see you. I shall hold on to this letter a few days longer and if Clinton does not catch up, shall trust it to the tender mercies of Cousin Sallie's Mail, which crosses at Natchez 3 times a week, so your letters if mailed would reach me regularly.

Monday 14 after dinner. I have been playing chess all this morning having beaten Capt. Webb, though he beat me the two last games. John Lesueur and Linn Watkins came last night having come by Okolona but did not bring me any of my clothes so I am minus drawers and don't know what I am going to do but I'll get along some way by borrowing as I have done. There is nothing new transpiring today. We heard some severe firing this morning and I imagine I can hear occasional guns now. I think that the fight will come off before long and when it does you will hear, I feel, the greatest victory that ever has happened on this continent. The Yanks are so situated that we will capture their entire supplies—Guns, ammunition, wagons, stores, everything and their army can only escape by squads. It cannot possibly get away in an organized state. I wish the fight would come off for I think it will bring an end to this sanguinary struggle and if it is my lot to be killed it may make very little difference whether I live one, two or three weeks.

I have got almost reckless as far as living is concerned for I *cannot* get home to see you and life here is really no life at all to me. I wake up and say lo! when will it be day and after daylight would God it were night. Thus time drags away rapidly it is true but heavily. Oh if I could only see you I believe I could then be reconciled to stay away for another six months. It is hard indeed to be separated from one's own family, from all he loves or has to love in this world. Suppose for argument's sake the war should last twenty years, I would then, if I survived it, be an old, old man of no account to myself or anyone else. Why then *unjustly* keep a man in the service when he only volunteered for 12 mos. Who is fool enough to believe that the three year men (or during the war) will be disbanded at the expiration of their term of enlistment. The "or during the War" clause will keep all *in*. I think I would be perfectly justifiable if I should desert or at least as much so as if I were to desert at the expiration of three years—I don't believe I shall ever do it although I feel it would be right nor do I believe it would be any disgrace if looked upon rationally. But I will endeavor to never give you cause to blush or reason for taunt for my child though I am resolved not to remain in the Army all of my life unless it is a very short one.

John and Linn came by Mr. Madry's and they made inquiries about me. Have you ever written to the Misses Matt and Add? They have never heard from you if you have. I intend to go and see them if I ever have an opportunity, but you must not be jealous, dearest. Your husband has never seen your equal. I went over to Wirt Adams Regt. on Saturday to see Nat Rudolph who is the brother of Miss Abbie. I learned his whereabouts last October but this is the first time I have ever been near that Regt. He was very glad to see me and I heard through him of all my Greenville friends. He promised to come and see me: they are encamped in an adjoining field, but he is even a more eccentric genius than She is. He wants to go home to get married, having been in service for 2 yrs. He said his Mother would be very glad to see me, as she often spoke of me in her letters. I did not bring up his sister at all. I used to have some right good times with him tho' he was always considered the scapegrace of the family.

It is thundering and has been showery this evening. The people here will make excellent corn crops if the season continues. You must write me dearest and mail letters regularly for they will make their way over to me much easier than mine to you. We had a rumor yesterday that Marmaduke had engaged the Yanks opposite Vicksburg on Tuesday last and whipped them severely. The Couriers spoken of heard the fighting but did not know who it was that was fighting. They started back this morning and expect to get back Wednesday night. They crossed the River and went up opposite the mouth of Yazoo and then recrossed the Miss. and made their way up on the north bank of Yazoo.

Now darling I must close this letter. I do so wish I could accompany it across to you. We learned yesterday that Capt. William Harrison's Company had run away and come down here and were going across the River to Louisiana. All had deserted but 4 men I believe. Capt. Harrison was endeavoring to get Gen'l Johnston's consent but if not said he was going anyhow. They have effectually played out I think. But dearest I have told you all I believe I have to tell. You know how my heart warms towards you. Write me often and tell me all the news. I'll send this by mail and if Jack Clinton comes in two or 3 days will write again. God bless and preserve you my own love. Give 100 kisses to our boy and love to your Mother father and all the rest. I am thankful that I was ever fortunate enough to call you my own dear wife. Good Bye dearest. My heart is yours. Votre seul,

Edwin.

Hd Qrtrs 1st Divis. Jackson Cavalry
Camp near Mechanicsburg, Miss. June 27, 1863

My own dear Sarah:

I started you a long letter last Monday by Jack Clinton who as I told you in previous letters was discharged but I fear he may have been captured as on Wednesday the Yankee Cavalry made a raid out and burned Brookhaven, the station on the N.O. & Jackson Road where passengers get off to go to Natchez. I do hope that Jack was not captured as I do not care about my letters being published in Yankee papers. This morning I understand that Maj. C. R. Riley formerly of N.O. but the Acting Commissary of Subsistence of the Brig. is going to Natchez to see his wife and promises to mail this letter there for me. Hoping therefore that it will reach you I will try and send you a short epistle, but have but little encouragement so to do as the last letter I got from you was bro't by Mr. Ratcliffe leaving date May 15th while Bates and Carter have letters from Minden June 8th. I don't know how they came but have an indistinct recollection of hearing some one say they were bro't over by Mr. Gregg. I feel sure you sent me a letter too if you knew of the opportunity but am afraid you did not. What would I not give for a letter from you to know at least that you were alive and well if nothing more. It seems as if every one was born to better luck than I am during this war at least. In times of peace I can make my own luck but here am a bond slave worse than any negro, in fact I would deem myself fortunate to exchange with any slave I ever saw.

I am tired out and fretted with the delay but at the same time must admit that I have not entirely lost confidence in Gen'l Johns[t]on, yet it seems very strange that we should have to wait till Grant fortifies as strongly in his rear as Vicksburg is in his front. I do not believe he intends to raise the siege by fighting Grant but to so harass him and cut off his supplies by means of the forces on the Western side of the River as to compell the siege to be raised and then attack the retreating columns of the enemy. The plan may be a good one to call into our aid the fierce heat of our Southern Sun and the effect of the swamp malaria on the hyperborean vandals with whom we are waging a war for existence, yet if it should cost us *Vicksburg* I fear it would also cost us the Confederacy for I do not believe we could hold *this army* after it falls.

Deserters are occasionally coming in to us but their papers say the same thing of our men. All the calculations made that large numbers of their men would leave in May etc. have all turned out fallacious. They never lack men, always have enough and we fight them at great odds every time. Van Dorn's fight at Thompson's Station is the only time during the war that I know of where we had the most men, of course we whipped them there.[20]

I do not believe they can take Vicksburg unless they worry out the small handful of men we have there. They have assaulted it some ten or 12 times with the same result, a disastrous repulse. I do not believe they will try that plan any more. They are now trying to mine the fortifications and blow them up and if we are not smart enough to countermine they will dig us out. Day before yesterday our Brigade moved south west 20 miles or more and tried to draw them out in a fight but they were too smart to bite at the bait spread before them. If they had come out we would have caught all their Cavalry. We rode

[20] On March 5, 1863, at Thompson's Station, between Franklin and Columbia, Tennessee, about 6,000 Confederates under Van Dorn and Forrest decisively defeated a Federal force of about 2,800 led by Colonel John Coburn. See Robert S. Henry, *"First With the Most" Forrest* (Indianapolis, 1944), 129–131.

some 45 miles and did no good. "Wirt Adams" Regt. fought them a few days ago and killed some forty or fifty, took 36 prisoners and one piece of Breechloading Artillery (a 4 pounder) one they stole from the Arsenal at Jackson. I talked with some of the prisoners and they talked as defiantly as you please. I told them they had not heard of Lee's victory North of the Rappahanock nor of our forces marching into Maryland and Pennsylvania & the (capture by Ewell's Stonewall Corps) of eleven thousand sent to reinforce Hooker. I do know one thing and that is that I don't intend ever to take any prisoners. I may but shall alter my mind if I do and I think anybody who should see the destruction they have caused in this country would applaud the resolution.

My letters now-a-days are very warlike but you must excuse them as I have nothing else of which to write. It is the only theme of conversation ever heard as we have nothing to do but listen to the bombardment and speculate upon this and that move that comes to our ears. We have orders now to have and keep on hand 6 days rations of provisions and 4 of forage. The wagons are hauling in the corn today and Samps Culpepper our Company Commissary has gone for other things, bacon & meal, if so we can find the former. The order says this is to be done in case an advance is made but leaves us in doubt whether it refers to the enemy or ourselves. The Cavalry is doing no good here only picket duty while the enemy is preparing raids throughout different parts of the State. We understand that Gen'l [Daniel] Ruggles defeated them in North Miss. a few days since, also Gen'l [James R.] Chalmers near Memphis capturing 400 prisoners. All the news (if so) is good but I fear it is for the purpose of encouragement just as Grant before his first attack told his troops that Richmond and Charleston were both in their possession, yet I dislike to think Confed' authorities would lie so wilfully. A cause must be desperate indeed that seeks alone to bolster itself up by falsehood. But let's leave this War question and turn to something more agreeable.

I have no letter to answer so I hardly know what to write. I took supper at a house last night and heard some music on the piano. It made me think of home and you. The lady, Mrs. Tuttle, sang very sweetly and her voice reminded me of yours. Capt. [Webb] & I sat on the piazza while Lynn & John went in the Parlor. We talked of our wives & homes, they had neither and I dare say we enjoyed it better than they. Yesterday was one of the warmest days I ever saw and last night until after midnight, then the wind rose and is blowing cool-ly now. The flies are most troublesome visitors. I believe they are more annoying than I ever saw them. One can scarcely breathe for them and eating is out of the question unless we have one or two brushes going all the while. Today we have a mess of Irish potatoes sent to us by an old acquaintance of Capt's but have no meat whatever to cook with them. Living is hard I assure you and I have fallen off lots but you know I can afford to do that and be gainer at least in your estimation, for you did not marry a great *pursley-gutted* man but a nice little man, didn't you? though you would be willing to take me back almost any way—wouldn't you?

Oh why must a man be separated from his family as some of us are while so many are allowed to remain with theirs. This war by no means bears equally on all and yet the stay at home speculators will be most courted and admired after its close. Money makes the Mare go always, and *will always do so*. You may say while in poverty "my husband fought a private through the war of Independence," while another woman will answer, "mine made a fortune in the War" and the Fortune will draw the admirers yes! and the friends too. This war will only increase the degeneracy of the times.

3 P.M. Well I'll try and finish out my page. I dreamed last night that I had lost my right arm and been discharged and had come back to you. I thought that if it had only been my left one I should not have counted the loss too great for the sake of being with you, but you know "Persons ain't responsible for what they say asleep." You haven't written me in a long time if the flowers we planted over our darlings graves have grown and flourished. I say "we" for I was there when they were planted over our daughter's grave. Our Noble Boy was laid away when his Father was far away and I scarcely know where they laid him. Oh how my heart bleeds to think that I'll see him no more forever. Why could he not have been spared at least 'till I got home, that I might have been at his bedside. But I will not murmur so, will turn to something else.

I do hope I shall get a letter from you tomorrow but as we have no

Post Office our letters are sent to Gen'l Cosby's Hd'Qrtrs and are brought by couriers from there. Your last was spelled Crosby and I am glad it did not go to HdQrtrs for they judge the Company by every straw as to intelligence. You had heard the name from some of the *Cavalry Ladies* who are not good authority for *spelling*. Give my love to your Father & Mother Lou & Cousin Mary and all the children. I think Lou might write again to me after the long letter I wrote her from Tenn. I read a beautiful piece of poetry composed by a Texan styled, "Oh He's nothing but a Soldier."[21] I'll send it to you to finish out this letter and I want you to send it to the Mount Lebanon Baptist and have it printed and a copy sent to you so you can preserve it in print. Please mail it to the Editor at once. I've written Dr. Crane a short note at the bottom and I hope you will get a paper and send to me, one to Mother. The other two as you please with.

But I must call the roll, and bid you good bye. God bless you my dearest and preserve you and our darling child. Write me often dearest and long letters. I don't think I shall write you again till I hear from you. A hundred kisses to my best beloved. Your affectionate, Husband.

[21] This poem, with no author given, appears in Francis D. Allan, compiler, *A Collection of Southern Patriotic Songs Made During Confederate Times* (Galveston, 1874), 28.

10

"We Cannot Make Much of a Stand"

Camp 4 miles in rear Mechanicsburg
July 10th 1863

My own dear Wife:

I wrote you a long letter yesterday but on sober reflection last night while all the Camps were wrapped in sleep I concluded that it was too wicked to send you and I have concluded this morning to write again. I have little indeed to write as news is scarce in this part of the Country. Vicksburg as you will already have heard has been surrendered to the enemy and 17,500 brave Southern men have laid down their arms and given up the stronghold, the key of the Confederacy.[1] It is almost impossible to tell the consequences but if Grant is wise Port Hudson will fall in less than a week and then Mobile, Selma, Montgomery, Atlanta, Augusta, Charleston. There is one escape and I am almost in hopes that Grant will pursue Johnston to Jackson as we learned yesterday that they were skirmishing at Clinton halfway between Jackson and Vicksburg. If we can keep them from Port Hudson till we can get there we may prevent such a series of disasters. God only knows what will be the fate of the Confederacy. I believe that as a power of the Earth it is conquered, but do not near believe the people are subjugated. I have little hope of the future.

But as an offset we hear of the total discomfiture of the Yankee Army in Maryland 12 miles from Baltimore at the Relay House some 30 miles north of Washington, having killed 4 Brig Gen'ls and severely

[1] Fay's figure on Confederates taken at Vicksburg was far too low. Actually 2,166 officers and 27,230 enlisted men surrendered to Grant's forces on July 4. See K. P. Williams, *Lincoln Finds a General,* IV, 420. The offsetting report of the "total discomfiture of the Yankee Army in Maryland" was, of course, erroneous.

wounded Col. Mead the successor of Hooker in command of the largest army on the Planet. Washington will doubtless be captured. Such being the case I have a faint hope that a compromise of some kind will be effected which may result in Peace. This is a faint hope but drowning men will catch at straws you know. The Yankee troops were told that when Vicksburg was taken they would be paid off, discharged, and go home, that peace would be made at once. Poor deluded, miserable wretches to believe a lie. How many thousands of their bones will bleach beneath a Southern sun ere they will see the dawn of peace. If Johnston whips Grant as he will if he can fight him outside his entrenchments the Yankee glory will be shortlived. God grant that he may get the opportunity.

Johnston was moving to relieve Pemberton and the time of the attack was to have been July 7th and Pemberton surrendered on the 4th alleging starvation as the cause. The 10th was agreed upon and the blame rests on Pemberton. Thus we have suffered from Southern men of Northern birth.[2] New Orleans, Vicksburg and the Confederacy all gone unless by a direct interposition of Providence. We hear that New Orleans is in our hands but it wont be long if Grant moves down the River. But a truce to War Matters, though a word more. I very much fear you will be visited by the Vandals before long for I know there is a lack of ammunition on the west side of the river and if so you may look for me home. I may come anyhow. I can't tell you, you need not be surprised to see me at almost any time. I feel sad to think that all my sufferings & toils are all lost to the Country all in vain. My first allegiance is to my family, my 2nd to my Country.

Mr. Minchew came last Friday but he brought me no letter from you. Others had received letters from Minden by mail since Caufield's return there, some as late as 19th but none for me and you can imagine how I felt. Tuesday I got yours of the 16th inst. and you don't know how rejoiced I was to get it, but at the same time I thought it was very tame & cool considering I had not had a letter for nearly two months. I thought it not an equivalent for the long letters overflowing with my heart's warmest love I had sent you weekly save on the march

[2] The allegation of Pemberton's treachery at Vicksburg, though utterly false, had wide circulation and acceptance in the Confederacy. See R. S. Henry, *Story of the Confederacy* (Indianapolis, 1931), 263–264.

from Tenn. I can very readily see how you surrounded with friends and supplied with your hearts desires can feel or rather cannot realize the longing, yearning for loving words of those who are deprived of every comfort cut off from friends and even intelligence of home. I know you thought your letter everything that could be desired and in fact it was quite a friendly letter not more and I think I ought to expect something more than friendship from my wife. You promised to write a long letter the next Saturday but I shall never get it I fear as everything is in such confusion now & I expect this is the last letter you will get from me unless I write by Minchew and there is no telling when he will start as he is trying to get a discharge for Gus and that may take him two months to get his papers through. Mr. Ward has sent up two sets of papers & he has not heard from them yet. I may get letters through to you in this manner but in no other as all communication by mail is or will be cut off and as for hearing from you any more I have given that out entirely, for no one will cross from that side to this now.

If some terms of accommodation are not come to between the contending powers this will be a war of extermination. I cannot keep from the War Theme, my pen is like Anacreon's lyre only its strains instead of those of Cupid belong rather to Mars bristling with his helmet and shield. I wish you to keep that pistol loaded and capped and if the Yankees come to Minden to wear it on your person, never be without it and the first one that dares insult you blow his brains out. This you must do or you are not the woman I married. I expect to murder every Yankee I ever meet when I can do so with impunity if I live a hundred years and peace is made in six months. Peace will never be made between me and any Yankee if I can kill him without too great risk. The Thugs of India will not bear a comparison to my hatred and destruction of them when opportunity offers. There can be no fellowship between us forever. I wish you were in Mexico. I would not be long in joining you and we would seek some abode in a South American state, but that climate would be unhealthy for Yankees as long as I stayed there.

I expect to send this letter by a Mr. Underwood of Harrison's Co. who will cross at Helena. He says he was in sight there the other day and saw our Guns playing fog with Yanks transports, though he is not a very reliable character and may have been mistaken. I hope he will get this letter across for me somewhere. I have written you a good many things lately that I wanted done but I don't know whether or not you have had them done or not. You wrote me something once upon a time about my hogs dying with cholera but did not tell me if we had any left at all nor one word about our cattle. I could never tell from your letters that we had ever kept house or had anything, whether we lived in a city or country, but I suppose you have so much to do in school that you have no time to think of these things.

The report has just come in that Bragg has fallen back to the Tenn. River, Rosecranz having whipped him or rather flanked him and caused him to fall back.[3] If it had not been for Bragg's incompetency we would have held possession of all of Ky. & Tenn. We have been thoroughly blessed with incompetents in this Western Dept. Jeff Davis thinks Richmond is Heaven or nearly so while the loss of Vicksburg is incomparably greater than 40 such cities as Richmond, yet the latter has been surrendered, the former held.

I am glad to learn that Thornwell is talking so plainly and glad too that his memory is so good. I recollect making him eat a crust and I presume it has been kept alive in his memory by Laura & others. Bless him, he bids fair to be as intelligent as our darling eldest born. Oh this accursed, infernal war, how I wish it could be closed now on some terms. I want to see my wife and child, they are a necessity to me altho I may not be to them. I *must come home*. Of course you have had the wagon fixed for Thornwell? I am very much afraid your being in school has proved much to his detriment and I fear you do not govern him as rigidly as you ought for he may be left to your sole control and management through life unassisted except it be by a stepfather. Poor child, his lot will then be a hard one for I have not seen a man since I have been in the army save one that was worthy the love of a good woman.

I am sorry to hear that Buys is among the missing; I hope he is unhurt and will come in again. Joe is a good fellow. I am sorry to hear that Jack Crichton was wounded for I had always hoped he

[3] Bragg, weakened by diversion of a part of his force to Vicksburg, was outflanked by Rosecrans at Tullahoma in late June, 1863, and forced to retire to Chattanooga. See Henry, *Story of the Confederacy,* 292–293.

would come out safe.[4] But I must close my letter, I know it is not interesting but it is the best I can do under the circumstances. I am glad to hear that you have so much flour. I wish we could get some for this cornbread will sour in 12 hours and we are required to keep two days rations on hand all the time. But I must write to Mother a hasty note to let her know I have not been surrendered at Vicksburg for she will worry if she does not hear. I want to write to Spencer too before long as I expect he is now in Chattanooga. I am tired of this eternal state of suspense. Whatever is to be done I want it done quickly. My love to your Mother, Father and Sisters. What did your Father go to Shreveport for? Don't let him neglect that matter of Spencer's. Good Bye dearest, Your husband E. H. Fay

Across Pearl River in rear of Jackson Miss
July 15th Wednesday Morn. Sunrise

After a night broken by the roar of our Heavy Artillery shelling the Federal camp I snatch a few minutes to write a word more on my letter by Mr. Underwood. I am well, they are fighting (skirmishing) and have been for the last four days in front of the breastworks in Jackson. We cannot hold the place and will fall back to Meridian in fact the wagons of some commands have already gone. The Confederacy is a foregone conclusion and I think a peace on the basis of some kind of a reconstruction will be patched up soon.

Mrs. Col. Scott has sent a request to Gen'l Grant to allow her to cross the Miss. River, a most humiliating request I think, but so it is. I may write by her if she goes as probably Mr. McLeod will accompany her. Van McKamie came to the company yesterday and J. M. Pearce but were so contemptibly mean that they would not let anyone know a word about them coming. I never want McKamie to speak to me nor do I intend he ever shall. We are ordered to saddle up and I shall have no more time to write. I don't know that I shall

[4] Sgt. Joseph G. Buys, Company G, 8th Louisiana Infantry Regiment, was captured at Chancellorsville, May 3, 1863. Private John Crichton of the same unit was wounded at Chancellorsville. Both were from Minden, Louisiana. Buys was exchanged three weeks after his capture. Both men survived the war. Booth, *La. Confed. Soldiers,* II, 208, 482.

ever be able to send you another letter while the war lasts but God will preserve you and take care of you my dearest one. Do take care of our only remaining lamb and keep him from harm as far as possible. If you ever get a chance to send me a letter do so certainly. Pearce mailed the letter you gave him to bring and I shall of course never get it. You must keep a letter written all the time so if you hear of anybody crossing you can send it at once. Oh if you were only on this side of the River what would I not give but I get letters from Mother almost as seldom as I do from you. Her last was 26 days coming. I have written her a short note this morning but I don't know when I'll get an opportunity to mail it for I don't think there is any mail from Jackson now.

Mother dear *we* will not live under Yankee domination for we will go to Brazil or some other South American country and live free from the accursed race. I shall never cease to hate them. Oh if I could only come home now and take care of my little family. The citizens of Jackson are encamped around us in this swamp as the Yanks shell the place during the day and they cannot stay in safety in town. Oh my dearest what will you do if I should never come back to you. I am sad this morning and confused for the roar of the cannon and the whizzing of shells is the only music that salutes my ear and it is pretty constant I assure you.

As far as clothing is concerned Mother has made me some she writes me and if I need I shall send Rich there after them. Do not feel anxious about me my dearest. If it is my *kismet* (destiny) to come back to you I shall do it, if not, why who can change the decrees of God. This is Turkish doctrine but some philosophy after all. There are many things I would say to you if I could only think of them but everything is in such a state of confusion that I can hardly think of anything. The smoke of burning powder is so dense that it "clouds in" the sun and we are fighting in the shade. There has been no general engagement yet though Breckinridge's Division cleaned out a Brigade of Yanks on Sunday. Took 300 prisoners and killed outright the balance but the valor of a few don't avail against hosts almost innumerable and so we will have to fall back. I think we will stand a while at Meridian and then fall back to Mobile, though we cannot make much of a stand at Meridian as they can flank us anywhere there and we may fall directly back to Mobile. They cannot keep up Communication with their base of supplies on a longer line than Jackson on account of our Cavalry.

But Mr. Underwood is almost ready to start and I must hasten to close. If the Yankees occupy our country you must be sure to follow my instructions in regard to keeping that pistol by you all the time. Don't move one step about the House even, without it and keep it dry all the time. Get some ammunition and practice for you may be sure you will need it. Be sure you do it. Lay aside all womanly fears and be a *heroine,* be my own noble, brave wife. And now dearest how shall I say Good Bye. This is in all probability my last letter to you. You know my deep overflowing heartfelt love for you. You know that I live only for you, and life without you would be only a blank. Take care of yourself and take care of my child. Be of good cheer and it may all come out for the best yet, tho' I dare not hope it yet. Give my love to your Father and Mother, Sisters and all my friends. I know not if I shall see any of them again but hope I may. Give a thousand kisses to little Thornwell and a heart full of love for yourself. You know that you have my all. Good Bye dearest. May God protect and bless you is the prayer of your husband who loves you dearly.

Camp Brandon Miss July 23d63

My own, own dear Wife:

This clear bright morning I seat myself under a Tent fly on a sack of corn with a half quire of paper before me to answer your last loving kind wifely letter which you sent over the River by Parson Clampit. Oh my own darling you dont know the well spring of love that gushed up in my heart towards the author of it. Yes my own dear Wife it was just such a loving letter as I love to receive. We heard on Saturday that there were letters for us in the 12th Regt. which was some 20 miles in advance of us and I accordingly detailed a man at once to go after them. I felt sure (when Mr. H. W. Menifee of our Co. showed me a letter received from Parson Henderson of July 3d) that I too had a letter there. I learned that Mr. Henderson was boarding at Mrs. Randall's, the first I had heard of it, and was glad enough to hear it, for I know that your Mother had a large enough family without taking boarders. I thought too that now Thornwell would be relieved of the bad example of little Harry, but was surprised that you did not mention the fact in your letter to me, but I presume you had previously told me in some of the letters I have not received. Why was the change made?

We were camped within a mile of town and about 12 M moved camp into town near a good spring but had scarcely dismounted before the booming of the army's cannon announced their approach. Then there was hurrying to and fro in hot haste and we dashed out on the Jackson road to where the fighting was going on.[5] I accompanied Gen'l Cosby across a corn field to an open hill where we could see the serried host of the vandal invader marching forth under their vaunted Stars & Stripes. I counted 8 Regts Infantry and one of Cavalry while we had only one Regt. Cavalry and two small Battalions. We skirmished with them for some two hours holding them at bay but at length slowly gave back, they following. This was the first time I had had an opportunity of witnessing all the proceedings of a battle and accordingly I remained behind with the skirmishers till the Yanks advanced a whole regt. through the standing corn to the brow of a Hill and poured whole volleys into about a dozen of us. Bullets rained thicker than hail and how it was that some of us were not killed I cannot tell. There was one man only slightly wounded.

We then fell back to town and I stopped to converse with some ladies till the Yanks nearly overtook me when I clapped spurs to old Jack and waved them a final adieu with my hat which drew a volley of Minnie balls after me. I rode through town slowly they following quite deliberately on the Eastern side. I halted with Capt. [George] Moorman, Gen'l Jackson's A.A.G. and a couple of pickets when the enemy run a 12 pdr. cannon and fired a round which dispersed us. I followed up the road and overtook the Command in camp 4 miles from town. Here I found that Capt. Webb had a letter for me and I assure you I was not long in building a fire by whose friendly light I could read the words of love traced by your loving hand.

[5] The action referred to occurred at Brandon, Mississippi, July 9, 1863, between Union forces of Brig. Gen. Frederick Steele and a portion of Gen. W. H. Jackson's Cavalry. See *O.R.*, XXIV, pt. 2, 530, 659–660.

Oh my dearest precious wife you know not how much I love you, nor how constantly day and night I think of you. My thoughts always revert to you every night when I stretch my limbs upon my blanket on the hard ground. Capt. Webb and I spread our blankets together but I tell you that although I like him as a bedfellow, I have slept with a *person* I like better. I was surprised to find the $50 bill in my letter and I don't know but I would have preferred to have had that much paper covered with lines traced by your loved hand than by lines of the engraver though they represented the above mentioned value. I did not need it particularly though it was acceptable.

We have drawn no money now for nearly 7 months and we see no prospect soon of getting any in the present perturbed state of affairs. The Yanks remained in Brandon all night burning the principal part of town and left on their way back to Jackson, which together with Canton they have burned up before. Ashes and charred remains of all kinds of buildings mark their course everywhere. Yesterday, Wednesday we caught thirty five of the robbers with two wagon loads of ladies dresses & underclothes robbed from some residences between here and Jackson. Killed 4, wounded 6, prisoners 35. Our loss one severely wounded. I was going out on a scout today but did not feel like a hard ride, or the true reason is, the wagon came up last night and as I could get paper I thought I would write you. I have sworn not to take a prisoner and I want to go out and kill some of them, will probably go tomorrow if I can get off. I sent out some lowells (corn sacks) and am having me a pair of drawers made. I am also going to have me a shirt made of the same. I am not suffering for clothes now, and there is some talk of our going to Okolona. If I do I can get my clothes I left there.

(Two P.M.) The enemy have left Jackson for one of our scouts has just come in who had been through the town and a part of our Brigade has gone in. I expect we will go tomorrow tho I hope not as I do not wish to witness such destruction as I know the vandals have perpetrated there. You cannot guess who is now sitting under the "fly" with me. It is one of my old scholars, Wm Boyle of the 9th Texas Cavalry, a Lieut. He has improved greatly since his removal to Texas and appears very well indeed. He is writing a letter to his mother &

Sisters now, will stay with me tonight. I am always glad to meet any of my old scholars. It is very pleasant for I thus have friends throughout the length and breadth of the Land.

I read a "Memphis Appeal" now published at Atlanta, Ga. which gives a letter from Gen'l Lee to Pres. Davis in which he states that he whipped the Federal Army more thoroughly in Pennsylvania at Gettysburg than ever on Southern soil and that his falling back to Hagerstown, Md. was in no way rendered necessary by any movement of the enemy but as a part of his plan. The Yank papers made us believe that Lee was compelled to recross the Potomac and a hundred other lies. Major Gen'l U. S. Grant has been made commander in chief of the armies of the U.S.A. in place of old Halleck. Thus has Pemberton's sin resulted in his advancement. He (Grant) will wish to figure for the Presidency and may adopt a new course of policy in regard to the war. I hope he may continue as foolishly as he has done heretofore for I don't think he is any General, and I am rejoiced that Rosecrans has not been the promoted one. The Yankees also claim to have taken Charleston but Beauregard telegraphed that he has driven them back. I hope before I close this letter that I may have some good news to tell you.

I fear the Villains will now try to overrun Louisiana and that they may come to Shreveport. If they should ever come to Minden I want you to secure me a flask of powder and hide my rifle for I am coming home certainly where I can certainly do more good than I can anywhere else. Do not neglect this matter now, for I shall depend upon you in the emergency and you must not fail me. The villains may be preparing for an attack on Mobile instead of the invasion of Louisiana and I do hope it is the former for I believe we can hold Mobile and I do not want them to overrun La. I will enclose a Brandon paper in this letter for you if I get no later news.

I am so glad you have some *neighbors* in next to us. I value the place at $500 more than before, besides they are Presbyterians and an accession to the church. I wish I was at home to know them. Have you done anything with your flower yard? It was in an awful state when I was there. I hope Mrs. Mitchell has kept it up. Do they make pleasant neighbors? I presume your Examination is over before this time and you are relieved from the cares and vexations of a school room. If you desire to teach another session just act your own pleasure in regard to it. Whatever you wish to do will meet my approbation you know my darling. You know my ideas in regard to all domestic matters. I would like to have my wife the finest spinner & weaver in the Parish and at the same time the most accomplished musician in the State. I know in Head work you cannot be surpassed and would be glad to find it the same in *handiwork*. You have improved greatly in the latter respect since our marriage and I attribute it entirely to your love for me. I do sincerely thank you for your expressions of love in your last and will take back everything I said about it in my letter by Underwood. Always express my own dear one the love you feel unrestrainedly. Do not keep back the sugar plums of married life.

Friday July 24th 1863. I have taken another sheet of paper dearest to write a few words more in time to have it ready for Mr. Minchew, for I think from the orders that have been issued we are going on a long march into *I think* North Miss. perhaps to Okolona and when we move Northward he will leave us. This will probably be the last letter you will get from me in some time. You can learn there if the mails cross the River and if they do you can write to me as often as you find time, they may perhaps find me out. I wish you had written me about the Letter stamps before the Post Offices were all broken up here. I could have sent you some, as it is I will try and send all I can get in the company. Ben Neal promised me some and if he has not disposed of them I'll get them. You only want stamps to put on letters sent by hand as you can pay postage on all mail matter. I do hope that our mails across the River will be resumed for I cannot bear the idea of being entirely cut off from the centre of all my earthly hopes.

I do hope I can get some appointment on that side of the River for this war may last ten years and I cannot afford to be separated from you so long, and as for a Confederate Soldier ever getting 60 days furlough to which he is legally entitled is all nonsense. This is just as much a Military Despotism as Yankeedom save in the matter of arresting citizens. No matter then that our soldiers are daily deserting by hundreds for they find themselves deprived of the rights granted them by Congress. This war on our part seems to me to be almost entirely directed on the principle of doing evil that good may come and I have looked for no permanent success to our arms while such a course is persevered in. I cannot believe we will prosper.

News has been received here that Lord John Russell has resigned his seat in the English Cabinet and Lord Palmerston taken his place. Earl Russell stated in the House of Lords that if the question of "recognition" was passed he would resign and later accounts say he has done so without stating the fate of the resolution. Something foreign may possibly save us else this war will be one waged till one or the other gives out. The party having the best wind to use a "turf" phrase, will win. I do not believe we will give it up while I look for it to become in a few years simply a guerilla war under a black flag. It would not surprise me if the latter was not raised in six weeks. Our worthy(?) Pres. Davis has called for Conscripts to 45 so all that labor has to be gone over with again and I hardly think he has men enough in service now to force his conscription. The day has passed since his Northern West Point pets have ruined our once flourishing Govt.

Did you know John C. Pemberton commanded the Mass. Regt that was stoned & mobbed in Baltimore. Yet such was the fact, and then was transferred to the command and entrusted with Vicksburg, the key of the Confederacy.[6] Oh my Country, my Country what stabs have you not received at the hands of your friends even your Parents. Is it wonderful that you die when stabbed by a parental hand. The picture is a mournful one. We are credibly informed through our scouts that the Vandal hordes have re-embarked on their way up the Father of Waters. God grant that my home may escape their desolating barbarism. I do not recollect whether I told you that John Morgan has crossed into Indiana with 8000 men and 12 pieces of artillery, such is the Yankee account but he will treat them with uniform Confederate politeness and not retaliate in kind.[7] I wish

[6] This was one of the many false reports about Pemberton that made the rounds of Southern camps after the fall of Vicksburg.

[7] For an account of Morgan's Ohio-Indiana raid, July 3–27, 1863, see Cecil F. Holland, *Morgan and His Raiders* (New York, 1942), 226–249. Morgan was captured on July 27, 1863, near East Liverpool, Ohio, and sent to the Ohio State Penitentiary, from which he escaped on November 27, 1863. He was killed at Greeneville, Tennessee September 4, 1864.

he would make their land a desert, but no, our policy is to treat savages to a civilized warfare. O tempora, O mores, O mia Patria. The zeal of thine house has eaten thee up I fear.

But now my own dearest I will say a word about our little Thornwell. You will in all probability be his only parent for eight or ten years if not always. You know how I want him raised but I fear you will not be strict enough. I think it was our strictness with our darling that made him such a good boy and so universally beloved. Last Tuesday was a sad, sad day for me, the anniversary of the loss of my best beloved save you, dearest, and my heart will murmur, murmur still. It has made me very wicked dearest I am ashamed to acknowledge but I conceal nothing from you I know "who art thou a man rebellest against God" but still it is so. I am not worthy to live. I am unfit to die. My heart has become harder than the nether Mill Stone. I have no love for anything save you and my child. Oh if this war was over I might feel differently but I never expect that day to come and I care little how things go. I am glad you are having Thornwell's wagon fixed. Yes, his papa would go to the "poss" and fix it if he were there. Do you think he still remembers me? Perhaps it would be better if he would forget me. I am glad you got the letters from Tennessee.

I had got so far and heard the call from the upper part of our camp "Come & draw your letters." I went up and found yours sent across by Mr. Hill which was mailed at Washington, Miss. and came back from Columbia, Tenn. It contained very little news save your plan of going to Texas. It will do you no good to run if the Demons come, but meet them *boldly,* pistol in hand. I could believe in the violation of the Young lady on Red River but not of their stripping her naked. I think the story is exaggerated though I have heard of worse things for instance at a house where there were two beautiful young ladies near Vicksburg, they took two negro women in the parlor before their young mistresses and sent in soldier after soldier till they had actually killed the negro women by *violation.* The low bred dutch some of whom cannot understand a word of English. Such are the troops they send against us and such devils incarnate they exchange for our soldiers, man for man.

But now they are drafting the good men and a two days riot has occurred in N.York City in which 50,000 men are said to be engaged, also in Hartford, Ct.[8] God grant the leaven may spread till the whole lump is leavened, but I fear their victories will discourage resistance. But all things must have an end and so must this war, some time or other.

We have just heard from Simeon Gray who was left at Columbia. He is at Rome, Ga. and is improving, has been pretty low with typhoid fever. You know Plunkett who tried to get a discharge for fistula. His papers went through as far as Bragg who sent him to Rome, Ga. He has done no duty for 12 mos. Some soldiers wont fight. Oliver Butler was left up in Tenn. also, having injured his foot (smashed it). Nothing has been heard from him. I expect you will see him in Minden paroled as I fear he has been captured. Thos. Gassaway is sick now but *I hope* not dangerously, also Ben Hardy. There is an excellent Hospital here and if we move will leave them here. But I hope they will be up again before long. I almost wish I could get sick and go to Selma to the Hospital. Would then stay at Sister's but even her kind offices as nurse would not compare with yours my own true loving wife.

I hope you got a letter I sent across the River by Maj. Railey of New Orleans whilom our Brig. Commissary.[9] It contained a copy of a beautiful piece of Poetry, viz. "He's nothing but a Soldier." I regret your not getting all my Tenn. letters as one would show the efforts I made to get to you, unsuccessful though they were. I am glad my darling to find that you have such confidence in your husband. He has never "soft soldered" you at all but *has* and *ever will* prove true to you, but I will have to get a "travelling divorce" if I cannot come home don't you think so? Eh, dearest? I could tell you some things if I could see you I cannot write. Will I ever see you again. Will I ever

[8] The New York City draft riots occurred July 13–16, 1863. At least 500 people were killed and much property was destroyed. See Shannon, *Organization and Administration of the Union Army,* II, 205–208. A recent popular account is Irving Werstein, *July 1863* (New York, 1957). Resistance to the draft occurred in Hartford, and an attack on the arsenal there was threatened, but did not materialize. See Shannon, II, 220.

[9] Probably Charles R. Railey, Louisiana Militia. See Booth, *La. Confed. Soldiers,* III, pt. 2, 237.

fold you again to my loving heart and print a love token on your lips. How many husbands and wives this cruel war has divorced for the time being and how many *for life*.

I hope you will use all your influence with Capt. Wimberly or any body else that can advance my interests there. I want to get some position on that side the River that I may be near you. On Gen'l Smith's staff or on Gen'l Taylor's. If I had any opportunity I could distinguish myself and win a name tho I do not court military fame. I want to be in some position that I can feel that I am rendering some service to the Confederacy. I have done no good so far and it is not my fault. I'll finish tomorrow.

Jackson's Division, Sunday, July 26th. I did not write any yesterday and have bad news to tell you this time. Rich was running my horse yesterday and ran against another horse and broke his left leg, both bones between the ankle joint and knee. I hauled him into camp and a Surgeon set his leg. I shall try and get a pass to carry him to Selma but hardly hope to make it. I regret it very much but I can't help it. I wish I had sent him across the River with Jack Clinton. It will be three months before he will be of any service to me. If I can get off I'll bring one of Father's negroes back with me. I feel badly this morning. Expect we will move tomorrow but where don't know.

Monday Eve. Yesterday I found a place where I this morning took Rich. Dr. Wm. Rober's in this place. He will be cared for there I think. I left $40.00 to ensure his attention. He feels pretty badly having to lie on his back, but must suffer.

My own dear One. I was much rejoiced last night to receive your long loving letter of June 25. It was dark but I assure you I soon got some lightwood and made a torch so I could read the lines traced by your loving hand. You don't know how much I love you and I believe it increases every day. I feel sure you would feel happy if you could just realize how much I do love you.

Well a piece of news. An order has been issued by Gen'l Johnston allowing one man in every 25 for duty a furlough and our officers *have ruled* that every man who has been home on any pretence whatever will not be allowed to go till the remainder have all been home.

Our Company has two men allowed and at this rate I am only a showing after 30 months. It makes no difference. I shall come home, leave or license when I have a mind to. I have submitted to military despotism almost as long as I intend to, and when I get ready I am coming for good. I want to get into service on that side and if I do not the Confederacy may go to the devil as for me for I will not support a govt. when my rights depend upon the caprice of first this Gen'l then that. My family are nearer and dearer to me than any Confederacy could be for when our Country fails we can find another. My first allegiance is my family, a second to the Country if it does not trample on my rights. But I will not discuss this question now.

Tuesday Morning 6 A.M. Dearest one. I got a letter yesterday from Mother but was an old one June 20th. I will enclose it to you so that you may hear from her. I presume you get no letters by mail across the River. I feel very badly that you did not get several letters I wrote from Okolona. One contained a copy of "Gen'l Bragg's March" written by the composer who was the most accomplished Pianist I ever heard play (P. Rivinac).[10] My letters from there were long long ones and I do not like to lose my labor. I believe your letters all at least that have crossed the River will reach me sometime. I am glad you and Lou got the Tenn. letters. I did not see Rector Smith.

So dearest you have seen one woman who you would be willing for me to marry (*that is if I must marry anybody*). I presume the lady named is an excellent one but would the lady have me a widower you reckon? She is not pretty but some good folks are not. But dearest I do not like this badinage on so serious a subject. God grant that you, my dearest, may live as long as I do. I have lived unmarried a number of years and I do not say I would not marry again if you should be taken from me, but I do not believe I should ever desire to, knowing that I could not find your equal. But of this no more. May our lives be long and happy after this cruel war has closed. We heard it rumored yesterday that France & Europe had recognized the Confederacy and that Gen'l Price has resigned.

[10] This piece, the full title of which was *General Bragg's Grand March,* was published in New Orleans in 1861, and later during the war in Augusta, Georgia, by A. E. Blackmar & Brother. See Marjorie L. Crandall, *Confederate Imprints* (Boston, 1955), II, 590.

So you wished once you were a man did you? But then you could not be *my wife*. Does it make you happy dearest that you are my wife? I am fortunate to be the husband of such a noble good wife. Oh, dearest if I could only come on that side the River where I could see you again. I must be transferred to that side to some arm of the service or I shall transfer myself. But I hope this war will close before long. It cannot in the nature of things last always. I wish our Company could be transferred to that side and Capt. Webb will make an effort (so he says) to get it over.

He has applied for a leave of absence which he will in all probability get and carry this letter to you. I intend to send a little letter in this to our dear little Thornwell because he wanted me to "ite him a lellie." I hope his wagon is fixed and he will take much pleasure with it. I wish I could see him now and hear him talk, but that pleasure is denied me. I do not believe I told you I had sold Jack my War Horse for $300. When Rich gets well I do not know what I shall do but I'll try and buy him a mule or send him home and get a pony for him there. His leg is getting on pretty well and the Dr. thinks he will be well enough to travel in four or five weeks. I do not think we will leave this place in some time now. Hope not. Tell your Mother I am glad that Mr. Henderson's residence in her family has had such a good effect. I am afraid when I come back I'll tease her back into her old habits. Am sorry your Father is so troubled about the Mill. Tell him to become disabled for a while and have me discharged to come home and attend to it. I must come home on some ground and *you must prepare the way*. Can you do it?

Thursday July 30th. My dearest I have just read two & half sheets of Foolscap which I have written over to you, but have not said the half of what I want to. As I left off the last talking about coming across, I will recommence that theme. I am fitted for the Engineer Dept. and I want an effort *strong* and *well defined* to be made by somebody to get me an appointment on somebody's Corps. I must have it. I cannot stay on this side with no prospect of seeing you for years. I want you to come across with Capt. Webb if I cannot get a situation on that side. Mother is anxious for you to come and I could occasionally get off four or five days and go and see you. I cannot, I will not be separated from you much longer even if I have to be branded deserter for it. I must and will see you.

Rich is doing very well and I hope will be able to get along in a few weeks. I intend sending him to Father's after some clothing for me when he gets well enough to travel. I told you I had sent some Lowells to have a pair of drawers made and they do very well. I could not get the shirts made but I am not suffering for clothing now. Capt. Webb's papers have not come through yet but mine to get a five day leave to carry Rich to Selma have been "approved," but the cars are crowded with soldiers and he is very comfortable so I'll not go to Selma.

Oh my *own darling one* how I wish you were on this side the River. I might see you occasionally—but then *consequences* might result which would not be *agreeable* and *not desirable* while the war lasts. What think you? I think that if the war should continue for 10 or 15 years longer our authorities would see the suicidal policy of not letting *married men* go home once a year at any rate. There will be few young soldiers, legitimate ones at any rate. There will be a great many otherwise wherever the army has gone. Have you ever heard anything more about Miss E—— P——s. We have heard all sorts of stories both in the 12th Regt. and in our company. I can hardly believe it yet though it is very generally believed.

There is a very nice family where I have left Rich—Mother & two daughters at home. One a widow in mourning with a little boy 18 months and a little girl about the age our little blessed "Dodo" would have been. She has *three* children just as ours were and is about our age. A very pleasant lady in conversation is Mrs. Reynolds. I have not talked with her any about her family but I presume she has lost her husband in the war. I do sympathize so much with her. Do you ever see Mrs. Hughes now-a-days and how is she getting along? and Mrs. Hayes, too. I cannot realize that Willy Cook is large enough to go to the War.

You say that you don't believe the people of Minden ever want me to come home and teach. I am glad they don't for I wouldn't teach in Minden Male Academy if I were there. You did not tell me what you thought of my letter to Pres. Davis through Hon. J. M. Perkins. The argument I think is irrefutable tho I have never had a reply to it. I fear it miscarried or it certainly would have elicited a reply. But I seem doomed to misfortune at least in this campaign. I think some of entering in the Confederate States Navy till the close of the War, what say you. I can't be permitted to visit you and I will be making "prize money" on board a privateer to support you and our child should I live to see its close, for I don't think we will be worth a dollar at the end of it. I feel gloomy *at times* at the prospect and wish you were out of the Confederacy in some foreign country and I assure you I would soon be with you.

But I must not write up all my paper today as it may be a day or two before the furloughed men get off. Geo. Monzingo & Newsom [Joel N.] Murphy drew the lots among the enlisted men to go. Mr. Minchew will go when they do if we do not move before their papers come back. I must fix up Thornwell a "little lellie" to send in this. I have 15 stamps I can send you and if the boys can get more I'll send them. It has rained every day for a week save yesterday. Night before last one of the most terrific storms, a perfect hurricane. Poor soldiers had a good time sticking it out and sleeping in wet blankets. Good bye for tonight.

Friday 31st 1863. I doubt dearest you can make out this *backwards* letter or not[11] but I will fill it out at any rate and if the boys do not get off too soon I will fill out another letter that I received last night from Mother and Sister. Dear good sister Sallie. You don't know how glad I am that she has at length got free from that old hell-cat with whom she has been living, but you will see from her letter her situation and rejoice with me.

I do wish dearest you were on this side the River and if there is any way and Capt. Webb goes over I want you to come back with him. You can come in the carriage as far as Natchez and make your way across to Brandon, thence to Selma by R. Road and Father will meet you in the carriage but if I can come across the River to you on any terms that you will approve, I had rather stay on that side. I fear it is uncertain whether I can by any efforts I can make on this side get across. If it could be arranged I will get a transfer to some company

[11] This part of the letter was written between the lines of a letter from Fay's mother to him dated June 20, 1863.

over there but I hate to leave the Company as Orderly Sergt. and go as private in Gibbs' or Young's Companies. Try dearest and see if I can't get an appointment through Mr. Wimberly or somebody else in some Depart. even if it is wagon master. But I presume my papers would not be approved except for promotion unless it was on the Engineers Corps. If nothing can be done, you must come over with Capt. Webb. and you will find a good home at my Father's where you are ever welcome as a dearly loved daughter.

Sunday Morning Aug. 2, '63. Dearest I have been disappointed in finishing this sheet by being absent in the country. I could not stand plain Beef boiled and bread. We had not an ounce of grease of any kind and I could not stand dry corn bread and beef so I got a pass and started out in the country with T. B. Neal after some flour. Rode 9 miles and put up for the night at a house and only paid four dollars apiece. Went to a Mill and got 50 lbs of flour at 35 cts. pr. lb. Got our dinner at a man's who is a true Southern man, cost nothing, came on back and a heavy rain coming we had to stop within 3 miles from Camp and paid $4.00 again, bought 10 lbs of Bacon at a dollar a pound so you see that at $12.00 pr. month I paid $8.00 for two nights entertainment. What is Confederate money worth at that rate. We have had no money for 7 months and I am flat again but you need not send me any more for we will draw and I don't want to be bothered. I found some very pleasant ladies at Mr. Taylor's where I got dinner, one who reminded me of Gus Long, a Mrs. Pearson, daughter of Mr. Taylor. I played a couple of games of backgammon with Miss Jennie H. Taylor, but with the success I always have and you know I am one of the best at that game.

We have a paper in Camp of the 30th inst. which announces the death of Hon. Wm. Yancey of Ala. I regret to hear of his death for he was my friend and I would have had no hesitancy in applying to him for any favors in the future. Poor man, he was as true to his adopted land as any man could be. A true patriot, a scholar, and a Statesman. His enemies accuse him of being ambitious and he was like Caesar for his country's good, not like Caesar for his own aggrandizement. Peace to his ashes. Requiescat in pace.

I haven't seen Rich for two or three days but am going to see him this evening and know how he is getting along. Capt. Webb will go with me. Old man Ward who stayed at our house is discouraged as being over age and starts home afoot in the morning. I will save this to send by some of the mounted men as I presume they will get there before he does. I am going to write a long letter to Sister Sarah this evening and will enclose yours of July 3d and in this way you can correspond with your Mother & Sister through me. News has reached here this morning that Morgan & his Men were not captured but one squad, 300, were captured in attempting to cross the river, but Morgan was tearing up, burning and destroying the Rail Roads in Ohio. We have been having rain every day for three weeks except one or two days. It has been the most sultry weather I ever felt. Nights, towards morning very cold, but still the health of the army is pretty good. We have one or two men a little sick. I have not seen Gassaway who is in the hospital for several days. Intend going to see him today. I will try and fill up Mother's other letter before the boys get off home. I apprehend that they will find no difficulty in crossing as a couple of the 2d La. Regt. crossed a few days since at Rodney and Capt. Webb will go that way if he goes. I hope you will come back with him.

Monday Morn, Aug. 3rd. My own darling Wife—Mr. Minchew said yesterday evening that he would start today but I don't think he will and I'll try and fill out this sheet. Mother as you will see will make me the clothing I need and I have written her to get me some socks as Rich has lost mine. I have only three pairs. I went to see him yesterday evening and his leg is growing together finely. The Cars come into Brandon now and just as soon as he is able to travel I intend to send him to Rocky Mount after my clothes.

I have written so much and at so many different times that I fear I shall say a great many things over 2 or 3 times. I know, however, my darling you will excuse it if I do. I know you love me dearest even as life itself and I am sorry when I think my last letter may have pained you. I wrote a long letter of four pages but when I came to read it over I burned it and wrote another. You'll forgive me my darling won't you and write me the whole feeling of your priceless heart hereafter won't you? You know not how I treasure the least word that expresses that your heart is all my own. You know that I love you above all things on earth and it is a happiness to feel that God has blessed me with so good a wife and I will try always dearest to love you as you deserve.

I have many things to write unto you if I could only think of them, but they escape me among the multitudinous calls that come upon me. If you make me some shirts, check or stripes, make them full across the breast and put plenty of buttons on them to hold them together so they wont gape and show my hairy belly. Watkins has just come from HdQrtrs and states that our Cavalry will be ordered to Okolona, Miss. in ten or 15 days. You may direct your letters in case you have an opportunity of sending any, to Brandon and they will be forwarded to Okolona if we are there. I do not think we will stay there long however and apprehend will go into West Tennessee. I send you 18 postage stamps that you can put on letters you write to me that come across by hand and by some one who is not coming to the Company. They will bring them without stamps. The five cent stamps are the same I brought from home and you have seen before.

Whenever I go to the Rail Road I think of your having passed over this same road and I feel as if I were walking in your footsteps. Do you ever think of me in that way? I hope your Father has invested Spencer's money in bonds. I have heard nothing from him since I saw him but intend writing to Chattanooga in a few days and I guess it will reach him. If all my hogs are not dead try and have them got up and see if you cannot keep up the stock. We are paying a dollar a lb. for Bacon here. I hope your Father will not sell any of ours. You had better see if you can't collect enough money of my accounts to buy *you* a *nurse*. I had rather have a negro than the money. Can't you buy Laura? Buy one of some kind if you can. How does Cynthia get on? Any prospects of an increase in her family? Tell your Father to write me what he is doing at the Mill and when you get a chance ask him if he really does believe Mr. Fay would pinch a woman's arm? Don't let him get the best of you that way. Your confidence is not misplaced I assure you.

But a word more about the getting on that side the river business. Where there's a will there's a way. If I can see Col. Sandidge and you will all elect him Governor I'll get off perhaps. But I have used every effort in my power on this side and they have been unsuccessful. You must exert yourselves if I come now. What say you and what says your Father? Can you help me in any way? *Do it if you can* or I must drag out a weary existence on this side. Come over dearest if I cannot come to you. I leave it all with you for I am helpless. If I could see Dick Capers and he would give me my position in his Regt. I would get a transfer to that Regt. as I think I could do that.[12]

Tuesday Aug. 4th. The furloughs of Murphy and George Monzingo have come back approved for thirty four days and as they start home this evening I will finish my sheet. My own darling one how it pains me to have to be separated from you so. I presume you have not heard of the death of Wm. L. Yancey of Ala. He died after an illness of weeks. John Morgan has recrossed the Ohio safe with his command into Western Virginia. Gen'l Loring's Division is ordered to Virginia so the 12th Louisiana will go there. There will in all probability be a grand Battle going on near Manassas by the time you get this and I am very much afraid Lee will be whipped as the enemy are massing Grant's and Rosecranz's forces there. The last news from Charleston is that we have repelled a very determined assault and the enemy acknowledge a loss of 1500 men killed. I had a paper to send you but some one has stolen it from me. Old Minchew has determined to stay and see if he cannot get Gus discharged, being under age. Joel N. Murphy, a Brother of Miss Eliza's says he will go to Minden and will see you, that he can bring me a couple of pairs of socks. Perhaps you can get Geo. Monzingo to bring me the undershirt.

I am going to make out the pay rolls this evening as we have a prospect of drawing some money. Tell Bud to send me his pony. I will pay him what he asks for him. I want something for Rich to ride and if the Yankees come over there they will take him anyhow. Capt. Webb's papers came back with the enquiry where he wanted to go, so they have to go through again before he knows. Those boys will only stay ten days so you had better commence your letters as soon as you get this and write a little every day as I have done in this. Oh my best beloved how I wish you were on this side the River. I believe you

[12] Colonel Richard L. Capers commanded the 5th Louisiana Cavalry Regiment.

are as safe where you are as anywhere in the Confederacy, but I might get to you sooner if you were on this side. The latest European news is very favorable to a recognition of the *Confederacy by France* and *I believe* an alliance is now on foot both offensive and defensive with her.

5 o'clock P.M. I have made out the pay rolls and now I will try and finish this sheet. We draw Bounty but I shall not draw it as I am determined to try the law and see if I am to be kept. in against the law. I shall make an appeal to the Sec. of War and see if I can't come on that side. I send you a newspaper of the latest possible date you can get the news and circulate it. It has rained the severest kind of a storm this evening and I am wet to the skin. Do write me long letters when you have an opportunity. I love your letters. I am afraid that you will never get through with this. You will see the news in the paper and you must judge for yourself of the state of the Confederacy. If you were safely out of it I should be rejoiced, for I would soon join you. I am wasting my life here with no benefit to myself or to my family. I see Dick Taylor thrashed Banks and I hope you all may be able to protect yourselves over there.[13]

Your examination is over and you are, I presume, at leisure learning to spin. You know my idea on that point. Oh my only beloved how I would I were with you, but will it ever be. Tell your Mother I am glad to hear such good reports from her. Boarding a preacher has done her some good. If I should come back I expect she would get back in her old habits. But it is growing dark. I'll have to stop. Kiss little Thornwell a hundred times for his Papa. My best love to your Mother and Father. I want him to write me a letter. Also to Lou and Cousin Mary too if she is with you. A kiss for Ella and Alice and a kind remembrance to Bud. He might write to me and I want you to make him do it. If I have forgotten anything I will try and remember it when I write by Mr. Minchew, who will not start for a week I reckon.

Remember me dearest in your prayers tho I am past praying for.

[13] On July 13, 1863, at Koch's Plantation, on Bayou Lafourche, a portion of Gen. Richard Taylor's command, led by Gen. Thos. W. Green, defeated a detachment of Gen. N. P. Banks' forces, commanded by Gen. Godfrey Weitzel. See *Battles and Leaders,* III, 598.

Remember I love you above everything else in this world and if I die your name will be the last I will pronounce with my lips. Your memory is ever near me and I shall ever love and cherish it while life remains. Good Bye dearest and may Heaven's richest blessings be showered on you and my child, shield and protect you from danger and grant that I may some day meet you again when I will never part from you. My whole heart is yours dearest. Edwin H. Fay.

Camp Brandon, Miss. Aug. 8/63

My own dearly Beloved:

Mr. Ward and old man Minchew *say* they will start tomorrow morning and so I have taken a small box on my lap, refilled my inkstand, seated myself on the shady side with my back supported by the trunk of a large red oak, to try and scratch a few lines of love to you. I do this more because I know you will be disappointed if you do not get a letter by every opportunity rather than because I have anything new or interesting to write. I have the expression of my love but that is not new though I flatter myself at least that it is interesting to you, for I do believe you prize my love above every earthly object, but you know too that you possess it to its greatest extent. I have not much time to write and if you don't get as lengthy a letter as you did by Geo. Monzingo I know you will excuse me, as it is now 4 P.M. and they *say* they will start at daylight. I have all my duties to attend to in the mean time but I will try and get over one sheet if it is among the things possible.

First let me tell you a little camp incident. While eating dinner [P. P.] Bates came down from the upper end of the camp and said there was a man with a wagon load of Melons for $5.00 apiece, that he said he was a Union Man and always intended to be and asked Capt. Webb's advice what they should do under the circumstances. Capt. said nothing and soon the wagon drove by our fly about 100 yards beyond us and the two companies gathered around and each got a watermelon, walked off and told him to charge them to Lincoln, U.S. etc. The Provost Guard paid him for three I believe $3.00 and he came up to Capt. Webb and *he* told him he didn't get his watermelons and if he could find them the men should give them up. I then asked him if he said he was a Union Man and he replied in the affirmative. I told him not one cent would he get from this Company & that I would report him to Gen'l Cosby. He left, got in his buggy, made his negro drive up the wagon and left town in a hurry. He said he used to live in Bossier Parish, his name was Locke. So much for $5.00 union Watermelons.

I wrote you in my last about Rich breaking his leg and my taking him to Dr. Rober's to get well as we expected to leave here at that time. I have been there frequently to see him and got very well acquainted with the family. A young lady about 18, Miss Rachel and an elder Sister, Mrs. Reynolds a widow, who lost her husband last September, the old Lady & the Dr. compose the family. Mrs. Reynolds is about your age and has three lovely children about the ages of our three. Her eldest a little girl reminds me so much of our darling boy. She *favors* him in the face somewhat. Her second is a little girl with the same round face our baby daughter had and her little boy 18 mos. old looks somewhat as Thornwell did when I last saw him, tho not so large. Poor woman! she told me of her sufferings the other evening and I could but weep with her. Her husband was taken sick last summer in the Swamp in Bolivar Co. north and between the Yazoo and Miss. Rivers. She went and bro't him home but her love and kindness could not prolong his life. She said she did not want her husband to go into the service for she knew he could not stand it, but he was a proud man and could not bear the jeers of others and volunteered—another victim of the inexorable tyranny of public opinion. Capt. Webb accompanied me there one day and tries to teaze me about taking on about the Widow because I speak freely of my regard for her, says he intends if he gets off home to tell my wife how I am acting and I reply that I am willing for my wife to know all my acts and I defy anybody to destroy her confidence in me.

Am I right in my boasts, I believe I am. Ladies have very few charms for me now and I do not seek their society for it revives all too keenly my reminiscences of home and my loved ones there, yet when I do meet a *lady* you know I try to enjoy myself as much as possible and you know how fastidious my taste is regarding what I esteem ladies. But few come up to my Standard and you know what that standard is. For fear you mistake, it is my own dear Wife. A lady to please me much must remind me of you in some particulars. I do not think any one I have seen compares with you in all respects tho I told Miss Alice White, a cousin of Misses Madry that if I were a single man she would have to say "yes" or "no" before that day passed. She was perfectly beautiful a *blonde* while Miss Mary Jane Robinson (you have heard me speak of) was a brunette & together they were according to their styles the most beautiful women I ever saw. They may both be the most beautiful women but they could never be as dear to me as *one* wide blue eyed woman I know who already rejoices in the appellation of *my dear Wife*. Does she rejoice in that appellation? I hope she does.

Last evening Capt. Webb and myself got a pass from Gen'l Cosby to go out in the Country some 9 miles to spend the night with an old friend of Capt. Webb's. We had got 5 miles of the distance when on turning round I saw "George" (Capt's Boy) coming post haste after us. He told us Capt's Bro., Dr. Webb from Ala. (Livingston) had come, consequently we turned back. He came to see the Capt. and is going back on the Cars tonight. He is a very pleasant sensible educated man. We lost a good Supper and breakfast by the operation but we will go again some time.

Rich is getting along finely his leg having grown together again, wants crutches but I'll not let him have any till he gets strong again. He dislikes to have to lie up but I am not sorry for him tho' I miss him very much. As soon as he gets able I intend to send him to Montgomery after my clothing. He can come to me though I have sold his horse. I wish I could get Bud's Mexican Pony here, they are the only horses almost that can stand the service. My Mare I ask $1000 for. She is the best saddle animal in the Brigade, but I want to send her home to raise colts from. I have changed her name to Hecate which I think suits her disposition better.

I have given you no War News in this and there is none save one rumor. Wirt Adams who is scouting near Vicksburg sent yesterday morning the following dispatch. "A Lady just from Vicksburg says the Yankees report the surrender of New Orleans to a Confederate Fleet and land forces under Gen'l Taylor. I also learn the same from scouts in the vicinity of Port Hudson." We do not put much faith in it however, though it is believed to some extent at HdQrtrs. I hope it may be so.

What say you dearest to my making an effort to get transferred to the Navy? I want to get on board the Florida or Alabama and be making something to support you and dear little Thornwell on. The crew of the Florida have made $50,000 apiece in hard cash so say the papers, and you know that they always speak the truth. If you will give your consent I'll endeavor to get into that service. I believe I wrote you that Gen'l Cosby approved furloughs for ten men of the Co. to go home but they came back disapproved by higher authority so it will take 3½ years for all our Company to get home. I have no idea of getting home before the close of the War and I have no idea that the War will close till Lincoln & Co. are dispossessed of their office. The English Cabinet rejoices that it did not recognize the Confederacy as there is no prospect of Reconstruction or entire Subjugation. I hate the English as intensely as I do the Yanks. We will come out in the end victorious I believe but there will be but few men left in the Confederacy to enjoy the Independence of it and they will be the Exempts from Substitution and otherwise. The Volunteers will all be killed.

We have heard from the Minden Blues. They went into the battle of Gettysburg 40 strong lost 6 killed and 18 wounded. Capt. Sam Webb wrote to the Dr. who is with us but gave no names so we don't know much about it. That company has suffered severely and so will all good troops suffer when contending against such odds. I don't know what this army is going to do. We draw nothing from the Commissary Dept. but a little yellow meal and poor Beef. Not a lb. of Bacon, nor can we buy any even at a dollar a lb. Poor Beef without any grease is poor eating and I have never complained till the last few days.

Tell your Father to buy all the Hogs he can and feed his toll to them and put up all the Bacon he possibly can. You might invest your money made teaching and speculate *lawfully, honestly* in some such way as that. I fear you will have to support yourself in some such way if the War continues. My wages, 32 pr. month won't support me.

I am *longing* again to get one of your good letters but I fear I'll have to wait a month till the boys come back who have gone across. I wish I had gone when Harrison's Co. did. But my sheet is nearly filled and I must close. Please answer everything in my three last letters that you think worth answering. Give all the love *you can spare* to your Mother & Sisters and remember me kindly to all friends who enquire after me. Kiss my dear little boy a hundred times for me and believe me my darling your affectionate husband, Edwin H. Fay

P.S. Capt. Webb has got his leave of absence and starts in the morning. I wish you would see him and perhaps he will bring a pair of socks for me. I do hope he will make some arrangements to get the company transferred and I want the people to help him. Be sure to write me some letters and long ones by him as he will stay a week longer than the others. I want a pair of Boots but not just yet as mine are not gone and I cannot take care of two pairs. Send Bud's pony by Capt. Webb for Rich will be just about able to travel by the time he returns, that is if he can spare him. Good Bye.

Camp near Clinton Miss Sep 2d 1863

My own darling One:

I have determined, after having debated the matter in my mind for some time to write you this evening though there is no telling when if ever I shall have a chance to send it to you, but as a chance may arise unexpectedly there will be no harm in having the letter written. Besides I want to talk with you any how as you have been in my dreams for the past few nights and I have enjoyed unalloyed happiness at least in dreamland if not in our almost gone Confederacy. I could not recollect my dreams I only knew they were very pleasant, that I was with the only one around whom my life centers.

Oh! this cruel war! and so fruitless in its results in behalf of our Independence. Tomorrow will be two long long Months since your last letter rec'd by me was written. Had I ever thought two months would elapse without hearing from you I assure you I should never have volunteered. The country might have gone to grass and we would have sought another home in some country where there was no war. Nine long weary months have elapsed since I last pressed a love token upon your lips and in all probability nine more moons may grow and wane before I again press a loving kiss upon them even should my life be spared, for the termination of this struggle is like the mirage of the desert, it seems to recede from the approaching traveller so seems the end of this conflict, every vestige of Republican liberty being taken away from the people of the North.

The election in Ky. has been carried largely in favor of the Administration by Abolition bayonets and 12 pdr Cannon and I very much fear a like result will occur in Ohio and that Vallandigham will be defeated.[14] If they gain another victory over the Confederate arms, his defeat is almost certain and I fear they will gain it even if they have not already done so at Charleston tho our last accounts made out a flattering report. Sumter's walls had succumbed to the enemy's 200 pdr rifle guns but a lining of sandbags 27 feet thick was impervious to the shot. Charleston may be burned and levelled but will never be surrendered says the Gov. of S.C.[15] Mobile I do not think will be attacked at present but I fear greatly that you will have a visit from the vandals when the waters rise if not before. You must get word to me if it should happen and hide my rifle with a flask of powder and a lot of balls & caps where I can find it and I'll be home in a short time. I can do more good killing there than lying in camps here. My efforts will do no good here and it grieves me to feel I am to be kept here away from all my bosom holds dear for no good purpose. If I felt I was doing any good or shortening the war in the least I could be better content with my lot. By the Bye I have been homesick lately and I should not tell you of it if I had not almost entirely recovered.

I have been having chills and fever several days though have had no chill for more than a week and yesterday and today I have felt very well indeed. The way of it was this. Aug. 10th the Brig. left Brandon to move to Raymond, as we supposed to camp and John Lesueur and I stayed behind for his Boy Sandy to put a pair of shoes on my mare and do some of the work in the shop. We did not get off till Tuesday

[14] Vallandigham was defeated by John Brough, the Republican candidate for Governor of Ohio, by a vote of 288,374, to 187,492. Roseboom, *The Civil War Era,* 421.

[15] The Confederates held Charleston until February 18, 1865, when Sherman's invasion forced the evacuation of the city.

Morning and rode 25 miles to Raymond to learn that the Brigade, save Wirt Adams regt. had gone on a scout towards the Miss. River with 2½ days cooked rations. Wirt Adams told us that the Yankees were crossing Big Black to follow Gen'l Cosby and we could not go on for fear they would pick us up. I remonstrated to no effect and he told us we could stay with his Regt. or return to Brandon. I learned that Zeb Rudulph of his regt. had gone home and as I had no acquaintance there I told him we would go back to Brandon and so started and went out to "Cooper's Wells" and stayed near there at a Mr. Thigpen's[16] till we learned 3 days after that Gen'l Cosby had gone to Rodney as we supposed to fire on the Transports when we put our dodging Wirt's pickets and riding 40 or 50 miles a day to catch up but we did not overtake the Command till they got nearly back to Canton.

The hard riding in the sun gave me the chills and on Friday we were reviewed by Gen'l Stephen D. Lee who as Maj. Gen'l takes command of all Cavalry of the Dept. after review I had a severe chill and on Sat. morning the 24th I started back to Brandon on business but was taken sick on the road at Mr. Taylor's (where I wrote you I went to get Flour from Brandon once.) I had high fever that evening and on Sunday Morning such a shaking chill that all the family came in to see me shake. It lasted about 3 hours when the fever came on and Miss Jennie Taylor, who looks just like you, bathed and rubbed my head for two hours till I had to just make her quit for I knew she was tired. My fever did not leave me till Tuesday Morn 3 o'clock although I rode to Brandon 12 miles Monday Morning and stayed at Dr. Reber's where I found Rich had left the Wednesday before on the cars for Rocky Mount in charge of Col. Layton, a son-in-law of Dr. Reber. Mrs. Reynolds about whom I wrote you keeps house and her parents live with her. She treated me with the greatest kindness and is one of the nicest and best women I ever saw. My chill did not come on next day tho the Dr. gave me some medicine but I put it in my pocket book

[16] Samuel J. Thigpen, who according to the 1860 Census, owned 5500 acres of land and lived in the Dry Grove community, Hinds County, near Raymond, Mississippi. In 1860 Thigpen was 27 years of age and had a wife, 29; a son, 6; and daughters, 3 and 1. Information provided by the Mississippi State Department of Archives and History.

and it did me as much good I think as in my stomach (at least it will last longer) and I had no other chill since though I have not been entirely clear from fever till day before yesterday. (Memo) If you have chills and fever wear some medicine in your pocket and you will recover.

One year ago today since we made our memorable retreat from West Tenn. after the Denmark fight, Sept. 1, 1862, the bloodiest fight on record for the force engaged and such another as I hope never to witness again. My hair almost stands on end when I think of it and my heart swells with gratitude to God for the preservation of my life through it all. Then arises the question whether He will preserve it thro the other dangers that beset my pathway. You say in one of your letters that you feel that my life will be preserved and that we shall enjoy each other's society again. We may and if I could *see any* prospect of a termination of this war I would feel so too but I am wasting the best part of my life and I am sad and lone and dreary. No wife, No child near me, and life even the longest so short at best. Oh, can I endure it much longer. The thought almost crazes me. I am so anxious to hear from you. I do hope something has happened that will call me across the River.

I have thought of another plan to get over. Let your Father see Kirby Smith and represent that I am necessary to carrying on the Mill and get him to address Gen'l Cosby to have me detailed for that purpose. It can be done and I can do the Country as much service in that way as any, or as I am now doing. If I felt I was doing any good I would not be so anxious to come. Drowning men catch at straws and this is the last plan I know of to get in your neighborhood unless the Yanks come and then I shall go anyhow, nolens, volens. But no more of this.

I got a letter from Mother and Brother William Henry on the 23 ult. He is at home and what he says and thinks you shall judge yourself as I will send his letter along with this if it goes by hand, the only way in fact it is possible to go now. I am looking for Rich back next week and I hope he will bring me a lot of clothing as Mother wrote me she had it made for me. Oh if you could only come over on this side the River with Capt. Webb I could then see you once more for I would get off on some plea and come see you. You would have to come right through our Camps to get to Brandon, the terminus of the Rail Road. You will see Capt. Webb but I know you will not accompany him. The undertaking will prove too great as there are no conveyances to be procured on this side the River and you can't travel without me you know anyhow. If I was over and had to return I know I could arrange to bring you across if you wished to come. Perhaps it is best as it is. I am tired of writing now and so will bid you Good Bye till tomorrow.

Tuesday Sep 11th, 1863 at Mr. Thigpen's near Raymond. You will think dearest that tomorrow has been a long time coming when you look at the date of this, but it has come and gone and I am here at Mr. Thigpen's trying to recover from another attack of fever and chills. I have missed them and am feeling much better and if I had any assurance that they would not return again in a week I should feel very well. Our Camp is still at Clinton and I am some ten miles from camp on a *two* days leave of absence tho I shall stay until I get better be it two or ten days.

I thought as I was riding down here the other day of one more plan by which I might get into service on the other side but I require an energetic coadjutor. From what I learn of Gen'l Kirby Smith from Van McKamie & Pearce I feel sure if you would go over to Shreveport and see him and tell him that your husband was exempt under the act of Conscription and that he was qualified as an Engineer (refer to Gen'l Rust and Lovell who both tendered me the position on their Staff) that he desired to be on that side that he might hear from his family and ask him for a place on his Engineer Corps or a position as *Independent Scout* for him, I feel sure you would get it. If he made you the promise make him give it you in writing and send me a copy of it and I'll be at home in two weeks after receiving it. I fear you will think it a great task to go see a Gen'l but he is no more than a man. The ladies here like to go to the Gen'ls for favors I judge, by the way their carriages flutter around Hd Qrtrs. I have no doubt you would gain your point. I'd rather be an Independent Scout than anything else, but it would be the hardest kind of service, but I could occasionally take Minden in my way. If I am asking too much of you dearest, don't do it, but I think you would be pleased with your mission when it was over. I could willingly stay away from you 12 mos. if I could hear from you, but to be cut off from hearing I cannot do it. If you should go to see Gen'l Smith tell him plainly everything, keeping back nothing. Tell him I am Orderly Sergeant of Gen'l Cosby's Escort and that I feel as if I was doing no good whatever, that I want some position where I could feel I was benefitting the common cause of our country. Something whispers in my ear that success will attend your effort. If he will promise me either of the positions mentioned I'll come across the River with or without leave.

I am tired of Cosby's drunkeness and Jackson's slothfulness. Since last writing you I have begun to believe that this war will not last very long in the year '64 and I believe it will close on account of the Franco-Mexican difficulty and the explosion of the Yankee financial scheme. I think want of finances and diplomacy will bring it about. Seward and Chase are each plotting for the Presidency in '65 and their antagonism may defeat the ends of both. Our latest news from Charleston was favorable. They had made a night assault on Sumter in 9 barges hoping to take it by surprise, but lost 100 privates, 18 officers prisoners and 4 out of 9 barges, our losses nothing. We have given up Morris Island, however, after moving the guns from Gregg & Wagner. Bragg has fallen back from the Tenn. River to let old Rosey cross which if he is not too wary to be caught in it will be a trap whereby Johnston will bag all of Rosecranz & Burnsides armies. Joe Johnston is there and I have confidence all will be well.

I received a letter from Mother and Sister Sallie the other day but I will not dilate upon what they say for I intend enclosing theirs in this to you. They drew again the other day for furloughs and the lots fell on Lancaster and Richard Ratcliff. Carter & Watkins drew and Watkins won but gives way for Carter so he will come and see his beloved Amanda. This will probably be carried you by him as he may get off before Lancaster does as the furloughs of the privates have to wait till they can certify that those that have already gone have come back. I wish I felt in the humor for writing but a slow 6 days fever with chills every other day don't fit one fast for letter writing. I have very little news to tell you for I have seen but two papers in two weeks except Yankee papers of the rankest Abolition dye, for instance the "*Cincinnati Commercial.*" A perfect tissue of falsehood from beginning to end.

We have been living tolerably well for some weeks. We bought some bacon and have been drawing the finest beef I ever saw and occasionally some flour & shorts, principally the latter. If any people deserve to prosper for patient endurance of suffering surely the Independence of the Confederacy is a fixed fact and at no distant day for several flags of truce have been inside the Yank lines and members of our Company have accompanied them and the vile villains have everything heart could wish. They live better far than they did at home in times of peace. No wonder then they carry on a war for plunder and rapine, they can command their soldiers.

I came off from camp and forgot my saddlebags and paper so if I write any more out here I will have to interline Mother's & Will's letters. I'll wait awhile and see If I can think of anything more to say to you. If you find letters interlined you must go from this to them. I do wish I could send this to you at once. How glad I'd be.

11

"Anything To Get on That Side the River"

Sep 19 1863. Still at
Mr Thigpens 4 mis South Raymond

My own darling Wife:

While lying on a pallet before the fire yesterday with one of the hardest shaking chills in came Julius Lancaster from camp some 14 miles distant with your anxiously expected letters by Capt. Webb and you cannot conceive my darling one how my heart did rejoice to have the pleasure of reading once more one of your loving letters. So many of them too. It did not quite take away my fever but it made it a great deal lighter than it would otherwise have been. The best was that after I had read all as I supposed and lain down, I rose to look over something again and I found the date Aug. 30th that I had not read at all so you see that was just like getting a new letter again. You don't know how I bless you my darling for thinking so much of me and I do not feel worthy of it, for I feel that you are a great deal better than I am. I do not know how to begin to answer your letters unless I do it *seriatim* which I believe I will do. I have just been reading all of your 5 full sheets and I find a great many things I would like to reply to in words oral for a reply in writing covers so much space, but my head is so bewildered and dizzy this morning from yesterday's and last night's fever that I feel hardly able to direct the pen at all.

This fact in itself is a reply to one of your objections against my coming across the River into service on that side. However, I only have chills with fever continuous from one paroxysm to the other, on this side, i.e. a chill every other day with fever during the meantime whereas if I was on that side I might have chills every day, ergo, I had better remain where I am altho I know I am doing absolutely worse than nothing for the redemption of the Confederacy.

I cannot call it "my country" for my Country would not permit Comd. Genl's to usurp all the power of Congress and make laws by their lordly edicts. The Confederacy under the present administration of affairs is no more than a *black patch*. I believe the day of Independence is dawning but we will then see the same political electioneering spirit as ever before. The Confederacy, and I say it with deep regret, will be as corrupt after 5 years as the old Union was. Southern men too above all others I look upon as entirely incapable of self government. But I'm running off the track. There's no use speculating about the future. Sufficient unto the day is the evil thereof.

But to answer your letter and first as to my advice about running from the Yankees. I have told you and I know it is the best way to meet them boldly, yes pistol in hand and tell them to their teeth that it is your place and you are determined to protect it. A gentleman in Brandon, ex-Col. of the 6th Miss. Regt. sat on his gallery with his double barrel gun on his lap and told the first one that molested anything that he would kill one of them at least and cursed them for cowardly robbers. One shot one of his chickens and he made him pick it up and carry it into his kitchen and then told the negro woman to cook it for him, that no cowardly Yankee thief should eat his chickens while he was alive. His was the only place in Brandon that was not plundered to a greater or less extent.[1]

A Lady in Tenn. told me that her husband being in the Army she was very much frightened when a Regt. of Vandals camped around her house into which they came ransacking everything. At length they demanded her smoke house key which she told them she had in her pocket and if they must go into her smoke house she would go with

[1] The person described was doubtless Dr. John J. Thornton of Brandon, Mississippi, who was elected colonel of the 6th Mississippi Infantry Regiment, on September 5, 1861. He was wounded at the battle of Shiloh and resigned from the army on May 25, 1862. He was noted as the one member of the Mississippi Convention who refused to sign the ordinance of secession. Information provided by Mississippi State Department of Archives and History.

them. She started, expecting to open the door to them, but when she stepped on the ground a new courage seemed, she said, to take possession of her. She saw about 75 in her yard and walked to the smoke house, put her back against the door, drew a pistol her husband had given her and told them they could only enter over her dead body. That the first that approached she would kill and ordered them to fall into line and call the roll to see who was brave enough to attempt it. They stared at her for a few moments when gathering fresh courage she told them they should every one leave her yard and the first Yankee that set foot in it again without her permission she would kill. They camped there 2 months and she was entirely unmolested.

So I say stay where you are, treat them, if they should come, civilly and whenever they overstep the bounds of civility have a pistol ready with a will to use it. You must have it not your Father. They will burn the Mill you may be sure of that unless your Father should see the Comdg. Officer at once and get a guard or guard it himself night and day. They will destroy our house unless someone is living in it, so you must keep some one living there all the time if Mrs. Mitchell has gone away. As far as your going to Texas is concerned to be outside their lines, hoping to hear from me, that is vain, for if they ever occupy Minden, and I hear of it I shall be there too just as soon as my mare can carry me there. I wouldn't miss the opportunity I would have for killing them there for anything. I'd be called a deserter a thousand times rather than miss that chance of lessening the number of the devils—

I am sorry dearest that you are so much opposed to my getting across on the other side of the River for I had flattered myself until the reception of your letters last night that the plans suggested in a previous letter would be carried out with a hearty earnestness. I am much obliged for your letter to Gen'l Smith but if you thought it such an undertaking to write him I don't know what you will think of my urgent request to go and see him personally and ask him to receive your husband either in his engineer Corps or as a private Scout. I then can base an application for a transfer and it will be granted and I can come back legally. You can tell him that my knowledge of the French language would be an advantage as a Scout in the Southern part of the State. If you will see him which you can do and get an acknowledgement of his willingness to receive me in either of the above positions I can then send up an application on this side for a transfer with a strong possibility of its being granted, and I furthermore promise that if you don't want me to come home for *particular reasons* that I will not spend *a night* at home till the war is ended. You must either do this or your father must get a request from Gen'l Smith to Gen'l Jackson or Lee that I be detailed to assist him in the Mill as he is grinding Govt. wheat, but understand that I am not going to leave the Army for I would report at once as a scout to Gen'l Smith. Anything to get on that side the River myself for there is no prospect whatever of the company ever coming over. I am determined to come on that side either by fair means or foul before another equinox.

Mr. Murphy did not come across the River but representing himself as a Capt. in the Commissary dept. got an order to report for duty on that side. He was 4th Sergt. and a *detached beef driver* and that is all the Capt. he was.[2] I don't blame him for staying on that side though for I would do it if I was over there. James Newcomb (Mrs Wimberly knows him) left the Company the day after Capt. Webb did and has not been heard from.[3] I expect he went home and went out to Texas with the Bennets. I understand Harrison's Company are favorites with Gen'l Smith and are gone to Mexico with some prisoners. If our Cavalry fell back to Vienna when the Yanks were only at Monroe I think that they need a good Company or two who have seen real service to come over and show them how far in advance of the Yanks to retreat. But this is none of my business.

I come now to another part of your letter and it is where you are so patriotic. I do not blame you dearest for feeling as you do but at the same time I assure you that *spoken patriotism* is cheap. I had fully as much of it at the beginning as you could have and perhaps have as much now as you have but I acknowledge it has considerably

[2] Muster rolls of the Minden Rangers show that 4th Sergt. Joel N. Murphy was on furlough in July and August and absent in September and October. He was then dropped from the rolls. Booth, *La. Confed. Soldiers,* III, pt. 1, 1099.

[3] Sgt. James L. A. Newcomb of the Minden Rangers was listed on the muster rolls of July and August, 1863, as absent without leave; on the September and October rolls as absent since Aug. 9, 1863. He was then dropped from the rolls. Booth, *La. Confed. Soldiers,* III, pt. 1, 1271.

cooled down. Had I been at home protected from the Summers rain and the winters' frosts with as much to eat as I had before the war, surrounded by my relatives and friends. If I could have lain down to sleep without being awakened by the bugle's shrill blast, if all I had known of war had been what I had read, I too perhaps could have said quite as loudly and as proudly too what is a man's home or family worth to him if he has no country? Ah me, if patriots at home only knew what it was to be a soldier they would cease talking about patriotism. Patriotism is only a word embodying some ill defined idea of something, I fear *patriots* know not what. I tell you all the romance of patriotism consists in words which thrill the feelings for a time and is mistaken for something real. If there was only one country on the face of the earth and if a man was compelled by powers beyond his escape or control to live in that one country then there might be some sense in the present senseless oratory about patriotism.

I know very well there is not a man in the Confederate Army today that is not kept there by some *interest or other* and there is no patriotism in it, tho it answers just as well just as long as they stay and fight. There is no such thing as patriotism where the rights of the private soldier are trampled on every hour. No it is brute force and fear of public opinion alone that now holds together the armies of the Confed. States. I am willing to acknowledge there is only one thing keeps me there and that is absolute hatred of the infernal Villains. But my efforts are paralysed and I can do nothing. In fact this Cavalry has done nothing since a year ago. Our Co. has done nothing and worse than nothing since the fight at Corinth last Oct. Do you wonder then that I am dissatisfied when I see the Confed. losing ground daily and feel that I am so situated that I can do nothing. Our Cavalry wastes its time in grand Reviews before Hardee & Stephen D. Lee and dress parades for a few lonesome and garish young ladies. Noble employment for a band of men. Men, some of whom too really desire to inflict some injury on the enemy, but they are not allowed to go out of camp.

You say I would not have near so easy a time over there. I do not expect it. If Gen'l Smith will make me a scout I do not expect ever to have a single day of rest, rain or shine, but I would then *know* that I was doing some good for the Country. I imagine I hear you quoting "and they also serve who only stand and wait." I cannot see things in the light you do for I have been an actor and you an audience. You say banish the word *"desert"* from your vocabulary etc. I would by no means consider I had deserted the service of the Confederacy if I should report to the Trans. Miss. Dept. for service. I am illegally held to service on this side the River anyway. I have never rec'd the $50 Bounty for continuance in service. I was too smart for that. I could not be roped in by that kind of a bribe. $50 was no inducement for me to re-enlist during the War.

As for living in the Confed States after the War just say to your Father that if they gain a nationality business may compel me to remain in them, but I'll never exercise the rights of citizenship and if there should be a reconstruction I would not remain in the United States longer than I could find a vessel on which to leave. I would not live a day in a reconstructed Union. I would not live in a Confed. composed of the Northwestern & Southern States. I am what I was in the beginning from first to last, a Secessionist to the backbone, deeper dyed than ever before. Isn't it a little singular of all the Candidates in Claiborne parish I am the only one on both sides who is in the Army.

But now to take up your letters in detail and to begin with July 28th. Well your letter by Maj. Johns has never come to hand and I seriously doubt his sending it. I don't think Maj. Johns was much of a Military man or he would have known there was only one way Gen'l Smith could get us across and that was by private request of Gen. Johnston to transfer us. I am very sorry that your Examination resulted so disastrously. Dr. Bright has certainly not got will enough of his own to successfully conduct a female college in Minden. When he was so vacillating I should have refused entirely to have anything to do with it had I been in your place. However Mrs. Drury Murrell's or Mrs. Carter's indignation are not insuperable barriers to your advancement. Mr. or Mrs. Carter will never burn up the world with their flashes of intellect. He is an earnest reconstructionist and if he was not in the army would be a traitor if the Yankees came where he lived. However now he is in the army he will be as conscientious in discharge of his duty as he knows how to be. I do not think Mrs.

Bright treated you very well in shifting the blame to your poor shoulders. Bought wit is dear but is cheapest in the long Run—

The next thing that I see is the charge of doubting your love in the Letter by Underwood. I feel that my subsequent letters have counteracted that charge. You know my darling that I have never doubted your love. I only thought you were too reserved in the expression of it and I felt blue as you certainly knew by the tone of my letters and should have excused it. I never have nor shall I ever lose confidence in your love tho' some of your expressions would lead one to think that you thought more of what you call your Country than of your Husband. I know you dearest and I love you and do not and never have distrusted you.

You didn't tell me that your Father had got the bonds for Mr. Spencer. Do not let him neglect at once. Spencer wants the Bonds. Let me know in your next. I think your Father's views right about going to Texas. If they overrun La. they will Texas so you'll have to keep running. I suppose you have heard of the death of Lowry Simmons at Gettysburg. I was surprised you had not heard it as I learned from Capt. Webb. Bob Smith & John Simon Williams wounded and some others you do not know.[4] I am glad Joe Buys got back safe and that Jack Crichton had got home. I wonder what Anneke got to stealing money for. I am sorry you paid Mary that money for Rich owes me much more than that and I am afraid I'll never get it—I have written you to do several things and you have never told me if you did. Did you ever get a letter sent by Maj. Reily of N.O. sometime in June, mailed at Trinity or Natchez. It contained a beautiful piece of poetry to be sent to the Mt. Lebanon Baptist for publication. "He's Nothing but a Soldier." You will see by Mother's letter enclosed that she will make me some clothing. I think if I can get over these chills I shall get along pretty well.

I have finished all the answers to July 28 & 29—In August 24th

[4] John Lowry Simmons, John Simon Williams, and Robert A. Smith were all privates in the Minden Blues, Company G, 8th Louisiana Infantry Regiment. Simmons was killed at Gettysburg, July 1, 1863, and Smith was wounded in that battle. Muster rolls do not list Williams among the wounded at Gettysburg. See Booth, *La. Confed. Soldiers,* III, pt. 2, 570, 628, 1103.

you say you wrote a letter to Gen'l Kirby Smith. I am glad my darling that you thought enough of your husband to exert yourself. I want you to make one effort more and this time *go and see* the Gen'l. I know you can effect my transfer if you will only resolve to go and try and I know you will do it my darling for my sake. I know you had rather I were near you in case of an invasion and you have it now at your option. I know I will not trust you in vain. I am glad you got the papers I sent. I wish I could send you some this time but I don't know that I can get any as we seldom see any papers though the last news we have is very favorable.

A fleet of 9 steel clad rams from England have passed into Wilmington and are there taking on crews.[5] I suppose the Yanks are beginning to despair of taking Charleston and the Fleet from England is exercising their wits. Six more are to sail from England so the Yankees say for N.Y., Boston, Phila. to bombard those cities. Bragg & Rosecrans will fight in a few days. Longstreet's Corps from Va. has reinforced Bragg and it is said Lee will plan the fight and lead the charge. If so the Yanks will meet with a more severe defeat than they have ever yet met.

Commodore [Matthew Fontaine] Maury has written a most excellent letter in which he says the prospects of the Confederacy were never brighter than at present. This is very encouraging coming from the source it does. The Franco-Mexican difficulty is perplexing the Lincoln dynasty. Maximilian ascends the Throne of Mexico and recognizes at once the Confed. and sends ambassadors to both powers. The U.S. have to surrender their Monroe doctrine and recognize Mexico, or France and Austria will declare War immediately. I think before the days and nights are of equal length again this war will have closed and *I believe* a total bankruptcy of the Lincoln Govt. will be the cause. I do not look to steel clad ships or Foreign Intervention to bring it about but the total discomfiture of the Yankee army now at Chattanooga will burst the grand bubble of Yankee finance and all will be well. I believe if I live to see next June I'll see my home in peace but I want to be on that side of the River when it comes.

In your letter of Aug. 19th at Mrs. Lesueur's I find nothing partic-

[5] This report, like most that Fay heard concerning activities of foreign nations, was false.

ular to answer. Did Lucy Smith lose both her children. I so infer from the way you write. As far as Parson Henderson is concerned I think it was good riddance for from what I have heard from him from members of the Co. who knew him he is not the man to suit me and is dreadfully *henpecked* to boot. Mother Shields didn't cry when they started away I know. Mr. Henderson had never mentioned the reasons of his leaving in any letters to the Co. and he writes to Giles Monzingo and Wafer Menifee. I am sorry you were disappointed in learning how to make a hat but the one I had cut down when at home is still good and I think will last another year at least. Sister Sarah could show you how to make, I daresay, a much prettier hat than Mrs. Andrews as she made them for Uncle Lloyd in Selma to sell. Uncle Lloyd is getting to be so penurious that he will hardly eat enough to keep alive. Is getting to be a Miser in his old age, enters readily with Weaver into all his speculations & extortions and is just what all the whilom Union men have proved to be who have stayed at home. Vampires sucking the life blood of the State. But I've been writing off and on all day so I'll put it away and try and write the other side before my chill comes on tomorrow.

Monday Morning Sept. 21st. Well dearest the chill came on me yesterday attended by cramps and was by far the severest I ever had but I have sent for a doctor and will take Medicine and try and keep off. The Dr. has just come and I find him to be Dr. Tulleston who used to live up on Flat Lick. He has given me some medicine but I have not much confidence in him. I shall lie abed tomorrow and take Quinine and will I hope escape my chill, but if I do and return to camp I have no security against their return and I shall probably have them all winter. But this is the healthy side of the River and I have had such good health all along I ought not to grumble if I am sick a little. Besides common chills never kill anybody and I'll get over them when the war is over. Don't feel uneasy about me at all. I guess I'll get along very well. I am not alarmed so you need not be.

I have not seen Capt. Webb and know nothing of the Minden news save what you wrote. I agree with you that this is not time to be having babies and I sincerely rejoice you are not in the same category. However I don't think you need ever fear being troubled in that line again. Should the Yankees come to Minden you had better sell or send off Cynthia for she is just whore enough to go to the Yankee camp if it is ever within 20 miles. I wish you would sell or swap her for a negro that would have children. You have not written whether you ever delivered my message or not to her.

I am truly glad that you have such pleasant neighbors in Mr. Black's family. It is certainly a great pleasure to you. I wish I had the pleasure of knowing them. You did not tell me if Capt. Webb came to see you. You promised a sample of your homespun dress but did not send it. The piece of poetry you sent me I cut out once to send to you but you did not get my letter. As to transcribing it I have not time at present and it is so worn out that I can hardly preserve it. I will send you a piece in exchange for it. The first time I see "Rivinac" I'll get him to copy his Waltzes for me and send you the Manuscript.[6] I can get no printed music short of Mobile and I don't expect to go there till the Yankees attack it in force which I don't think they will do till they meet with much better success at Charleston. I hear this morning that Bragg is pursuing Rosecrans and long ere this letter reaches you will be fought the battle of our Independence, the decisive one in the Valley of Tenn. I expect the bloody battle is coming off today.[7] Oh for something to close this war and I believe it is coming—

I shall send some of your dear letters to Mother and Sister Sarah whom I'll write to this evening. I do wish I could get some newspapers to send you but cannot. I will not be able to write Thornwell a letter this time but tell him why didn't he send me Dick to ride in the War. I would like much to have some of his big water melon but cannot come now. It remains entirely with Mama whether I come or not. It will take 3 years to furlough our Company at the rate they are going on now and I will be one of the last men to come. I want to get a transfer and have already told you how I can obtain it. You ask me if John Lesueur is engaged to one of the Misses Madry. He was when

[6] P. Rivinac, composer of *General Bragg's Grand March* and other musical pieces. See Richard B. Harwell, *Confederate Music* (Chapel Hill, 1950), 75, 77, 92.

[7] The Chickamauga battle to which he refers was fought on September 19–20, 1863. Bragg's forces won the great victory over Rosecrans that Fay hoped for, but it was not followed up and it had little effect on the course of the war.

we left there but he came by there on his way down from Tenn. and I don't know what was the result—it was Miss Mattie. Did you ever write them as I asked you to? I have not heard from them in a long time.

I am sorry to hear of so many deaths particularly of children. It seems as if we were not the only sufferers. There is no use in my trying to become reconciled to the loss of our darling one. I cannot for his death is as great an affliction to me as it was a year ago. I miss him in every thought of home. I cannot become reconciled to his loss. But of this no more, there seems to be no justice in Heaven above or on Earth beneath. Blind chance now seems to be the ruling power.

I feel much more cheerful now than when I wrote the letter by Underwood but it grieves me to hear of such men as John Ray Slack etc. welcoming the Yankees. If Slack acted as you wrote me I reckon him no longer on my list of friends. I wish you had told me who you were going to elect for Governor. The time will soon come John Ray can never hold any office in La. after this war, but I must bring this letter to a close for I have an opportunity of sending a letter to Mother tomorrow. I may write between the lines on Mother's letter that I send you. I am much obliged for the kind remembrance of the Lesueur family. I am very sorry Lou didn't send my letter I don't think I shall soon write her again if that is the way she treats me. Didn't you leave out some of your letters? How is it Mr. Wimberly isn't conscripted and numerous others. Get Mr. Wimberly to go over to Shreveport with you when you go to see Gen'l Smith. Now don't think you can't go and plead your husband's case. If I was going to be hung couldn't you plead for me or would you be too modest. But this may be a life and death case. I feel as if I was coming across by some means or other before another Christmas. The Mill, or a transfer must bring me over.

Give my best love to your Mother & Father. Ask Mother Shields if she don't wish she had taken my advice and not boarded a preacher? A kiss for Lou from me and love in abundance to the other children. What has become of Bud. I hear nothing of him. I am afraid he is getting to be a vagabond having no school to go to and I know he wont work at all. I am glad you had Thornwell's wagon fixed. Yes his papa will buy him a pony and he can prove it by mama now. A hundred kisses for him and my whole heart for you my darling wife and may God preserve and bless you. Your affectionate husband, Ed.

Friday Morn Sunrise Sep. 24, '63

My Own Darling:

I improve a few moments this morning to add to my already well filled letter that I send it by Bob Thompson to Camp for Julius Lancaster to carry as soon as his application for furlough comes back "approved." He promised to come by this way but for fear of an accident I send it into Camp. And first my dearly beloved you will rejoice to hear I have broken my chills for two days and think now that I shall be permanently relieved from them. I am still at Mr. Thigpen's where I have received every kindness and attention that could have been bestowed on an own Son by his Mother. He is about my age and lost his wife some 2 years ago. He has two lovely children, 8 & 6 yrs.—brother & sister. I wish I had time to give you *incidents* of their kindness but I haven't time this morning—

I have also some glorious news to tell you from Gen'l Bragg. He attacked "old Rosey" last Sat. 19 and drove him back 11 miles capturing 50 pieces of Artillery and on Sunday 25 pieces more still driving them back. Our loss is 6 Brig. Gen'ls, viz. [John] Gregg (Texas) [Benjamin Hardin] Helm, [John B.] Hood (Tex.) [Daniel W.] Adams (La.) mortally wounded & missing.[8] Monday the battle was renewed but we have not heard the result yet but expect the enemy were driven into the Tenn. River. The battle commenced near Ringgold, Ga. You must see Julius Lancaster when he comes and he can give you the latest news if I don't have an opportunity of coming to see you on paper again before he starts. There is a good deal of dis-

[8] Fay's information on casualties was only partially correct. Three Confederate brigadiers were killed at Chickamauga—Preston Smith, Benjamin Hardin Helm, and James Deshler; four were wounded—John Gregg, Evander McNair, Daniel W. Adams, and John C. Brown. John B. Hood, a major general at this time, lost a leg. See *O.R.*, XXX, pt. 2, 24.

satisfaction in the Company and if you can get Julius by himself make him tell you. *I* am not the cause.

And now my own beloved about Gen'l Kirby Smith. You must see him and get him to give you a showing upon which I can base an application for transfer and if he is willing to accept me as scout tell him I have a friend who I am anxious should come with me and a verbal promise that he will receive him will be all that is necessary. It is Bob Thompson. Be sure that I hear from you in regard to this matter on Lancaster's return for I cannot wait much longer. Now don't think dearest that I am imposing too great a task upon you. Ladies over here think nothing of going and making personal application to Gen'ls. for what they want and I'll tell you another thing *they get it too,* so can you if you will only try. Get some one to go with you and don't give up for a seeming repulse, but Gen'l Smith is a fatherly old man and will treat you with a great deal of courtesy. Tell of the offer I had from Gen'ls Rust & Lovell to give me the appointment of Engineer on their Staffs but I prefer to be an Independent Scout.

I am so glad my own dearest that you wrote me so much about our own little Thornwell. I am very glad to hear that he thinks so much of his Papa. Bless him, papa loves him dearly and longs to see him. You must read my letters to him often and it may do him some good. I beg you dearest that you will make him obey you implicitly in all things. Don't let him get into a habit of fretting and having his own way. Make him mind and let him know it is done in accordance with my wish. I hope you will teach him his little prayers and make him say them every night.

I have been reading the Memoirs of Rev. Dr. Judson and I do think he was a devoted Christian if his letters and Dr. Wayland don't belie him. I do wish I could be like him in some respects but I am afraid I never can. I do thank you my own loved one for your serious solicitude for me and I wish I was more worthy of it but I fear it is too late for much reformation for me. If this war was over and I was with you perhaps your influence exerted daily over me might do some good. Rejoice with me dearest for I believe this war will cease before another twelve months roll around. I feel very sure of it and if I can only live through this war all will be well. I am sorry you arn't willing for me to join the Navy. You had better get me on the other side. If you don't I may go, there is such a call for men for the steel clad fleet now in Cape Fear River.

Give much love dearest to all for me. Tell your Mother I am mighty anxious to hear her voice again. I am glad she has got pleasanter neighbors than Mrs. Kenmore. Do take care of yourself dearest. Write me long, long letters. God bless my wife and child. A dozen kisses for Thornwell and a hundred for your sweet lips. Your affect. husband.

E. H. Fay.

Friday 2 P.M. Miss Oct 2d 1863
In Camp 8 mis N.W. Clinton

My own darling:

I have just come into Camp and find Carter and Lancaster are going to start in the morning across the River and I will write a few more lines to add to the already full letter I sent to them to carry a week ago. I believe I have entirely recovered from the chills not having had any since Tuesday week. I spent a very pleasant time at Mr. Thigpen's after I got well enough to ride about. Now don't feel uneasy about me dearest for I don't think I shall be sick any more. I know I wont if I can possibly get on the other side of the River and it all remains with you.

If Gen'l Smith will receive me as a scout I will come over by transfer honorably, but I will tell you a secret *if you will keep it* and it is that I would not be surprised if a large part of the "Minden Rangers" did not come across before Christmas. This *is secret* for you. If I can come to report to Gen'l Smith as Scout or Engineer I can come with a good face but I fear I shall come anyhow if I don't get that. They are closing down on the system of furloughs and grant only one now for 15 days only. Men will not stand that and desertion will go on as before and I don't blame them. A man's family is dearer to him than anything in the world, at least mine is & 40 Confederacies may go to the devil if I am to be kept away from all I hold dear during the rest of my life. If I can't live with my family I don't want to live for living in this world don't pay even at the best. If I could only hear from you weekly or semi-monthly I could stand it but to be cut off entirely and have them shut down on furloughs to boot I can't stand it. You must see Gen'l Smith and send me his answer by return of the boys. I must come.

We have been getting good news from Bragg and I enclose a copy of the Dispatch to Gen'l Jackson. It has not yet been confirmed and is doubted by many. I hope it is true. Bragg's victory will carry the elections in the N.W. States and that I think will be one of the preliminaries of peace.

Capt. Webb bro't me 2 pr. socks and an undershirt for which, my own dear wife, please accept my warmest thanks and my best love. I never put on anything you made for me without thinking of you, and dearest if you only knew how my heart wells up in love to you you would prize it. Oh my wife and boy what would I not give to be with you once again but *will it ever be,* is the question. I cannot feel that this war will last another year but the idea of being away from you for another is horrible. I must believe Gen'l Smith will receive me and if so I'll see you before many moons roll around.

The command have just (last night) returned from a five days *forced* march after Yankees and are pretty near used up. Julius can tell you about it. I want you to go and see him. I wish your Father would have Henry make me a Horse Brush out of some of the Gin Bristles. Make it oval in shape and in one piece and as thick as the holes can possibly be made. He can screw a thin piece of plank on the back to keep the threads from wearing. Julius will bring it to me. I know of nothing else you can send that they can bring unless you can think of some small something that I do not, a *long* letter and a note from Gen'l Smith will be the most acceptable things they can bring me. But it is getting towards dark and I must close.

Give my love to your Mother & Lou and all the rest. I wish I had time to write you a longer letter but I'll send one of Mother's to fill up. Oh dearest how I hate to say good bye, but I must. Do take care of yourself dearest, be careful of your health and take care of little Thornwell. Kiss him many times for his Father. Write me a long, long letter and believe me your loving Husband, Ed. H. Fay.

3rd—Good Morning Dearest: Frost last night and everything killed in counties above this. I think Lancaster will bring me a couple of overshirts if you will see him and have them made for me. I Love you darling. My heart is all yours. Do give me long letters and all western news. God bless you, Edwin

Camp near Brownsville Miss
Oct 8th 1863

My own dear Wife:

Another of the very seldom opportunities of sending letters across the River having occurred I embrace it gladly and have seated myself at a *table,* the first in many a long day (having written most of my last letters to you on my memorandum Book and it resting on my knee, and will endeavor to fill this sheet by the time Mr. Thompson a nephew of R. E. Thompson of our Company starts, which will be in a few days. I have very little new or interesting to write and yet I fancy I can fill up a sheet with matter interesting to you even though it contains no novelty.

First and foremostly, I have had no chills for over two weeks though I have been in camp almost a week sleeping in the open air in the frost and dew. I have felt very well and strong but am afraid to boast lest the insidious chills crop up and surprise me. I hope I may keep perfectly well till I can hear from Gen'l Kirby Smith and in case I can come over the River I think I can keep perfectly well. You cannot imagine my dearest one how tired I am of staying on this side the *branch* and it is almost a year since I saw you. Little did I think when we were married that the time would ever come when I should be absent from you a full year and yet it will probably be more than a year before I see you even under the most favorable circumstances, that is granting I got a chance to come over this winter. I think if Rich had been with me while I was sick at Mr. Thigpen's I should have come home on a short furlough anyhow, but I was afraid I would get sick and could not come back on this side and I did not want to leave my negro. I have heard nothing from him since Sep. 3rd, the letter I have already sent you but am looking for him in camp next week. I sent a letter last Sunday by a Mr. Sims near Palestine who was going directly to Prattville. I wrote them to send Rich by him to me as I am in great need of him and his leg is well enough by this time I should think if it should ever be.

I have just finished dinner and although I have eaten more than I ought sitting in camp and taking no exercise yet I am as hungry as a wolf and believe I could eat up a little hog if I had him nicely cooked. Speaking of eating, we are drawing excellent rations now and have plenty, get fresh pork and mutton and Beef too and have been buying potatoes at $1.00 a bushel, so you see there is no danger of our starving just now. How long this state of things will last I am unable to say.

I expect our Brigade will remain in this neighborhood all winter unless the Yanks should make an attack on Mobile which I have no idea they will do. We can hear of nothing from Bragg's army though we have papers as late as Oct. 4th. Rosecranz is still in Chattanooga fortified with four lines of entrenchments, but Bragg has a heavy Battery on Lookout Mountain 2/4 miles from the town which entirely commands the place. We hear a rumor too that Gen'l Stephen D. Lee. has with his cavalry in the Northern portion of the State taken Memphis but this I think only rumor though he has gone there for such a purpose as we all know. He may be going to cross the Tenn. and get in Rosecranz's rear. Suffice it to say he is on the "War Trail," while *we* poor *we* sit on our own be——ds and do nothing at all. "They too may serve who only stand and wait," but I want to do the rest of my service west of the Miss. and if you are only successful in your mission to Gen'l Kirby Smith I shall do it. You don't know how anxious I am for Carter's and Lancaster's return that I may know my fate.

Col. Wirt Adams has been appointed Brig. Gen'l and Gen'l Cosby is now absent ostensibly to see his wife in Ga. but I think to get a situation with Gen'l [Simon B.] Buckner whose A. A. Gen'l he used to be and Adams will then take command of this Miss. Brigade in which case I think our Co. will look out for itself and embrace its opportunity to join a La. Regt. on your side. This is speculation but may prove true after all. The enemy have almost concluded to abandon the siege at Charleston. Their letter writers are already preparing the minds of the Yankee people for an abandonment of the siege. They acknowledge that their Iron Clads are a failure and they are terribly exercised about a Confederate fleet. Of the latter I hardly know what to think as I have heard it talked so long and no sign yet though I have it on very good authority that some are already at sea. I am anxiously awaiting the result of the election in Ohio which comes off Oct. 13th. If Vallandigham is elected Governor I would bet all I am worth that we have peace before 6 months or at least a separation of the North Western States from Lincoln's domination. Oh if it would only come I believe I could remain *semi*-contented even away from you the other 6 mos. and you don't know how hard that is.

Yesterday I read some half dozen letters written from Valparaiso, Ind. by a woman to her husband in Vicksburg. I cannot describe them in this letter for my pen would blush to even copy such vulgarity as some of them contained. One would certainly form a very exalted opinion of the Yankee nation to judge from the letters captured both from their soldiers, home & from their wives to the army. I have never yet seen a decent Yankee letter and I have read many since I have been in the Army.

Our Company has been receiving some new recruits. Thos. Randle and Geo. W. Scott, a Bro. of Col. Scott, have both been transferred from the 12th La. Regt. I expect you have heard of the death of Maj. Loudon Butler comdg 19th La. at the battle of Chickamauga on the 20th September.[9] We have heard nothing from Parson Scott's Company but learn by the papers that the 19th La. "*suffered heavily.*"[10] So much for news up to this time.

I lost my pocket inkstand the other day & really I would not have taken $10 for it for I don't know where I am to get another unless you find that one of Bud's, a box-wood turned like a small barrel and send to me, I think it is at the shop, by Julius L. The Rivinac Waltzes you mentioned in your last I will try and get. He (Rivinac) is not

[9] Butler was a lieutenant colonel at the time of his death. Booth, *La. Confed. Soldiers,* II, 204.

[10] The 19th Louisiana Regiment on September 20, 1863, according to the report of the commanding officer, lost out of 349 who went into the fight, 28 killed, 106 wounded, and 19 missing, a total of 153 casualties, or 40%. *O.R.,* XXX, pt. 2, 224–226.

with the Brigade at present but the first time I see him will try and get him to copy them. It is impossible to get any sheet music this side of Mobile or I would send you one or two pretty pieces. "The Officer's Funeral," a song is very pretty. I can send you the words and air but have not the accompaniment.[11] Perhaps you have it. Write me.

Friday 3 P.M. Mr. Thompson starts in the morning and I will fill this sheet and send you a couple of newspapers besides, the 6th & 7th, the latest in camp. I will not attempt a summary. When you have read them please send them down to Col. Lewis *with my compliments!* for I may want to use him some time or other. I cannot but hope you will be successful in your mission to Shreveport for I dreamed that I came home last night and you don't know how I enjoyed your meeting kiss. Oh how happy I was till I waked and found it all a delusion. I do think if I live through this war that we will live far more happily than ever before (tho' ours was as happy a life as one could well desire) for we will then know how to appreciate one another's society more than ever yet we have done.

Our boys went out with a flag of Truce and I sent five dollars in gold down and bought two oil cloths and would have got a pair of Boots if Ben Neal hadn't thought them too small. I could send you a Chicago Times but Yankee papers lie so confoundedly I wont send it. I am glad you are learning to spin. I learned while I was at Mr. Thigpen's. The shirt and socks by Capt. Webb I got all safe. I was in hopes I should find some little note tucked away in it somewhere, some surprising little love token, but I fear the realities of married life have taken away all the sentimentality you possessed when a girl. Have they done so? I was disappointed but I breathed a prayer to heaven to bless the dear one who was clothing *"her own volunteer"* by the labor of her hands. I have not tried on my things yet but I know they'll all be right. There is a rumor that we will move northward and take Memphis but it is all buncombe I think.

Write me a long, long letter by J. W. Lancaster, tell me all the *gossip* tho' I know you are not given to retailing that. Tell me all the

[11] This piece, by "the Hon. Mrs. Norton," was published in several sheet music editions during the Confederacy. See Crandall, *Confederate Imprints,* II, 624–625.

smart things Thornwell does and says. Tell Lou I hunted in vain for her letter in your last envelope. What is Bud doing? You seldom mention him. Give my best love to your Mother and tell her I want her to have you & Lou weave a nice piece of Cotton goods to make me a suit next summer. The coat I want with a band around the waist and a pleated body, infant waist I believe they call it. They are all the fashion among the Cavalry for even dress uniform. What can your Father have me a pair of Boots made for. Mine are pretty good yet and may last me this winter yet I fear I shall go barefooted before spring if I don't come on that side the River. I'll make them last me as long as possible. My hat is as good as when I left home tho a little dirty. I learn that Hyder Kennedy is safe but have heard of no one else that you know of the 19th. Tell John Lesueur's friends that he is well—that at present he is out having some Blacksmith work done. He is pretty well provided for in the clothing line.

Saturday Morning. News has come in that Wheeler has captured Murfreesboro with a large amount of Commissary Stores. A letter has just come from the 19th La., Capt. Scott's Co. has come out all right except A. K. Wilson and Ant. Morris of Athens, but Charley is waiting and I must close. God bless my dear family and keep and preserve them. Affectionately, Ed. H. Fay

At Mr. Thigpen's Oct. 23, 1863

My own dear Wife:

I learned from a La. acquaintance in Wirt Adams Regt. that I would have an opportunity of sending a letter across to Monroe by one of the old "Phillips Rangers" in five or six days & as I am detained here by a hard cold rain I thought I would commence a letter to you at any rate as I know I have a much better opportunity of writing here than I have in Camp. You will want to know how I came to be here and I will tell you.

I came out to buy a mule for Rich to ride as Smith Bennett will not consent to let me have Old Jack back again. Mr. Thigpen sells me a fine young mule 5 yrs old for $200 & he has a mare here that I am trying to buy for $600 for the purpose of sending over the river to you for a buggy animal. I am afraid he will not let me have her. I also came for the purpose of having my boot patched and foot measured for another pair for which I am to pay $80. You see shoe leather is quite an object in this part of the world, and I don't know what poor soldiers are to do another year if boots get much higher. I had worn the boots you sent me 374 days yesterday and I think they will last perhaps three months longer, tho' when boots have to be patched I think they are about done. I calculated on going back to camp this morning but a cold sleety rain has set in and I am determined I will not expose myself to the weather when I can help it—and as I am beneath a most hospitable roof I shall stay—

You don't know how astonished I was when the other day (Sunday) as we were hurrying on from Canton towards Livingston in order to meet the Yankees, to find a stranger who enquired if I could tell him where he would meet Gen'l Cosby's Escort. I told him he had met one already when he handed me two letters one for Capt. Webb and the other I recognized by the color of the envelope as coming from the one dearest on earth to me. I devoured its contents greedily and you don't know how much my heart went out towards my own dearest one. The letter of ten days before, that you spoke of I have not received. The date of this was Sept. 29 and is the only one received since Capt. Webb left. Whoever bro't over the other must have mailed it at Port Gibson or Fayette and as there is no regular mail from that part of the country I have not got it. This will also explain why I cannot send letters to you thro' Lieut Truly or Messrs. Roebel & Co. of Fayette. If mails ran regularly there I would write you every week but I have not the paper or envelopes to waste on uncertainties. Every opportunity I have I will improve and you can hear from me once in two months by furloughed men anyway and if other chances offer I'll also embrace them at least till I come across the River. I am counting quite confidently on the success of your mission to Gen'l Smith and am living in hopes of seeing you before Christmas. A year ago today I left Vicksburg for Monroe on my way to you and as the thought of my having been away from you for a whole year comes up I can hardly contain myself but feel almost as if I would start at once for you—

But I must tell you of the trip we had after the Yankees.[12] Last Thursday morning our scouts announced the Enemy coming and all was bustle and confusion loading up our wagons and sending them to the rear. We saddled up and drew up in line of battle across our camp. Capt. Bowie of Adams Regt. was on picket and held them at bay all day but lost one man, an old Ala. acquaintance of mine, Charley Drummond from Greenville, Ala. a Mess Mate of Zeb. Rudulph. Poor fellow he was a good soldier and the bravest among the brave. We lay in line of battle that night and next morning the pickets falling back the enemy advanced and planted a battery within 1000 yards of ours and one of the fiercest artillery duels of the war commenced. We silenced the enemy's battery and they commenced flanking us on the right and left when we fell back about a mile and awaited their approach. About 100 skirmishers held the column at bay all the rest of the day. We fell back at night some two miles and the Enemy, 10,000 strong, only advanced 2 miles in two days though only opposed by 1000 cavalry and a battery of four Guns. They had 30 pieces of Artillery and 2500 Cavalry. They took (Saturday Morn.) another road and found Gen'l John W. Whitfield and his Texans on it supported by Col. [John L.] Logan's command. They skirmished all day near Livingston while we went to Canton and next morning started early to reinforce them. [General William] Loring's Division of Infantry was waiting near Canton but Sunday morning or rather Saturday night the Yanks got wind of it and started back towards Vicksburg at a double quick. We cut them off on their right flank at the Baker Creek ground but they had their wagons guarded on both sides with a double file of Infantry and our officers deemed it not prudent to attack them, so we lay still and let them pass by unmolested.

There were murmurings loud and deep from the soldiers of the Brigade because the Yanks escaped us. They brought out 300 wagons some loaded with entrenching tools and telegraph wires evidently intending to take Canton and occupy it, but they met such stubborn

[12] The objective of the series of skirmishes which Fay here describes was to repel the Federal expedition from Messinger's Ferry (on the Big Black River) to Canton, Mississippi, October 14–20. Brief references to these actions appear in *O.R.*, XXX, pt. 4, 754–760.

resistance from our Cavalry that they concluded west of Big Black was a safer place. They told citizens on their retreat that we had 30 thousand infantry fighting them. We lost four killed and ten wounded in our Brigade, and ten or 15 graves of Yankees we have found on our battle field. What the losses were in the other Brigades I have not yet heard. We were five days in the saddle and two without rations. When we came out on the field at Baker's Creek in the rear of our enemy we halted for some time and I found in the road a piece of cracker that some Yank had bitten and thrown away and after trimming it with the edge of my knife I ate it greedily and I have seldom tasted anything better. Some fifteen minutes after Sandy, John Lesueur's boy came with cooked rations. You don't know how glad we were to see him. Gen'l Cosby was absent to see his wife and Col. Adams was in command.[13] We fed him and Capt. [W. F.] Bullock, A.A.G. and I don't know when I have seen men eat more heartily than they did.

Gen'l Cosby got back to camp about four hours after we did. He went to Chattanooga while he was gone and I think he will endeavor to get a command under Gen'l Buckner and if he does our Company are resolved to cross the River on our own hook. If you only succeed with Gen'l Smith I'll come over any way and I think I'll be satisfied on your side where I can hear from you and dear little Thornwell.

We have heard some good news from your side but hardly dare believe it though it has been confirmed several times—that Dick Taylor has captured Gen'l Banks and staff and 15 Regts. Yanks & Negroes. Gen'l Lee has defeated Meade in a 3d Battle of Manassas and captured 2500 prisoners.[14] Meade had fallen back to Alexandria —but as offset to all and more than offset too is the news that Ohio & Pennsylvania have both gone Republican, so Vallandigham is defeated and the last hope of Constitutional Liberty is buried in the

[13] The reference apparently is to Brig. Gen. John Adams, who commanded a Confederate Cavalry brigade in the operations described. See *O.R.,* XXX, pt. 4, 754–756, 759.

[14] The reference may be to the battle of Bristoe Station, October 14, 1863, but in that action Gen. G. K. Warren repulsed a Confederate attack and inflicted some 1,378 casualties while suffering only 546 losses among his own men. See *Battles and Leaders,* IV, 84. The report of Banks' capture by Taylor was false.

overwhelming grave of Lincolnism and darkness. I had rather Lee had been defeated than Vallandigham for I could then have forseen some end to this unhappy war and now I see none whatever. If John Brough is governor of Ohio Lincoln will go on unrebuked and his acts of usurpation will be acquiesced in and there will be no termination to the war without some outside influences are brought to bear. Pres. Davis has done one thing I like, viz., revoked the exequaturs of all English Consuls in Confederate ports and recalled Mr. Mason from England. I am glad he has shown the manliness to no longer dance attendance at the Court of our worst enemy.

From Bragg's army we learn nothing save that he occupies Lookout Mountain and can easily shell Rosey's Camp. Wheeler has captured 700 wagons with their loads and Stephen D. Lee is at Columbia, Tenn. with about 7000 Cavalry threatening Nashville. It is rumored that Gen'l Bragg says he wants the Yanks to send their whole army to reinforce Rosey for he wants to capture all at once, but I expect the next news will be that he is falling back again to Ga. I have no confidence at all in him though Pres. Davis has been there to view the situation and was at Jackson, Miss. yesterday and I expect will review the Cavalry tomorrow. I hope not, however, for I don't fancy reviews at all.

I am sorry that I cannot send letters to you by way of Fayette but I will have opportunities occasionally of sending by other means. I expect ere this you have had my letters and papers by Mr. Charley Thompson. I hope so as I wrote you a long letter which I don't want lost. I am sorry to hear that you have soldiers camped so near you and am afraid that they will not raise your opinions of Confederate soldiers but am glad that you show them some attention and invite them to meals sometimes.

But you ask me about going to Texas? I gave you my views in a previous letter and it is only necessary for me to answer one of your reasons for going. You say if you stay inside the Yankee lines you cannot hear from me. Now I would ask in the name of Common Sense how do you suppose you would hear from me if the Enemy occupied Minden and you in Texas. If you stay at home and the Yankees come I will come to you for then I can kill more yankees in 2 days than I can in 2 years here. Every house you don't want burned must be inhabited by somebody and as to losing negroes & stock it would be well to send them off, but if you abandon your house rest assured you will find only a heap of ashes on your return. If you will act boldly no harm will come to you and if Mrs. Mitchell should leave our house you must occupy it sure or *some white person* or they will burn it sure. Your Father had better disable the Engine and Mill to keep them from burning the shop. His gin materials had better be removed to his lot, if he wants to save them. But I am giving advice that I don't believe it will be necessary to follow for I do not think even for a moment that they will ever occupy Claiborne Parish. I have told you what I judge best for you to do and I think you will agree with me that I am right on reflection.

But about the entering the naval service. You have quite mistaken the nature of the service. The "Florida" has never fired but one gun in anger since the war began and that was at the Ericson some 60 miles off Sandy Hook so you see I will be in no danger more than on land and really not in so much—and if I am to be separated from you as I am I had rather be at sea than on land and then I can support myself which I can't do in the Army. My wages will hardly keep me in boots let alone clothing. If I can be transferred to the Florida I don't think you will object very seriously and my time for making application is short if I can't be transferred to Gen'l Smith's command. 'Tis my own convenience and not money making that influences me. I have been thinking suppose the war should last ten years longer what would life be worth to either of us, after being separated so long? I am not patriotic, I confess, enough not to wish you were in Mexico or near there, that we might emigrate to some other country. I cannot live separated from you on this earth very much longer. I had rather be dead at once. This war will not end during the life time of Seward & Lincoln I don't think and they both bid fair to live a long time yet. Mine is the general opinion of the army and there are gloomy faces enough I assure you.

Mrs. Webb wrote Capt. that she was going to Texas and he is distressed about it, thinks she had better remain at home. His letter was Oct. 2 and Maj. [Thomas C.] Standifer did not bring them across the river. You surrounded by friends and relatives do not begin to imagine the loneliness I feel at being separated from you so long.

You seem to regard it as a light thing but I had rather die than endure it for two years longer. Curse the country and govt. too. If it destroys my happiness what advantage is it to me. I am selfish I acknowledge and lay but small claim to what is called Patriotism. I am willing to sacrifice part of my happiness for my Country's sake but not all of it. I think his family is a man's first care and 2d his Country. But no more on this theme. I am sorry to hear of so much sickness throughout the country, but if it was only the English that died it would not matter much as they were of no advantage to the Country anyway.

Exempts. Speaking of Exempts. I must relate a little anecdote about Bethel (D. H.) Hill. A soldier in W. H. T. Walker's division applied for a furlough. Gen'l Walker disapproved but respectfully forwarded to the HdQrtrs of Gen'l Hill where it was endorsed as follows: "Approved for the reason that a brave soldier ought to be allowed to go home whenever practicable, else all the children born during the war or within the usual period afterwards will be the offspring of the cowards who remain at home by reason of substitutes or other exemption." The soldier went home.[15] I have a notion to apply for a furlough and attach that scrap to it which I have clipped from a newspaper and send it up and I believe Gen'l Johnston will approve it. But I don't want a furlough but a transfer to that Department.

About Neuse Murphy, I have already written you that he was a *beef driver* and I want the girls to tell him to put some (3) strips of rawhide on his collar instead of gold lace.[16] You say the conversation turned on me. I can't see how it could have been very interesting for Mr. Murphy *hates* me more than any one living because I used to

[15] Gen. Daniel Harvey Hill, who was deprived of a lieutenant generalcy and the command of a corps because of difficulties with Bragg growing out of the Chickamauga campaign, had a gift for caustic phrase. Another story that made the rounds of Confederate camps told of Hill's endorsing a bugler's request for a furlough with the comment: "Disapproved—shooters before tooters."

[16] This is Sgt. Joel N. Murphy of the Minden Rangers, referred to by Fay in his letter of Sept. 21, 1863. A cavalry sergeant's rating was indicated by three yellow stripes, usually worn on the sleeves, but sometimes on both sleeves and collar. See *Atlas to Accompany the Official Records of the Union and Confederate Armies* (Washington, 1891–1895), Plate 172. See also Fay's letter to his wife, December 18, 1863.

plague him nearly to death. He falls in love with every girl who treats him politely and is without doubt the most consummate *fool* I ever knew and as far as my giving him Miss Gussy Bright I would hardly mention his name on the same day I called hers. You must tell her for he will be sure to tell her I did it. A lie does not stick long where his vanity is concerned. I regret very much your acceptance of a present from him but what is done is past and can't be recalled. I want to warn Lou against him for he is engaged *according to his own account* to one Miss and one Tenn. young lady. But I have wasted too much space on him already.

If they need a Post Commissary in Minden it is an office I would like to fill and I think Mr. Murphy will be recalled on this side the River. Gen'l Rust would do anything for me he could and if you need any assistance in getting me across he will gladly render it.

I have read your letter all over and I believe answered all of it except Thornwell's message. Papa will bring him a whip & a "poper" too but he can't bring a "gogger." Papa thinks often of him and wishes he could see the dear little fellow and Papa hopes he won't be sick any more but will be a good boy.

What do you do for shoes now? I am so sorry your Father and I did not begin a Tan Yard. It is the most valuable piece of property now that one could own. You never wrote me if you got the postage stamps I sent you. In fact my darling you have neglected to answer several inquiries made in some of my last letters. I presume it was an oversight on your part. I have inquired several times what had become of Bud but you have never answered me. I expect my letters are too long or you have too much company to read over my letters more than once and so you forget little matters. You mention "Miss Texanna Phillips," who is she for you to speak as if I knew her. What has become of Miss Emma P——? I have heard contradictory stories in regard to her. I am sorry to hear of so much sickness about Minden. Hope your Father is quite well now, and also the rest.

Rich brought me from home two shirts of heavy cotton jeans and two pairs of drawers of the same, 3 prs. of socks & two yellow check, gingham pocket hdkfs. The overshirts you made me are all worn out. I am thinking of sending Rich over with the next men furloughed & sending a pair of pants Uncle Lloyd cut as a pattern, to have a pair made by, but I think perhaps I have enough to last me this winter. Wish I had a good warm vest. I wore my other out and threw it away and now I need one and a pair of gloves, knit, not crocheted, but I hope to come and get these things before long as I have bought transportation for Rich if I conclude to go. He is still lame and will always be as his broken leg is about a quarter or half inch shorter than the right one. He has diminished his value $500 by his foolhardiness besides the inconvenience he has put me to. I wish I had sent him home from Mechanicsburg as I first proposed.

But I must close. Give my best love to your Mother and tell her she must have the fatted calf killed when I come home. Ask your Father if he don't want me detailed to help him grind Govt. wheat at the Mill? Love to Lou, Ella & Al—as Bud will never write me a line or send me a message I have none for him. Good Bye and may God bless you my dear wife. Ever yours, Edwin H. Fay.

Don't put such long directions on your letters: Edwin H. Fay, O.S. Cosby's Escort Care of Capt. Webb, Jackson, Miss.

Nov. 2d 1863
Camp near Brownsville

My darling Wife:

I thought long before this that my letter written at Mr. Thigpen's would have reached you but I am glad that I have another opportunity of enclosing a sheet in the same envelope. I dreamed of you my dearest last night and if I was superstitious I should have been very unhappy today, for I dreamed that you were dead and oh the desolation of my heart, no one can realize, till I was sufficiently awake to feel that it was all a dream. I had been talking to a Mr. Noland, who has joined our Co., (a nice gentleman) of our little Will Ed. and had told him that when I first parted from you I had thought it possible that I might never see *you* or *Thornwell* again but felt that if I survived the service to return home I should certainly find him.[17] Alas! vain are the expectations of man. That conversation was the

[17] Muster rolls of the Minden Rangers show that Avery Noland joined the company at Clinton, Mississippi on September 24, 1863.

source whence I traced the dream. It distressed me so I did not sleep any more, but with the light the impression passed away and I hope it was only an impression.

But I have some news to tell you. When I was sick at Thigpen's Sidney Killen and [Williamson] Jones went to Capt. Webb and told him that I was only playing off that I did not stay with the company and urged him to reduce me to ranks, that they, one or the other had to do my duty and ought to draw the pay. This coming to the ears of my friends, Bob Thompson and others, and they (Jones & Killen) making the proposition, Bob and others joined in and *talked against me* and proposed that all the non-commissioned officers should resign. When they agreed to it, Bob got on his horse and came out and told me about it. He said they had attacked me and he had been around and found I could easily be elected again, but wanted me to resign and to get them to do so and that we would beat them for any office and thereby reduce them to ranks.

I consented and Capt. Webb granted the Election which came off on the 29th ult and they were beaten to the tune of 16 to 34. I had no opposition tho' Sidney wanted to run but found he had no chance. He was first Corporal, Bates 2d, Culpepper 3d, & Jones 4th. He ran for 2d Sergeant against Jim Simmons and Jones for 3d Sergt against Ben Neal. Sam Culpepper had been Co. Commissary for a year and we wanted to run him as 5th Sergt without opposition so that by virtue of his office he might continue Commissary, but he went over to the Killen Clique and the morning of the election disclosed he would run for 3rd Sergt and then we beat him too though we were anxious to make him Commissary. Bates was promoted to 1st Corporal. We carried the whole ticket though there was almost as much excitement as during the Secession question. I said Killen & Jones both went to Capt. Webb—I don't know that Killen did but Jones spoke the sentiments of both. I have never seen men cut down so before and I feel truly sorry for them, but they should not have aroused my friends by plotting against me. They had Capt. Webb's influence too except against me for he is a true friend of mine and can't get along without me. The Non Com officers are now J. H. Simmons 2d Sergt., H. W. Menefee 3d, Jack B. Henry 4th, [Thomas B.] Neal 5th- [Pascal P.] Bates 1st Corp., [John M.] Pearce 2d, [Benjamin G.] Brantley 3d, and Thomas Monzingo 4th. Mat Killen, [J. L. A.] Newcomb & [Joel N.] Murphy used to be Sergts. but all deserted. So much for Company excitements and news.

We have had some very cold rainy weather but today the heat in the sun is very oppressive, tho the boys are almost all playing ball out on the parade grounds in front of camps. I wrote you I could not get Old Jack back but I have bought a valuable young mule for Rich to ride. I am going out to Thigpen's Wednesday or Thursday to get my boots, would go tomorrow but learned that Capt. Price of Homer had bro't a sack full of letters for our Co. & I feel so sure I have one that tomorrow being our mail day I won't go off. Oh I do so hope I'll get one.

Friday Nov. 6th Well darling I was disappointed. Your letter did not come so on Wednesday I got a pass and went to Thigpen's after my boots—I had not been gone long before Gen'l Cosby sent for a man to go to Montgomery, Ala. Capt. Webb sent after me but the messenger did not find me so Capt. went himself and I got cut out of spending four days at home, two disappointments and failing to get my boots, a third, but it is all for the best I reckon.

I have just got a letter from Mother, the 29th Oct., which I will send you. Do you want more stamps if so let me know and I will send them tho I hope you will send me what will bring me to that side. I have been copying a piece of poetry for you that I sent you once before and you never received also the words of a very pretty piece of music just to fill out the blank. I cannot get any Music in sheets or would send you some. I do hope I shall soon hear the music of your voice. I would write you the rumored news but have sent you so many false ones that I'll wait a few days for confirmation as I don't expect to get this off for some days yet.

Oh my darling I do not know how I can stay away from you any longer. A long, long year has elapsed since I pressed you to my loving heart. I cannot stay much longer. I must come to you or you to me. I'll write more and send you a list of losses in the 19th La. Regt. Good Bye

Brownsville, Nov. 7, 1863

Dearest, I have just learned that Mr. Waters of Wirt Adams Regt. starts tomorrow morning across the River to Monroe. I will send you two letters, one containing Mother's letter and the song and the other my letters. I am very well. We have just moved camps below Brownsville, near Bolton's Depot. I wish I could send you a paper and perhaps I may as I have one of the 4th inst. will if I can find anything to do it up in. Do write me as often as you can find an opportunity of so doing. There are persons frequently crossing if you only knew it. I expect to write again in a few days by Thos. Gassaway who will come on furlough & Nacy Meeks. Goodbye dearest. It is so dark I cannot see to write more. May God bless and protect my helpless wife and almost orphan Boy. Your ever true and affectionate husband,

E. H. Fay

12

"I Am Tired of Doing Nothing"

Camp near Clinton, Miss. Nov. 13th, 1863

My own darling Wife:

Well Julius Lancaster, [J. J.] Carter & co. came to camp about 4 P.M. yesterday and I got your letters and I can exclaim with you "Blessed be letters" but would beg permission to add to the quotation when they contain the news we expect but when one's heart has been set for seven long weeks on receiving what would enable him to revisit all that are dear to him then to be so sadly disappointed, oh! that sickness of the heart may you never know. You remember the Fable of the farmer and his sons reaping the field of wheat which contained the nest of a Lark. Had I known that such were to have been my fate rest assured I should have never made the request I have made in my letters.

I am sorry my dearest one that you have been deluded with the idea that anyone save yourself would have sufficient interest to obtain my transfer to that side of the River. If I had supposed Col. Lewis' *letters* to Gen'l Smith would have effected anything I should have addressed him at once, but I have been long enough in service to know that *you* & *you* alone could effect anything. Had I not known it do you think I would have asked you to do anything that I know your timid disposition would so revolt at. I am sorry dearest that my insane desire to see you led me to overestimate your boldness. I had been reading of some ladies who during previous revolutions did a great deal to preserve those they loved and I am very sorry dearest that I imposed such a task on you. I knew no one could accomplish it but you and I thought I must go to you or die—All hopes are now blasted and I have no hope whatever of seeing you till the close of the War (if I should live) and I never expect to live to see the end for I very much fear that our Son whose young life commenced in these troublous times will have to shoulder a gun in ranks ere the termination of this war. There is no hope of my getting a Furlough for there are 25 members who have been decided to be entitled to draw furloughs before me and then I am to take the chances with twenty five others so I have no hope of getting home on Furlough in 2 years at least and I am determined not to remain in the Confederacy for 2 years longer without seeing you.

I have now given up all hope of getting a transfer and intend making application to be enlisted on board some vessels that are being fitted out as privateers. In fact I have been speaking about it today to Maj. [Paul] Ravesies, a member of Gen'l Cosby's Staff, and he says he thinks he can procure me a situation as he lives in Mobile but don't think the Vessels will be ready for sea before February next. I hope dearest you will give your consent for if I am to be separated from you as I am now, I had much rather be on board a privateer.

I am perfectly satisfied that you all on that side the River know nothing about this war, you can't realize it at all. You know so little of military matters if you believe that through the influence of Mr. B. or anybody else an able-bodied man could receive an appointment from Gen'l Johnston's Commissary. Why they are turning out of office every able-bodied man out of every Department on this side the River and I could no more get into any of them than I could fly and you know I can't do that else I had been with you long ago. It is only able-bodied officers who failed of re-election who can remain at home and get Offices. My last hope having been dissipated I have not determined positively what I shall do but if I can do nothing for the Confederacy here and I have done nothing save being an expense to it I might as well be in Mexico or South America. I am tired of doing nothing. I want an opportunity of killing the damnable villains who pollute our land. I don't want a position in the Engineer Corps or any Dept. half as bad as I do an Independent Scout. Then I have an opportunity to carry out my maxim that *paroled* Yankees never come back to fight. An easier place than I now have I don't expect to find and I am not hunting easy places now, but I am determined to be within hearing and *seeing* distance, too, of my family or be dead to them during the War. Of the former of these propositions I have no hopes, of the latter I will make what efforts I can with your consent.

You speak in your letters of having written me many things that I know nothing about. You make allusions to matters that I know nothing of. For instance Wade Barrington's wife. You have never mentioned his marriage in any letters I have received. The gossip is what I have long looked for. I am only astonished it did not occur in 9 mos. after he began to get about. Your letter by a Mr. Wertman never came to hand and you ought to have known that a d——d Dutchman would steal the Stamps off letters sooner than mail them. I have already acknowledged the receipt of one by Maj. Thomas C. Standifer in a letter by a Mr. Waters who mailed it in Monroe if he crossed safely. July 3rd, Sep. 5th, Sep. 29th, Nov. 4th are the only letters I have recd. from you. I mean the Envelopes containing these as latest dates. On the other hand I have asked you a great many questions in letters that I know you have received and yet I get no answers. Your letters all seem written in the greatest haste and as original and not in reply to mine. I do not complain as yours have been very welcome to me anyway and so highly prized even with the disappointment.

Speaking of it you cannot imagine how mortified I am at being compelled to acknowledge to some of my most intimate friends the failure to receive a showing from Gen'l Smith upon which I could base an application for transfer as I had confided to them upon what my hopes were founded. I almost knew he would not refuse you and told them who would be my messenger & how sanguine of success I was. Lt. Carter had told them that Col. Lewis made the application and they see how signally I have failed. It is only known to 3 men however but yet I am much mortified as well as disappointed. I am very sorry my own dearest one that I was so thoughtless as request you to undertake such a task. Alas ! deceitful are human hopes. I thought I should accompany the present furloughed men home, viz., Lt. Watkins, Mr. [John F.] Dunn, and J. D. H. Taylor from Comie Bluff. They go but I remain.

I understand from Lancaster that there are plenty of Mexican Ponchos or blankets for sale in Minden. I want you to buy for me one certain and send back by J. D. H. T. or Watkins. They are worth $200 on this side and my shawl is most worn out. I learn that they can only be bought from soldiers. If so please get Mr. Wimberly to get it for me.

Monday Morn 8 o'clock (16th) My own darling one, I thought I would finish this yesterday but was sent outside the pickets toward the Yankees on some business which being finished I went on an independent scout down to see the Yanks, on my return I wandered over the Baker Creek battle field and such sights as met my eyes I never wish to see again. I saw where the vandal foe buried our men by just throwing them in gulleys and throwing a few brush and a little earth over them. The rains have washed them bare and their bleaching bones are now protruding thru the rotten jeans which once clothed their brave and manly limbs. The eyeless sockets in the whitening skulls only confirmed me in my resolve to never spare any of those monsters who for desire of gain invade our lands. Even large white oak trees are killed by Minnie balls.[1] I saw one that I estimated had 300 in it and in one rail on a fence behind which the Yanks lay I counted 38 balls fired by our men. Yankee graves were as thick as you could wish to see behind that fence too. You have never seen a battle field dearest and you can form but slight opinion of the thoughts that come rushing through one's mind. Those poor bleaching bones of our men once belonged to forms as intent and full of life as mine and they now lie where no fond Mother, Sister, or wife know it. They may indeed be aware of their death but not of their burial place. I thought too what would be your feelings had I been one of that number and my resting place unknown to you. I then thought that your grief would in time pass away and that perhaps in time another would occupy my place in your affections and have the right to press you in his bosom and call you his own.

But a truce to these sad reflections and a return to pleasanter themes. I left 3 five dollar gold pieces with a lady who is going into Vicksburg, to buy me a pair of boots, ditto guantlets and a couple of

[1] The battle of Baker's Creek or Champion's Hill, near Vicksburg, was fought on May 16, 1863, between the forces of Pemberton and Grant. It was a hotly fought battle in which the Federals, out of some 29,000 men, suffered 2,254 casualties and Confederates lost 2,181 out of 20,000 effectives. See Thomas L. Livermore, *Numbers and Losses in the Civil War* (Boston, 1900), 99–100.

silk handkerchiefs. Gold is worth $1.50 in greenbacks in Vicksburg so I sent $22.50 after my things. I hope I will get them particularly if I come home on transfer. I do hope Col. Lewis may be successful and do not let him give over his efforts. Since Carter has told me I do have some faint hopes of it being carried through. But if I could only have sent up the application so as to come with the present furlough men I would have had company but I can come alone very well if I can *only come*. I dare not place much confidence in coming lest I be disappointed and a disappointment now would almost kill me.

You ask me what I think of the trade of the house for the negroes. I don't know what to say to you except that I want you to act just as if you were a widow in your own right. You know I place implicit confidence in your judgment. I have no idea we will ever live in Minden again should I survive this war, and consequently wont need the house and lot—Yet I want you to act your own judgment in the matter and I shall be perfectly satisfied. Oh I must tell you of a trade I made Saturday. I sold $1.50 in silver for $30 in Confederate Notes. Wasn't that a good Trade?

But I have to go now with a "Flag of Truce" to Big Black—I send this by Mr. Hart, a brother of the one who stayed with us, he is on his way to Texas on Furlough—I will write again by Watkins in a few days. I'll send some papers if they come from Brandon in time but I will not get back before tomorrow but will make arrangements to have them sent. But I must get ready to go now. You don't know how I hate to tell you goodbye dearest, if I only knew I should come across the River in a couple of months I should say good bye for the present with a light heart, but I'll hope on—and may come. Give many thanks to Lou for her letter and much love to your Mother & Father. I am obliged for the letter he wrote me. The Govt. pays 25 to 30 cents for pork on this side. Good Bye dearest, your loving husband,

E. H. Fay.

My kindest regards to your kind friends Mr. & Mrs. Black & family. I am very glad you have such dear friends and such pleasant neighbors. Our place is worth now a $1000 more than it was before they moved there—I wish I knew them. Hope I will have that pleasure before very long. Kiss dear little Thornwell for his Papa. I wrote this intending to send it by Watkins but as I have this opportunity hurriedly finished it and do not intend it as an answer to yours.

Camp near Clinton Miss Nov 19/63

My own darling One:

I sent you a letter Tuesday morning which I suppose is crossing the river today and if I mistake not closed by telling you that I was going down to Big Black bridge with a "Flag of Truce" to see the Yankees. Well we went down till we came to the Pickets when we were halted and our papers were sent in. They would not allow us inside their lines and night coming on we came back 1/4 mile and camped. Kept up a strict guard all night and next morning about 10 A.M. here came Col. [Daniel] McCook and his Major of the 24th Illinois Infantry attended by three Lieuts dashing up on stolen horses. One of the Ladies recognized the horse that McCook rode as her own saddle horse that they had stolen from her when out here before. She was after the horse then. They brought out a couple of bottles of whiskey and tried to get the Ladies to drink but they would not and even considered it an insult. They would not allow the Ladies to go in and so failing of our object we bid them good morning and they returned to their camps while we took the opposite direction and reached camp just at dark. I did not speak to any one of them but treated them with dignified contempt.

That Col. McCook was the Brother of the Gen'l Robt. [L.] McCook who was killed while riding in an ambulance near Huntsville, Ala. last Fall. He introduced himself as "the Bro. of the celebrated Robt. McCook who was murdered by guerillas." I wanted to murder him all the time he was talking to the women. He had no respect for their feelings by his conversation towards them. I thought it all arose from his association with negroes. My opinions of the Villains were not raised by what I saw of them under the "Flag of Truce." I don't want to go again.

I do not recollect whether I told you that I had sent some gold into Yankeedom (at Vicksburg) to buy me some boots, gauntlets, & silk hdkfs. If I only knew that an order for my transfer was on the way I would send in and try and buy for you my dearest such little articles as I thought you might need. If I come I shall try and bring you a pair of shoes for I presume you need them as much as most anything. But that "if." Oh would I could know that it was on the way. I would then have some hope of seeing you. Oh if your letters could only have contained the application. I could then have sent it up at once and by this time it would have returned approved and I could have brought you this letter instead of sending it by others. Thos. J. Gassaway & Nacy Meeks start tomorrow morning and I am hastening to finish this letter that I may send it by them to you. Oh my darling how hard it is that I have to send to you and not *come to* you.

I had a long talk with Carter last night and asked him about the conversation Col. Lewis had with Gen'l Smith. I am afraid Gen'l Smith does not take much interest in the matter. I don't want this matter ever to rest till I get a transfer and you must importune Col. Lewis continually till he procures it. I felt so sorry when I got your letter that you had trusted it to other hands and I am afraid I wrote you a letter not as kind as it ought to have been but I know you will forgive me when you consider how disappointed I was. I expected when I made the request that he would give you a statement of his willingness to receive me into his service and upon that I would base an application for Transfer. Capt. Webb and Gen'l Cosby would approve it and it would go all the way through. As it is I shall live in hope that Gen'l Smith has sent it to Gen'l Johnston and that it will come *down* to me instead of go up from me. I do want to get on that side before the River rises so I cannot cross. If the order for my transfer comes I shall go to Okolona for my clothes in my valise before I start home. It will delay me only a few days and I want to get that silver spoon.

There are so many going over now that I wish I had something pretty to send you, but I have not so you must take the will for the deed. I will send the latest papers we have received from Mobile, the "Evening News" 13th. I have two copies and send one to Col. Lewis with my compliments—you must send it to him immediately if he is at home. If you would prefer to come on this side and Mr. Black can through his influence with the Chief Commissary get me a place I can get you across. Vehicles do cross the River now for I have seen them and I can arrange to have you brought over, but unless I could get a position where I would be stationary I would prefer to come to you rather than the other way. This war will be of indefinite duration I am afraid for I see less prospect of a close now than ever before, though a *rumor* is now circulating through camps that Bragg has gained a great victory, particulars not given. News from Virginia informs us that Hoke's and Hay's Brigades of Lee's army were surrounded and all killed or taken prisoners so I fear the "Blues" are now inmates of Northern prisons—I do hope they escaped as 800 are said to have done so.

Of course you have heard of the Northern Elections, how Vallandigham was beaten by bayonet-controlled votes, as also of Republican gains wherever there have been any elections. Judgment has fled to brutish beasts there and men have lost their reason and their liberties too. I am glad to hear that Banks considered Dick Taylor too strong for him and his retrograde movements. I do hope your country will not be overrun but have my fears. However, Minden is safe unless they capture Shreveport and I don't look for that. Col. Lewis applied for a position on the Engineer Corps for me but if I come over I shall try and be an independent scout in the Swamp that I may kill some of the Yankee negroes and Yanks too.

I shall enclose in this 50 Postage Stamps for I presume stamps are getting scarce with you. You can distribute them among your friends and I will send 50 more by Lt. Watkins—I enclose in this a notice of a bi-weekly mail between Shreveport and Brandon. It commenced its regular trips last Monday. When you have no opportunity of sending by hand that mail is next safest plan. That net overshirt is a very handy thing and is much admired. I don't like the color though and the yarn is not twisted hard enough for service. If you could see the shirts Mother sent me you would not think I needed much overshirts.

But I had forgotten to answer your letter—I want to know who it was that told you that Michelet's L'Amour was an impure book. I did not think so when I read it nor do I think you will consider it so.[2] I am rejoiced to think you have such good neighbors in Mrs. Anderson &

[2] The work referred to is Jules Michelet's *L'Amour,* first published by L. Hatchette, Paris, 1858. An English translation, by J. W. Palmer, of the 4th Paris edition, was published by Rudd and Carleton of New York in 1860.

Mrs. Black. I wish I could know them. It is some inducement to remain in Minden after the War. You speak of sending me a sample of Cousin Mary's dress. Your letter never reached me and I could not tell you how I liked it. You asked me to tell you how I liked the idea of selling the house & lot. I leave that entirely up to you. I trust your judgment. I want you to have self reliance. Act in all matters just as if you were a widow in your own right. I think the trade will be a good one as you represent it. I want you to trade Cynthia off if she wont have any children. Rich says Father has given Sister Sarah Victoria that mullato child of Martha's. You recollect her. I must go and claim my share.

I insist that Thornwell's request shall be granted and that he shall not wear clothes any more, but breeches. I want him to have some when I come. As for the pony—I expect it will be a bad chance to get him a pony but if I can find one I'll swap my mule for it. Does your father want another Mule? Does he want any shot gun caps? I can get them for $3.00 pr. hundred. Did I tell you about some body stealing my pistol, belt, cap box and all. I had $1.50 waterproof caps that I was going to send. The pistol was worth $125.00. So you see I have had some bad luck. If I come over I shall buy me another, if not don't want any. Shall send a Smith's patent rifle by Lt. Watkins if I cannot exchange it for a Maynard.[3] You have never told me anything about Bud—what has become of him? Tell Lou I am much obliged for her letter and hope to answer it in person ere long—

As far as new music is concerned it is impossible to get any unless I knew the name of the particular pieces and then I could send inside the Yankee lines for it. If I can find any I'll send it. I saw Rivinac and he promised to copy some of his Waltzes for you. I'll send up tomorrow to Livingston and get it if he has done it, but Gassaway starts early in the morning and so I cannot send it by him but will send by the others who I expect will start in 6 or 8 days. Did you get the poem "Oh He's nothing but a soldier." If not I have a copy which I will send you. I have sent you some scraps several times but you have never acknowledged the receipt, tho I know you must have got them as you did the

[3] Illustrations of the Maynard and Smith rifles (carbines) may be found in the *Atlas to Accompany the Official Records of the Union and Confederate Armies,* Plate 173.

letters. My last letter from Mother I sent you and it has been nearly three weeks since I wrote her. I am expecting to hear tonight by Ben Neal if he gets back from Atlanta. I believe I wrote you how nicely I got disappointed in a trip to Montgomery by being out in the Country. I hope I will not be disappointed in coming to you. You must go and see Gen'l Smith yourself if he has done nothing, when you get this. Get your Father to get him to have me transferred to assist him in grinding Govt. Wheat. Do something or I will go to Mexico.

Head Qrtrs. Cosby's Escort, Nov. 24, '63
Near Raymond, Miss.

My own dearly beloved Wife:

I had hoped my dearest to write you some good news in this letter but my "honey of hope" is turned into the quinine of disappointment this morning by the return of "my papers" from Gen'l Jackson for proper address they having been addressed to Capt. Webb requesting a transfer to Corps of Engineers of Lt. Gen'l Kirby Smith. Gen'l Jackson says that it must be addressed to "Sec. of War, C.S.A." and I have accordingly in pursuance of his instructions rewritten and sent up "my papers" to James A. Seddon Sec. of War, C.S.A. Capt. Webb approved and *earnestly recommended* and Gen'l Cosby *approves* also, and Hope again plumes her pinions for flight till aforesaid papers can be forwarded to Sec. of War. I hope they will go through all right but am determined to have two strings at least to my bow and shall therefore send similar papers to Gen'l Smith for approval to be forwarded from him—I have also applied to Capt. Harrison for a position as Adjt. in his Battalion which I understand has been organized at Shreveport. I think that amid all the multitudinous methods some one may prove successful. Still the disappointment is great for I had hoped to be at home by Christmas but now I fear it will be Christmas before I hear from Richmond. However it is all for the *best* I suppose but I cannot see how. It I had the approval of Gen'l Smith I should feel sure of its approval by Sec. of War. I'll hope for it on the strength of *my* request until it comes "Disapproved." But no more on this subject I pray, I imagine I hear you say. Well so be it. I'll turn to another tune.

I have written you so frequently of late that I have but little to write and nothing new or interesting. I can only repeat the uninteresting story of my love and that so many sheets have contained that I fear that it has already brought satiety and palls on the appetite. There is a great dearth of news at present. I have just seen a paper of the 21st inst. and learn that Longstreet has captured Knoxville and 1600 prisoners. Wheeler has defeated and utterly routed the cavalry of the Enemy capturing 600 prisoners.[4] The sum of news is very favorable and I presume ere many weeks the enemy will be driven from Tenn. Charleston holds out remarkably. The enemy attacked Fort Sumter in barges and when hailed, replied with a volley of oaths, followed by a volley of musketry. They were speedily driven to their Monitors for refuge. So much for news up to date. There is a rumor of the capture of a Courier from Burnside to Grant stating "that he had only 10 days rations and God only knew where the next was to come from." It was first reported to come from "Thomas" but the paper of the 20th says as above—

I have written you several letters lately some two weeks ago, one by a Mr. Waters to be mailed in Monroe, La. another by Lt. Hart and some 6 days ago a long one by Thos. J. Gassaway. I hope you have received them all for they will compensate in some small degree for yours. I am sorry for the Letter I wrote by Lt. Hart for I fear you will think I blamed you for not going to see Gen'l Smith. I do not blame you dearest but I believe if you had gone I should now be on my way home. As it is if I can come at all I shall not be able to get home before the 1st Jany. if I should live. There is a Maj. Lacy going across with Dispatches and I send this letter by him. I only have time to write a line while he is saddling his horse.

The 25 today. Longstreet occupies Knoxville and a Despatch to

[4] These reports were erroneous. Longstreet's unsuccessful siege of Knoxville, November 17–December 4, 1863, was climaxed by a costly and futile assault on November 29. Wheeler, who assisted Longstreet in the Knoxville campaign, experienced some minor successes in the preliminaries, but won no such victory as that reported by Fay. See *Battles and Leaders,* III, 693–698, 732–733, 748–749 and John P. Dyer *"Fightin' Joe" Wheeler* (Baton Rouge, 1941), 143–148.

Jackson, Miss. that Thomas has retreated from Chattanooga. I was not very well today, had a severe spell of sick headache last night. I hope I am not going to be sick. Lt. Watkins will cross the River I expect next week and I'll try and write a few lines by him. I send a letter to Col. Lewis enclosing proper papers for a transfer to Gen. Smith's Department with the request that he sign it and forward. I wish you would go right down and ask Col. Lewis to inform Gen. Smith that Jackson's Division, Cosby's Brigade (Gen'l Johnston's Army) which I neglected. Good Bye Dearest. God Bless you, Edwin. Kiss Thornwell.

Camp near Bolton's Depot S.R.R. Nov. 30, 1863

My darling Wife:

So many letters have I sent you lately that I have very little new or interesting to write you but know that if anyone coming to Minden failed to bring you a letter you would feel distressed and to save your feelings I will endeavor to scratch over this sheet anyhow and I do not apprehend you will be by any means displeased at the receipt of it when you recognize the handwriting. I do wish I had subject matter to make you an interesting letter to pay for yours but so few conveniences have I for writing and in such haste I have it to do that I make but a poor out of it and to any eye less charitable than the eyes of love I would hesitate to send such scrawls. I remember during the Mexican War reading, rather hearing read a letter from a soldier written on a Drum Head and thinking what an awful place it must be to write on but I have used so many much worse places than a drum head that I think now he was very fortunate, for a drum head is one of the best writing tables I ever saw. Most of the letters you have received have been written amid noise and bustle on my Memorandum Book on my knee having to slide my paper along every time I crossed the longitude of my Book. Today I am supporting my paper on a blank book "Company Book" just the size of the paper with my legs "a la Turque" and said book and paper resting on my lap, and in regard to my letter I say as Peter said anything new or interesting have I none but such as I have give I thee.

The weather, the prolific theme or commencement of most conversations is as cold as any Greenlander could reasonably wish. Our Hog Meat froze so hard last night that our slaves had to cut it with a hatchet this morning. Ice formed an inch and a half on our water buckets. My two blankets by the help of the heavy jeans coat you sent me last winter kept me very comfortable before the large log heap fire built in front of our fly. Today is as beautiful and clear as ever dawned on earth. The Sun with his beams is quite invigorating and with the excitement produced by a strong cigar I have tried to arouse my mental powers but they have lain dormant so long that nothing I believe save your immediate presence can rouse me.

You have no idea to what extent smoking is carried on in camp and that too with tobacco at $5.00 pr. lb. but I cannot learn to smoke a pipe much to your delight I have no doubt. I believe I should have learned if it had not been for you, but I thought I should dislike it very much if you should learn to use snuff and you had the same cause if I should get to using tobacco. I saw a beautiful lady a few days ago but she spoiled her beauty by having in her mouth an everlasting snuff swab. She was a married lady whose husband had been discharged from the army on account of Consumption. Her name was Cherry. She reminded me of my old sweetheart somewhat in appearance. By the Bye, Her brother, Zeb Rudulph, went home on furlough some time ago. He saw his Sister there and said she made many inquiries after me. He is very much like her and his Company say he is as crazy as a loon and he is one of the most singular acting and talking fellows I ever saw and I think his sister is as crazy as he is. I am more and more thankful every day I live that I made the escape I did. God indeed orders such things for the best, for I really believe I have the best wife in the world and if she were only a little more demonstrative of her affection in words (she is in deeds) she would be without a single fault in my eyes. She is good enough and too good too for me—But I must not flatter her. I'll tell her what I think when I see her which I hope will not be long, first—

I believe I wrote you in my last that my "papers" had to be sent up to the Sec. of War. I have every reason to believe that they went up "approved" as far as Gen'l Johnston's Head Quarters and I have but little doubt that they received a favorable consideration there which will pass them with the Sec. of War. I only regret that it will probably take them so long to return that I shall not be able to cross the River before Christmas. If I could only eat a Christmas dinner with Mother Shields it would recompence me in great measure from some of the many privations of camp life. You will have to go with me when I report to Gen'l Smith and ask him for a furlough for me for I can only stay at home one night on my way, but as I have never had a furlough I have no doubt but he will grant me one. But I am raising hopes in your mind which may perhaps never be realized. I may never get across the River till the War ends and that I can form no conclusions about.

In fact I cannot see how the war can end in five or six years for Bragg has been driven back from Chattanooga with the loss of some of his artillery and now occupies the old battlefield of Chickamauga. It is telegraphed however that he killed 20,000 of the Yanks and by reports our loss at 5000.[5] I have sent to Jackson for some late papers which I will endeavor to send you. It is reported that Longstreet had entrapped Burnside at Knoxville, Tenn. and the latter had surrendered. It is certain that he has him closely invested in Knoxville with only 10 days rations and the rumor is entitled to more credence on that account. This is the best and the worst news we have had on this side. I may get some more tomorrow & will send it to you if I do.

Rivinac has sent me three pieces of music which I will send to you by Lt. Watkins and also a song I had copied for you "The Officers funeral." I expected to get Rivinac to write an accompaniment for the piano but will send it now and you can make one yourself. I wrote you about the Music Ben Neal sent home by Watkins. You must go down and see Mrs. Murrell and see it—I intend to get some for you before I come if it can be found this side of Mobile. I shall send you a book too if he can carry it, entitled "No Name" by some English

[5] Livermore in *Numbers and Losses during the Civil War,* 106–108, gives Union casualties for the Chattanooga battles November 23–25, as 753 killed, 4,722 wounded, and 349 missing—total 5,824; Confederate casualties he gives as 361 killed, 2,160 wounded, and 4,146 missing—total 6,667. The battle of Missionary Ridge on November 25 was a crushing defeat for Bragg and was followed by his voluntary relinquishment of the command of the Army of Tennessee on December 1, 1863. See Horn, *Army of Tennessee,* 303–304.

Author unknown and if you get it you must promise to send it to Mrs. Laura N. Simmons at Athens.[6] It belongs to Jim Simmons her husband and I only got it for you by your making that promise. You can send Bud up almost any day. He will like the trip. I think you will like it. It is different from anything I ever read.

I sent my last letter by Maj. Lacy of Va. who was carrying despatches to Gen'l Smith. I hope you will get it though it was written in great haste and contained very little news. I have I expect rewritten a good deal of it in this. I shall also send a pair of pants for a pattern to cut me some by to send back by Gassaway or some one. I want them cut just like the ones sent except the pockets to be put right in front, about two inches below the waistband cut right through the cloth in front. Mr. Lloyd was going to cut these so (I send the ones Sister Sarah made) but was afraid I would not like them, since which time I got the Uniform pair and the pockets were as described above and I like them very much. An inch and a half below the waistband will do. I need a pair of pants very much. My uniform pair are too small in the waist to wear with any comfort. If I knew I would come home before long I would not ask you to send me any but it is very uncertain and I do not know where I can get another pair. If I don't send these pants you can make me some anyhow and put in the pockets as described above. The last pair you made me did not fit very well but you know fitting is nothing anyway for everyone says "He's nothing but a soldier." If I should get on Gen'l Smith's Corps of Engineers I should like to dress a little nicer than I have been doing in the Cavalry Service but it is no matter. I've dressed well enough. It is not dress makes the man any more than it does the woman.

Mrs. Thigpen was so pleased with the scraps of your dress that she sent in for a square of it to make one like it by. I am going out there tomorrow and will give it to her, I forgot to send it to Mother in my last letter. I have written two letters to her but have received no answer and I cannot account for it. I shall write again before long if I do not hear by tomorrow's mail. An order has just come in to be ready to move by 3 P.M. and as our destination is kept a profound secret I am afraid we are going to move out of this country. I hope

[6] *No Name* was a novel by William Wilkie Collins, first published in London in 1862.

not however, for I have some gold in a Lady's hands that I want to get before we go, that I sent in to get boots at Vicksburg. If we move John Taylor and Watkins will not get off in several days and I may get an opportunity to write more. I shall send $5.00 more postage stamps which you can keep or dispose of as you see proper. Do you want a pair of Shoes? If you do I think I can have you a pair made and bring you if I come.

I hope we are not going way up in North Alabama but fear we may. I may get to go to Father's if we do, but I don't want to get away from the Miss. River. I do hope I shall get a letter from you before long but how it is to get across I do not know. I'll leave the rest of this page to write you on should anything turn up before they get off. I reread several of your old letters last night and as I have no safe place to put them I put them in the fire. It hurts me to burn your letters containing words of love but I think under the circumstance it is best and consigned them to the secret keeping flames. Your words of Love are engraven on the tablets of memory so I need not the medium of written words to remember them. The rest I shall probably write with pencil. Good Bye now dearest one.

(Friday Dec. 4th) Well dearest we did not go far away as I feared, only moved camp 6 miles and are now back again in the same Camp having stayed away only two days. I have just made out the payrolls for July & Aug. and drawn my $64 and as John Taylor leaves in the morning have seated myself to write you the rest of this letter. You don't know my dearest how much I want to see you and when anyone starts across the River I almost take wings and come to you. I awake 3 or 4 times before daylight every morning and spend the time thinking of you and wondering if in the silent watches of the night you ever think of me. Do you ever dream of lying in my arms your head pillowed on my breast? Do you ever think that I while lying on the cold ground am thinking of you, wondering if you "miss me at home." You spoke of your bed being 'ours' when I was there. You may claim it all for I fear I shall never be there or if I should be am so wedded to sleeping on the ground that I will give up my share to you.

But I must tell you the news. Bragg has fallen back to Ringgold,

Ga. ambushed a Division till the whole Yankee Army passed by when they fired upon them and the Yanks turned tail for Chattanooga.[7] I will send you a paper telling of Longstreet's capture of Burnside at Knoxville and Lee's driving back Meade in Va. I am more and more hopeful for the Confederacy than I have been in some time and I don't know why for Bragg has been forced back *whipped,* although the advantage is with us. There is a rumor in camp that Bragg has been relieved of his command and Hardee supercedes him. I don't think he will do much better than Bragg. Time will prove. I am encouraged to believe that this war will end next year, but I hope I will get across before long myself. If I do wont there be a joyous meeting between somebody.

About the Novel, "No Name." I have had a copy given me and will send it to you and so you need not trouble to send to Mrs. Simmons. The character of Moral Agriculturist is the best drawn of any character I ever saw. I hope you will like it. The pants I shall be unable to send I reckon as the boys will have all they like to carry but if you can send me a pair I expect John D. H. Taylor will bring them if you will write him at Scottsville. He will start back the 1st week in Jany. I rec'd a letter from Bro. Will H. which I will send you in this envelope. Lt. Watkins furlough has not come yet. I hope Watkins papers will come tonight. Capt. Webb is calculating to send George (his boy) across with Lt. Watkins and I may not send the Book till then. I have done it up, however, and send it. You will get it from Walnut Creek. Lt. Watkins has *stolen* my late papers and done them up in a package. If he has, he promises me that when his Brother reads them he will send them to you. I want you to send for the Mississippian Dec. 1st and "Mobile Evening Telegraph" of same date.[8] But I must close. Give much love to Mother Shields, Lou and the rest. I commend you my dearest to the kind care of our Heavenly Father who will protect the widow and the Fatherless. Kiss my boy. 1000 for yourself. Truly & lovingly yours, Ed. H. Fay

[7] This is a distorted report of General Patrick Cleburne's gallant rear guard action against Hooker, near Ringold, Georgia, November 27, 1863. See Horn, *Army of Tennessee,* 302.

[8] The *Daily Mississippian* was published in Jackson, Mississippi. For a time in 1864 it was issued at Selma, Alabama, under the title the *Morning Mississippian.* See Crandall, *Confederate Imprints,* II, 872.

Waterford, Miss. Dec. 7th, 1863

Gen'l S. D. Lee has just completed a splendid raid on the Memphis & Charleston R. Road.[9] On the 1st Dec. he attacked the enemy with Ferguson's Brigade, drove them into Pocohontas and induced them to assemble their forces there. On the 2d he marched on Saulsbury, found it evacuated, tore up two miles of track and crossed Gen'l Forest to his District, 4th he moved on the enemy in front of Moscow, attacked and drove them back with damage. McCulloch's Brigade of Chalmers command drove them into a huddle on the Bridge over Wolf River & slaughtered them. Many were drowned trying to cross the River. 300 Yanks and horses driven into the River which was filled with dead horses and Yanks. 50 prisoners were captured. Ross's Texas Brigade displayed great gallantry in cooperating with Gen'l Chalmers charging on the Right. Col. [W. F.] Slemons 3rd Ark Comdg. Brig. of Chalmers Comd. acted in conjunction & same day took and destroyed Lafayette Station, running off the Guard. Then moved down the road and destroyed the Bridge over Gresham's Creek capturing the guard & destroying Stockade. Col. Steele also burnt the Bridge over Cypress Creek near Chevalla. Lt. Col. Harris, 1st Miss. Partisan Rangers wounded. Capt. Grimes killed. Our loss twenty five killed. Vidette.

List of Captured Minden Blues[10]

Capt. [Samuel Y.] Webb. Sergts [Jos. G.] Buys & [William H.] Bailey
Corps. [John M.] Lancaster & [Covington L.] Burnett
Privates—John Boykin, Ed. Bailey, Thos Berry, G. W. Daffin, Josh Grounds, Dave Hadley, Thomy Judge, Wm. C. Morrow, Thos. E. Morrow, Jesse Morris, John McIntyre, Moses Strickland, E. Strickland, John Simeon Williams, Richd. West, James Vick
Escaped unhurt—N. J. Sandlin, Corps. Burnham & Geren. Privates, A. Bun [?], Bob Long, Mack Lewis, Wils Morrow, Marshall Mont-

[9] For reports of the operations to which Fay here alludes, see *O.R.*, XXXI, pt. 1, 242–254.

[10] The members of the Minden Blues (Company G, 8th Louisiana Infantry Regiment) here listed were captured at the battle of Rappahannock Station, Virginia, November 7, 1863. After the action, 13 officers and 149 men were listed as missing, most of whom were captured. This represented nearly all the officers and men who went into the battle. See *O.R.*, XXIX, pt. 1, 626–629.

gomery, Sol Strickland, Ramon Rodriguez. *Wounded;* John Lyons, James Nolan, John Pinkard, Lyons lived only 26 hours, Nolan shot through body—probably die—Pinkard was shot through both thighs & lost two fingers.

The above was received by Capt. J. Y. Webb from N. J. Sandlin, 1st Lieut. He remarked that they had a very narrow escape, only one pontoon for all to cross—but I was determined to escape or die—This was at the fight at Kelly's Ford. Ben Neal wants me to say that he was told by a Chaplain that the 8th La. was not in the fight, wants it corrected so people wont think he told the lie. Mrs. Capt. Webb has the letter. Sandlin wrote enclosed in hers. I send you a Jackson Mississippian of Dec. 2d and an Atlanta Appeal of the 18th. Will try to get others by the time Watkins gets off. Gen'l Hardee declines the responsibility and it is rumored that Gen. Joe Johnston has been appointed in Bragg's place. Bragg asked to be removed so it is said.

Bolton's Depot, Dec. 8, 1863

My own darling One:

It would be difficult dearest for you to conceive the pleasure I experienced last Sunday night on returning to Camp to find a letter traced by your loved and well-known hand though the pleasure was alloyed in a great measure to learn it was here Saturday morning when I left camp to go out in the country, near Palestine. Julius Lancaster had some relatives of his wife living near there and as I had frequently passed the house and knew where he lived I accompanied him. We went to Mr. Thigpen's and I took my coats out to have the cuffs and collars trimmed with yellow flannel (Cavalry stripes). His Mother did the work and I borrowed an old coat of his and went to Mr. Patterson's where we stayed all night. Were very hospitably entertained till after dinner when we left for camp where we arrived just after dusk.

I was disappointed in not getting my boots, the old Irishman being drunk. Thigpen had kicked him out of his Shop. The boots were cut out all ready to be made. I expect I will get them next week. I had been in camp for two hours and was just getting ready to go to bed when Jack Kenny said to me "I have a letter for you Mr. Fay that I got at Hdqrtrs the morning you left." I thought it was from Mother as I was looking for a letter from her, but as I ran my eye over the Direction I "*hollered*" right out, "From home."

Oh dearest you can't imagine how glad I was to find "that Mrs. Harper had told Lou that Gen. Smith had written to Richmond for me"—You will find by letters you will have received that I had already sent up papers to Sec. of War for transfer. I shall look daily till I hear from there and shall welcome with Oh so much Joy an order "to report with as little delay as possible to Hd Qrtrs of Gen. Smith Trans Mississippi Dept." You may not think I was glad but I did not sleep a wink that night. I fancied myself already in your arms and if I closed my eyes I could see yours beaming on me in true affection. Oh how long the time will seem before I reach you. If I cannot get home by Christmas, should I get off at all, I shall go to Okolona after my valise and that will delay me a week but in the meantime I shall have you a pair of shoes made as a present for you.

I forgot to tell you that Julius and I were invited to Christmas dinner and if we can get off we will go. I shall send this letter by Lieut. Watkins who says he will start in the morning but I hardly think he will for he is not in a condition to travel. What his disease is I will tell you when I see you. You can *imagine* in the the meantime. Did you ever receive my letter with the poem "Oh he's nothing but a Soldier." I've sent it twice but you have not acknowledged it. I hope you have for Lt. Watkins has hooked my copy and sent it off and I cannot get it again easily.

I want to know what position Mr. Black occupies as you say he made application to Gen'l Smith for me on the Engineer Corps? Is he an Engineer? If he is I want to be with him and if not to be an Independent Scout. You speak of my getting a furlough very often but military matters & men must be very different on that side from this if I can. Furloughs are things of rare occurrence on this side and as to buying one from any single man in the company that is simply impossible. There being only one man in the Company who loves money well enough and he has already drawn his and used it—Richard Ratcliffe, Loye's Substitute. [William] Crocker (Englishman) might do it. I will try him but if I get across at all I shall hear from it before the next drawing.

What made you dream my face was shaved clean, my beard is longer than ever it was and is splitting and breaking all up so that it does not increase much in length. My hair is all coming out and I have scarcely enough to cover my head. I am going to let you trim my beard when I come. I am sorry that you have never received the Ambrotype sent you from Corinth.

I was glad to hear of the Defeat of the Yanks at Opelousas and am obliged for the report of Gen'l Taylor. We had the news in our papers but did not know as to its reliability. Also of the Occupation of Brownsville, Texas. As for news here we have little more than I last wrote you by Mr. Taylor but hope to get some late papers today as we have sent to Jackson for some. The battle of Chattanooga was a terrible blow on the Yankees and we have heard that Grant was falling back across the Tenn. River. It is rumor, yet I believe it. Longstreet has really captured Burnside's army and A. P. Hill from Va. is marching with a strong column to reinforce him so he will be able to meet Grant's whole army should it go after him. Grant is said to have lost 40,000 men in the late fight, ours less than 5000. Bragg is removed and Hardee is temporarily in command. It is thought Joe Johnston will assume command there. Gen'l Wirt Adams has captured Natchez so it is said and a large amount of negroes & stores. The news from all quarters is favorable. I had heard of Mildred Thomasen's marriage and I don't think it came *any too soon.* I am glad you & everybody else like your dress. I gave Mrs. Thigpen a piece of it to make her one like it. Miss Mattie & Miss Texana seem to be frequent visitors of yours. I am glad you like their society. Miss Gussy too, tho I thought she was a little stuck up when I saw her. I am glad you are anxious to learn to spin. I saw Mrs. Patterson Sunday with a dress that I thought a beautiful striped Poplaine but on examination it proved to be cotton of her own manufacture and she showed me a jeans suit made for her husband, the prettiest Jeans I ever saw. She showed me a lump of opium she had made too.[11] Verily

[11] The opium may well have been made for use in Confederate hospitals. When Surgeon General Samuel Preston Moore learned that a good grade of opium could be obtained from red garden poppies, he directed medical pur-

the *heart of her husband delighteth in her.* I felt that I knew you could do so too if you would only set your mind to it. She was an intelligent well educated woman and to the question if she did not think her education enabled her to make better jeans, she replied "I know it does."

As to your going to Texas. Had you not better wait till I come home and then go together during my furlough? I would like to go and then we can camp out as I prefer that to living in a house. About the sale of our house and lot I have written you to do just as you please. If Slavery should be destroyed by this War, Our House & Lot will not be worth anything to us. If the negroes should run away and go to the Yankees we would lose everything. If we have peace in a year or two the negroes will be more valuable than the property and yet they might die. I cannot decide either way. If the Yankees come to Minden they will burn the House. I leave it entirely with you, with this observation "I don't believe the war will last another 12 mos." I shall be perfectly satisfied with whatever you do. You must cultivate self reliance to a greater degree and learn to depend upon yourself, for I may not live thro this War and you must take care of your own.

Of Will Lewis I had already heard and am not surprised at Neuse Murphy for he courted every girl he saw while in the army and some were fools enough to love him a little and promise to marry him. Why did you not write me by Jim Henderson even if it were only a line? I am [sorry] your Father has consented to board Jno. T. Hayes & wife. I like Mrs. Hays but it costs too much to board folks. Board is worth $300 pr. month over here for man and wife and I wouldn't board any man who *owed service* to his country. Am very glad you enjoyed the Meeting spoken of in your last and would have liked to have been with you though I fear it would have done me very little good as I am past recovery, I fear. So Mrs. Wimberly has broken up housekeeping. I wondered at her doing it crippled as she was. I thought she ought to have stayed at the Drs.

I think I sent you Rivinacs Quicksteps 1 & 2.[12] I sent his Medley

veyors throughout the South to urge Confederate women to grow these plants. See H. H. Cunningham, *Doctors in Gray: The Confederate Medical Service* (Baton Rouge, 1958), 150.

[12] Blackmar of New Orleans published P. Rivinac's *Our First President's*

Quickstep I know and that is pretty. I don't think Mr. Dittmer can make me boots at $100 nor you any more shoes at $30 either. Thank you for notice of election but you did not tell me who was elected Clerk of the Court. I agree with you that meat will be scarce and I don't want your Father to make any return of mine, if I have any, for they *have no right to take a soldier's meat.* It rained hard last night and is cloudy and cold today and I think we shall have bad weather now, of course it will rain and raise the River if I am to be transferred to that side.

You say that Thornwell is quite different from his Bro. I wish he was like him. I fear and indeed I know that he will be spoiled, ruined entirely, raised as he is with his little aunts and Bud. The very years in which he needs his Father's care he is deprived of it and should the war end will be past recovery. This grieves me very much for our darling boy was just what I would have him trained to my notion, but he must be taken and the other deprived of my care, just when he needs it. The one had a foundation laid which could not have been destroyed and so the foundation laid for the other can not be broken up.

What terrible effects this War has produced. Where do the Couriers who stay at your Father's go to, and do you know how Gen'l Smith sends despatches across to this side. The mail line has commenced I believe from this side but I fear it will not continue long. I expect I shall cross above Vicksburg when I start. I am sorry I did not make the application for transfer last summer and I could have been across before now. I will leave this blank space for tomorrow. I write you so often that I can with difficulty fill a sheet.

Thursday morning, Dec. 10. Watkins starts today and I will send you by Capt. Webb's boy, George, the old pants so you can cut the others by them. I enclose in this the latest despatches. Longstreet is reported falling back into Va. I send a Mobile Evening News of the 4th which will give you the latest we have on this side. We heard yesterday of a victory of Gen'l Green on Bayou Plaquemine on your

---

Quickstep in 1861, and in 1864 Blackmar of Augusta published his *Medley Quickstep.* No reference could be found to "Quicksteps 1 & 2." See Harwell, *Confederate Music,* 75, 92.

side. I am going to send into Vicksburg for a couple of pairs of shoes for you which I will bring if I get off. I will send also a quire of paper and then you can use the blank bills of Lading. I expect to bring a ream of it when I come myself but I must close. Give much love to all for me and believe I love you *truly*. Kiss our boy for his papa. Yours affectionately, Edwin.

Hd Qrtrs Rocky Mount Jany 1st 63 [64]

My own darling One:

The first cold, cold day of '64 I seat myself by the parlor fire in the "old castle" to indite a letter to you, my own, my darling wife. I have just read a piece of Mr. Hempstead, "To My Wife" and if you wish to know exactly my feelings towards you get Mrs. Harper's copy of his Poems and read this piece. I expect you will be surprised to find this letter dated Rocky Mount, but your surprise will be lessened when you hear all the causes that bro't me here. I got a letter from Mother saying that Father was failing very rapidly and was anxious to see me before he died, so I drew up an application for leave of absence for (15) days and Gen'l Johnston & [Stephen D.] Lee being present both signed my papers "Approved" and I started at once, Dec. 19th for Rocky Mount.

At Meridian I stopped over and by my intercession got William Henry (7) days leave from the Commander of the Post and bro't him with me. Dunham got leave from his "boss" for the Christmas Holydays and so the three Boys all came home together. I planned a pleasant surprise for our Mother & Grandma, but it was all broken up as Mother was at Jack's House to see Aunt Maria and Dun and Will both went in there and found Mother. I was going to the house first and after the surprise was over (say some 20 minutes) Will was to come in from another direction and I was to be as glad as anyone to see him. Dun was to come in after and we were both to be glad to see him as if we had not met. We landed at Duncan's Ldg. and walked out 4½ miles. Reached there just as the Sun rose and got out home just after breakfast. Folks surprised but very glad to see us. Found Father suffering from severe cough and I fear very much he is going into consumption though I leave him much better and have some hopes that his life may yet be preserved many years. He has failed a great deal since I saw him last March but is the same good Father still. He has frequently expressed the wish that he could see you and Thornwell and he thinks a great deal of you.

It is now 11 A.M. and I am expecting to start at 1 P.M. to Washington to take a Boat for Selma on my way back. I tried to get transportation by way of Mobile that I might stop a day in Greenville to see some of my old friends but they could not give it that way so I go back by way of Selma and will see Sister again. I tried to have her come up with me but Sam would not let her and I did not press the matter as you could not be there and you are one of Father's children. I saw Cousins Will & Eliza and they both send very much love to you. Will has gone to Richmond to see if he cannot get permission from Govt. to take out a cargo of cotton to England to buy machinery for the Factory and he wants me to go with him which I have promised to do if he will have me detailed by the Sec. of War. I would like much to go but don't suppose I can get off, so you need not worry about it.

In camp 2 miles west of Brownsville, Miss.
Dec. [Jan.] 9, 1864.

My own darling: A week has elapsed and a week big with events too, to me, since I stopped writing at the summons of the dinner bell. I have changed my locality by some hundreds of miles and am back again in the bustle of Camps. Came down to Washington and saw Mrs. Price and her daughter and the little girl, our *"Willy gone"* loved so well. How sad to think he will never see her more. Others children are spared but ours must needs be taken. Truly the ways of Providence are inscrutable and past finding out.

Came down on the Cherokee, Capt. Jesse Cox, found her crowded with soldiers from the Tenn. & Va. armies on furlough. Came down with Jay Wheat's widow & Miss Sue Hale, *the deceived.* Reached Selma just at daybreak. Took breakfast with dear Sister Sarah in her own little home. Ran over to see Add just for a moment before the

Cars left. Saw Mrs. Ann Godden you have heard me speak of from Marion, Ala., rattled off on Cars for Demopolis and reached Meridian in an old box Car at 11 P.M., no fire that cold night. Soon reached Camp of 1st Ala. Regt. and found Will asleep. I ought to have gotten there at 7 P.M. Slept balance of the night with him and took 7 A.M. train for Jackson, Miss. which reached at 5 P.M. Found no Rich or horse and so paid $5.00 for supper & bed at a one horse hotel in Chimneyville as the Yankees appropriately denominate Jackson, Miss.

Next morning raining and muddy but as I was due in Camp I took my saddle Bags, heavy with sundry bottles of Blackberry Wine & Pepper Catsup & started up town to see what I could find and luckily found two QrMaster Wagons going right to camp. It rained and froze all day, but I got here safe and dry to find Gen'l Cosby had resigned and asked to be transferred to the Trans Miss. Dept. Capt. Webb had sent up a petition to be allowed to go with him, from neither of which have we heard yet. Gen. Polk gave his consent for Gen. Cosby to go but referred the whole matter to the Sec. of War. My papers sent up came back "Disapproved" and Johnston has been ordered to the Command of Bragg's Army and Gen. Polk commands this Dept. I have heard nothing from Gen'l Smith's application for my transfer and I fear Mrs. Harper was mistaken in regard to it.

You have but little idea unless you have experienced similar how cold the weather has been during this month. I just came in when I commenced this letter from sliding on a pond frozen sufficiently thick to bear a horse. Our Co. have had fine fun for several mornings. I have had but one fall as yet and not serious *except to the ice*. The poor, poor soldiers suffer such weather. If we are not allowed to go with Gen'l Cosby but are ordered to a Regt. on this side, I believe it is the intention of every man in the Company to report across the River. Those who always opposed before are right up for it now and I hope we shall come. Capt. Webb was as anxious as any one at first but when I spoke about it to him the other day he spoke of ordering me under arrest. I defied him to do it & thus the matter dropped. When the matter became noised abroad through camp the only two men who were opposed to going said if Capt. Webb vaccilated in that way they were determined to go and leave him. So I think we will but don't know, as our Co. are not noted for firmness or decision though I believe they stand pretty well in a fight. I hope they will come and I shall do all in my power to bring it about.

I send this letter by Sergt. Jas. H. Simmons of Athens as he, Willson [Williamson?] Jones, Doc. Brantley and Lt. Martin all start tomorrow. Simmons & Jones have bought furloughs from other men. Gassaway & Meeks have not returned to the Company and we fear they may have been captured.[13] It was the fact of expecting letters by them from you my only beloved that brought me back to camp as soon as I came, for Capt. Webb and every one else thought I had 20 days leave. I am greatly disappointed in not hearing as it is now most two months since your last was written, Nov. 14th '63. While in Selma I bought eleven pieces of music for you for which I paid $11.00. Some are very pretty. I hope you will like them. One "My Wife & Child" I bought especially for its title and for you—Nine Songs and two Marches—Lee's & Stonewall's.[14] The Officer's Funeral too, I send. If you wish you may sell some of the pieces but must make your money back. They are worth $2.50 pr. piece if you sell them. I hope you will like the selections.

And, too, darling I send what I know you will want and that is our darling boy's picture. I send it with many injunctions respecting its preservation for I wish it to reach you safely. I shall tell Jim Simmons to carry it in his pocket and if he should be taken prisoner to preserve it with his life. I know your heart will well out with love towards me my darling for this present if it reaches you safely. Little did we think when his picture was taken that ere he doubled his then age his manly little form would lie mouldering in the dust. *Our Child must be taken.* We had given our heart's idol once and another sacri-

[13] Privates Thomas Gassaway and Nacy Meeks of the Minden Rangers had left the company on 38-day furlough November 28, 1863. The muster roll for January and February, 1864, shows them "absent without leave." Later records show that they were paroled at Gainesville, Alabama, May 11, 1865. See Booth, *La. Confed. Soldiers,* II, 983; III, pt. 1, 938.

[14] "My Wife and Child" by Henry Rootes Jackson, written while the author was in the Mexican War, was published in 1863 by Dunn and Selby of Richmond, Virginia, and Columbia, South Carolina. The marches sent home by Fay were probably "General Lee's Grand March" by Herman L. Schreiner and "Stonewall Jackson's Grand March" by Schreiner and Charles Young. See Harwell, *Confederate Music,* 75.

fice was demanded—I cannot feel that it is just—Our noble boy might have been spared it appears to me—

But I must tell you of our Christmas dinner. Mr. Robinson invited the whole family and all save Father and Mr. Brown (Leander) went. Mrs. Robinson had all her daughters and grand children there—only 45 in all at table. A very nice dinner and your husband—par eminence, the *favored guest*. Martha & her Mother both vied with each other in their attention to your "caro sposa"—I was greatly flattered especially when Mrs. Robinson told me very confidentially that *married life* did not *agree with "Sister"* (Martha) that she had never had any health since she was married. I just thought I was too lucky to live long. I had made such an escape but I am sick of this foolishness. Martha's attentions were flattering to me not to her husband. I felt I had a far more sensible wife.

I saw Mrs. Ticknor but did not see Hatty or Ellen. Hatty had been confined and Ellen would be soon. Cousin Eliza had lost her baby but I think from her complexion will have another in six or seven months. Miss Ellen Norton sent me her *"best love"* but as she did not include "Sally Fay" I told her I could only return *"kind regards."* Did not see Mrs. Hastings but him in the Bank. His head & whiskers are as white as driven snow. Grandma made me a pair of pants of Factory Kersey so I am at present well provided. Mrs. Sayre did a good many little things for me. She is such a nice lady I wish you knew her.

Oh if you had only come back with me I could have seen you now twice since I have, but then *you might have been as Hatty and Ellen*. Oh what would I not give for a letter from you today. Must it be that I am never again to see you. Does your patriotism still buoy you up that you are willing to be separated forever from me for the sake of the poor broken down Confederacy.

The Confederacy has acted in such bad faith that I am not surprised that anything should happen to it now. My confidence has now gone entirely. The present Congress is totally inadequate to the issues bro't before it. They have passed a Bill putting in *all persons* who have Substitutes and will in all probability extend the Conscription from 15 to 50 years.[15] If the North does not "go up" in the next twelve

[15] The act making persons who had furnished substitutes liable to military

months the South assuredly will. Intoxication, Madness, & Speculation seem to rule the hour. Speculation and the haste to get rich is ruining everything. The Yankees cannot conquer us but we are fast conquering ourselves. Confederate money is worth only four cents on the dollar in Montgomery and Mobile. I bought two yards of yellow Flannel for the company to trim their coats at $20 pr. yard. Your "Music" is all I bought for myself. I wanted to buy some *staff buttons* for my coat but could not afford to pay $25 pr. dozen for them.

Father went to Montgomery with me Dec. 30 and bought a negro woman "Charity," Gus's wife. I tried to persuade him not to buy her as she is too old, *past breeding,* but he said she kept Gus straight and as he dreaded to be left alone with Gus in his badness, I did not offer much opposition. I could have prevented it but did not. I told him I had rather pay $2000 for a 15 yr. girl than $1500 for her. I got an insight into all his affairs so that I can manage them as I expect I shall have to do before many years. Father has failed a great deal since I last saw him. He had a dreadful cough when I first got home but he got better after the long walks we took in Montgomery in the rain. I was much afraid it would prove fatal to him but on the contrary the exertion did him good and I left him almost entirely recovered from his cough and said that he felt better and stronger than he had for some months. I think the effect of my presence did him a great deal of good. He spoke frequently of you and how hard the separation one from another of us was. He wished I might be with you and we both with him and Mother. He thinks you a model wife and spoke of your going to Prattville with me with hearty approval of your conduct but thought I was wrong in requiring it of you until I explained the whole matter to you. Said I had a *noble wife*. You don't know how happy it made me to hear you praised by my parents or any of my friends.

Yes, darling one, it makes me proud of you. But will I ever see you again? is an oft recurring question with me now. My hopes are almost

---

service was approved January 5, 1864; that extending the conscription to 17-year-olds and to men from 45 to 50 was approved February 17, 1864. Both laws aroused much protest and neither brought many men into the army. See A. B. Moore, *Conscription and Conflict in the Confederacy,* 45, 309, 358–359.

gone. I shall try another application for transfer if Gen'l Smith's doesn't come soon. I must have something on which to base a hope of seeing you or I cannot live much longer. I fear if I interline these pages you will be unable to decipher it so will fill the marginals and close for this time. You might write me once a month and send by *Shreveport* in Mail paying 40 cents postage. Have seen Shreveport dates Dec. 16, that came in that way. Saw them on the 29th ult. in Atlanta Papers, so you see there is some communication. It is two months nearly since I have heard from you and what sorrow may not these two months have produced for me on that side the River. You, on whom my life almost entirely depends may be dead and our only remaining boy, too, may have been taken from me. But I pray God I may be saved that sorrow many years. I enclose a short letter from Mother to you. She had several letters to write before I left and had not time to write more. She was not very well, troubled with Leucorrhea, so father told me. You know what it is? How is your health now? As good as you could wish? Give much love to Mother Shields & the children all from me. I haven't time or paper or I would write to Lou. Did you get the paper sent by Lt. Watkins? and have you got all the things I have sent you by furloughed Men? Good Bye. May God bless and preserve my wife and child is the prayer of your husband. E. H. F.

3 P.M. Jan'y 9, '64. Is it possible that the whole year of 1863 has passed and I not have seen the idol of my heart in that time. What is a country worth that keeps a man away from his family, from all his heart holds dear without any prospect of ever seeing you again. The end of this just though cruel war is farther off in prospect than it was the 9th Jan. '63. Now no prospect of an end save in disruption, total and complete of Yankee Finance. They have proved themselves far more able financiers than we, even though it was on the Robert Law scheme of the French Revolution. We may be able to hold out Twelve months longer but I don't think the Yanks can with the pressure on them. The Presidential Campaign is already beginning to open in their papers. Grant & Lincoln are the candidates. Lincoln determined not to permit an election. But I want to see you, the Yanks may go to the Devil. I wish you were in Mexico and I would soon be there too.

I must come home. Do see Gen'l Smith and get him to make application for me if he has not done it. If he has, get him to send up an inquiry for I certainly should have heard of it before now. Oh, "can I never more behold thee Never more hear thy gentle voice again." I have just bargained for a furlough that a young man is to get in 50 days. $500. I can borrow the money. I have $300 due me here. If my transfer would only come now. Good Bye my darling. "Zoe mou sas agapo."

13

"I Was Received Very Kindly"

Shreveport, La. Mar. 28th '64

My own dear Sarah:

I have this morning received orders to proceed to make a reconnaissance of all the Roads leading from the Main Road from Shreveport to Greenwood in Row of Townships 17 north and south to Texas line. I am about starting on this Tour, my first as Assist. Engineer. I would send you a copy of my instructions if I had time but as I have not, will keep it till I see you. I spent last night with Mr. Goodwill, dined, supped and breakfasted with him & Dr. Nottingham. The Dr. went around to Dr. George's with me and I applied for Board and expected to go there for dinner but as I am ordered off shall not. I have no idea how long it will take me to make the aforesaid reconnaissance but will try and do my best.

You must write me care Capt. Black, Cotton Bureau, so that I may find it on my return to this place. I am almost as anxious to hear from you as I was on the other side of the River. Tell your Father that Duroc's back is improving and I think I will cure it. Also tell him to get rid of all his Confederate Money before July 1st, '64 or he will have to fund it in 4 prct. 20 yrs. bonds.[1] The Yanks have gone back so it is reported. Gen'l Green has joined Taylor some say with 10,000 mounted men. I say with 5000. Everything is stirring here. I have but little time to write and nothing new save the fact that I love you dearly

[1] The law requiring holders of Treasury notes to fund them in 4% 20-year bonds, or exchange them for new notes at the rate $3 of the old for $2 of the new issue, was passed on February 17, 1864. For details of the act see Richard C. Todd, *Confederate Finance* (Athens, Georgia, 1954), 74–79, 112–114, 126–127.

more dearly than ever. One item of news. They are to have a grand Review of Price's Troops here today but I cannot stay to see it. I shall expect a long letter from you by the last of the week certain. If you should see or hear of Clarence Bright see if he cannot arrange it to have me with him. Kiss dear little Thornwell for me and accept all my love for yourself. Love to Mother & Father Shields and all the children. Truly your devoted, Ed.

Opelousas, La. Apl. 10th 1864

My own dear Wife:

You have doubtless heard from Mr. Linfield of my visit to Shreveport, La. I got across the swamp very well and was received very kindly by Mr. & Mrs. L. He read me a large part of his "fast day" Sermon, a most excellent and telling discourse. Next morning was engaged with Maj. Oliver, fixed up everything satisfactorily and managed by dint of hard begging and a little *lying* in collecting one thousand dollars from Col. Douglass. Mr. Linfield said he could not have sold the account for that much on the streets. He paid me two $500 bills. I am going to turn them into gold. I could not get one dollar of my pay or commutation and found there was no money in Shreveport or the Trans-Mississippi Department. Maj. Oliver had none and don't know when he will get it. Got on the "Texas" by dint of hard running at 4 P.M. en route to Alexandria. Ran down to Devil's Elbow and carried away a part of one wheel and had to lie by all night to repair. Got to Natchitoches next night at 11 P.M. and Alexandria at 4 P.M. on Friday. Stayed with Capt. Montgomery and at 9 A.M. left for Opelousas, came down to Bayou Cocodrie and built a raft swam my horse and got here Sunday eve at 3½ P.M.

Found all right here but business greatly accumulated and I have the sore eye so badly I can hardly write even to you. Caught a severe cold on board Boat and settled in my eyes, so I know as a good wife you will excuse me from a long letter. I am very well bodily save the opthalmia—but mentally I am not—for I feel so anxious about you and dear little Thornwell that I can hardly think of anything else—I thought of you all the way to Shreveport and my visit seems to me almost like a dream. I cannot live without you and you must come down here some way or other. Everything is fully leaved out and it is a most beautiful country dressed in its livery of greens. I have not seen many of Mr. McConnell's friends yet but his trunks have gone up. Mr. Huston has got home, came just in advance of me from Alexandria one hour—I asked Maj. Heard to forward them at once and he promised by Ambulance to Mrs. Black. Tell him he must write me. It rained on me almost all the way, but I kept dry. Do dearest write me often and tell me all the news and spare no efforts to get down here in some way. Give much love to everybody for me and kiss our darling many times. Do try and come. God bless my darlings. Your own, "Ed."

In Camp 17 mis West of Camden
Tuesday Apl 25

My own dear Sarah:

I am going to write you a letter not just because I feel like it for I assure you I do not, but because I know a letter will be a pleasure to you and because, too, I know not that I will have another opportunity of writing you soon. But I suppose my movements "since I last pressed your lips to mine," will prove interesting. I waded through [General John T.] Walker's Division and reached Parson (?) Sheas where I saw Mrs. Randle and Abe Monzingo's sisters all to look at the "sojers." At Old Johnny Crow's stopped again, saw Tom Jones and John Murrell and saw no one that you know till I reached Old Sammy McRees', here I stopped for information and he invited me to spend the night. Learned that he had lost his wife only a month before, she having come down to Minden to the Concert, taken cold and died of pneumonia. Called on my friend Dan Gladden and made my way that day 27 ms. to within 7 ms. of Magnolia.

Next morning went into town, found Capt. [R. M.] Venable gone up the Road towards Camden at Gen'l Smith's HdQrtrs. Found Mrs. Tanner, your Mother's cousin, she is living with her niece I expect, Ben Johnson's wife. Treated me very kindly, made many enquiries about your Mother & Father, not many about you, which I of course did not like, spent a half hour very pleasantly, mounted Charlie and wended my way 12 miles to Gen'l Smith's HdQrtrs, found Maj. Douglass[2] who welcomed me like an old acquaintance and showed me "our" Camp. Capt. Venable put me to work at once & I had not ¼ completed my report before he wanted me to saddle up and accompany him to the front. We went some 10 miles and spent a pleasant night in bivouac with Col. [Robert R.] Lawther of Missouri, comdg Cavalry Regt. in [John S.] Marmaduke's Brigade. In conversation found both he and Capt. Venable were bro't up after the strictest sect of Presbyterians almost the only ones I have met in the Army.

Next morning went down almost in sight of Yankee pickets, made a reconnaissance and returned to Camp, Capt. Venable having taken another road. Next morning was ordered up the River above Camden to go as close as possible and went some 2 miles beyond our pickets, took a cross road and cut off the advanced post of the enemy, made two Yanks throw down their guns and ordered them up to me. Started but dashed into woods seeing I was alone and made their escapes. Captured their guns and turned them over (Enfields) to our pickets, reported to Col. [Nicholas W.] Battle comdg outpost and he accompanied me and we advanced to within 100 yds. of Enemy's reserve & tried to draw their fire but were unsuccessful. Col. Battle paid me a very high compliment but I am too modest to repeat it, in regard to my bravery. Urged me to come the next morning and we would go into the outskirts of Camden but I was under orders and had to return to Camp, got back Sunday at noon, HdQrtrs having been moved to this place. Spent the rest of the day in Camp and next morning was ordered to reconnoiter a location for a Military road 4 ms. in advance of our pickets and inside Yankee lines. This I accomplished successfully and got back to Camp last night about 9 P.M. Today have been making out reports all the morning and am winding it up by this letter to you. Sub rosa: Venable seems to think a great deal of me, asks me to join blankets with him so we sleep together when I am in Camp. So much for my "Engineering" as you express it in one of your letters.

By the by I got your last the moment I reached Camp from Mag-

[2] This must have been Maj. H. T. Douglas, who was chief engineer of the Trans-Mississippi Department. See *O.R.*, XXXIV, pt. 3, 768.

nolia. I thank you most heartily for your long kind letter and wish I had something interesting to write you. I suppose you have already received my reply to Miss Mattie's note though one of your reasons failed and I *won the bet,* as I did also another bet in regard to Lieut. Hardie of the Cotton Bureau being an engineer. I asked Mr. Black about it on Sunday but forgot to tell you. So you see that you owe me $100 now, but you are a bad debtor and am afraid I shall not get my pay at least *in coin.*

Well, I presume you have heard of the Capture of a Forage Train of Steele some 12 miles of Camden on the Washington Road—[Major General Frederick] Steele occupied Camden on Friday before I came from Shreveport and on Sunday he sent out for forage and subsistence.[3] Our Cavalry permitted them to go out and load their wagons & on their return attacked them, drove them off, captured all their wagons and 4 pieces of Artillery. They had 500 negroes and the Choctaw Indians were turned loose on them and in a few minutes they had killed 480 negroes and scalped them, taking only two negroes prisoners. These only lived a short time. The 2500 Yanks effected their escape through the eagerness of our men to plunder the wagons. A shamefull neglect of discipline prevails on this side the river. Our lines are gradually drawing around Camden and if Steele does not *steal* out we will capture him entire. I think Gen'l Smith's plan is to invest the place and starve him out. A courier was captured the other day

[3] Fay's account, somewhat distorted, is of an engagement at Poison Springs, near Camden, Arkansas, April 18, 1864, between a Federal foraging expedition commanded by Col. James M. Williams and a Confederate force commanded by Brig. Gen. Samuel B. Maxey. Williams' force, numbering about 1,200, suffered an overwhelming defeat, and lost four artillery pieces and the entire forage train of 198 wagons. Williams reported 301 casualties, of whom 182 were from his Negro regiment, the First Kansas Colored Volunteers. This regiment went into action with 463 men. Both Williams and the commanding officer of the Negro regiment reported that the Confederates killed colored prisoners, including the wounded. Maxey's troops included Col. Tandy Walker's Second Indian Brigade (1st and 2nd Choctaw Regiments). No mention is made of the Indians scalping their foes in this engagement (though scalping did occur at Pea Ridge), but Tandy Walker tells in his report of an Indian private in the pursuit jumping astride one of the guns and giving a whoop, "which was followed by such a succession of whoops from his comrades as made the woods reverberate for miles around." For reports of this fight see *O.R.,* XXXIV, pt. 1, 743–757, 841–849.

with despatches from "Banks" ordering Steele to fall back to Gaines Landing that he (Banks) had met 75,000 at Mansfield and been compelled to retire. I hope we shall capture the whole of his forces and no doubt we will. I think it will not be many days before we have a fine batch of prisoners.

I hope so and then I am coming down to Minden and get my horse. Charley has done pretty well but my infernal saddle has raised a boil or two on his back. I have exchanged saddles and it is getting better. I don't know what I shall do next but I hope I may get work near you before long. I am anxious to see you for I have several things to tell you. I wonder what you are doing now. I would like much to come in and see you. I hope you are well and dear "Nornah Fay" too. Wish you would have my horse well attended to, have him curried every morning. Tell Bud to take my rifle up to Mabry and have it fixed, the lock repaired and barrel dressed out, rifles recut. If I had it with me I could kill squirrels and we could live a little better. We are living harder here in the front than ever I did before except at Corinth.

All of your questions I answered when I was with you and as I have not your letter by me I shall not attempt to answer it. I wonder if you [are pregnant] but of course you cannot tell yet. I hope it may not be. What say you? But I must close for all our ink has given out and paper too. Mrs. Turner said that if she had any way she would go down and see your Mother. Be sure to write me and direct to Care of Capt. Venable, Gen'l Smith's HdQrtrs and I will get it. I shall send this by Courier but have no idea when you will get it. I have been very well since I left you, think my Sabbath at home cured me. Write me one of your good long letters and write to Spencer and tell him what disposition you have made of his money, get Mr. Black to invest Spencer's now—interest bearing in 4 pr.cts. I think he has three or four hundred bills not bearing interest. Do you write to Jane and she will send it to Spencer. Did you write the letters you promised me to Mother & Bob Thompson? Hope you have and sent them across by Gray and Menifee. Have they started yet?

It is very warm today and I have been in my shirt sleeves all day. That rotten lining of my coat is all wearing out. See if you cannot get me some more yellow trimming for cuffs and collar. I shall rip off the old. Wish we "our party" could camp near Minden. I would get several things that I could carry in Wagon—Please knit me another undershirt the first chance you have for I need it badly. I will try and keep you informed of my wants from time to time. You can write me care Capt. Venable at Gen'l Smith['s] Hdqrtrs and the letters will follow me wherever we go.

What is Bud doing. He ought to be at a good school somewhere but I don't know where he could go. If I get to surveying with Compass and chain I shall want him for chain bearer and I will then teach him Engineering in one of its branches. Do you see or hear anything from Dr. Gibson or Cotton-Headed Joe. Of course Lou does from the latter. Tell her I bid her beware for as pretty girls as she have been flirted with. Beware of men Soldiers in particular, though I am much pleased with "Joe." Ask Dr. Gibson if he dont want to transfer to Topogl. Engineers, if so maybe I can work it—though I am afraid he could not see Ellen very often unless he moved her to Minden. He had better do it anyhow as that is a Central point. How does your Mother's garden come on and your Father's corn. Give much love to all the family. I may put in a few words in pencil. I love you my dearest one, more and more every day and hope this cruel war may soon be over and I live with my darlings again. Truly & lovingly, Yours "Ouphe."

Wednesday Morn. Ordered to front today. Gen'l Smith moves his HdQrtrs 9 ms. from Camden. My old saddle has worn out my breeches in front, not mine but the one I exchanged—plague take saddles anyhow. How do you do this bright morn. Much love and hundred kisses to you and Thornwell. Yours ever and lovingly,

Ouphe.

Camden, Ark. [Apr.] 28th, 1864

My own dear One:

I am here in Camden on my way to Dallas Co. and having to wait for the approval of my orders by the *lazy* officials of Gen'l Price's Staff I will drop you a few lines as I learn at the Post Office that there is a mail running to Minden. I find that it will take me nearly four months to complete the Survey ordered but I am to return once (when half done) to Lewisville with permission to come by Minden and "make up my work" there. I shall probably not be at home as soon as I told you in a previous letter but you must write me at Princeton, Dallas Co. if there is a mail which I will learn at the Office when I mail this and let you know. We have stirring *official* reports of Gen'ls Lee & Beauregard in Va. I presume you have the same but somehow I'd rather see it in print. I can realize it better. A Memphis Bulletin in town, I am told, estimates Grant's loss on his left almost 100,000 men —I don't believe anything that paper ever did state. Steele it is said is removed, didnt learn his successor, as also *Banks "idem."*

I spoke of Bud's coming—I presume he will not until I come back —Try and have everything done for me when I come. I will stay a week with you but fear it will be July past the middle before I see you. Write me as soon as you get this, all the news in a good long letter. Tell me all about *yourself* and everybody, a real gossiping letter to cheer me in my lone rides through the woods. I have verbal permission from Lt. Hodges to go to Little Rock if I deem it prudent. Tell me what little saddle bags articles you want in case I go there. But the officials have come and I must get off across the Ouachita. I hope more strongly than ever that the dawn of peace is not far distant. But I must bid you Good Bye till I meet you again. Love to all and the whole envelope full of kisses for yourself & Thornwell. Affectionately, Toujours votre, Ouphe

Direct to Princeton, E. H. Fay, Topographical Engineers.

Princeton Ark May 3d 64

My own dearly Beloved:

I steal a few minutes this morning to write to you before starting for Lewisville Ark. I am ordered there on reconnaissance of road from this place—Well—I suppose before this reaches you, you will have heard of the Battle of Saline River[4]—We overtook the enemy on Sat-

[4] The engagement to which Fay refers was the battle of Jenkins' Ferry, on the Saline River in Arkansas, April 29–30, 1864, between Confederate forces

urday morning and fought him on a Swamp or marsh where our poor boys had to march through muddy water waist deep—Walker failed to carry out orders and the enemy escaped but destroyed his transportation, some 200 wagons—He cut down 150 before leaving Camden—The morning before after writing you I was ordered on reconnaissance near Camden and learning that the enemy had evacuated I went into Camden. Saw Maj. Douglass and he countermanded Capt. Venable's orders and said we might remain till he ordered up Capt. Venable. Mr. Sanders, Asst. Engr. & myself had a good time. I'll tell you all about it when I come home—I have not time to tell you now. We lost very heavily, much more so than the enemy—3 to one—the negroes charged a sec. of Artillery unprotected crying "No Quarter." The horses were all killed and four or 6 men—There were a good many negroes killed & wounded. Mr. Halsey, Asst. Engr. will take this to you and if you see him can tell you all about the fight. Gen'ls Scurry & Randle were both killed.

But I must saddle up—Good Bye my dearest. I love you dearly. Kiss our boy for me. Write me at Shreveport, Care Capt. R. M. Venable. Yours and yours only, Ouphe

Lewisville, [Ark.] May 22d/ 64

My own dear Wife:

I have gotten hold of a small ½ sheet of paper and will hasten to give you a short description of the time past since leaving you. I stopped at Mr. Dick Roby's by invitation from him passed up by Capt. Strange and went up by Walnut Hills, thence Sunday Night I spent with Judge (Capt.) Harris. Here I was entertained in style and Judge accompanied me to Lewisville next morning. Here Lt. Hodges said he did not expect me to have returned by some days so I wish I had stayed longer with you my own dear one. Monday evening I left on reconnaissance down below Lewisville and saw your Mother's uncle Thom K. Smith. Here I spent some hours and took dinner, was treated very kindly, saw Mrs. Stamps, his youngest daughter (Susan).

---

of Lt. Gen. Kirby Smith and Federals commanded by Maj. Gen. Frederick Steele. For reports of the battle see *O.R.*, XXXIV, pt. 1, 669–671, 782–835.

She sent much love to your Mother's family, *to all of you*. She has three children, Ella, eldest, Anne and Baby, *will have another soon.* Passed by Dr. Smith's and saw his wife—did not see him. She sent much love to her kinfolks that she had never seen and expressed herself anxious to know them. Spent Friday night with Judge Harris and took dinner with Mrs. Dr. Bacon. The Dr. was gone to Texas with his negroes but she was looking for him back every day. She sent much love to you all and is very anxious to see you all. I have been treated very kindly by all of our relatives here and I like them all very much. I wish you could come up here and see them. Mrs. Bacon lives on the plantation 14 ms. from Lewisville. She said if I got sick I must be sure and come there. If I could see you I could give you all our Conversations but have not space here—

I expect to be sent East of the Washita to Dallas Co. to make a survey of the whole County. I wish I did not have to go so far from you. I am anxious to hear from you, as not a word have I had since I left you and you were not very well. I wish if Bud has not gone to do something that he could come up to Princeton and ride the country there with me—I think that his health is very poor & the exercise of going about with me would be very beneficial to him. I will pay a part of his expense if he will come. If I take the whole County it will take me four or five months to complete the survey and I shall have to come back to Lewisville once when I have half done and then I will come down and see you—I will run away and spend a few days with you. I feel anxious about you, your cold was so bad. I, too, have taken a cold from sleeping on a feather bed but I am not very bad off. My appetite never fails me and as long as it holds out I think I am pretty well off.

Monday Morning. There was so much talking yesterday I could not finish my letter but will try and do it now. I expect tomorrow to start to Dallas Co. and I wish Bud could come up there and go with me. He would have to come by Camden and to Princeton where he would hear from me from Esq. Gray. I shall make my Hd Quarters at Princeton. I wish I knew who to tell you to direct letters to at Camden. I do not. So send to Capt. Venable at Shreveport and request him to please forward by Courier if he can do so.

We have been hearing rumors of a great deal of good news here lately. Gen'l Smith reports at Shreveport that he has official information from Gen. Lee that he has killed, wounded and captured 40,000 of the enemy, 100 pieces of Artillery—Our loss 10,000—That Grant's & Meade's armies are completely discomfited and demoralized.[5] God in his infinite mercy grant that the infamous wretches may be compelled by their sad experience to make proposals for peace for I want to live with those who are near and dear to me once more—

I wish I had my summer clothes it is getting so very hot up here. I am afraid I shall have to quit the Engineer Corps—Capt. Venable limits our expenses to four dollars pr. diem and when not on duty does not pay our expenses at all. Quite a number of the Assistants are leaving him on account of his Economy I am sure. I will suit him in that line for my expenses up to this time have not been half what I hear others reporting as theirs. I do not tell what I expend.

By the by we have some news here that Gen'l Joe Shelby has captured the Yankee Gen'l [John M.] Thayer and 3000 prisoners between Little Rock & Fort Smith.[6] This is deemed reliable here. God in his mercy has favored our Arms this Spring. We can hear nothing of Banks' movements below. I fear he has escaped as we understand that Churchill's Division is coming back.

Be sure and have everything ready for me by the latter part of June —I hope I can come home to you then and I will leave my heavy clothing there. I wish I had Rich with me, he would be of great assistance though I can get along pretty well without him. If he went to the Yankees I hope they have killed him ere this. Did you mention his leaving in your letter to Mother. Try and keep posted as to the whereabouts of Capt. Webb's Company and let me know. If Bud can't come and stay with me try and get him to come and bring me some news from you. I am so anxious to hear how you are and to hear

[5] The reference is to the bloody Virginia campaign beginning with the Battle of the Wilderness, May 5–7, 1864. In the month beginning with the Wilderness fight and ending with Second Cold Harbor, June 3, 1864, the Army of the Potomac suffered about 55,000 casualties. See Bruce Catton, *A Stillness At Appomattox* (New York, 1953) 55–164. For Grant's losses see *Battles and Leaders,* IV, 182.

[6] This report was erroneous. For a popular treatment of Shelby's colorful career see Daniel O'Flaherty, *General Jo Shelby* (Chapel Hill, 1954).

from Amma too. Judge Harris' wife asked me many questions about her. She is a sister of Eli Harris' wife of Claiborne Parish. I told Gertrude when she wrote to Lou to be sure and ask her how the Battery came on but told her nothing more—I do hope dearest that you are quite well and that your health may be graciously preserved. I do love you above every earthly object and cannot live without you. I must close by sending my best love to your Mother and Father and all the rest—Write me all the news and save all the papers you can get hold of for me so that I can be posted when I come. Be of good cheer dearest and keep up your spirits for my hopes of a speedy termination of the War are growing brighter every day. Take good care of our child and *be sure to see nothing but what is beautiful.* I send much love and would many kisses but fear the effects of evaporation. Good Bye. May God bless and preserve my wife & child. As ever affectionately, Your

Ouphe.

Lewisville, July 17, 1864

My own dear Wife:

I have rubbed out the old pencilling on this tattered and torn sheet, there being no paper in the Office on which to write letters. But to my text. After leaving you the 2d time I called at the College to see if Clarence was going—found he was not so rode on and after passing Milton Smith's overtook old George Monzingo going after a negro, rode with him till we crossed the bayou at Cypress brake and stopped at Old Man Smith's 7 miles from Minden—here saw Dora Griffin, I suppose, never recollecting to have seen her before but she knew me and Uncle George called her "Dora" so I suppose it was her. Took dinner and rode on three miles but it was so hot that I was obliged to stop in the shade. Took off my saddle and found my "pad" had raised great whelks on Duroc's back and determined to turn round and come back home and get my gunny sack. Slept on it a few minutes and found the whelks would go down so saddled up and rode on to Capt. Strange's. Here I stayed all night and paid five dollars.

Next morning rode on and after crossing the Ark. Line met "Thibideaux" who told me that Lt. Hodges had become alarmed about me.

I rode on four miles and stopped at a log cabin in the woods which was the neatest house I ever saw. I asked permission to lie down and sleep and she gave me a pillow and I turned down a chair and slept for two hours. In conversation I found she was a lady I used to know in Alabama, a Mrs. Butler. Rode on to Judge Harris' and stayed all night. Found his little "Staton" quite sick with bilious fever. Saw Dr. Smith who was tending on him—Gertrude left ½hour after I got there going two miles to stay with a lady to go to Walnut Hills to attend an examination the next day. Judge was anxious to have me stay all day with him but knowing Hodges' anxiety about me I started on and got here about 10 o'clock. Found all my confreres here—

I got your letter giving an account of Amma's death. I was glad to get it for you write me better than you talk to me. Your letters are always very welcome even if they are old and I have seen you too before getting them. They do me good.

I start tomorrow for Dallas Co. again. Have just read the Caddo Gazette of the 15th inst. and find the news very cheering and in fact am pretty well convinced that McClellan has spoiled his chance for the Copperhead nomination which comes off 30 Aug—your birthday, I believe. I don't want such an intensely Union man, as he seems to be, to be their nominee. But God will work it all out for the best in some way I believe. I want to see the Yankee nation without a Govt. enjoying what they are so fond of, a state of Anarchy and confusion.

Sumpter Lee has just come in to see me and we have had a long talk. He was quite sober. I do not know how I shall fill out this letter to you, for I have nothing to write and I have commenced with such narrow lines that it will require a great deal. When I finish Dallas I expect I will come by and see you again but don't know. Will see when the time comes. 'Tis so very hot that I dislike to ride this weather but shall take it in the fore and after parts of the day and lie up in the middle of it. I wish I had my woolen clothes for I verily believe they are cooler. I heard from Shreveport that in about a month "they" would have the best article of Confederate Gray ever brought there. I want Mr. Black to buy me enough for a fine suit for I do think I am entitled to something from C.S.A. Speaking of C.S.A. I wish you to examine accurately the first $5.00 new issue you see and see if you can detect those three letters eighteen times on the back of the note, if you can I will make you a present some of these days.

The *example* Lt. Hodges gave me about the hats was as follows—If I pay $5.00 for one hat what must I price it for so that I can fall 10% and yet make 10% on the money laid out. Another—a pond 73 miles in circumference. A travels round it at the rate of 10 ms. pr. day B—8 ms. pr. day; C—5 ms. pr. day—all start from the same point and in same direction. When will they all be together and how many times will each one have gone round the pond? Do you understand spherical Trigonometry? Brush up on it for I thought I knew something about it but find I do not and want you to teach me. I am rusty in almost everything since I have been in this infernal war. I am getting more and more tired of it every day.

I wish you would write a letter to Mother your first leisure opportunity and tell her that the letter mail with 40 cents postage is now open. I saw a letter that came by it a few days ago. I am very anxious to hear from home for I feel anxious about Father. Tell her to leave a letter with someone in Montgomery to send by hand to us also to put on 4 stamps and direct it *Via Meridian* to Minden and we will get it. Now don't neglect this request of mine, write the letter and keep it on hand ready for the first opportunity. Tell your Father that the new order of the Treasurer makes all straight about the new issue question and that he can get all of his old off. If he will buy up a quantity of Salt he can exchange it for wheat. Money wont buy wheat in this county. I will try in Dallas. I can hear of no negroes for sale in this part of the country. Did you write me two letters while I was away before? I don't know hardly what to say about directing letters. You might direct to Camden and I may get it. Write me a good long letter. I hope our little Thornwell will have a very light attack of measles if he has them at all and think he will hardly have them. Write me if you can hear anything from the old company and try and find out. I may not come to Minden till after returning to Lewisville.

Be sure and teach Thornwell his letters. Do not neglect him a single day. I think he will do anything for praise and will therefore learn quite fast. Let him know all his letters and spell some before I come again, if I can come. I hope your Father has got his boiler fixed ere this and is grinding again. Judge Harris wants to know if there is any place he can buy or rent near Minden in ten or fifteen miles. Says he is tired of Ark. and must be where he can educate his children. Write him and let him know. I expect he will come down to Minden before long. He will bring Gertrude down. Wish your Mother could board her. Write me one of your good long serial letters, tell me all the news. Give much love to your Mother & Father. Hope she succeeds in the indigo business. Take care of my chess men dearest. I foolishly left them on the mantle in the Parlor. Kiss Thornwell for me and *Pray for me dearest.* Yours most affectionately, Edwin.

Lewisville, Ark.
Monday Morning July 18/64

Dearest & best of Wives:

A despatch (telegraphic) came up from Magnolia this morning from Camden the 16th, stating on the Authority of the "Memphis Bulletin" of the 10th inst. that on the 7th inst. Ewell's Corps was at Hagerstown, Md. and Breckenridge's Corps at Greencastle, Penn. Lincoln had called for ½ million of men to resist the invasion.[7] A despatch from J. E. Johnston to S. D. Lee that by draft and volunteering he, (Lincoln) was getting 50,000 men pr. day. Grant had telegraphed to Washington City for 40,000 men as the Rebels were in heavy force on his flank. This came over the Wires, but how could the Bulletin know anything of a despatch from Johnston to S. D. Lee. It might know of the invasion of Penn. & Md. but only published this as an offset. Besides how could Gen'l Johnston know how many Yankees per diem increased the ranks of old Abe. Depend upon it that part was manufactured. It wound up by saying that the Archives had all been removed from Washington City. It is not definitely known whether Little Rock has been evacuated or not. Oh, Judge Harris wants you to send him all those Yankee papers by mail. Shall not start till tomorrow as must have my horse shod.

[7] The grossly exaggerated report here summarized by Fay was inspired by General Jubal Early's Washington raid, July 4–20, 1864. See *Battles and Leaders,* IV, 249, 492–499.

I do long for this War to close, for I am heartily tired of it. Will try and write you a short note week after next. Don't be disappointed if you do not [get it] however. I'll come and see you as soon as I can. Don't forget the Gray Cloth before it is all gone. I want a vest too. Now dearest I must bid you good Bye again. Oh how hard it is, I want to be with you all the time. Don't forget any of the requests I have made of you, try and comply with them all. See if you can't get a dressed buckskin from somebody [for] Dr Patillo to make me a pair of Gauntlets. I need them and will more when cool weather comes. I wish you and your Mother could come up and see your Ark. kinfolks. Kiss little Thornwell for his "Dear Faver" and accept a heart full of love for yourself. Yours only and yours Ever, Edwin.

Engineer Office [Lewisville, Ark.]
Aug 22d 64

My own dearest:

I stop a few moments this Monday morning to finish out Bud's letter to you. He has told you all the news of our trip up here so I will not reiterate. He has gone down to Judge Harris as there was not much in the office to interest him while I was finishing up my maps. Left Sat. morn will be back Wednesday—There is no news here save the Capture of Fort Smith by Gen'l Maxey & Gano.[8] The Yanks are said to have left Little Rock also but the latter lacks confirmation. Yesterday we got the Caddo Gazette but had nothing we had not previously had from Extras. There is a rumor too via Camden that Hood has defeated Sherman & is at present driving him back towards Chattanooga.[9] If true this is glorious. I have very little fears for Mobile as it is certain that Taylor's forces have crossed the Miss. River.

[8] Fay's reference apparently is to a demonstration made against the Federal garrison at Fort Smith, Arkansas, July 31, 1864, by Confederate forces of Brig. Gen. Douglas H. Cooper. The Confederates did not capture Fort Smith. See *O.R.*, XLI, pt. 1, 29–36.

[9] Fay is in error about Hood's defeat of Sherman. Atlanta was under a siege that lasted until September 2, 1864. The Confederate defeat at the Battle of Jonesboro, August 31–September 1, caused the evacuation of the Georgia capital. See *Battles and Leaders,* IV, 314–344.

I was paid for 3 mos. service on Saturday $375 in $5.00 Notes. I wish you had them that they might be funded at par. I think it is a great swindle of Capt. Venable's that we are not paid in new issues. Lieut. Hodges had no option in the matter else I would not have received it. On the other side you will find in pencil a copy of a letter sent to Capt. Venable expect to hear from him tomorrow or next day. I expect to be sent to Ashley Co. just as soon as I get my Maps completed which will be the last of this week. Bud will accompany me, he is getting along very well. Says he has found out my secret in getting along—I enter a house with such quiet dignity that every one thinks I am someone great. He will go and see Mrs. Dr. Bacon and I told him to ask her if she didn't have *some flannel for you,* said he wouldn't do it.

I want you to write me as soon as you get this and tell me all the news. If I go to Ashley Co. I may have an opportunity of getting some Yankee goods. I am told there are calicos in Shreveport at $17.00 pr. yard and Gov. Allen sells to soldiers wives even cheaper. You had better go over. I shall send this to Lieut. Sanders and you can send your letter in the same way. Hope your father has entirely recovered and that he has consummated the trade with McDonald. I am looking for a letter from you. By the by I got both those letters you sent to Princeton on my arrival here.

Tuesday eve. Well I have just completed all my Maps and now have nothing but my reports. Bud has not got back yet. Look for him tomorrow. Have heard from Alexandria. Maj. Douglass is throwing a Pontoon across the Miss. That beats Grant all hollow. Capt. Boyd goes across with Gen'l Taylor. Our Cavalry have not started to Missouri yet but are preparing. This is a dull place & I am so busy I have not much to write you. There is nothing of interest here anyway, hope I may get a letter from you before I leave. I dreamed of you last night. Hope you are quite well. What has your Father done about that trade. Hope he will make it. How do you all get along? Have you commenced your piece of cloth yet, or my second undershirt? My love, I could write to you always if writing were not such dull work. I want to talk to you my best & dearest of wives. Give much love to your Mother & Father and the rest. Kiss Thornwell for his "dear Faver" and God bless and preserve you my dearest. Yours lovingly, Ed.

Lewisville, Ark. 26 Aug. [1864]

My own darling One:

I have just received from Adjt and Inspector Gen'ls Office, Richmond, Va. under date Mar. 14th 1864, Special Orders No. 61, viz. Sergeant E. H. Fay of Capt. Webb's Co. Gen'l Cosby's Escort is hereby transferred to the Engineer Bureau and will report to Richard M. Venable, Capt. & Chief of Topl. Bureau Dst, W. La. & Ark. By Command of Sec. of War. John W. Riely, A.A.G. so you see my darling that I am all yours yet—no longer Cavalry but *Engineer* now. Rejoice with me. It was done too before I thought of staying, so you can tell all grumblers I am regularly transferred. Capt. Venable writes me that he will be glad to employ Bud just as soon as he resumes *instrumental examinations* and promises to give me—but I'll send his letter so you can see. Lieut. Hodges has ordered me to Ashley Co. Ark. and to the Miss River also to see if I can get any Stationary for the Office—start today—Am very sorry I have not heard from you before leaving—as now for five or six weeks I shall not be able to hear. Will return by way of Minden. Bud was delighted with his kinfolks and they, I think, pleased with him. He has not got very homesick yet. Hope you will all keep well. Wish you had this spare money I have got about me for it is terribly in my way. Bud says he wants to write a few words [to his mother], so Good Bye my dearest, Lovingly, Ed.

Dear Mother:

I wrote Sister Lou a letter a few days ago. I have not received any word from home since I have been in this sweet hole. Since I wrote to Sister Lou, I have been to see all our relations and am mighty pleased with them all. I spent two days and nights with Dr. Smith and family. I enjoyed myself very much. I also spent one day with Aunt Em (Mrs.

Bacon). She asked me a great many questions about you all. When she told me Good Bye she kissed me. They all call me Cousin Johnny. But enough about kinfolks.

We will leave this evening for Ashley county a long way from here. I expect to see the Big Branch and maybe a gunboat before I get back home. Don't get uneasy about me. Has Sister Lou heard from Mr. Holmes since I left. Tell Pa. I want him to move to a deer country after the war is over. I have not heard any news since I left home except rumors of the evacuation of Little Rock by the Feds. Give my love to all. Kiss Thorny for me. Good Bye, Your Son, Johnny W. Shields. [The following paragraph fills out the sheet on which the preceding letter was written.] Sarah: If you can send a letter to me at Bastrop, Morehouse Parish I may perhaps get it before we get home and may not. Lieut. Hodges wants me to get paper & pencils for the Office and gives me carte blanche leave so shall try and see our friends the Guerrillas before we come back. I cannot bring much on horseback but what can I bring you—needles, pins, hdkfs., etc. Take good care of Thornwell and kiss him every day for his papa. We are just going to call on Mrs. Dr. Chandler (Miss Julia Sullivan) that was. Good Bye, with love to all, Lovingly, Ed. H. Fay

Bastrop La Sep 4th 1864
At Mrs Whetstone 3 ms North of

My own dear Wife:

Bud and I are at my old friend's Mrs. Dr. Whetstone. Got here yesterday about 2 o'clock, have an opportunity of sending this letter directly to you and now write on account of Mrs. Whetstone. She has a daughter, her youngest "Susan" and she is very anxious to send her to Minden and wants me to urge Mother Shields to board her—I wish Mother Shields would do it. I think she is a sweet girl and would be very little trouble to you. I want you to write to Mrs. John A. Whetstone at Bastrop, La. and let her know. She will want to know price of board, tuition, etc. If Mother Shields cannot board her can you find her a boarding house, must if possible? She does not wish to board in the College. If so make the arrangements for her, conditional of course. Tell Mother that if she boards Coz. Gertrude, I hope she will consent to board this young Lady for me.

I have just left the memorandum of the things you wanted with a lady of town who promises to *try* and get them. I don't know but I may be disappointed in getting them but hope not. Shall try up in Ark. also. Am going to stay with Capel Robinson, a Bro. of Hunt, to-night. Bud is getting on thrivingly. Has been stuffing Scuppernong Grapes all day. I send this letter by Dr. Robards who will call on his return from Shreveport for an answer. You can write to us here by him and I will get it on our return from Ark.

We have no news here save a Yankee negro raid to Floyd Carroll Parish. Bud sends his love to you all and so do I. Give love to Thornwell and a dozen kisses from his Papa. I would write more but Dr. Robards is waiting. Good Bye and God Bless you my own darling, Yours, Ed.

Show Dr. Robards all attention necessary for my sake. I fear you cannot comprehend this but must try—Do urge Mother to consent to board this young lady.

14

"I Cannot Afford To Live Here"

Opelousas, La. Jan. 1st 1865

My own darling One:

As Capt. McCandless has arrived and starts for Shreveport via Minden this evening I will write you a short letter by him—and it is needless for me to say I regret I shall not have the time to make it a long one for I love to write to you my darling quite as well as you love to read my letters and today I was calculating to write you a long letter to pay for the simple note you got from me from Alexandria.

I left there as I told you on Tuesday and came out with Judge Baillio (pronounced Baio) where I was generously entertained. Here I met Mr. Drake from Lake Bistineau, Rep. from Tensas, Dr. Gibson's friend who was exchanging Jeans for Sugar. Thence down Bayou Boeuf through Cheneyville and learning where W. W. Crawford lived 7 ms. from my route, turned out and stayed all night. Himself and wife were very glad to see me and design starting up to Mt. Lebanon on Tuesday next to live during the War. He will return to his pastoral duties there. I passed through one of the most beautiful countries in the world but one which has been entirely desolated by the vile foot of the invader until it has almost become a desert. I meandered down Bayou Boeuf to Jesse Andrus, a gentleman to whom we sold a Mill once, a very hospitable old gentleman of Va. extraction, who born in La. had seen four different Governments. The Spanish under Gayoso, Gov. Genl., the French, the U.S. and lastly the Stars & Bars of the Confederacy. He lives 7 miles above Washington.

Friday about 11 o'clock I reached Opelousas which will probably be my home for some time if I can get commutation for Quarters and Fuel, if not I cannot afford to pay what I am paying, $210 pr. month for Board. The old Bachelor with whom I board says he will board me for $15.00 pr. month in hard money but that he can buy nothing for confederate money and really it is of no use to him. I furnish my own rations at that. I have a nice room, bed, etc. not much to eat, two meals a day that will prevent my getting fleshy again. If the Post Quartermaster is only authorized to pay commutation I can get along very well. There are two or three officers on duty here. Capt. Taylor from Marshall, Enrolling officer, Lieut. Morris, Post Q.M. and myself. I find every one disposed to give me all the assistance in their power and I think I shall be pleased with the place. Have not got me an office yet but expect to in two or three days as soon as Judge Mouton returns, who has the only desirable one in town unoccupied. Capt. McCandless has done all my riding for me so I run no risk of Jayhawkers and it is quite a relief to my horse.

He informs me that there are large stocks of goods at New Iberia and Franklin but can only be bought for Specie and as I have only $10 I cannot buy a very large lot. There is nothing for sale here save a few green oranges and if I could buy them for State or Confed money would send you some by Capt. McCandless. I hate to spend my gold for meat which so soon perisheth. Flour is worth Six dollars a pound in State money here and State money is considered better than New Issue. If I had a load of Flour I might get some goods in Franklin. The provisions you put up lasted me for dinner all the way and I just gave away to the negroes a doz. biscuits left over and some sausage. I ate dinner every day but one from it, that day I dined at Mr. Payne's of the firm of Payne & Harrison, N.O. the day before getting to this place. I found it 90 miles from Alexandria here by the Bayou Boeuf tho to have come through Chicot and the pine woods it would have been only 75 but the Bayou Cocodrie Swamp was represented so bad I preferred the other.

I had a singular dream at Mr. Crawford's, thought you and I were standing on the back gallery of our house looking through the hall, a buggy with two ladies and a child and nurse drove past and looked in as if they were going to stop, smiled as if they recognized us or rather me. I drew back from observation and they drove on to the Mill turned and came back & a servant brought back a scrap of paper on which was the single word "Settle" written signed Electra. I remembered neither the circumstance nor the allusion but as it seemed to be some one who knew me I ran out of course and invited them in but could not recognize the Mother and she would not tell me her name so I could introduce her. 'Twas someone I had known but could not tell who. I introduced you and while in the quandary awoke nor could I recall the dream to finish it. 'Twas singular wasn't it.

This is the New Year and I am far remote from you. I do hope another New Year if we are spared I will have you with me wherever I am. I do miss you so much. It is almost as bad as being across the Miss. River, only I am not so much exposed to danger both seen and unseen. I love you my dearest but am afraid to tell you of it so much lest it nauseate you. Now let me hear from you often and as soon as you are able after the event let me have a long long letter from you. Remember me to Mrs. Black and Mrs. Anderson. I would like much to see them. Tell your Father that the 65 Saw Gin sent Thos Texada was moved out by the Yankees and is now standing in the weather. The Box is over it yet, however, but they have stolen the brush band. I tried to get it moved under shelter but could not. I hope you will all entertain Capt. McCandless to the best of your ability as he is a very nice man. Tell your Father so, invite him to stay over night. Give much love to your Father and Mother and Ella. Kiss my dear little Thornwell a hundred times for his Papa. I cannot buy negroes for Confederate money here. Good Bye dearest. Dearly & affectionately yours. Ed. H. Fay

Opelousas, La. Jany. 7, 1865

My own darling One:

Alone in my office at 5 P.M. this Sunday evening I seat myself to write you a letter. I have had nothing from you as yet & am much disappointed today, our only mail day during the week, in not hearing from you my love. I hope you have gotten my letters and believe you have even if I have not received yours. You cannot imagine how lonesome I feel down here in a strange land without you and the feeling is only redoubled by not hearing from you. I will not complain however for I know your situation, and that you feel very little like writing.

This morning I went to Church and heard Mr. Henry White preach, who you will all recollect as one of Mrs. Black's boarders during Conference. A tolerable sermon delivered with some degree of Eloquence that would be pronounced by some as great, but it contained no sound thought but a good deal of imagination. I did not expect very much and consequently was not greatly disappointed. He is a good man though I believe and that will cover a multitude of faults in preaching. I was introduced to Revd. Mr. B. F. White his Brother who has charge of the Male and Female Schools in this place, a very pleasant and agreeable man and an earnest educator I think. I dined with him and sat down at a table with some 35 or 40 young ladies which reminded me very forcibly of old times. Was also introduced to the Rev. Mr. McConnell of the Presbyterian Church Presbytery of New Orleans, an old acquaintance of Mr. H. M. Smith of Shreveport "Post Chaplain," also of Mr. Ford of Minden. He is a refugee from the parish of Terre Bonne and a graduate of the University of Dublin in Ireland though you would never suppose him an Irishman from brogue or looks. He is the most manly handsome Man I have ever seen I think. I am anticipating great pleasure in his acquaintance if my very onerous (at present) duties will allow me time.

You cannot imagine how busy I have been, making out reports and getting things in working order. Have just got all my reports for Dec. last completed and started when the whole business of five Parishes for 1865 comes in upon me to look over, correct, and take Duplicates of, before being turned over to the money Collector. I have no Clerk yet and am doing it all myself. I would pay pretty roundly for a good one just now but can offer no inducement to any one not connected with the army for board here is so high that I cannot afford to live here long at present rates. I want an excellent pensman, at least as good as I am and a great deal better if I could find him. Have written to Maj. Oliver[1] to see if I cannot get Lestrapes, his Clerk. Have not got an Office of my own yet either, though will try and do it this week. I find a large preponderance of the population here French and Catholic and the society is not very pleasant but what do I care for society when I am as busy as I expect I shall be for some time to come. I am

[1] Maj. S. D. Oliver, Quartermaster Officer for La., assigned to Gen. Kirby Smith's Trans-Mississippi Department. See *O.R.*, XXXIV, pt. 2, 986.

inclined on the whole to like the place for I am resolved to be content wherever I am.

There is only one drawback and that is your absence. Were you here it would indeed be home to me for indeed it is true " 'Tis home where the heart is" and you know dearest where my heart constantly resides. I am told that couriers are getting very particular about sending private letters. You can write a note and get Lieut. Sanders to send them for you. He will endorse them for you as if they were his own. Have thought of you a great deal in the past week and shall continue to do so until I hear of your safe delivery from the terrible trial through which you are about to go. I feel you will be aided and assisted from above and that all will be well. If this reaches you ere the time I beseech you have no gloomy forebodings for I am always hopeful, seldom despondent if I do get pretty mad sometimes.

Tell your Father I wish he could send down a load or two of Flour. It readily commands 5 or 6 dolls. in New Issue or State money or 15 or 20 cents in silver. I think I could send back loads of Sugar if there is any demand up there for it. There is very little currency down here save specie and I have seen more gold since I have been here than during the war. I have seen no flour bread of consequence since I left home.

But I must close my dearest, as it is getting dark through my window though only little after 4. Give my kindest regards to Mrs. Black, my love to Mrs. Anderson. Would send love to Mrs. Black but she is a married woman and Mr. Black's friendship is esteemed too highly to lose. Love to your Mother & Father and Ella, don't forget Sue & Kate also. To my own dear little Nornah Fay I cannot send enough love. I am so sorry I did not send him some Oranges by Capt. McCandless. I'll not lose another opportunity if any are to be had for what is the use of money except to minister to our enjoyment. Did you know that one pair of my drawers I bro't down were almost eaten up by the Mice in your Bureau drawers. You had better see that your own clothes are not all eaten up.

Oh darling, do write me often. I prize your letters very highly. Clip the despatches from the Gazette and send me.[2] We get awful Yankee

[2] Probably the *Caddo Gazette,* a weekly published in Shreveport, Louisiana, 1841–1869.

accounts down here but I do not begin to believe them. Mother, as soon as you are able please don't neglect Thornwell's lessons. I am anxious he should learn to read and then don't care about his being crowded. Please don't forget it. Did I tell you that Maj. Venable was very anxious to have me with him in the Heavy Artillery at Alexandria, but said he had gotten so badly defeated and had put me to so much trouble before in the other application he was afraid to try. When my commission comes from Richmond then I shall try and get nearer you. Oh darling how I want to see you but have to close. Your truly affectionate husband, Edwin H. Fay

Tuesday. It rained so yesterday I could not get this off but will try and get it off today. Send all your letters to Maj. Oliver & he will forward them to me. I get letters from him in 4 days.

[Opelousas, La.] Sunday Night Jany 15, 1865

My own dear Wife:

Some two hours after I had despatched my last letter to you came one dated Jany 2d conveying to me the grateful intelligence as Mrs. Gibson expressed it "Unto us a child is born, unto us a Son is given."[3] Oh Mother you cannot imagine the inexpressible relief to my mind when I learned that it was "Well with the Mother that it was well with the child." I was in Capt. Taylor's Office (the letter having been handed me on the street by the Courier and it was raining) or I think I should have jumped for joy when I heard that you were doing well —"had not missed a meal"—even though you had gone through a fiery trial. The terrible forebodings you had, and had expressed to me before I left you, although I laughed at and made light of, still caused me to feel gloomy because I know well how all powerful is the force of the imagination. You can imagine too how surprised I was that an event I did not look for until today should have come off two entire weeks previous. Glad too was I that we had one child born on the 1st of Jany., Grandma's birthday. Indeed it was a day of gladness for

[3] Fay's third son, Edwin Whitfield, was born January 1, 1865. He referred to the infant in subsequent letters as "New Year."

though I do not believe in dreams I had had some quite contrary to my usual custom and they were quite ill-omened. I never did believe in dreams and I shall less hereafter. Many thanks to Mrs. Gibson for her kind letter. I only wish she had told me more about you.

I suppose Thornwell feels very proud that he has got a baby to crow over Mrs. Black. Poor little fellow, I hope he will always love our New Year's Gift as well as he does now. By the By you must call him *New Year of 1865,* something of the kind it is your privilege as it was not "Blue eyed Mary." I do feel so thankful that you have been spared and that too it came off so as to relieve you from your trouble two weeks earlier than expected, but I do not feel thankful that I have as yet only received one short letter and that not from you since I left almost four weeks ago. It does appear as if some one might have written as postage by the Courier line is cheap. I fear you have written and the Courier thrown it out. If they have I'll raise such a din of war in their ears from HdQrtrs that for the future they will be more careful of letters directed to *Capt.* Fay, one of the advantages of the "Three Bars" as you see.[4]

How I wish I could be with you! I don't think I ever wanted to see you as badly in my long absence on the other side of the Miss—and you may take it all to yourself too and not attribute it to the young stranger for you know when I first begin to like babies and he is not quite old enough yet, but you yourself I want to see for I have a thousand questions to ask &c. I shall look anxiously tomorrow for a letter from your own hand for it only takes five days by courier from Minden. I get communications from Maj. Oliver the morning of the 4th day after date.

But of myself I suppose you would like to hear. I cannot give you a very good account for my head is roaring so with quinine that I can hardly write. My old companions gave me a slight admonition to prepare quarters for them last Thursday was a week ago, but I reinforced my works with quinine (a pill bah!) and they drew off discomfited I had hoped with the intention of abandoning the siege, but on Thursday last they surprised my fortifications, and Comdg. officer

[4] One of the several differences in rank insignia adopted by the Confederacy was the use of three bars (worn on the collar) instead of two, to designate the grade of captain. See *Atlas to Accompany the Official Records,* Plate 172.

having been on duty the night before at a *Gumbo* party in a cold room and coming home in a very cold frosty night at 1 A.M. he forgot to examine his defenses and they seized him by storm. He *shook* them off however, cast from Molasses and sulfate de quinine some (ten) cannon balls and prepared to defend the works when they renewed the attack. The balls were shot clear enough but were *mined* and *blown up* before taking effect. The fortress succumbed but not without a severe struggle and yesterday the Commandant kept his bed maturing plans for tomorrow when he thinks he will be successful. Should he be, he will inform you.

Today I attended the Methodist Church again though did not know till I got there that Mr. McConnell our Presbyterian minister was preaching in the Episcopal Church. Heard Mr. B. F. White, the principal of the school and bro. of Mrs. Black's White. Was invited to deliver a short address to the Sunday School and partly consented but will be unable to do it from the fact that my Blanks have come from Alexandria and I shall have so much work to do during the week that I shall not have time to prepare for it. Besides Mr. McConnell preaches in Washington six miles distant and if the weather is good I will exercise myself and horse I think in going to hear him. I fear I shall have chills all the week tho, so I'll not be able to complete my work but hope not.

Want it provoking to find my box of Blanks had been here for two weeks and I almost spoiling for something to do and the trifling French Hotel keeper would not tell me a word about it saying he thought I would call when I wanted them. That's French politeness. I have before me on a plate some pop-corn cooked with sugar done in regular French style very different from Maj. Caldwell's stuff and in my overcoat pocket some two hundred Pecans put in there by a young gentleman to whom I loaned the coat last night. I wish I could send them and some oranges, too, to you and Thornwell but I have no way to send them. There are a good many little things in town but they can only be bought with specie—I have $10 and any little things you want I can get but remember that $10 don't go far. There is considerable trade with the Yankee lines but nothing but specie or cotton. Bank money goes for 3 to 1 in specie. I will buy some coin if a good opportunity offers and then I can buy you a calico dress for I presume you want that more than anything else Hey?

Wednesday Morn 18th. I am not very well this morning. Have not heard a word from you yet. Met Thos. Crichton yesterday. Am going to take medicine today. Will write you next Sunday. Do write me weekly. What shall I do if I can't hear from you. Kiss Thornwell and New Year for me. Lovingly yours, Edwin H. Fay.

Opelousas, La. Jany. 21st, '65

My own dear Wife:

Here it is the twenty first of January, just a month since I left home and save a short note from Mrs. Gibson not a word from you. I do not know what to think of it. I should think if you were not able to write yourself you might at least get some one else to do it for you. Just imagine yourself for one moment in my place and think how you would feel to hear not a word for almost a month? I cannot find it in my heart to blame you for I cannot persuade myself that you have not written, yet I know not how it is that I cannot get letters. Last night three packages came to me from Shreveport and I felt so sure I had a letter in one of them from you that I could hardly wait till I could get a candle lighted to break the seals, but no, no letter from Minden. But I'll still hope on.

I have been very busy the past week with work in my office and the chills together, tho yesterday evening I agreed to knock off and take a ride and see if that would not assist the Quinine I had taken. I had partly promised Br. McConnell to go with him to Washington to attend church this morning, but fearing I would have my chill I declined going to remain overnight but rode with him to the edge of Town Limit and promised him if I missed my chill and the weather was favorable I would ride in this morning to hear him preach. He supplies the pulpit of Revd. Mr. Bradley, the Methodist Minister there. It is very cold and drizzly this morning and I do not deem it prudent to go out so you may thank the weather for this letter.

As we were riding along yesterday I was telling Mr. McConnell of the school in Minden and I find him half inclined to take it if he can get it. I think the people of Minden & vicinity would do an excellent business to get him. He is a graduate of Belfast, Ireland and a *most excellent* classical scholar and withal a *rigid disciplinarian.* Boys will have to walk a chalk line with him. I am very anxious for the Trustees to employ him as I feel sure he will fill the Bill. He taught some time in the public schools in New Orleans and that is guarantee enough of his capacity. Mr. Black knows him and so does Mr. Ford who was one of his examiners for admission into the Presbytery. I shall write Dr. Quarles about it to go with this and I am very anxious for him to get the place.

I understand Jack Crichton has been sent back from Va. on Surgeon's Certificate of Disability. I want him for a clerk and you must try and get word to him in some way, to send me a copy of his certificate approved by the Enrolling officer of his Parish. I did not intend writing much this morning only to let you know that I escaped chills again, but for how long (?). I shall continue to write you every Sunday even if I do not hear from you. Please make arrangements with Lt. Sanders that if any letters come directed to him from "Office of Tax in Kind 4th Dist." that he will send them to you *unopened.* I can then send my letters to you direct. Let me know the arrangement. Your letters if properly directed would come to me direct through the Courier line from Minden. I could get them in five days. Do try and write me at least once a week and oftener if you can. I don't know how long I shall be here as there are various rumors of Yankees—though shall stay till I see them come in. Give much love to your Mother and tell her I haven't seen but once biscuits since I left home and that was at supper the other night at Parson White's. I wish you could manage some way of sending me the "John White" Book.[5] Kind regards to Mrs. Black's family when you see them. If Mrs. Black wants to send letters to the City I could perhaps occasionally get them carried through if sent to me. Kiss Thornwell a hundred times for

[5] The reference is to a genealogy of the maternal side of Fay's family, written by Allyn S. Kellogg and printed for the family at Hartford, Connecticut, in 1860 under the title *Memorials of Elder John White, One of the First Settlers of Hartford, Conn. and His Descendants.*

Papa and New Year too. Write often, my love. *Yours very affectionately* Edwin.

Opelousas, La. Jany 29, 1865.

My own darling Wife:

I was indeed rejoiced last Wednesday Morning to get your long looked for and anxiously expected letter of the 18th inst. You cannot imagine what a joy it was to me for you have never been left by me for a whole month without any letter, but I should not complain for you speak of a letter previously sent by Hines Mitchell which I have not yet received. Alexandria is 90 miles from Opelousas in winter and only an occasional mail, at the option of the driver, pretending to once a week but oftener making the trip once in two or 3 weeks, so your letter by Lieut. Mitchell will probably never reach me. I have nothing new or strange to tell you this morning so will answer your letter in detail which by the by you did not do for me for you mentioned having received none of my letters and you certainly replied to none—I believe though you did mention the shoes so I infer that at least you got that letter.

I regret very much that you should have chided yourself for your last words to me but think you decided rightly in regard to reproving one when in the heat of passion, and an hour's running after a vicious horse is calculated to throw the greatest equanimity of temper off its balance, whiles mine was decidedly upset and has not gained its equilibrium yet as far as the horse is concerned. True I regret my wife should be thrown in almost as great a passion as I was and without cause on her part, but my love for you is so close a veil that it screens all your faults.

You have doubtless long ere this received the letter written in answer to Mrs. Gibson's and have had my views on the subject of the new baby and you must surely have taken it for granted that he was an unpleasant theme to me for in your letter you are strangely reticent in respect to him only mentioning in the end of your letter that he was addicted to long naps, whence I conclude that no matter what his looks may be he is at any rate a healthy and well disposed baby. As far as his name is concerned if you don't like those already suggested there is no haste about it. Give him something that will serve as a designation. I am very sorry you suffered so much though you do not mention it and I only infer it from the tenor of your letter. I wish you had written me more explicitly. How in the world was it dearest that you made such an error in your "reckoning." I rejoice however that it happened when it did, only wish I had been there to have soothed and cherished you by my aid and presence but military law recognizes no family for any under Brig. Genls.

I am very glad that dear little Thornwell is so delighted with his new brother though I knew he would be and tried to prepare him beforehand, you know with what success. I am very glad too that he remembers his father so well and is so fond of him. His Father loves him too, dearly and sends him an hundred kisses in return for his 16. I am very glad to hear that you have recovered from your bowel complaint. I do hope you will speedily recover both your health and strength for when I am assured of your health I can better bear the long and tedious separation from you. You speak of telling me some things when you see me. You had better write them for I have no idea you will see me before sometime in July if then.

Speaking of Miss Gussie and Capt. Fauntleroy, he has some cousins down here in Opelousas who are not greatly impressed with him. Dr. George Hill to whom we sold a Mill once, a real old Dr. Eagen[6] sort of an Irishman, good company & has taken a powerful liking to me because I can quote Horace & Homer. Says, I am told, that "I am the most intelligent young man he has met since the war began and ought to be promoted at once." Am sorry you did not tell me about Mrs. Gibson's dress though it could not be worse than I all along expected. I am only sorry that Mrs. Black had anything to do with it. You speak of having had so much company but don't tell me who it was. I suppose Lou was delighted to see Mr. Holmes and expect she will be for marrying next, for goodness knows she wants to bad enough. I am sorry for Dr. & Mrs. Gibson. If I or

[6] The reference may be to Dr. Bartholomew Egan, who during the war was appointed superintendent of a Louisiana State Laboratory for the making of indigenous medicines. See Jefferson Davis Bragg, *Louisiana in the Confederacy,* 233 ff.

rather you were keeping house she should have a home until the close of the War.

By the by it is the opinion here that it will end in the spring. The Yankee papers (the only kind we get) are teeming with stories of recognition. I put no confidence in Yankee stories however. I am still very much in need of a clerk and I would at once apply for Mr. Neil but am afraid he could not live on the $100 per month I am allowed to pay him. I will however enclose an application in this to him and if he has a surgeon's certificate of disability and thinks he can stand it, can come. Maj. Oliver has refused to let me have Lastrapes not being able as he says to supply his place. As regards the position Mr. Black spoke of. If I understand it from what Mrs. Gibson wrote it is a superintendance of Post Qr.Masters for Northern & Eastern Texas that would necessitate a continued riding. I am too pleasantly situated here to accept that unless I can be benefitted in some way more than I can now see. The stories about Jayhawkers had grown considerably before they reached Minden. They once did reign here & hereabouts but have been routed and driven off long ago.[7] Twenty two were caught at one time since I came here & their *Major, Dr. Dudley* was killed with five others at another time. You need have no uneasiness on my behalf as I think I am quite as safe here as in Minden.

I have just been to Church and heard a funeral sermon from Revd. Mr. McConnell of a young man who was shot in a drunken brawl in a Coffee house in town some weeks since. He lived nearly a week and gave evidence as far as human judgment goes of a sincere repentance. I don't believe in, or at least, I think a death bed repentance in *very bad taste* to say the least. To cheat ones Creator out of all the service due him to the last moment and then claim the advantages of a crucified Redeemer, God must be more tender than I am accustomed to regard him if he often makes a practice of accepting such a magnanimous offering. But then the Thief on the Cross! Quien sabe? As I was going to Church called by the P.O. and got your note by Mitchell. Thank you dearest for that "urgency of heart" that compelled those not very willing eyes & hands to pen me even

[7] For a brief discussion of the depredations of guerilla and jayhawker bands see, Bragg, *Louisiana in the Confederacy,* 198–201.

so short a note, even though I did not get it till today. I am truly sorry to learn that you had suffered so much and am equally with yourself thankful you were spared by a protecting Providence. I am glad that you are able to be up and about.

Have heard nothing from Maj. Botts but don't know but I might be induced to accept the position for if I am not allowed Commutation for Quarters & Fuel here I cannot stay. There all my expenses would be defrayed by Govt.—Tell Thorney I don't want him to buy any more babies unless he can buy a *little girl* for a Sister from Dr. Patillo. Am sorry he bought a flat footed Baby but am glad it is dark haired. I never saw a baby in my life but what had tapering fingers. Tell "Nornah" Papa would come home in a minute if he could but Maj. Oliver wont let him now. He must be patient a while.

You want me to tell you all about my boarding house. The man to whom the house belongs shot a boy trespassing on his grounds and killed him, was thrown into jail and the Yankees turned him out when they came and he fled to Texas leaving his house in charge of an old gentleman, an old overseer. We live tolerably well. I have a comfortable bedroom and the servants on the place are very attentive but I have to pay such enormous board though the old gentleman has agreed to board me for $150.00 pr. month. In fact I told him I could not pay any more. That is $10 pr. month over and above my pay but if I can draw such commutation as they do in Alexandria & Shreveport I can live very well. Confederate money is almost valueless but is better than State money. Proximity to the Yankee lines makes gold & silver almost the only currency. I could board for $15 pr. month in Specie. Confederate money will not pass at all below this point.

But I have filled out a long letter and now must close. I could talk a week but I write so much during the week that I can hardly hold a pen on Sunday. I write from Monday till Sat. Night. Give much love to all our friends for me. Tell Sue I shall have to beg off from my promise to take her home. I can't get home myself. Kiss our babies for me a dozen times. Much love to your Mother and Ella. Kind regards to your Father. Tell him I am not near whipped yet, nor must he be. It will all come out right after a while. Hood did not retire but was ordered out of Tenn. and Lee will get Sherman yet. Will have peace in the Spring if not before. Give my kind regards to Capt.

Webb and also Mrs. Webb. I am glad to hear of his safe return home. If I could send you and dear little "Nornah" some oranges I would do it. I haven't eaten one myself yet. I am sorry I cannot get any shoes. Maybe I can draw some from Govt. as I have to make a requisition for clothing for my men before long. I hope also one of these days to get me a suit of Grey. But I must write to Mr. Neil and dinner is almost ready. I want Jack Crichton[8] for a Depot Agent if I get Neil for clerk But I must say goodbye my dearest one. 1000 kisses for you from your loving husband, E. H. Fay.

I send the letter to Mr. Neil to Capt. Brigham, Post Quartermaster Tax in Kind at Monroe by courier. I send you back your Stamp uncancelled, preserve it. I wish you would send to Maj. Oliver that small bottle of *Carmine Ink* that is upstairs and has never been opened. It is on the mantle I believe. It was when I left I know. Ask him to send it to me by *Courier*. I wish it very much. I had a slight chill again last night and fever all night but intend to escape tomorrow night (Tuesday). They are nothing serious, lighter chills than I ever had before. Goodbye dearest one. I send this to Maj. Oliver this morning by Courier.

Opelousas, La. Feby. 5th, 1865

My own dear loved One:

"It rains and rains and is never weary" and though the poet goes on to say "some days must be dark and dreary" I will endeavor to enliven a part of this by holding sweet converse at the distance of a week with you.

I wonder if it has rained as much at Minden as it has at Opelousas for the past Month. It really seems as if we had nothing else down here since I have been here. In fact it has rained almost without cessation here since last Tuesday and it is fast making me sick and disgusted with the country, so much mud and water. I long for the piney woods and sandy land any place where you and my children are. It

[8] Probably John M. Crichton of Minden, who was a private in Company B, 8th Louisiana Infantry Regiment.

really seems to me as if I had been absent from you for six months instead of as many weeks and I believe I am quite as anxious to see you as I was while east of the River. Oh why must I be separated from all my heart holds dear. This infernal War, will it never close. If I could only hear from you weekly or even once in two weeks I should be better reconciled at our separation, but I have only received two letters from you, by Lt. Mitchell, and of the 18th Jany. I looked anxiously yesterday for a letter but none came and I fear me now the waters will be so high that none can come even though they be on the way. I know not whether you will get this but it gives me pleasure to write it so here goes.

I hardly know how to fill out this sheet unless I draw you a picture of my every day life. I rise at 7 or 7½ in the morning from a good moss mattress, dress, wash and brush my teeth, fix up in a most fastidious manner and read till 8½ when we have breakfast of beefsteak, corn bread and sweet potatoes, sometimes a piece of ham or bacon, cooked very well and washed down with a glass of water. Milk or coffee being exploded theories of living. On rising from breakfast I draw on my gauntlets and with as martial air as I can possibly assume march down four squares to my office to attend to my day's labor which consists in writing business letters, giving information to parties inquiring about their tithe receipts, overhauling reports of various assessors and agents, copying the same after rectification, until 2 P.M.—then dinner of pork and cabbage, gumbo, beef in various forms, but often wild duck baked. There are the greatest abundance of wild ducks in this "grand prairie" that I have ever seen. Negroes bring them in by horseback loads.

There is a mulatto that a number of years ago when a good negro could be bought for $1000, brought $2200 and his master says that he gave him a gun and in two years he brought him back all the money killing ducks, geese and other game. I have seen him bring in 60 & 70 ducks and geese by 10 o'clock in the morning. He has an ox and a horse trained to feed along near the edge of a pond with which the prairie is filled & he walks along by its side till he gets 15 or twenty ducks huddled together (as they are not afraid of a horse (loose) or ox they will swim along as if nothing were near). He told me he would not fire at less than ten in a bunch and he sometimes kills 25 or 30 at a shot. These he brings to town and sells at $5.00 a piece in State money or 25 cents in specie.

But I have wandered from my subject. After dinner I return to my office till 5 or after and then come back and read by candle light till 8 or 9 and go to bed. I have done a good deal of reading there being quite a valuable collection of books in the house, have read four volumes of Washington Irving's works, a volume of the Spectator by Addison, which has many good things in it. Thus my life goes on in one unvarying round, no variety and no diversions in it. If you were with me I could be quite contented here, but you are not and where the treasure is there will the heart be also. This morning when I got up I took a good bath (which I generally do twice a week) and I feel very well. The wind has got round in the North and in 3 hours we have had a taste of vernal spring and icy winter. I think I have recovered entirely from my chills as I have not had any for some time. I attribute it to *aletinena,*[9] eating only twice a day, for we have no supper and now that I have got used to it think it does very well.

Oh what would I not give to see you this morning. I wrote you in my last that I had little hope of seeing you before July, but Maj. Oliver has written me that he hopes before long to have some money for his department and I hope when he gets it he will order me to Shreveport after my share and then I will come and see you. I have been thinking lately what I should do after the War is over if I should survive it and have built many castles "en Espagne," but I will not tell them till I see you which I hope to do some of these days. I feel a great deal of anxiety about Thornwell—I am so anxious he should learn to read. I do hope you will be regular and systematic with his lessons. Do try and teach him to read and then I don't care about his being urged forward. If you teach Thornwell, I'll teach Newyear if I have time. I wrote enclosing a requisition for clothing for my men at Maj. Oliver's suggestion and I hope soon to get some. I included in it a suit for myself and Capt. McCandless says he will get me one in Shreveport and send to you, so I hope to get two suits of grey.

Did your Father get pay for the Iron from Engr. Dept? If I had that money down here I could speculate and double it in two months.

[9] This term could not be found in medical dictionaries. Fay must have coined it.

New Issue is very scarce and gold in a few weeks can be bought 5 for 1 to pay taxes of '64. I shall use Spencer's money if I can when I come home. I must do something to make a living for my pay wont support me. When the weather and roads get good I am going down to Franklin and round to Lake Charles & may go to Beaumont, Texas—I wish I could take you with me. Hope you have heard from Father, Mother and Mr. Spencer. I am anxious to hear from them. Has your Father heard anything from Ga. lately? I have heard nothing from Maj. Botts in regard to what Mr. Black told you. I wish I could be transferred into Capt. Black's Dept. or to Shreveport or somewhere so I could see you frequently. I don't mean to stay long with you for I saw how unwelcome I was to some of the Family when last home. Have you moved upstairs yet? I want you to before I come home. What has become of Mr. Linfield and who is in our house?

Yesterday & today were quarterly meeting but it has rained so today that I presume there has been no service. Was so busy yesterday I could not go. Mr. B. F. White has quite a flourishing school here. Tuition old prices, parents furnishing provisions. I see by the Gazette of 27 that Dr. Bright has sprung up on board to $100 pr. month. 'Tis too bad. He will break down his school. I suppose that is done to support his new Virginia son-in-law.

Kind regards to my friends Mrs. Black and Mrs. Anderson, to Mrs. Gibson, especially if she is with you. Tell Sue I heard from Missouri the other day. Ella must learn her algebra and Latin well. Do you have any more trouble with Cynthia. How does the Mill get on. Have the castings come yet. I hope now the soldiers have gone you are not so much bothered. Tell your Father to buy you a negro girl for a nurse *at any price* and I will pay him if I live. You must have a nurse of your own. I don't like the idea of hiring. If I could go to Ala. I could get you a first rate one and I want to go next summer.

But now dearest I must say goodbye. Write me often. Just put your letters into the Courier office addressed in an official capacity and they will reach me. Take good care of our darlings. A hundred kisses to you and them. Lovingly yours, Edwin

15

"Great Peace Rumors"

Opelousas, La. Feby. 19th, 1865

My own dear Wife:

Many many thanks for your dear letter of the 8th, which reached me the 15th and I assure you it was quite unexpected for I had not dared look for one so soon. I am very glad indeed that you have at length discovered the new way to this place for your letters. I think those sent through to Maj. Oliver must have lain a long time in his office before being forwarded to me or perhaps you sent them by mail to Shreveport, if so it must have taken them a week to go. I am getting more reconciled to my lot down here if I can hear from you in six days. It almost resembles a conversation compared to those lengths of time that I have not heard from you in times that are past and gone.

I am very thankful for such a full description of the baby, our little New Year's gift and I am glad he looks like you, but I fear that as his hair has already begun to change so his features will after a while and that like our little "Nornah" he will look more like Papa than Mama. Am sorry that Thornwell is jealous, you must be guarded in your actions before him towards the baby. I want him to love his little Brother dearly, tho' I don't know that I want *him to buy any more babies unless a little sister*. You must be sure to tell him that I can be his papa just as much if I am the baby's papa too and that I am glad "movey has two childs." I had inferred from what you wrote about his preferring to sleep to seeing Mr. Marvin, that he was a very quiet, phlegmatic child and am somewhat surprised at his nervousness—

Thank you for local news but I had most of it before from Dr. Quarles. I regret very much dearest that you are so troubled as regards your health—I wish you would not be imprudent and I think the egg custard you ate was certainly the worst thing you could possibly have taken. Be prudent and diet yourself and try and preserve your health for my sake for you know not how much I love you. I wish you had some good London Porter and would take it. I think my health is completely restored as I have missed my chills so long I have forgotten how long ago it is. I ride out every two or three evenings with Mr. McConnell on horseback for evercise. He will start up to Minden the last of this week or the first of next. I will try and send you some oranges & a tucking Comb. I can get a nice Buffalo one for $4.00 silver and I think I can buy it at five for one before long. There is going to be a great demand for New Issue here before long. As for the spurs and Boots for Nornah he must wait till I can get them and he get older—I don't think he is quite a man yet. The Pony I would buy if Mother would promise me that she would take regular exercise on him too. I can buy a very nice one for $500.

Mr. Lackey has surely got frightened early in the day—if he thinks Yankees will get to Minden. I think it is the scariest town I ever saw. I am truly thankful that Mr. Linfield has gone to Shreveport for he always looked on the black side of affairs and kept your Father in hot water. Does he keep his horse in Shreveport? I enquire for if I should come up I would ride his horse over, should leave mine in the Public Stables at Alexandria in charge of Capt. Montgomery, but why speak of it when I have no idea I can come before July when the River will be low. I hope to have you down here before that time. It would cost you a $100 to come from Shreveport to Alex. on a boat, it would be cheaper to come by land in a two horse wagon if you possibly can. I only offer these things as suggestions. You ask me if I draw soap and Candles &ç. nothing but blue beef and meal, and very little of that. Living is rather hard but sleeping is very good only I have to sleep alone without you and you know I don't like that.

Oh how I wish you were with me. Have you procured a nurse yet? Hope you will write me next time that you have sold our place. I shall move down to this country if I don't go back to Ala. when the War closes. Mr. McConnell wants me to go down to Houma in Terre Bonne Parish and open a female school. They have a fine academy which cost $14,000 and a good Presbyterian Church there and want a Teacher, at present in Yankee lines.

We have had great peace rumors for two weeks but a N.O. paper of the 13th inst. says our Commissioners have returned to Richmond having been met by Lincoln with the ultimatum that we return to the Union and give up the Institution[1]—I have had no faith in it from the beginning—I think Pres. Davis should have had Blair tried by a Court Martial and hung as a spy the very day he first came to Richmond.[2] They should make the first overtures and propose recognition before I would allow any one of their envoys in my lines. The raid to Bastrop and Monroe I suppose has fizzled out. Harrison of course ran. I saw a man who was in Monroe at the time and he says 200 Yankees were all that came. I do think if Gen'l Smith don't cashier Harrison he ought to be displaced though I believe it is Buckner's business legitimately.[3] Tell your Mother for me that in this country where every body knew him, Dick Taylor has not a single friend that I have met yet, nor does anyone accuse him of being a military man.[4]

I saw Thomas Crichton yesterday. His Co. and another are detached and sent to Vermillionville in Lafayette Parish, also one of Dr. Nottingham's sons. My coat is wearing out and I expect you had better make a tearful appeal to Major Heard and see if you cannot get me a suit of Grey or trouble Capt. Black with it as he is the Agent for Foreign Supply. Maj. Oliver wont do anything for me. Capt. McCandless will do all he can, at least he promised me to, but fear he has forgotten it. I need a suit and must have it somehow or other—The lock of the baby's hair I could not find. Did you open the envelope after first sealing it? for I thought from the looks it had been opened—any rate the hair was not in it. I met a cousin of Dr. Gib-

[1] These rumors were inspired by the futile conference at Hampton Roads, February 3, 1865, between Confederate representatives Alexander Stephens, John A. Campbell, and R. M. T. Hunter and the Union leaders, Lincoln and Seward. See Coulter *The Confederate States of America,* 551–552.

[2] Francis P. Blair visited Richmond twice in January, 1865, on unsuccessful peace missions. *Ibid.*

[3] Brig. Gen. James E. Harrison, who had just been promoted to that grade, at this time commanded a brigade in Lt. Gen. Simon B. Buckner's District of West Louisiana. See *O.R.*, XLVIII, pt. 1, 1371. No report of the raid mentioned by Fay could be found.

[4] Criticism of Lt. Gen. Richard Taylor probably derived in part from his difficulties with his superior, Gen. E. Kirby Smith. See Joseph H. Parks, *General Edmund Kirby Smith, C.S.A.* (Baton Rouge, 1954), 403–431.

son's, Mr. F. Richardson who is one of the Couriers stationed at this place—quite a nice young man. I send you back your same envelope that came on yours of the 8th and enclose one directed to myself that you may put your next in, to let you know that I have envelopes. The Dept. has been only tolerably liberal in furnishing me stationary.

But it is church time and I must go and hear Mr. McConnell preach his farewell. Wish you could just step into my Office this Sunday Morning and see me. I have an Office with the Dist. Tax Collector. Have heard nothing from Mr. Neil yet fear the Raid will prevent it. Wish he could come along as I need him very much now. Give my love to all my friends. Write me often and long letters for I do dearly love to hear from you. Tell Sue I don't think the Yankees hurt Bastrop much from what I have heard. It was only a reconnaissance to see if the Divisions that had left Minden were not attempting to cross the Miss. River. Kiss dear little Nornah for his Papa a hundred times and New Year too. Be sure not to neglect Thornwell's lessons. I want him to learn to read. I am so glad he has missed his chills. Give him the Iron mentioned in my last. Take good care of him & yourself too. Many kisses to you dearest from, Yours devotedly "Ed."

I have just heard an excellent sermon from Mr. McConnell "Ye are the Salt of the Earth"

Opelousas, La. Feby. 26, 1865

My own darling:

Last Tuesday according to expectation came your dear letter of the 16th inst. but it was written one day later than I expected on Thursday instead of Wednesday. Six days from you seems quite near indeed thanks be to the much abused Courier line. I for one am ready to declare that it is a great Institution. Notwithstanding your letter gave me great pleasure it also caused me great pain, for you know not what a grief it is to me my own dear one to hear of your ill health and I am beginning to be really alarmed about it. I am afraid that your inactivity and neglect of exercise during your pregnancy has seriously impaired your health. You do not tell me what is the matter or at least you seem not to know, say that Mr. Wimberly and Mrs. Harris say you have dyspepsia. What do they know about it. Have you no physician? You speak of taking Bismuth and Iron. Whose prescription is it and why do you not consult the best medical advice to be obtained. Oh dearest do try and preserve your health for my sake, you know it was one of the reasons I was always so proud of you that you had always such excellent health. For my own part I think if you would take gentle but *regular* and even after a while vigorous exercise I can but believe you would soon recover. Do dearest one try it, even borrow Mrs. Craven's pony and try horseback riding, try and overcome your fears for the sake of your health. I am determined to buy you a pacing pony at any price if I can find one. I cannot, you must not have your health ruined by sitting moping in the house all the time. I'd rather you had never had any children in the world than to have your health ruined by it. You speak so despondingly too that it makes me most miserable. If it is dyspepsia you have, eat regular ashcake not very carefully washed from the ashes and no fresh meats and I'll warrant you a cure.

You must not keep the Box of Sardines for me and deprive yourself of the pleasure of eating them. I wish I could come home and see you and the little ones. I am afraid you have not received one of my letters in which I wrote you that you must come down here and spend the summer with me. I am determined if I can find a boarding place for you and you can manage any way to come down, to have you with me. I will be allowed Commutation amounting to $450 per month with my pay and that certainly ought to board us. We could keep house on a small scale with it. If I could get an ambulance I would put my horse and old Bob in & bring you down. I intend asking Maj. Oliver for a leave of absence before long but have but little idea he will grant it, if he don't I am going to get on my horse and come anyhow. I cannot remain quietly here and hear of your ill health. I cannot endure it.

I am very glad indeed to learn that after the many efforts I have made I have at last through my friend Capt. Black obtained a suit of Greys. I hope Capt. McCandless may succeed too for I need both suits. I am sorry that your Father has not collected that money from the Engineer Dept. I would defer it till Col. Douglass comes back. What has happened that the road through the swamp to Shreveport has become impassable? I shall have to get off the Boat at Campto or Adkins Landing as it is nearer than round from Shreveport. I fear that you have failed to get some of my letters as you do not seem to know that I wrote some six or eight weeks ago to Father and Mother of the birth of our little "Kainettee" or New Year. You ask what his name would be in Greek. There is no single word meaning New Year, but "kainos" and "etee" mean it & the above name I think will do for our boy but would be better for a girl—I do not think the Express Mail is stopped for I hear of its going from Alexandria occasionally. I am surprised that you don't hear from our parents in Ala. I fear they don't write.

As for Politics or news I think it is the most disgraceful thing in the world that any Commissioners should have met Lincoln & Seward at all unless the latter had signified a readiness to acquiesce in our ultimatum. 'Tis the height of folly to propose anything else to us.

I am glad, as I know you were, to hear that I had created a favorable impression upon those people in Jefferson Co., Miss. They are very nice people. I wish you knew them. Though it has been my lot to find friends wherever I have been. I think, though don't know, that I am pretty popular down here. So your Mother has sworn off from keeping boarders has she. Why she'll take Kate Hardy just as sure as the sun shines. And she can't get along without Martha Moseley. Cant you devise some way to get a two horse wagon and come down here next month. If you can fix up the plan and let me know it I will come after you. I do feel really sorry for Mrs. Gibson. Why don't she go over to her cousin's at Mansfield. I met the other Mr. F. D. Richardson, the uncle of Dr. Gibson. He was much rejoiced when I told him that John Gibson was at our house. He thought he was dead. He lives down in St. Mary's Parish and has kindly invited me to spend several days at his house. He seems to be a very nice gentleman and I would like to go. It seems that Miss Rudolph is quite a ubiquitous character. I think she needs a protector or guardian. Mr McConnell I hope will be with you before long tho he may be delayed to get his baggage up to Alexandria. If he can make any arrangements he will start up to Minden on Tuesday.

I regret very much that I could not get Mr. Neil for I need a Clerk very much. I made an application for another man. I enclose a little letter for Nornah Fay that I wrote him. It is a beautiful day, yesterday being the first day for a week. This is the greatest country for rain I have ever struck. I got a letter from Maj. Botts the other day but it was about a horse and not about that business in Texas. Give much love to all my friends for I see by the Gazette of the 17th inst. that Lieut. Carlisle has been married. I suppose Lieut. Sanders has got back and taken command, so I will send this to him and ask him to forward it to you. I regret very much that so many were killed in the 12th La. Regt. How was Bob Scott killed? He was an aid of Gen'l Stuart. Write me all the news. What! has Mrs. Black fallen out with the College that she is going to have a private teacher. I fear that Dr. Black is fast playing out. Poor Eli—his children will ruin him for a time and I fear eternity. I want Mr. McConnell to preach as often as possible. He will preach out at Butler's school house too as he says he wants to preach every Sunday. I will send you some things by him. Do you want a pair of scissors? If so I can get you a pair for $2 in specie. But now dearest I must close. Good Bye and a thousand kisses from your affectionate, "Captain."

Opelousas, La. Mar. 3d, 1865

My dear, darling Wife:

Your painful letter of Feby. 25th reached me some two hours since and I have immediately written Major Oliver that I begged him by all he holds dear to order me at once to Minden. It will take eight days for me to hear from him and if he grants me the leave as I expect he will, i[t] shall not be many days before I clasp you in my arms. I applied the other day to Maj. Oliver to order me to Shreveport just as soon as he obtained any funds for me but after reading your letter I wrote him and put it in the Courier Office at once. Oh, Mother you don't know how much anguish I shall endure until I hear from you again. I have spoken to my Friend Old Dr. Hill and he says Dr. Pattillo is giving you the right treatment, in fact he recommended the same to me before I showed him your letter. He says and I heartily endorse it "that you must wean little New Year and do it at once, too, not to once a day but entirely" for I had rather lose a dozen babies of his age even if it were necessary (which *weaning* by no means implies) than one wife whom I love as dearly as I do you. No, Mother, everything must be done to preserve your health, it must not be risked for even little New Year. Dr. Hill also says that a gentle friction from a rough glove continued for half an hour every morning over the region of the bowels will be of great benefit to you. You should take gentle outdoor exercise in an open buggy every fair day. If I can come home I think I can get you well. I can take better care of you than any one else. Oh, darling I am so uneasy about you. If I could come to you in one or even two days I would not wait for Maj. Oliver's assent, but as it will take six days, you must not look for me before the 20th of this month. The roads are awful but I shall ride almost night & day after I get started.

I have an excellent man who is gen'l agent for this Parish, an old customer of Wm. Shields & Co., Mr. Isaac F. Littell who has acted as my clerk and can attend to the business almost as well as I can, so my business will not suffer during my absence. I thought when I last wrote you that Mr. McConnell would have been off before now for Minden but he can get no transportation for his trunks to Alexandria and consequently will not get off I fear before I do. I think I shall take a Boat at Alexandria and come to Adkins Landing and ride out from there. I think that will be the quickest way I can possibly get to Minden. I wish I could exchange posts with Capt. Floyd so that I might be near you at least till you recover so that you can come down here with me. I am going to make arrangements to get boarding for you, if I can, and I hope you will be well enough to come back with me if I can find any conveyance for you. I calculate my presence will inspire you. I fear you are low spirited and that is having an injurious effect upon you. You must cheer up and look lively for I don't want to find a skeleton when I come home. I am going to bring you something when I come that is nice. If I could get them to you would send down to the Bay and get some nice oysters for you. Hope you have eaten your Sardines. Am glad Dr. Pattillo sent you some Partridges for I do hope that they will do you good. I am grateful to him for his kindness to you.

So Lieut. Sanders has returned, now I am sure my letters will go to you direct, tho I am sorry you did not get mine of the 12th. I think I sent that to Maj. Oliver. He was very remiss about your letters to me. Tell Lieut Sanders that all letters endorsed "Tax in Kind" directed to him are to be forwarded to you unopened. I am obliged to Lou for her letter but have no time to answer it now. Much love to your Father & Mother. Tell the former that if he can save the Flour and I can get a wagon, I can make four or five hundred dollars in gold on one load. It will sell readily here at twenty cents per pound in specie. Two thousand lbs. would bring 400 in specie, a six mule team could make the trip in 18 days—and I should bring it back with me when I come. Kiss dear little Thornwell for me a heap of times and little New Year too, and darling Mother, a whole heart full of love to you. You are my life, my all. Do try and cheer up and let me find you improving. Ever yours, Edwin.

Opelousas, La. [Mar.] 13th 1865

My own dear Wife:

Yesterday was your day for a letter but as I was absent from home I did not write and have accordingly stolen an hour from my work this Monday evening to pay you my weekly due that it may be only one day behind, i.e. if it meets with no delay on the way. But before I tell you of my whereabouts yesterday I must beg leave "en parlance Commerciel" to acknowledge the receipt of your dear letters of the 25th ult and 2d inst. The former reached me some 20 minutes after I had sealed up your last in an official envelope to Maj. Oliver (Tuesday), or I would have endorsed on the back the arrival of yours. On Thursday last yours of the 2d came directed by yourself and forwarded by Lieut Carlisle. It came in 7 days, the quickest trip any of yours have yet made. You can't imagine how grateful I was for two letters in one week and the last contained answers in advance to many of my questions in my last. Thank you for them.

With yours of the 2d came one from Dr. Quarles who I think used Miss Sallie for an amanuensis tendering Mr. McConnell the school at Minden. I went over to his boarding house and told him (Thursday eve.) stayed till 11 o'clock giving him the dots about Minden & vicinity. I was careful and spoke very disparagingly of no one. He has since told me that it was one of the pleasantest evenings he had spent in Opelousas. He will come up very soon and wants me to come up with him but I cannot leave without orders from Maj. Oliver and though I am as anxious as anyone could be I hate to ask him for leave of such a length as would pay for my 6 days trip up and 6 back. I would want to stay two weeks at least but I cannot be gone over 2 weeks from my Office until I get a well trained Clerk. I hope Maj. Oliver will get some funds for me soon and then he will order me up to Shreveport perhaps, then I can see you for a few days at least. I intend when the roads and weather get favorable, Providence permitting, to have you come down here. I have appealed to Gen'l Buckner and he has orderd Commutation to be paid so that my monthly pay is $140 pay proper, 3 rooms $30 each 3 cords wood $75 pr. cord —$455 pr. month, that will board us I reckon. The only difficulty will be getting you down here but we will try and arrange that matter when the time comes.

If you were with me I should be just as favorably situated as I cared to be, though if all the news we hear down here is correct we will have peace before long and I shall then be with you again never to leave you again for any length of time till death does us part. Oh, Mother, with you and steady employment I could be happy anywhere; without you a golden palace with ambrosia and nectar would afford me but little pleasure. I have been kept so busy since I have been here that I have had no time to become homesick and it is only at night when I lie down and cannot find your head resting on my arm that I miss you so much. But there is a good time coming some of these days if we live to see it.

I regret very much that your Father did not close that trade at once for those negroes and am glad you took the responsibility to try & carry it out. I am always glad of any evidence of your self reliance and anything that you may do in my absence you know I will ratify. I hope it may yet be brought about. I have tried to buy you a negro girl down here but no one will sell a negro for anything but specie and at very high prices at that. I have no hope of getting anything down here for Confederate Money, though they now have a Tax Collector and New Issue will rise. I hope to buy gold at 5 for 1 in a few weeks. I will look for a Comb for you so as to send up by Mr. McConnell, if there is one here but fear I wont be able to find one, there is very little here of anything. I have been looking for some small birds eye calico for shirt bosoms but can find none. However I have looked not much.

On Saturday one of my Gen'l Agents for the Parish of Lafayette came up and insisted I should go down and spend Sunday with him. So we started about 3 P.M. and rode some 14 miles down to "Grand Coteau." Sunday I went to the church of St. Charles college (Jesuit) and attended celebration of Mass. Heard a sermon in French but could understand but little as he spoke so fast. Had some first rate Music with an organ accompaniment. It was in a French family I stayed but they could speak English too. The house was situated in the edge of a prairie that extends 100 miles to the Gulf of Mexico without any timber. Oh I wish you could have seen the sunrise Sunday morn on that boundless prairie as level as a floor. How I did wish you were with me to help me enjoy it. But no, I could only determine to try and give you a description when I did see you. I cannot write it.

You say that you don't wish me to spend that gold for fear I am taken prisoner. There is no danger of that I don't think for if the Yankee comes I shall fall back with some four of five trusty men westward and hang upon their rear & destroy everyone that falls into my hands. There is no doubt that a great expedition is fitting out in New Orleans for somewhere: some parties say that it is for Mobile, others for Red River. I don't think they will try Red River again this spring, wish they would. But it is getting dark & I must stop. I will finish in the morning.

(Tues Morn.) I do not like to hear of Thornwell having so many chills. You must give him 4 drops of Tincture of Muriate of Iron. So Dr. Hill says and it would not hurt you either. He says if you will give it to Thornwell regularly he will have no more chills. It must be done by all means. I'll send by Mr. McConnell some oranges to him if there are any, if he will take the Iron like a man. But don't promise him too certainly lest I fail in it. I am so sorry dear that you are troubled so much with bowel complaint. You must certainly stop it for chronic diarrhoea is terrible. Am very sorry that you have caught cold in your breast but am glad you were mistaken in regard to the thrush. I knew all the time it was only the effects of pregnancy. If you want me to come home you had better carry on your correspondence with Maj. Oliver and ask him if he cannot order me up to Shreveport on some business before long. Hey? I would make the application myself but dread the long trip whereas if he orders me up I am entitled to transportation for myself and horse on a boat from Alexandria. However you need not act on the suggestion unless you are very anxious for I cannot very conveniently leave till I get a good Clerk. Though I will have very little to do after two weeks except for the 1st 6 days of each month. So I leave it entirely with you.

I am sorry Mrs. B. and Mrs. A. have treated you so cooly. What is the matter? What did David do? Tell me why did they bring Wallie back. They will have a good school in Minden now and there will be no need of calling on Texas. I do hope every body will be pleased with Mr. McConnell. He knows and esteems Mr. Linfield. I send you in return for your Dispatch a printed copy of a piece of Poetry that I had published in the Opelousas Courier. You can keep it. I wish I had another copy for Judge Harris. I am sorry your Father did not get that money for that Iron. I would complain to Gen'l Smith about it. I would like a part of it down here, for I could make money trading—I wonder if there is no chance for me to get a pair of shoes made up there somewhere. Ditmer has my measure. My boots have given out and I am reduced to my old shoes. I will buy some specie and then I can get shoes. Tell me what Bank your $100 Bill is and then I can tell you what it is worth and whether or no to send it. Some bills are good and some not, for what reason I do not know.

I am going in April down to the Gulf and get some oysters and fresh fish. I wish you were fond of them you might come and go too. Be sure not to forget to hear Thornwell's lessons regularly. I am very anxious to have him learn to read. Saturday I had a present of 3 linen collars that fit me tolerably well. I shall need some more socks some of these days and if you can make a trade with old sister Jones have me a couple of undershirts knitted. As for flour I could get it from Alexandria but I care little about it. As I wrote you before we neither have coffee genuine or any other kind. I have heard nothing from Maj. Botts yet and I hardly expect to. I shall write Capt. Black in a few days but not in relation to that. Give much love to your Father & Mother for me. Take good care of New Year and Thornwell. Write me by Courier direct from Minden getting Lieut. Commanding the line to frank or endorse your letters. I shall direct this to care of Lieut. Carlisle. Now dearest, write often and accept a heart full of love from your affectionate husband, Ed.

Please say to your Father that as he controlls old Ditmer to please have him make me a pair of Shoes of light Kip. Ditmer has my measure. I want them sewed—you have the thread I bro't from Arkansas but it must be boiled in weak ley [lye] before it is fit to use. I want them made with bottoms just like boots and nails on the outside of the heels if some of those 8 penny in the Dairy house have to be broken off—I want them made with Scotch bottoms and thick double sole.

Opelousas, La. Apr. 16, 1865

My own darling:

Almost two weeks have elapsed since I left you and not a word have I had. It does seem to me that under the circumstances I would have found means to get a letter to you, though I make all due allowances for your ill health producing disinclination to write. I am sure you have never yet realized how much your letters cheer and refresh me, or I would never have an opportunity of complaining at not getting them. I have felt vey anxious respecting dear little Thornwell after leaving him so sick but as I always account no news good news I sincerely hope he is better, indeed quite well. I felt great uneasiness in regard to him and could only comfort myself by reflecting that a kind Father would not deprive us of all our children. It really seems to me that I love my children better than most Fathers and as for that matter my wife too, that I am constituted for depth of affection, yet there are but very few persons that I sincerely love and you at least know who is first and foremost among them.

I came very near seeing you again ere this reaches you for on Wednesday last I received a letter from Maj. Oliver stating that he had $40,000 to be divided among the four Districts and that if I could leave my District conveniently to come to Shreveport after it. If Duroc's back had not been sore I think I should have started right back. As it was there was a gentleman going right up from here & he agreed to bring down the money for me. Besides I am very busy just now making out my quarterly Report and could not well leave. I would have come anyhow but feared you would not have been ready to come with me and I could not have thought of coming back without you. I called on Thursday evening on Mrs. Houston and there learned that Howell Bond, that friend of Mr. McConnell's who was sending teams down for his family would not start before the last of this Month. If so that is your best chance. They made many inquiries about Mr. McConnell and Mrs. Aycock wanted to know if he had seen Miss Maples. I told her no, but he had seen several ladies with long hanging ringlets and his heart had almost been taken by storm.They were very glad to hear of his success, though Mrs. Houston had not gotten his letter by Mail.

I am still boarding at the same place for Mrs. Smith has taken some school-boys to board, so Mr. White told me. I have not seen her yet, except to see her at church today. I called and *partially* engaged rooms for you at Mrs. Dunavants yesterday. She would not tell me her price but agreed to send me word tomorrow. I fear we shall not agree for I am not willing to give more than my wages and commutation and Confederate Money has gone to nothing here though even here is better than in Shreveport for specie can be bought for 20 for 1 and in Shreveport it is 40. I fear owing to the great mismanagement in every Dept. our country is gone and that henceforth it will indeed become a civil war by guerrilla bands.

Oh if you and the children were safe in Mexico, I would feel so much easier. We will have to emigrate to a foreign Country and you had better prepare your mind for it. Were it not for you and the children I would delight to fight them as long as my life lasted. I am thinking some of resigning and going back into the Ranks. You must write me when you think you can come down here and perhaps I can get a conveyance to meet you in Alexandria. Much love to all.

Kiss our darlings for me. I am too blue to write more. Your loving husband, Edwin H. Fay

Opelousas, La. Apr. 23, 1865

My own dear darling:

I was so very anxious yesterday that I could not wait the arrival of the Courier who distributes letters but as the hour for arrival had passed I closed my office and went around to the other street and found the dispatches from above had not arrived, waited some time and as I had never been in the Court House determined I would go up. I clambered up into the dome which has been used before as a signal station for the Yankee army and outside of which they had built a platform for that purpose. Here raised far above the trees or houses of the town I had an uninterrupted view of the surrounding prairie as far almost as the eye could reach in every direction. Here and there dotted over the wide expanse could be easily discerned small motes of timber, artificial of course, embowering within its shade the old French style of house or some "cajen" cabin bedaubed with the mortar made from the mud of the prairie, owing to its tenacity to being mixed in large proportion with the long gray moss of the forests which hangs like the grizzly beard of some fanciful giant of the olden time from the limbs not only of the *giants* of the forests but also from the "wee bairn" of the same whenever that forest is lucky enough to be found near. Wood indeed is a scarce article here. But to return. I also descried from my aerial perch the dimly defined outline of the expected courier some two miles distant coming in a "lope" from Washington. My vision here ended for I determined at once to descend, for the words of Virgil had resounded in my ears since I have overcome the obstacles to the ascent "Facilis descensus Averni," but I wanted no broken bones in the matter and was therefore more deliberate. I effected my "descensus" "without loss of life or limb" and soon after reaching the ground the Courier came.

I possessed myself of his bag and almost the first letter was the well known envelope containing your long looked for though highly prized letter. Indeed I had become really alarmed at your long silence. My anxiety in regard to Thornwell was very great and I had frequently blamed myself for leaving him and after I received Maj. Oliver's letter ordering me back to Shreveport for my share of the money I was sorry I had not remained one week longer, but, I was, I confess very anxious to leave for notwithstanding all were apparently glad to see me, still they were just as apparently glad for me to leave. I am very anxious my blessed one to have you come down here, but since the news we have lately received, Confederate Money has lost almost all the little value it once possessed. I can get board and a room at Mrs. Dunavants for $15.00 pr. month in specie or its equivalent which I expect for us all and a servant would be 900 per month in Confederate. Twenty for one is the equivalent here. I have some hope though I have said nothing yet that I can get room for you at Mrs. Houston's where Mr. McConnell boarded. Talk with him about it. If he had married, I was told by a gentleman, that he and his wife had made arrangements to board there. I do not know if it is true.

Mrs. Aycock is going to Shreveport in May and perhaps we can board there. My Father's house was ever an asylum for the distressed yet when I, his son, have a family in distress no one lends us a helping hand. You say you "have no money and will not ask your Father for a single dollar" and yet will not tell me the reason. Was that done like my wife, would I have kept anything from you? I have money now, that I could send you, if I had any way to do so, but I dare not trust it to the Courier line and don't know how I am to get it to you. I would have bought you a calico dress in Shreveport, went to the store three times but it was so crowded I could not get in so had to give it up as I could not wait all day for my turn. You can come to Alexandria on a Boat for $100 and I can meet you there with a conveyance if I knew when you would get there. You could come to Adkins Landg. and take the Boat. If you have to come that way you had better bring a load of flour and I'll send up a wagon. Flour will bring specie here at 15 or 20 cts. per pound. 2500 lbs of flour would pay our board for 12 mos. I don't want you to feel you are dependent on your Father, for our stock of various kind he has all the benefit of. Cynthia more than earns her board and I think I am entitled to a small share from the mill at any rate. If I was out of the Army dearest, I could easily make money enough to give you everything you wished but while this war goes on I am bound hand and foot and can make nothing but my pay and can't get that. But if you can devise any way to get it to you I can send you 1000 dollars easily.

You must write me often, your letter was ten days coming to me. I regret to hear of Mr. Lackey's misfortunes and to think the Presbyterians acted so shamefully. What excuse does Mr. McConnell give for his course. I am heartily rejoiced that Egan beat Watkins, the election went all right down here too. You say my visit was almost like a dream, it was a reality to me indeed. I am free to admit I did not enjoy it as I anticipated, but still my love for you was not diminished nor do I think it ever will be. I am very sorry you were disappointed getting a letter from Shreveport but Mr. Linfield promised me he would write your Father next day so I thought you would learn why I did not write. I wrote you immediately on my arrival here and that was the first opportunity. I am very sorry you were disappointed. I forgot to tell you that with your letter came one paper containing the news of Lee's surrender, which a N.O. paper of the 20th now contradicts and of Sewards and Lincoln's death which is a fixed fact. I have not seen as much excitement for many days as there was.

Thank you for the piece of your dress but it is not what I would have selected for you. It may make up prettily however. Thank dear little Thornwell for his kiss. I was about buying him a pony but thought I had better keep the money if you came and if you did not I could not send it to him. I do hope my own darling that you will soon recover and that the way may be opened for you to come to me. I long for your society. Kiss dear little Nornah and New Year for me and give love to all. Kind regards to Mr. McConnell. Your loving husband, Ed. H. Fay

Opelousas, La. May 5th 1865

My own blessed One:

It is Friday noon and as I have agreed to go fishing tomorrow and will not return till Sunday evening I hasten to write you a short letter. My health is good but I am not in as good spirits as when I last wrote you. Then my dearest I thought that you would soon be down here with me but now I think there is more probability of my being with you soon.

'Tis useless to disguise the fact that Gen'l Lee has sold the Confederacy. A wholesale proscription will follow and I will have to leave my country on your account. Were I a single man I would fight them forever but you are dearer to me than any country and I must make arrangements for your protection and support. Tell your Father he ought to require specie for his flour. Confederate Money will not buy anything here now. I cannot even get shaved at the Barber Shop for it. It will require it to take us to Brazil where we will have to go for I never intend to take any Green Back. Save everything you can that can be converted into specie. Poor Father, Mother & Sister how my heart bleeds for them in this their day of calamity. Boats I understand are running regularly from Montgomery to Mobile. Oh my God why dost thou so afflict my beloved country. Is thy arm shortened so that it cannot save. I firmly believe that the Confederacy will gain its independence but it will be when *every man* is forced by Yankee tyranny to take up arms. I cannot wait for that time but must just as soon as I am released from the Army I must hasten out of the Country.

I wish you to be cheerful and light hearted for I by no means give way to despondency but it is well to be prepared. The news we all get is from Yankee sources. If President Davis would come over here and take command and issue a heart stirring proclamation I think with the recruits he could get in a short time he could hold out for ten years and worry the Yankees into a recognition of the Confederacy. Would I were in Kirby Smith's place, my name should rank beside that of Washington as a 2d Pater Patriae. Don't show this letter to your Father but cheer him up. Give much love to all for me. Kiss our dear ones for their Father. I wish you would ask Maj. Oliver to give me a 40 days leave of absence that I might come home. I want to see you very much. Good Bye and may God bless me and mine, Lovingly,

E. H. Fay

Opelousas, La. May 10, 1865

My own dear Wife:

With heavy heart I write you again. I cannot endure the suspense of not hearing from you. I have been looking anxiously for a letter for nearly a week but as yet none have come, and as the Couriers are under "marching orders" I fear I shall not have another opportunity of sending you a letter. The papers of the 8th contain an account of the surrender of Dick Taylor,[5] the paper is three miles from town and as Parson White proposes to drive me out in his Buggy I am going to see it.

(Thursday Morn). Well I rode out to the Camp of the 7 La. Cav. but the aforesaid paper had been forwarded to Alexandria and I could find no one with sufficient intelligence to tell me what it contained. They said "that Taylor surrendered on the same terms as Johnston with the exception that Yankee soldiers in our Army shall be allowed to return to their homes in the North." I fear me the next thing we shall hear will be the surrender of Kirby Smith even if it has not already taken place.[6] My poor downtrodden Country! what can thy sons do who are true to thee. Exile alone awaits them.

In a foreign land dearest we will have to seek an asylum. My heart bleeds. I know not what to do. I have no funds to pay our passage to Brazil. Three long years have I been separated from you but I fear it is only the Commencement of a separation. I can go to Brazil alone without money and I can make a home for you but then the long tedious separation. When shall our sorrows have an end? Truly the Lord has forsaken his people—I fear the subjugation of the South will make an infidel of me. I cannot see how a just God can allow people who have battled so heroically for their rights to be overthrown. I can't I wont believe that my country is subjugated. Were it not for you dearest and our darlings I would imitate those noble spirits Mosby and Wade Hampton who have retreated into the fastnesses of the

[5] Gen. Taylor surrendered all remaining forces east of the Mississippi to Maj. Gen. Edward R. S. Canby, at Citronelle, Alabama, on May 4, 1865. See *Battles and Leaders,* IV, 411.

[6] The Trans-Mississippi Department was formally surrendered on May 26, 1865. The surrender was signed not by Kirby Smith, but by Lt. Gen. Simon B. Buckner. See Parks, *General Edmund Kirby Smith, C.S.A.,* 476–478.

mountains and swear to lay down their arms only with their lives, but you are dearer to me than country and beneath another clime we will found a "Nova Troja" where there may be peace and happiness yet to be found.

I suppose ere this you have received my letter telling you I was boarding at Mrs. Houston's. I find it very pleasant tho' not so convenient as at my old place. But I have not told you of my trip last Friday. I went down into Lafayette & St. Martin's Parish, stayed at the house of Mr. Zenon Broussard. I was entertained very handsomely. Feasted on strawberries, cream & clabber, went fishing but was disappointed in getting any. I enjoyed myself very much and have promised to repeat my visit but that is uncertain in these uncertain times. But I must close this letter as it is almost time for the Courier. I do hope I shall get a letter from you today. Mr. White has just come and asks me to go to Washington to Rev. Mr. Bradley's Sunday School celebration—he is waiting. Good Bye dearest. God bless and preserve you my own beloved. Kiss our darlings. Your loving, Edwin.

Opelousas, La. May 13, 1865

My own dear Wife:

I have written you several letters this week, but I cannot get over the "kakoethes skgibevoe" and so must trouble you with another line even though three weeks (nearly) have elapsed since I have had a word from you. How is it? Do you not write me? Have you forgotten my address? Have you forgotten your husband? Have you determined to give him up, separate or go in a convent? Have you heard he was dead, and about to marry again? Have you lost your reason and cannot write? Are you too sick to write? Are you dead? All these questions save one have come into my mind. Daily I await the arrival of the Courier and daily I am disappointed. Hope deferred indeed maketh the heart sick. I want to see you and be with you more now than ever before, since our marriage—though the remembrance of my last visit is not very pleasant for you had never been sick before when I came home. I sympathize deeply with you my darling in your affliction and I do not mean that I did not enjoy my visit but before when I have left you I always looked back upon the pleasures I have enjoyed in your society and they were bright spots but now when I revert to my last visit I can only think of your ill health and it is not as pleasant a retrospective as formerly. Have I explained myself so as to be understood and not misapprehended. If so I am glad.

Both my last letters were written in such haste I did not enjoy them at all and it is to that want of enjoyment on my part that you are indebted for this letter and also to the fact that I am anxious to make another proposition in regard to our correspondence. One thing is evident that your letters do not reach Maj. Oliver for his communications reach me regularly and he will certainly send them, so as I can get *no letters* when you write once a week perhaps if you write *twice a week* the matter might be improved and I occasionally get letters at least once a month. Mrs. Houston writes her husband twice a week and he is only in Alexandria and I am sure you who are at more than double the distance might do it especially as I furnished you with a sufficiency of paper. Suppose that you try it for the sake of experiment.

I attended an auction the other day and purchased a nice comb like the one I carried you only the top was ivory like Mrs. Dr. Gibson's. I paid silver for it thinking you or Lou might have it, for 75 cents. It is quite a pretty comb and quite durable. I bought an India rubber one for myself for 25 cents. If I could get it to you I think I could get you a bottle of pretty good brandy. I wish you would write to Capt. Black and see if he could not give me a situation with him. Confederate Money will buy nothing here, not even a glass of rum. I cannot pay my board except with tithe provisions and now people wont pay their Tithes preferring to pay in Confederate Money which is worth only one cent on the dollar. I shall have to resign and go into ranks if I cannot get in some other position.

Tell Joe for me that if he could live here I would be rejoiced to have him here with me. He has a good many friends in Opelousas. I am boarding as you know at Mrs. Houston's and I enjoy the society of the Ladies very much. Quite a contrast to the Bachelor's Hall where I previously boarded. How is Mr. McConnell getting on—I hope he is pleased. Tell him that a certain lady *with* curls is as fond of dancing as ever *even now*. I should be glad to hear from him and I will answer. Though I presume Mrs. Houston keeps him posted. Tell Dr. Pattillo that several gentlemen went out yesterday where the overflow had run all the ducks out from the Miss. & Atchafalaya Rivers, killed 101. Want that a pretty good hunt. One of them has just sent me a nice saddle and I have just taken it out home. But I had nearly finished my letter and said not a word about news.

We have nothing reliable here. Everybody but me is whipped. [Lucien J.] Dupré the Congressman from this district comes back thoroughly whipped. I don't think all is lost by any means yet, if Gen'l Smith would only prove equal to the emergency he might inscribe his name highest on the Roll of Fame. Oh if I had his opportunity. Now I am ambitious. If your Father has Specie it would be better for him, if the Yanks make a demonstration on this side, to move to the very western part of Texas, but as they believe the rebellion already crushed they will not be hard and will probably spare his Mill—and he had better stay. I wish I could see him. Bud and Joe must preserve my rifle if I cannot come home. Bud must make as many balls as it is possible for him to do and bring with him Scrap though I hope to be in Minden before any Yankees get there. If not he must do as I have directed. I hope Gen'l Smith will not surrender though I sadly fear he will be compelled to for want of a currency. If he had a few millions in specie we could certainly win our independence. We hear Pres. Davis is in Shreveport with a part of his Cabinet & Commodore Semmes. Poor Charley Reed couldn't run the "Webb" through though he tried hard. 'Twas a gallant act and gallantly carried through. He is reported having gone to Sea in a fishing Boat. I hope he will turn up all right and make the accursed foe hear from him upon the high seas yet.

Do you hear anything from Montgomery? Poor Dear Mother & Father, what will they do. I wish I could aid them. My faith in God is bound to be destroyed if the South is at last subjugated. I cannot, will not believe it. I did not intend to say a word about the "State of the Country" in this but I do not know how long I may have an opportunity of writing you by Courier and I know you would never get it by Mail and I wanted to tell you about my Gun. I am cheerful, not cast down and am determined never to surrender myself. When you write me, write good long letters semi-weekly and I will do the same. This makes four letters I have written you since hearing from you. I hope you got the Diaper Pin I sent you. Give much love to your Father & Mother for me. Remember me kindly to all my friends. Tell everybody I say "Never give up the Ship." Kiss our babies for me. My dear little Thornwell I hope is a good Boy and minds his Movey and is learning to read. Don't neglect his lessons dearest. I remain as ever I have been since I first pressed your lips to mine. Your true, faithful & Loving Husband

Opelousas, La. May 14, 1865

My own beloved One:

Yours ultimately of the 6th inst reached me this morning. You don't know dearest how it makes my heart bleed to feel that you are suffering so. Have you weaned little New Year? I hope you have, you never will recover without it. Discard all medicines. Have some Dewberry roots got washed clean, bruised and soaked in water you drink. Eat nothing but farinaceous food, take moderate exercise and my word for it you will improve. Go up to Mrs. Webb's if you possibly can, enjoy yourself all you can under the circumstances, and cheer up. Put your trust in God. I can lose my country, but not my wife. Cheer up. Don't get low spirited and I will suddenly pop in one of these days before long, before you know it. Since getting your letter this morning I have made application for leave of absence for fifty days and expect I'll get it. Yes darling if you could only be well I could bear all other afflictions. You are so very dear to me. I wrote you yesterday and it went up today. I hope this will start early tomorrow. Now dearest will you follow my prescription thoroughly. Do try it. Little New Year must be completely weaned. Then you will have no canker sores, a sign your bowels are getting better. I am no doctor but that is the best thing you can do.

Mr. Houston in a letter says that officers there, Alexandria, say they will be disbanded in 8 or 10 days.[7] I can hardly believe it

[7] For the widespread demoralization among Confederate soldiers in the Trans-Mississippi Department in May, 1865, see Parks, *General Edmund Kirby Smith, C.S.A.*, 473 ff.

after the patriotic address from Gov. Henry W. Allen and from Gen'l Harry Hays, but there is no telling. Scores here rejoice at it, i.e. the giving up of the Confederacy. Poor father & mother & sister. A. J. Smith's villainy in Montgomery, Frederick Steele in Selma. Poor President Davis, how my heart bleeds. I hope the Yankees will pass an act of banishment against every Confederate Officer, then they will have to furnish transportation to Brazil.

Please make Lou write, you dictate every twice a week. I am so anxious to hear from you often. How did L. B. Watkins get a 60 day furlough. I don't believe it, but between us this is. Better make friends of every body, we may need them. O dearest how I long to pillow your head upon my bosom and nurse you back to health. I believe I can do it if I can get there. I would come anyhow without waiting for "leave of absence" if things were not in just such a state and it would be said I deserted in the hour of danger. I am more circumspect now than usual.

But it is growing late. I must close. Kiss our dear little ones for their Papa and know dearest and believe how much I love you. Your ever loving and affectionate husband, Ed.

At Mrs. Houston's 25 May [1865]

My best beloved One:

I have on hand in my Depots 1600 weight of excellent Sugar and 32 lbs Tobacco, the Courier line has deserted. I have no orders from above nevertheless I shall start home just as soon as I dispose of this produce, which I hope will be next week or as soon as possible. I am very well and very anxious to be with you. I do not intend to fall into Yankee hands if I can help it on my way up to Shreveport for I will never accept a parole from them. I shall fight them to the last. But I must close as a gentleman is waiting. God bless you and yours. Lovingly from you know who ———Do not look for me till I come.

Appendixes and Index

Relatives and Acquaintances of Edwin H. Fay Mentioned in the Letters

1. Edwin Fay—Father of Edwin H. Fay. Born Barnard, Vermont, September 22, 1794; graduated Harvard, 1817; later moved to Georgia, and in 1820 to Alabama; taught school, practiced law, and became a planter; during the war lived at plantation "Rocky Mount," near Prattville, Alabama.
2. Harriet Porter (White) Fay—Mother of Edwin H. Fay. Native of Verona, New York; educated at Emma Willard School, Troy, New York; a deeply religious person.
3. Will Ed—William Edwin Fay, eldest child of Edwin H. Fay. Born 1857; died July, 1862.
4. Thera—Eleutheria ("Dody") Fay, second child of Edwin H. Fay. Born 1859; died 1860.
5. Thorny—Thornwell Fay, son of Edwin H. Fay. Born Minden, Louisiana, March 13, 1861; died Houston, Texas, March 31, 1932.
6. Edwin Whitfield Fay ("New Year")—Son of Edwin H. Fay. Born Minden, Louisiana, January 1, 1865; died Pittsburgh, Pennsylvania, February, 1920.
7. William Henry Fay—Brother of Edwin H. Fay. Member of First Alabama Infantry Regiment; captured at Island No. 10, April 7, 1862; exchanged after five months' imprisonment at Camp Butler, Springfield, Illinois; he and other members of his regiment helped complete Confederate defenses at Port Hudson early in 1863 and then stayed on to man the heavy artillery there; captured when Port Hudson surrendered on July 9, 1863; paroled and exchanged; killed by Federal sharpshooter near Atlanta, August 3, 1864.
8. Sarah (Sally) Stoddard—Sister of Edwin H. Fay. Married Sam Stoddard, who was in the Confederate army early in the war but was discharged for ill health; lived in Prattville area during the war; children were Will, Almon, and Harriet.
9. Dunham (Dunnie) Fay—Youngest brother of Edwin H. Fay. Sixteen years old when war broke out; put to work in government saddle and harness shop in Selma in 1863 to avoid conscription.

10. Will Fay—Cousin and intimate associate in pre-war years of Edwin H. Fay (Fay's mother in one of her war-time letters referred to Will Fay as "our adopted child") ; his wife was Eliza; during the war he held an administrative position in a factory at Prattville.
11. "Grandma"—Edwin H. Fay's maternal grandmother, Elizabeth Porter. Born in Connecticut January 1, 1786; moved to Selma, Alabama, in the antebellum period and was living there during the Civil War.
12. Spencer—Almon Spencer, Edwin H. Fay's best friend. Classmate of Fay at Harvard and taught with him at Minden Male Academy; Spencer and his wife, Jenny, and their child moved from Minden to the Prattville area when the war broke out and he became a member of Semple's Battery, Army of Tennessee; in Bragg's Kentucky campaign and the battle of Murfreesboro; hospitalized for illness in Chattanooga, August, 1863.
13. William Shields—Father-in-law of Edwin H. Fay. Owned and operated cotton mill and corn mill factory in Minden, Louisiana, in which Edwin H. Fay was a partner.
14. Sarah (Whitfield) Shields—Edwin H. Fay's mother-in-law. Close relation of Governor James Whitfield of Mississippi.
15. "Bud"—John Shields, brother of Sarah Shields Fay. He was sixteen in 1864; Fay tried unsuccessfully to get the Engineer Bureau of the Trans-Mississippi Department to employ John Shields as his helper; Bud did accompany Fay on one of his trips, but in what status is unknown; after the war John Shields became a prominent lawyer in Greenville, Mississippi.
16. Lou—Lucy Shields, younger sister of Sarah Shields Fay. Was about seventeen and a student in a girls' school at Columbia, Tennessee when the war began; lived with her parents in Minden during the war; married Joseph Holmes, a Confederate soldier from Mississippi.
17. Dr. Bright—J. E. Bright, D.D. President of the Minden Female College, 1862–1871.
18. Captain and Mrs. Wimberly—F. D. Wimberly and wife, of Minden. Neighbors and friends of the Shields and Fays; Wimberly was the first captain of the Minden Rangers but returned home in June, 1862, after the company was reorganized.
19. Dr. Patillo—W. C. Patillo, a Minden Physician. First lieutenant of the Minden Rangers until the company's reorganization; returned home in June, 1862.
20. Rich—Slave and body servant of Edwin H. Fay. Apparently ran away to the Yankees in 1863 or 1864.
21. Cynthia, Henry, Lizzie, Laura, Gus—Household servants owned or hired by the Shields or the Fays in Minden during the war.

A Roster of the Minden Rangers

(September, 1862–February, 1864)

Prepared from All the Extant Muster Rolls[1]

Name	*Rank*	*Time and Place of Enlistment*[2]	*Remarks*
Webb, Junius Y.	Capt.	Apr. 4, 1862, Monroe	Commissioned Capt. on May 18, 1862
Watkins, L. B. (first name appears as both Linn and Lynn in the letters)	1st Lt.	Apr. 4, 1862, Monroe	Commissioned 1st Lt. on May 18, 1862
Martin, Nathaniel M.	2nd Lt.	Apr. 4, 1862, Monroe	Commissioned 2nd Lt. on Sept. 1, 1862
Carter, John J.	2nd Lt.	Apr. 4, 1862, Monroe	Commissioned 2nd Lt. on May 18, 1862
Fay, Edwin H.	Ord. Sgt.	Apr. 4, 1862, Monroe	Promoted to Ord. Sgt. in June, 1862; trfd. to Engineer Bureau, Army of the Trans-Miss., Mar. 14, 1864; promoted to Capt. and apptd. Asst. Q.M., Army of the Trans-Miss., Dec., 1864
Killen, James M.	2nd Sgt.	Apr. 4, 1862, Monroe	Reported unfit for further duty by Surgeon, Mar., 1863; dropped from rolls thereafter

[1] Fay frequently refers to members of the Minden Rangers who are not listed on the official Roster. Many of these men can be found on the unofficial Supplementary Roster, which immediately follows this official Roster. When the company was reorganized in late May, 1862, some members returned to civilian life, while some transferred to other units. This fact explains the omission of their names from the official Roster, which covers only the period after the reorganization.

[2] Unless otherwise stated, place of enlistment is in Louisiana.

Name	*Rank*	*Time and Place of Enlistment*[2]	*Remarks*
Rathburn, Lysander (first name appears in letters as Lynn, Linn and Lyne)	3rd Sgt.	Apr. 4, 1862, Monroe	Died of pneumonia at Salem, Miss., sometime in early 1863
Newcomb, James L. A.	4th Sgt.	Apr. 27, 1862, Grand Junction, Tenn.	AWOL after Apr. 11, 1863; dropped from roll
Murphy, Joel Newsom ("Neuse")	5th Sgt.	Apr. 4, 1862, Monroe	Absent after Aug. 5, 1863; dropped from roll
Killen, John S.	1st Cpl.	Apr. 4, 1862, Monroe	Paroled in May, 1865; residence: Claiborne Parish
Bates, Pascal P. (Pack)	2nd Cpl.	Apr. 4, 1862, Monroe	Paroled in May, 1865
Culpepper, Sampson W.	3rd Cpl.	Apr. 4, 1862, Monroe	Paroled on May 11, 1865; residence: Bienville Parish
Jones, Williamson S.	4th Cpl.	Apr. 4, 1862, Monroe	Paroled on May 11, 1865; residence: Bossier Parish
Bennett, John J.	Pvt.	Apr. 4, 1862, Monroe	Listed as "Absent. Sick" from Nov., 1862, to Apr., 1863
Bennett, Smith W.	Pvt.	Oct. 20, 1862, Salem, Miss.	
Brantley, Benjamin J.	Pvt.	Apr. 4, 1862, Monroe	Paroled on May 11, 1865; residence: Claiborne Parish
Butler, Oliver M.	Pvt.	Apr. 4, 1862, Monroe	Captured June 20, 1863; released from U. S. hospital at Pulaski, Tenn., May 22, 1864; not heard of since
Cahill, John P.	Pvt.	Apr. 4, 1862, Monroe	Placed on detached service by order of Genl. Beauregard, May 28, 1862
Caufield, David W.	Pvt.	Oct. 20, 1862, Salem, Miss.	
Clinton, John A.	Pvt.	Apr. 4, 1862, Monroe	Not listed on rolls after Dec., 1862
Crocker, William	Pvt.	July 1, 1862, Priceville, Miss.	
Darby, Stephen H.	Pvt.	Apr. 4, 1862, Monroe	Paroled on May 11, 1865; residence: Bossier Parish
Duffard, Theophile (Tofield)	Pvt.	Apr. 17, 1862, Grand Junction, Tenn.	Detailed as Commissary Sgt., Aug. 31–Dec. 31, 1862; whereabouts unknown after Jan., 1863; dropped from roll

Name	*Rank*	*Time and Place of Enlistment*[2]	*Remarks*
Dunn, John F.	Pvt.	Apr. 4, 1862, Monroe	AWOL after 38-day leave in Dec., 1863; presumed to have been captured; paroled on May 11, 1865; residence: Claiborne Parish
Eastland, Horace W.	Pvt.	Apr. 4, 1862, Monroe	Placed on detached service by order of Genl. Beauregard, May 28, 1862; captured May 22, 1863; exchanged in July, 1863; future whereabouts unknown
Evans, Robert G.	Pvt.	Oct. 28, 1862, Salem, Miss.	Residence: Claiborne Parish
Gallagher, Scott	Pvt.	Oct. 14, 1863, Brownsville, Miss.	Paroled at Gainesville, Ala., May 11, 1865; residence: Perry County, Ala.
Garrett, John H.	Pvt.	Apr. 4, 1862, Monroe	Reported as sick, Sept.–Oct., 1862; reported as "Absent. Under arrest" for Sept.–Oct., 1863
Gassaway, Thomas J. (sometimes spelled "Gazaway" in the letters)	Pvt.	Apr. 4, 1862, Monroe	Hospitalized in Brandon, Miss., Sept.–Oct., 1863; paroled on May 11, 1865; residence: Claiborne Parish
Geren, Thomas R.	Pvt.	Apr. 4, 1862, Monroe	Not listed on rolls after 1862
Gray, Simeon	Pvt.	Apr. 4, 1862, Monroe	Paroled on May 11, 1865; residence: Bienville Parish
Grounds, Jesse G.	Pvt.	Apr. 4, 1862, Monroe	Promoted to cpl. during course of the war; paroled on May 11, 1865; residence: Claiborne Parish
Hardy, Joseph B.	Pvt.	Apr. 4, 1862, Monroe	Paroled on May 11, 1865; residence: Bienville Parish
Hartzog, Joseph F.	Pvt.	Sept. 8, 1863, Clinton, Miss.	Paroled on May 11, 1865; residence: Hinds County, Miss.
Henry, Jackson B.	Pvt.	Apr. 4, 1862, Monroe	Promoted to sgt. during course of the war; paroled on May 11, 1865; residence: Claiborne Parish

Name	*Rank*	*Time and Place of Enlistment*[2]	*Remarks*
Hodges, Edward W.	Pvt.	Mar. 12, 1863, Okolona, Miss.	Paroled on May 11, 1865; residence: Bossier Parish
Horton, Joseph M.	Pvt.	Aug. 15, 1862, Guntown, Miss.	Listed on Dec., 1862 as "Absent, prisoner on retreat from Abbeville"
Hudson, John W.	Pvt.	Apr. 4, 1862, Monroe	Wounded in action and on absence with leave, Sept., 1862
Jacobs, L. L.	Pvt.	Aug. 2, 1863, Brandon, Miss.	Substitute for James H. Williams; hospitalized on Dec. 20, 1863
Lancaster, Julius W.	Pvt.	Apr. 4, 1862, Monroe	Exchanged prisoner in Oct., 1862; promoted to 2nd Sgt. in 1862; trfd. to Jackson's Cavalry Division in 1864; paroled on May 11, 1865; residence: Claiborne Parish
Lesueur, John A.	Pvt.	Apr. 4, 1862, Monroe	
McArthur, Allen M.	Pvt.	Apr. 4, 1862, Monroe	Captured May 3, 1862, at Corinth, Miss.; exchanged Nov. 11, 1862; absent, under arrest, Sept. and Oct., 1863
McClendon, Alfred D.	Pvt.	Feb. 27, 1863, Monroe	Paroled at Gainesville, Ala., on May 11, 1865; residence: Ouachita Parish
McKemie, Sylvania G. (probably the Van McKamie of the letters)	Pvt.	Apr. 4, 1862, Monroe	Listed as sick in Sept., 1862
McRee, James J.	Pvt.	Apr. 4, 1862, Monroe	
Martin, Alexander	Pvt.	Sept. 24, 1863, Clinton, Miss.	Paroled at Gainesville, Ala., on May 11, 1865; residence: Claiborne Parish
Meeks, Nacy	Pvt.	Apr. 4, 1862, Monroe	Hospitalized, Sept.–Oct., 1862; trfd. in 1864 to Provost Guard of Jackson's Cavalry Division; paroled on May 11, 1865; residence: Claiborne Parish

Name	*Rank*	*Time and Place of Enlistment*[2]	*Remarks*
Menifee, Hardiman W.	Pvt.	Apr. 4, 1862, Monroe	Promoted to sgt. during course of the war; paroled on May 11, 1865; residence: Claiborne Parish
Minchew, Augustus F.	Pvt.	Apr. 4, 1862, Monroe	Discharged by order of Gen. Cosby in Aug., 1863; returned to duty in Jan., 1864
Monzingo, George W.	Pvt.	Apr. 4, 1862, Monroe	Listed as sick in Sept. and Oct., 1862
Monzingo, G. Whitfield	Pvt.	Apr. 4, 1862, Monroe	Paroled on May 11, 1865; residence: Claiborne Parish
Monzingo, Giles	Pvt.	Apr. 4, 1862, Monroe	Paroled on May 11, 1865; residence: Claiborne Parish
Monzingo, James	Pvt.	Apr. 4, 1862, Monroe	Paroled on May 11, 1865; residence: Claiborne Parish
Monzingo, Lewis	Pvt.	Jan. 15, 1863, Grenada, Miss.	
Monzingo, Samuel A.	Pvt.	Apr. 4, 1862, Monroe	Paroled on May 11, 1865; residence: Claiborne Parish
Monzingo, Thomas E.	Pvt.	Apr. 4, 1862, Monroe	Paroled on May 11, 1865; residence: Claiborne Parish
Morrow, Peter Y.	Pvt.	Apr. 4, 1862, Monroe	
Morrow, W. O.	Pvt.	Apr. 4, 1862, Monroe	Paroled at Gainesville, Ala., on May 11, 1865; residence: Claiborne Parish
Mullins, D. P.	Pvt.	Sept. 26, 1863, Clinton, Miss.	Paroled at Gainesville, Ala., on May 11, 1865; residence: Jefferson County, Miss.
Neal, Thomas B.	Pvt.	Apr. 4, 1862, Monroe	Captured, June 3, 1862, at Boonville, Miss.; returned to duty in Oct., 1862; promoted to sgt. during course of the war
Noland, Avery	Pvt.	Sept. 24, 1863, Clinton, Miss.	
Oliver, Alexander Browder	Pvt.	Apr. 4, 1862, Monroe	Not listed on rolls after 1862
Pearce, John M.	Pvt.	Apr. 4, 1862, Monroe	Promoted to cpl. during course of the war

Name	Rank	Time and Place of Enlistment[2]	Remarks
Plunkett, Joseph W.	Pvt.	Apr. 4, 1862, Monroe	Absent with sick leave, Sept.–Dec., 1862; back to duty by July, 1863; detailed to Hospital Corps, Nov., 1863
Randle, Robert	Pvt.	Apr. 4, 1862, Monroe	Paroled on May 11, 1865; residence: Claiborne Parish
Randle, Thomas	Pvt.	July 6, 1861, Camp Moore	Paroled at Gainesville, Ala., on May 11, 1865; residence: Claiborne Parish
Ratcliffe, Isaiah	Pvt.	Apr. 4, 1862, Monroe	Paroled on May 12, 1865; residence: Claiborne Parish
Ratcliffe, Richard (sometimes spelled "Ratcliff" in letters)	Pvt.	May 28, 1862, Baldwyn, Miss.	Paroled on May 12, 1865; residence: Pointe Coupee Parish
Scott, George W.	Pvt.	Jan. 19, 1862, Jackson, Miss.	Listed on rolls through Feb., 1864
Simmons, James H.	Pvt.	Apr. 4, 1862, Monroe	Promoted to sgt. during course of the war; paroled in May, 1865; residence: Claiborne Parish
Taylor, Daniel	Pvt.	Mar. 12, 1863, Okolona, Miss.	Paroled at Gainesville, Ala., in May, 1865; residence: Claiborne Parish
Taylor, John D. H.	Pvt.	Apr. 4, 1862, Monroe	Promoted to cpl. during course of the war; paroled in May, 1865; residence Claiborne Parish
Taylor, Needham B.	Pvt.	Apr. 4, 1862, Monroe	Wounded in hand by accidental gun shot; paroled in May, 1865; residence: Claiborne Parish
Thompson, Robert E.	Pvt.	Apr. 4, 1862, Monroe	Paroled at Gainesville, Ala., in May, 1865; residence: Claiborne Parish
Ward, Henry H.	Pvt.	Apr. 4, 1862, Monroe	Discharged from service, July 20, 1863, by order of Genl. Johnston

Name	*Rank*	*Time and Place of Enlistment*[2]	*Remarks*
White, Irby	Pvt.	Apr. 4, 1862, Monroe	Paroled in May, 1865; residence: Claiborne Parish
Williams, James H.	Pvt.	Apr. 20, 1862, Delhi	Discharged upon furnishing a substitute, Aug. 2, 1863
Wimberly, John C.	Pvt.	Apr. 17, 1862, Grand Junction, Tenn.	AWOL, Sept.–Oct., 1862; hospitalized in Monroe, Dec., 1863

Supplementary Roster of the Minden Rangers

This unofficial Supplementary Roster is taken from Harris and Hulse, *History of Claiborne Parish, Louisiana.* The source from which the list was compiled is not known. The date is apparently prior to the reorganization in May, 1862, as some of the men listed below remained with the unit while others joined the 13th Battalion, Louisiana Partisan Rangers. Those names which do not appear on the official Roster are marked by an asterisk. Those names which are probably, but not certainly, identical with names on the official Roster are marked by a double asterisk. Errors in spelling have not been changed.

*Wimberly, F. D., Capt.
*Patillo, W. C., 1st Lt.
*Harper, A. G., 2nd Lt. ("Bert" and "Burt" of the letters?)
*Hamilton, Joe, 3rd Lt.
Webb, J. Y., 1st Sgt.
Bates, P. P.
Bennett, John
Bennett, S. W.
*Blackman, Jeff
**Brantley, Dock (Benjamin J. ?)
Butler, Oliver
**Cahil, ——— (John P. Cahill ?)
*Carter, J. J.
**Caufield, D. C. (David W. ?)
*Caufield, J. M.
**Clinton, Jack (John A. ?)
Crocker, William
Culpepper, S. W.
*Darby, James
Darby, Stephen
*Davis, W. A.
**Duford, Towfield (Theophile Duffard ?)
Dunn, John
**Eastland, William (Horace W. ?)
Evans, R. G.
Fay, E. H.
*Fuller, B. F.
*Fuller, J. D.
*Fuller, William
Gallagher, Scott
*Garion, Thomas
Garrett, John H.
**Geren, T. J. (Thomas R. ?)
**Gossway, T. J. (Thomas J. Gassaway ?)
Grounds, J. G.
**Hardy, J. F. (Joseph B. ?)
*Hart, R. J.
Hartzog, Joe
Henry, J. B.
*Henry, J. F.
Hodges, E. W.

Hudson, J. W.
*Jones, Alfred
**Jones, William (Williamson S. ?)
**Killer, J. M. (James M. Killen ?)
*Lackey, John
**Lancaster, Jules (Julius W. ?)
**Laseur, J. L. A. (John A. Lesueur ?)
*Leary, Jim
*Loy, John C. (John C. Loye of the letters)
Martin, Alex
Martin, Nathaniel
*Mayberry, William
**McArthur, ——— (Allen M. ?)
McClendon, A.
**McKemie, J. G. (Sylvania G. ?)
McRee, J. J.
Meeks, Nacy
**Midchew, A. C. (A. F. Minchew ?)
*Monzingo, Abe
Monzingo, G. W.
Monzingo, Giles
**Monzingo, J. J. (James ?)
Monzingo, Lewis
Monzingo, S. A.
Monzingo, Thomas
*Monzingo, White
Morrow, P. Y. (same as Peter Y.)
Mullins, Dan
*Murphy, Ninus
*Nelson, Buck
*Nelson, Thomas
*Newsome, A. W.
*Noal, T. B.
Noland, Avery
*Nolen, A.
Oliver, A. B.
*Peters, Lewis
**Pierce, Murphy (John M. Pearce ?)
Randle, Robert
Randle, Thomas
Ratcliff, Isaiah
Ratcliff, Richard
Simmons, J. H.
*Simmons, Dr.
*Smith, Milton
*Smith, William
*Stanley, Thomas
*Stewart, J. J.
**Taylor, D. M. (Daniel ?)
Taylor, J. D. H.
Taylor, N. B.
Thompson, R. E.
*Wafer, Cicero
Ward, H. H.
Watkins, L. B.
White, Irby
Wimberly, J. C.

Chronological List of the Fay Letters, April 6, 1862–May 25, 1865

1862

Chap.

1 Quartermaster Room, Monroe, Louisiana, April 6, 1862
On Board Steamer *Alonzo Child,* 35 Miles below Memphis, April 8, 1862
Grand Junction, Tennessee, April 11, 1862
Camp Wimberly, near Grand Junction, Tennessee, April 13, 1862
Camp Wimberly, Grand Junction, Tennessee, April 21, 1862
Camp Grand Junction, Tennessee, April 25, 1862
Camp Grand Junction, April 26, 1862

2 Corinth, Mississippi, May 5, 1862
Van Dorn's Headquarters, 2½ Miles from Corinth, Mississippi, May 14, 1862
Camp Churchill Clark, Mississippi, May 20, 1862
Camp Churchill Clark, Mississippi, May 25, 1862

3 Camp Churchill Clark, Mississippi, May 27, 1862
Houston, Chickasaw County, Mississippi, June 5, 1862
Priceville, Mississippi, June 10, 1862
Tupelo, Priceville, Mississippi, June 15, 1862

4 Near Headquarters, Army of the West, Camp Priceville, near Tupelo, Mississippi, June 18, 1862
Camp Priceville, Mississippi, June 23, 1862
Camp Priceville, Mississippi, June 27, 1862
Camp Priceville, Mississippi, June 29, 1862
Camp Priceville, Mississippi, July 1, 1862
Camp, 4 Miles from Priceville (No date, but text indicates letter was written between July 1 and July 6, 1862)
Camp near Priceville, Mississippi, July 6, 1862
Camp Maury, Mississippi, July 13, 1862

5 Camp Maury, Mississippi, July 18, 1862
Camp Maury, Mississippi, August 2, 1862

Camp Maury, Mississippi, August 9, 1862
Camp Louisiana, near Guntown, Mississippi, August 13, 1862
Camp Louisiana, Mississippi, August 16, 1862
Camp Louisiana, Mississippi, August 19, 1862
Camp Louisiana, Mississippi, August 21, 1862
Mrs. Blackburn's, 7 Miles East of Holly Springs, August 26, 1862
6 Camp on Wolf River, La Grange, Tennessee, September 5, 1862
Camp, Baldwyn, Mississippi, September 11, 1862
Iuka, Mississippi, September 18, 1862
Baldwyn, Mississippi, September 25, 1862
Tupelo, Mississippi, September 26, 1862
2½ Miles from Ripley, Mississippi, October 7, 1862
Coldwater, 4½ Miles North of Holly Springs, Mississippi, October 12, 1862
Camp, near Salem, Mississippi, October 18, 1862
Camp, North of Tupelo, Mississippi, November 29, 1862
7 Camp Rust, 3 Miles East of Grenada, Mississippi, December 9, 1862
Camp Rust, Mississippi, December 14, 1862
Camp Rust, Mississippi, December 16, 1862
Camp Rust, Mississippi, December 18, 1862
Camp, Grenada, Mississippi, December 21, 1862

1863

Grenada, Mississippi, January 1, 1863
Grenada, Mississippi, January 4, 1863
Grenada, Mississippi, January 5, 1863
Grenada, Mississippi, January 13, 1863
Grenada, Mississippi, January 18, 1863
8 Grenada, Mississippi, January 24, 1863
Grenada, Mississippi, January 27, 1863
Okolona, Mississippi, February 12, 1863
Okolona, Mississippi, February 22, 1863
Okolona, Mississippi, February 27, 1863
Okolona, Mississippi, March 9, 1863
Exchange Hotel, Montgomery, Alabama, March 15, 1863
Rocky Mount, Alabama, March 20, 1863
Selma, Alabama, March 23, 1863
Camp Cosby, Spring Hill, Tennessee, April 11, 1863
9 Camp Cosby, Spring Hill, Tennessee, April 20, 1863
Camp Cosby, Spring Hill, Tennessee, April 23, 1863

Camp Cosby, Spring Hill, Tennessee, May 9, 1863
Camp Cosby, Spring Hill, Tennessee, May 20, 1863
Decatur, Alabama; Columbus, Mississippi; Louisville, Mississippi; Kosciusko, Mississippi; Canton, Mississippi; May 24, 1863–June 5, 1863
Canton, Mississippi, June 13, 1863
Headquarters, First Division, Jackson Cavalry, Camp near Mechanicsburg, Mississippi, June 27, 1863

10 Camp 4 Miles in Rear, Mechanicsburg, Mississippi, July 10, 1863
Across Pearl River, in Rear of Jackson, Mississippi, July 15, 1863
Camp Brandon, Mississippi, July 23, 1863–August 4, 1863
Camp Brandon, Mississippi, August 8, 1863
Camp near Clinton, Mississippi; Mr. Thigpen's near Raymond, Mississippi; September 2, 1863–September 11, 1863

11 Mr. Thigpen's, 3 Miles South of Raymond, Mississippi, September 19–September 21, 1863
Mr. Thigpen's, near Raymond, Mississippi, September 24, 1863
Camp, 8 Miles N.W. of Clinton, Mississippi, October 2, 1863
Camp, near Brownsville, Mississippi, October 8, 1863–October 15, 1863
Mr. Thigpen's, near Raymond, Mississippi, October 23, 1863
Camp, near Brownsville, Mississippi, November 2, 1863–November 6, 1863
Brownsville, November 7, 1863

12 Camp, near Clinton, Mississippi, November 13, 1863–November 16, 1863
Camp, near Clinton, Mississippi, November 19, 1863
Headquarters, Cosby's Escort, near Raymond, Mississippi, November 24, 1863
Camp, near Bolton's Depot, S.R.R., November 30, 1863–December 4, 1863
Waterford, Mississippi, December 7, 1863
Bolton's Depot, Mississippi, December 8, 1863–December 10, 1863

1864

Rocky Mount, Alabama, January 1, 1864; Brownsville, Mississippi, January 9, 1864

13 Shreveport, Louisiana, March 28, 1864
Opelousas, Louisiana, April 10, 1864
Camp, 17 Miles West of Camden, Arkansas, April 25, 1864
Camden, Arkansas, April 28, 1864

Princeton, Arkansas, May 3, 1864
Lewisville, Arkansas, May 22, 1864
Lewisville, Arkansas, July 17, 1864
Lewisville, Arkansas, July 18, 1864
Lewisville, Arkansas, August 22, 1864
Lewisville, Arkansas, August 26, 1864
Mrs. Whetstone's, 3 Miles North of Bastrop, Louisiana, September 4, 1864

1865

14 Opelousas, Louisiana, January 1, 1865
Opelousas, Louisiana, January 7, 1865
Opelousas, Louisiana, Sunday Night, January 15, 1865
Opelousas, Louisiana, January 21, 1865
Opelousas, Louisiana, January 29, 1865
Opelousas, Louisiana, February 5, 1865
15 Opelousas, Louisiana, February 19, 1865
Opelousas, Louisiana, February 26, 1865
Opelousas, Louisiana, March 3, 1865
Opelousas, Louisiana, March 13, 1865
Opelousas, Louisiana, April 16, 1865
Opelousas, Louisiana, April 23, 1865
Opelousas, Louisiana, May 5, 1865
Opelousas, Louisiana, May 10, 1865
Opelousas, Louisiana, May 13, 1865
Opelousas, Louisiana, May 14, 1865
Opelousas, Louisiana, May 25, 1865

Index